A History of the Cherokee Nation

New Directions in Native American Studies Series

Liza Black and Colin G. Calloway, *General Editors*

Rachel Caroline Eaton attended the University of Chicago, receiving a master's degree in 1911. After revising her first book, *John Ross and the Cherokee Indians*, for her dissertation in 1919, she was awarded a PhD in history. (Family photo collection.)

A History of the Cherokee Nation

Rachel Caroline Eaton

Edited by
David Berry, Martha Berry, and Patricia Dawson

University of Oklahoma Press : Norman

This book is published with the generous assistance of the Wallace C. Thompson Endowment Fund, University of Oklahoma Foundation.

Library of Congress Control Number: 2025021180

ISBN: 978-0-8061-9606-0 (hardcover)

A History of the Cherokee Nation is Volume 26 in the New Directions in Native American Studies series.

The manufacturer's authorized representative in the EU for product safety is Mare Nostrum Group B.V., Mauritskade 21D, 1091 GC Amsterdam, The Netherlands, email: gpsr@mare-nostrum.co.uk.

The paper in this book meets the guidelines for permanence and durability of the Committee on Production Guidelines for Book Longevity of the Council on Library Resources, Inc. ∞.

The editors dedicate this book to
Aunt Callie

Contents

Illustrations

A Tribute to
Rachel Caroline Eaton

Martha Berry

I do not remember a time in my life before Dr. Rachel Caroline Eaton
was a hero to me. Although she passed a decade before I was born,
she, her accomplishments, and those of her sister were woven into
my earliest understanding of what it means to be a Cherokee woman.
Unlike most people when they learn about Dr. Eaton, however, I
knew her as "Aunt Callie," my grandmother Mattie's older sister.

Rachel Caroline Eaton had no children of her own. Before she
died of breast cancer in September 1938, she must have reflected
on the few things she could pass on to those she loved. She had
no property, no wealth. She had devoted her life to education and
history, the pursuit of neither being especially rewarding in an outward sense. The Great Depression was at its height, and she could
leave little—her personal Bible from her days at the Cherokee
Female Seminary, a book called *One Hundred and One Famous Poems*
with notes and clippings tucked inside, her personal marked-up
copy of *John Ross and the Cherokee Indians*, a few photos of herself and
family members, and a nondescript box of papers. To her sister and
brother, and to their children who simply called her Aunt Callie,
she could leave nothing of worldly value. But in her passing, with a
simple bequest to a favored nephew, she made sure her life's work
would continue to influence lives in generations to come.

The books and the boxed manuscript were entrusted to Grady Lee York, her sister Mattie's middle son, who held a special place in her heart. Several years before, in consideration of Grady's need for a college education and Callie's yearning for inexpensive lodging where she could finish writing her book, the two struck a bargain: She and Grady would share a small apartment in Tulsa. Callie would cook, clean, and take care of things, while Grady attended the University of Tulsa by day and worked in a Tulsa bank by night. The arrangement fulfilled its purpose, but Grady would say later he sometimes chafed under the intense pressure placed on him by his aunt. Callie Eaton had a keen interest in his success, and she prodded him to work harder and to do better—as professors often do with students they regard highly.

By the time of her passing, Callie saw the results of their labors coming together. Grady was a young Tulsa banker, newly married, struggling but managing to stay upright in the midst of the Depression that had taken its toll on so many fellow Oklahomans. The box she entrusted to him contained her success—this rough, heavily edited manuscript. She asked him to "someday" get it published, although she knew the entire family couldn't have scraped together enough money to do it in those cash-strapped days.

The manuscript remained with Grady for nearly sixty years. After the Depression came the war, then children and work. Grady wrote to publishers, but for a time there was little interest in books about Native Americans. And even when there was interest, the manuscript was too rough. So, it languished in a box amid the accumulation of years of living, working, and then retirement. When I took a renewed interest in my Cherokee heritage and in Callie Eaton's manuscript, it emerged again—in 1997, almost sixty years after her death. Either by chance or by fate, I had fallen in love with and married a professional editor years before. David Berry, who took on the job of editing Rachel Caroline Eaton's manuscript and preparing it for publication, is a newspaper editor, now retired, with forty-four years' experience in writing and copy editing.

Which brings us to the question: Why study a history of the Cherokees written in the 1930s? The answer is that no other writer of history today can have the perspective Rachel Caroline Eaton had when she wrote her book.

A History of the Cherokee Nation was written by a woman whose grandmother came west with the Cherokees driven from Georgia. She was Cherokee, a member of the Ward family, six generations removed from Old Hop, a principal leader of the Cherokees around 1750. She was born during Reconstruction, witnessed the fiery destruction of the first Cherokee Female Seminary in 1887, laughed with Will Rogers, and saw the coming of the railroads to Indian Territory. She experienced the time of the land runs, the controversy surrounding the Dawes Commission, and the chaotic days prior to statehood. As an educator and historian, she gained a perspective few others can have. She lived much of the history she writes about and fills in, with rich detail, that period across which many writers prefer to skip.

Rachel Caroline Eaton was proud of her culture and worked her entire life to study and pass on to others the rich history of the Cherokee Nation. A poem she wrote in 1931 to be the club collect of the Tulsa Indian Women's Club clearly illuminates her devotion to the Cherokee people.

> Let us be wise, in wisdom ever growing,
> Steadfast and firm, the needful things to do;
> Walk calm, serene whatever winds be blowing;
> Attain the heights yet touch the lowly, too.
>
> Let us be true; sincere in word, in thought, in action;
> Free from all pettiness of soul and mind;
> And fair, devoid of prejudice or faction,
> Let us be wholly just, supremely kind.
>
> We pride of race would cherish veneration
> For ancient knowledge, wisdom, legends, lore;

Would throw the torch, each future generation
To grasp and pass, as in the days of yore.

We would hold aloft the banners of the Tribesmen,
Lest trailing they be trampled in the mire;
Signal, "Up ye Peace Chiefs, War Chiefs!" to the Clansmen;
"Sunset; comes Twilight! Build up your Council Fire!"[1]

RACHEL CAROLINE EATON

Most books are dedicated to a person who helped the writer accomplish what they set out to do. This book is dedicated to the author, Rachel Caroline "Callie" Eaton, from her family. We salute her lifelong dedication to education, her efforts to capture and pass along the history of the Cherokee people, and her painful struggle to prolong her life until the completion of her book. We also recognize her ability to capture the spirit and wit of the tribe, which endures—indeed thrives—today in modern-day Cherokees. We believe she would be thrilled to see the revived Cherokee Nation as it exists today.

Thank you, Callie. We hope you like what we have done with your book.

Martha Katheryn (York) Berry
Cherokee National Treasure

Introduction

Rachel Caroline Eaton, Cherokee Historian and Fire Carrier

Patricia Dawson

As a child growing up in the 1870s, Rachel Caroline Eaton sat by the fire in the evenings, listening to her grandmother's histories. As Eaton acknowledges in the preface to this book, Lucy Ward Williams was "one of the last of the fireside historians of her tribe, whose enduring loyalty constrained her to repeat, hours on end, the traditions and the history of her people until they were rooted and grounded in the memory of those who were privileged to know her." Women have always carried the fires of the Cherokee Nation. Long before Euro-Americans established universities on Turtle Island,[1] Cherokee women have been historians, intellectuals, and powerful leaders in their Nation. Like others who came before her, Rachel Caroline Eaton (1869–1938) was a scholar, activist, historian, educator, Cherokee intellectual, and fire carrier.

In addition to her early education from her grandmother, Eaton attended Cherokee Nation public schools, graduated from the Cherokee Female Seminary in 1887,[2] and went on to earn a PhD from the University of Chicago in 1919. She was likely the first Native American woman to get a PhD, but she was by no means the first Cherokee historian, and she applied her own Cherokee methodologies to her academic work. Eaton developed a network of Cherokee historians, led by women, and she was a strong Cherokee nationalist who fought for the sovereignty of her Nation throughout her career. She brought public attention to the Trail of Tears[3] with her tireless efforts in education, activism, and the publication of her first book, *John Ross and the Cherokee Indians*, in 1914. Her lifelong study of Cherokee history culminated in her second book, *A History of the Cherokee Nation*, which she penned toward the end of her life. This book was meant to be a comprehensive history of the Nation, and she herself had lived through much of the history she writes about. In the preface of this volume, she eloquently states, "The purpose has been to write this history of the Cherokees from the standpoint of a citizen by blood, reared in the nation, heir to its traditions, and beneficiary of its tribal institutions." Rachel Caroline Eaton drew from her own Nation's long intellectual tradition to develop histories legible to both community members and outsiders, and today's readers can learn much from her use of Cherokee methodologies centered around carrying DhW/atsila, weaving good ᎤᏃᎮᏍᎩ/kanohesgi, and practicing ᎦᏚᎩ/Gadugi.

Eaton's reference to her grandmother as one of the "fireside historians" points to a Cherokee story that teaches the centrality of women as fire carriers for their Nation. Long ago, the land was without DhW/atsila/fire, and the animals were cold. Then the Thunders sent DhW/atsila/fire into a hollow tree far out on an island. Animal after animal tried to bring back DhW/atsila/fire, but none could accomplish such a difficult task. The Raven flew over the water, but DhW/atsila/fire scorched him, which is why his feathers are black. Next, the Screech-Owl went, but DhW/atsila/fire burned his eyes and turned them red. Racoon tried, but DhW/atsila/fire exploded in his face, which is why he has those little rings around his eyes. Many others tried, but each one failed. Finally, the Water Spider offered to go. She spun thread from her belly, then made a bowl and placed it on her back, and she went over the water and put a tiny coal of DhW/atsila/fire into her bowl. She was the only animal who successfully made it back, and that is how the Cherokees got

DhⱤW/atsila/fire. When Cherokees relight the sacred fire, women are the ones who carry the fires back to their homes.

This story still holds an important place in the family today, and I first remember learning it through the work of Martha Berry, who tells (hi)stories through her beadwork.[4] In Cherokee culture, women are the fire carriers. In this story, DhⱤW/atsila/fire reflects the life of our Nation, and women are the ones who care for it and regularly regenerate it. All of these women were fire carriers. The Cherokees are a matrilineal society, so children's connection to their Nation and clan traditionally came through their mothers, not their fathers. By subtly referencing this story, Eaton pointed to the generations of women in her family who had passed down knowledge, presenting this form of education as the basis of her authority as a Cherokee historian. This intergenerational transmission of knowledge was built around oral (hi)stories. In Cherokee, ᏬᏃᎮᏍᎩ/kanohesgi, a word for history, also means story, and Eaton's work reflects a Cherokee understanding of historical methodologies centered around story.[5]

Eaton came from a long line of strong Cherokee women and men, and the stories of her ancestors shaped the narratives she penned. In addition to her grandmother, who survived the Trail of Tears, Eaton had relational ties to Nancy Ward/Nanyehi, Beloved Woman of the Cherokees, an important eighteenth-century leader who was one of the most famous women in the history of the Nation. She presided over women's councils, held a seat at the National Council, acted as a diplomat, warrior, and political leader, and was skilled in speaking to both Cherokee and Euro-American audiences.[6] Eaton's mother, Nancy "Nannie" Elizabeth Ward Williams, was named after her. Eaton was a descendant of Old Hop and Moytoy and was related to Attakullakulla.[7] Her strong political voice reflects her family's heritage, and her pro-John Ross leanings seem to have been influenced by her family as well.[8] Eaton's mother married George Washington Eaton, a white man who made the town of Claremore, Cherokee Nation, somewhat famous by marketing sulfur-infused well water as "radium water," promising a multitude of health benefits for the skin.[9] For Rachel Caroline Eaton, this "discovery" must have simply reinforced her belief in the benefits of the Cherokee practice of Going To Water, for in chapter one of this volume, she proudly points out Cherokee medical uses of water.[10] While Eaton's white ancestry likely helped her gain acceptance in white academia as a professional historian, her Cherokee kinship circles helped her understand Cherokee history from an intimate perspective.

Eaton always maintained a dedication to both education and scholarship. After graduating from the Cherokee Female Seminary in 1887 and Drury College in 1895, Eaton went on to teach at the Cherokee Female Seminary and Cherokee public schools. She received her master's degree from the University of Chicago in 1911. She published her first book, *John Ross and the Cherokee Indians*, in 1914, which she revised slightly to form her dissertation in 1919, the year she received a PhD in history from University of Chicago. Her book was subsequently republished in 1921, which spoke to the demand for her writing. As John Rhea notes, the 1914 and 1919 versions varied slightly, but the 1919 and 1921 versions were the same.[11] This book covered Cherokee history from around the beginning of the nineteenth century through the aftermath of the Civil War, with a brief discussion of earlier time periods. It serves as a foundational text in the field of Cherokee history and Cherokee studies more broadly. Following the success of her first book, Eaton continued writing to both academic and public audiences, publishing her article "The Legend of the Battle of Claremore Mound" in the *Chronicles of Oklahoma* in 1930, as well as writing several articles for the *Tulsa World* in the 1920s and 1930s. In 1920, the year after she received her PhD at the University of Chicago, Eaton became the first woman superintendent of schools in her home county, and she served two consecutive terms. Her degrees opened the door for a career at universities in the United States, including Trinity University, where she served as a dean,[12] and other institutions, such as Lake Erie College, but she always maintained ties to her community, and she spent much of her time researching and teaching in her Nation. Eaton campaigned for women's suffrage and was active in Cherokee and Oklahoma politics and various clubs and networks organized by Indigenous women in the early twentieth century, such as the Tulsa Indian Women's Club and the Indian Women's Pocahontas Club.[13]

Eaton devoted considerable space in *A History of the Cherokee Nation* to discussing the development of Cherokee Nation educational institutions, and her insights came partly from her own experience and partly from her participation in the networks of intellectuals these institutions helped train. By the time Eaton was born, the majority of school-age children attended Cherokee Nation public schools. As Cherokee historian Julie Reed notes, these were secular schools run by the Cherokee Nation government and financially supported with tribal funds, which contrasted greatly with the largely privately funded schools in neighboring communities and other areas in the United States.[14] The establishment of the Cherokee Female Seminary and Cherokee Male Seminary, which first opened in 1851, offered opportunities for citizens to attain higher education without leaving their Nation. The education plan largely followed Euro-American curriculums, though it did so within a Cherokee context.[15] Upon graduation, scholars like Eaton were well-prepared to continue their education at US universities if they chose to do so. Eaton showed a considerable amount of pride in these Cherokee Nation institutions. Because the Cherokee Nation government had control over its schools, students had much better experiences than those who attended assimilationist boarding schools run by the US or Canadian governments or various religious organizations. As Eaton points out in chapter 22, "Indians are endowed with the ability to impart as well as to acquire knowledge, and the fact has long been recognized that the Cherokees were ever their own best teachers." While schools like the Cherokee Female Seminary taught in the English language and often followed Euro-American education plans, they were Cherokee Nation institutions. The Cherokee Female Seminary gave space for Cherokee girls and women to develop strong communities and to replicate women-centered education in an institutional environment, as Eaton's book attests to.

Throughout her life and career, Eaton was surrounded by networks of strong Cherokee women, including other historians.

Central to Eaton's methodologies was the Cherokee value of ᏎᏏᏯ/ Gadugi, or the community coming together for mutual benefit.[16] Eaton knew that good Cherokee scholarship should be done in community, and Cherokee women have practiced research methodologies centered around kinship and ᏎᏏᏯ/Gadugi. In an article on Cherokee domestic science, Eaton declares that Cherokee women had a long history of practicing "real research work" in making decisions for their household communities; providing for their families after wartime devastation of crops; in rebuilding their Nation after the Trail of Tears; in their knowledge of agriculture, natural science, and foodways; and in passing on traditions to the next generation.[17]

These networks of scholars, activists, intellectuals, diplomats, artists, and more have always been an essential part of Cherokee society, from the pre-Removal women's councils that flourished under the strong leadership of women like Nancy Ward/Nanyehi, to the Indigenous women's clubs that Rachel Caroline Eaton and her contemporaries belonged to. The Cherokee Female Seminary lent itself especially well to the continuation of Cherokee women's networks, and Eaton openly discussed the fact that she was not the only historian with ties to that institution. In chapter 20, Eaton cited fellow Cherokee Nation citizen Narcissa Owen, who wrote a book "much prized for its contribution to Cherokee history," and emphasized her role as "Auntie Owen" to the many women she taught music to at the Cherokee Female Seminary. As an artist, historian, musician, educator, and community member, Auntie Owen became a model of "Cherokee womanhood." The Cherokee Female Seminary was a place where Cherokee women could teach the next generation of scholars on their own terms, even if most Cherokees chose a different approach to education. Another graduate of the Cherokee Female Seminary, Wahnenauhi, or Lucy Lowery Hoyt Keys, also wrote her own Cherokee history, which was published by the Smithsonian Institution in 1889. All three of these women began their manuscripts by noting the source of their authority: oral (hi)stories passed down by elders.[18]

Rachel Caroline Eaton was at the center of Cherokee historical scholarship at a time when professional, academic history was dominated by white men, and she helped organize a community of Cherokee historians led by women. In 1908, Eaton founded the Sequoyah Historical Society. Most of the founding members and all the officers were women, and the following year, the society joined the Oklahoma Federation of Women's Clubs, with Eaton serving as the official delegate.[19] Emmet Starr, a Cherokee genealogist and physician who would later go on to publish his own histories, was also a founding member of the Sequoyah Historical Society. Eaton became the first president of the society, and her own research interests seem to have driven much of its agenda. This was not an amateur history club. The Sequoyah Historical Society worked together to collect historical documents and material culture, concentrating on the history of "the former Indian Territory." The society emphasized histories told by community members, rather than outsiders, noting, "The history of East Oklahoma can be better and more intelligently collected by East Oklahomans than by our western neighbors." The society invited both Indigenous and white inhabitants of "the former Indian Territory" to join, but excluded all others, such as Black individuals, from membership, noting, "The members will be Indians and Caucasians only." The society may have helped many Indigenous community members to develop and promote their own historical narratives, but, dominated as they were by elites, there were glaring limits to their efforts at inclusion.[20]

Throughout her life, Eaton emphasized the importance of Cherokee history written by Cherokee people, and she herself wrote "from the standpoint of a citizen." The second half of this volume covers history that Eaton herself experienced, and she does not hide her viewpoints in her narrative. She had graduated from Cherokee Nation public schools and the Cherokee Female Seminary. She had learned about Cherokee history and culture from her grandmother and listened to (hi)stories from many other citizens. She had experienced personally the devastating effects of allotment and the end of US recognition of the official Cherokee tribal government. She knew that her own methodologies gave her greater insight than the pro-colonization viewpoints of many of her contemporaries in white academia.

One of the most valuable contributions Eaton's work offers today's academic scholars is her early use of Indigenous methodologies in academic publications. Long before the ethnohistorical turn in academia, Eaton was using Cherokee methodologies. She centered Cherokee values and concepts like ᏍᏏᏴ/Gadugi and carrying the fire. She described her scholarship as both "history" and "story," weaving together ᎤᏃᎮᏍᎩ/kanohesgi from her community's many ways of storytelling. Eaton described her methodologies at the beginning of an article about the Cherokee-Osage Battle of Claremore Mound that took place in 1818 right outside her family's land in what came to be known as the Sageeyah[21] community in Cherokee Nation:

> This story is a composite of many sources. The warp is authentic history based on the written records and on the hill which stands as the immutable background of this tragic encounter; the woof is fashioned of legends, traditions and fireside tales passed by word of mouth from generation to generation . . . but the fabric woven of these elements is shot through with the memory . . . embroidered with the imagery of one whose childhood was spent under the shadow of the historic hill.[22]

Eaton's focus on "fireside tales" certainly mirrors her description of her grandmother as a "fireside historian." For Eaton, good Cherokee history begins with the (hi)stories and perspectives passed down by ancestors and elders. These perspectives are not simply meant to be added as an afterthought or a rubber stamp to an academic monograph. Eaton's work was always close to home, and her (hi)story came from a lifelong study of place and material culture. In an article focusing on the history of another Cherokee space, Eaton spoke briefly yet eloquently of "the gift of 'listening silences,'" knowing that places tell their own stories to those who know how to listen.[23] In her discussion of Claremore Mound, Eaton remembered studying various objects left at the site, such as "arrow heads, battered tomahawks, and bits of colored beads."[24] She talked about daily life, foodways, and the role of women in supplying the warriors. Eaton was aware that Euro-American scholars privileged written documents and did not view oral (hi)stories as "authentic history." This separation of "legends" and written documents, stories and histories, oral histories and Euro-American archives did not make sense to Eaton. She frequently insisted on drawing upon all of these, as they are all part of ᎤᏃᎮᏍᎩ/kanohesgi. Eaton consistently wrote (hi)stories in a way that incorporated Cherokee perspectives and methodologies while simultaneously attempting to translate these perspectives to Euro-American audiences. One of her goals was to influence Euro-American academic and public perspectives on Cherokee history and contemporary politics. Eaton skillfully wove together (hi)stories that were legible to both Cherokee and non-Indigenous audiences. While Euro-American academic historians could point to her use of archival sources, Cherokees could see a much more robust narrative that privileged Cherokee elders as historians and Cherokee methodologies as the foundation of her work.

Embracing her role as a public intellectual who believed (hi)stories should be told in many ways and circulated to wide audiences, Eaton wrote several deeply researched articles for Oklahoma newspapers such as the *Tulsa World*. In chapter 28, Eaton fondly remembers the importance of the *Cherokee Advocate*, the Nation's bilingual newspaper, in bringing community together. After the US government shut down the *Cherokee Advocate*, Cherokee intellectuals such as Eaton turned to Oklahoma newspapers to do what so many of their forebearers had done since the beginning of *The Cherokee Phoenix*, the Nation's first newspaper. Eaton told Cherokee (hi)stories to both Indigenous and non-Indigenous audiences. In her article about Cherokee domestic science which appeared in the *Tulsa Daily World*, Eaton wrote extensively of the history of Cherokee women's foodways, praising "the intelligence of the Cherokee woman" both before and after Removal, and arguing that women were at the center of Cherokee community, kinship, the economy, and history. Eaton knew how to cite elders and oral (hi)storians from the community in ways that would identify them to Cherokee audiences but not necessarily to non-Cherokee audiences, as in the case of one unnamed descendant of Nancy Ward, "at whose feet many young tribesmen have heard the wisdom of the ancients."[25] Especially interesting is Eaton's three-part series for the *Tulsa World* on the Cherokee history of the area surrounding Fort Wayne and Beattie's Prairie. While their headlines, likely written by the editor, were designed to attract the attention of Euro-American audiences, her articles position Indigenous (hi)stories at the center of the place now commonly known as Oklahoma, and they weave together oral (hi)stories and archival sources to tell Cherokee ᎣᏍᏓᎥᎢ/kanohesgi on its own terms. She was not afraid to call out Euro-American sources for their biased prejudice while praising Cherokee historians such as Narcissa Owen, and she called the US military fort "at its best . . . a thorn in the flesh," while celebrating Cherokee history and lifeways in the area.[26]

As Eaton was placing the Cherokee Nation at the center of history, fellow Cherokee author John Oskison declared that Oklahoma, particularly Claremore and Norman, was quickly becoming "the literary center of America." He described Eaton as one of three important members of "the literary colony of Claremore," also featuring fellow Cherokee authors Will Rogers and Lynn Riggs.[27] The famous comedian, statesman, author, Hollywood actor, and storyteller Will Rogers had once proposed to Eaton's sister, Martha Paulyne Eaton York, but she turned him down because, as family oral history puts it, "Will's a brash young cowboy and I'm not going to marry a brash young cowboy!" Aside from would-be intimate ties, the Claremore literary circle, the networks of Cherokee women intellectuals, and the literary community across the Cherokee Nation worked to fight against Euro-American encroachment, pursuing what Daniel Heath Justice refers to as the Beloved Path, with diplomatic strategies of building peaceful relations, and the Chickamauga Way, featuring strong resistance.[28] For Eaton, the center of scholarship was not in academia, but in Cherokee community. It was in the Cherokee grandmothers passing down stories to the next generations, the Sequoyah Historical Society and the networks of Cherokee women who gathered their own community archive, the

Claremore literary circle, the graduates of Cherokee schools and seminaries, and the elders who "shared with many young tribesmen . . . things not yet found on the printed page."[29] Eaton was one of many authors and intellectuals who worked together in the spirit of ᏍᏏᏯ/Gadugi to fight for strong Cherokee futures.

After a long career in research and education, Eaton submitted *A History of the Cherokee Nation* to the University of Oklahoma (OU) Press in 1935. After some significant delays, the press ultimately decided not to publish it, accusing Eaton of "bias" and noting that she had a "too partisan, pro-Cherokee point of view."[30] Instead, the press decided to publish the work of Morris Wardell, a white settler, revealing the bias of the academic publishing world at the time. One of the readers tasked with reading both Eaton's and Wardell's manuscripts was Grant Foreman, a historian who had worked for the Dawes Commission[31] and was thus unlikely to appreciate Eaton's Cherokee perspective on allotment.[32] Despite accusations of bias, Eaton's publications constitute serious historical research, and her second book presents significant insights into Cherokee history. Eaton's work influenced future scholars and helped pave the way for Indigenous women in academia. Choctaw historian Muriel Wright noted that Eaton's first book "received much favorable comment not only for its subject matter but for its style and presentation. It is still considered one of the authoritative studies on the life of this great chief of the Cherokees."[33] But while scholars such as Kirby Brown, John Rhea, and Farina King have continued to study her work, Eaton died of breast cancer in 1938, leaving her second manuscript unpublished.[34] The many subsequent attempts by the family to publish it were unsuccessful until an increased acceptance of Indigenous methodologies and the work of Indigenous women intellectuals renewed interest.[35]

Eaton likely believed it was impossible to be "too pro-Cherokee," and she worked hard to promote Cherokee nationalism in a way that white academia could understand. Eaton conducted her graduate work in the 1910s during the Progressive Era, and her work reflects some of the values common in academia in her time even as it seeks to subvert them. Eaton emphasized narratives of progress, a long-standing strategy of Cherokee intellectuals and diplomats. Throughout the nineteenth and early twentieth centuries, Cherokees argued that they fit the Euro-American definition of "civilization" and should therefore be respected as a sovereign Nation.[36] As a strong Cherokee nationalist who had lived through continual assaults on Cherokee sovereignty, Eaton took up the narrative of progress in an effort to change US public sentiment. At the time, racism was rampant in academia, and many held to ideas of social Darwinism, believing that the supposedly "savage" nations of Turtle Island had not progressed as much as "Anglo-Saxon civilization" had. Eaton criticized these beliefs in the preface to her first book, and she named her third chapter in this volume "A Century of Progress," pointing to the continual innovation of Cherokee citizens. By doing so, Eaton flipped Helen Hunt Jackson's description of US atrocities against Indigenous victims, often described passively in her book *Century of Dishonor*. For Eaton, showing pride in Indigenous innovation and Cherokee nationhood was a way of promoting Cherokee nationalism.[37]

While Eaton's text is full of descriptions of "progress," she subverts Euro-American ideas of "progress" and "civilization" and offers her own Cherokee-centered version, one that promotes Cherokee values and traditional knowledge. In chapter 2, Eaton notes that Cherokees had already established their own tools of "civilization" long before Europeans appeared and only made changes when it was useful: "That they so long remained conservative to European ideas and appeared to disdain things alien was not owing to lack of mental acuteness. It was because their own tools and institutions were so admirably suited to their mode of life that they did not feel the need of better ones." While Eaton sometimes used words like "civilization" or "progress" to describe Cherokee innovation, she remained critical of Euro-American symbols of "progress." She deplored, for instance, the environmental impact railroads had on the Cherokee Nation, and viewed them as tools of colonization. She instead credits Cherokee institutions, innovations, and intellectuals as being instrumental to Cherokee well-being and "progress." Even modern scholars have much to learn from Eaton's habit of promoting Indigenous knowledge throughout her work. In chapter 3 of this volume, Eaton refers to one of her ancestors, Attakullakulla, as a "native scientist." And in her first book, instead of simply pointing out the lack of Euro-American doctors assigned to the camps during Removal, Eaton called attention to Cherokee medical knowledge and noted that Cherokees had their own forms of medicine but were not allowed to practice it.[38] Cherokees were not in need of Euro-American versions of "progress." They had their own traditions to draw on, such as the concept of ᏍᏏ/Gadugi, which can be seen in Eaton's descriptions of the community coming together to rebuild after the Trail of Tears and the Civil War. According to Eaton, it was Cherokees themselves who were the arbiters of "progress," and her narrative centers Cherokee concepts and values in a way that her Euro-American contemporaries in academia frequently dismissed.

Eaton's use of the language of "progress" centers the Cherokee idea of renewing the fire, and this idea has been carried forward by generations of Cherokee intellectuals. In one of the greatest literary achievements in history, Sequoyah invented the Cherokee syllabary in 1821, prompting the rapid development of print culture. *The Cherokee Phoenix* began in 1828 as a bilingual newspaper that allowed Cherokees to share their strong literary tradition with the world. Elias Boudinot took the title of the newspaper from a non-Cherokee story of the phoenix. At the end of its life, the phoenix would regenerate itself from fire to "rise from the ashes" anew.[39] This idea of renewal and regeneration comes from Cherokee ceremony of renewing the fire, even if it also served the diplomatic strategy of portraying the Cherokee Nation as "progressive" and "civilized." This idea was both a diplomatic move that took up the rhetoric of "progress" used by many Euro-Americans, and a strategy that subverted the prejudice so central to Euro-American ideas of "progress" by demonstrating a strong Cherokee nationalism in what Joshua Nelson terms "progressive traditions," or what Daniel Heath Justice refers to as the Beloved Path.[40] Rather than fit the

Cherokee Nation into Euro-American ideas of progress, Eaton, like many other Cherokee intellectuals, fit the rhetoric of "progress" into Cherokee ideas of renewing the fire.

Eaton's influence extended beyond academia to reach popular understandings of Cherokee history. Along with other Cherokee women such as Ruth Muskrat Bronson and Narcissa Owen, Eaton called attention to the Trail of Tears.[41] Those outside the Cherokee Nation know this episode in history as the Trail of Tears partly due to her tireless work as a historian, educator, and activist. While her first book spent considerable time discussing the rebuilding that took place following Removal, Eaton's discussion of the Trail of Tears received the most attention, and her chapter on the subject was taught in college classes as an example of good prose.[42] Much of Eaton's description of the Trail of Tears in this volume is a condensed version of her first book, but a significant addition is her use of the term "concentration camp" when describing the conditions at the camps Cherokees were imprisoned in for months before the long marches commenced. Eaton died in 1938, well before some of the most infamous Nazi concentration camps were liberated, but during her lifetime, there were many concentration camps across the globe. Such terminology would have negatively compared the United States to other regimes, perhaps adding one more reason why OU Press considered her book to be "too pro-Cherokee."

Eaton ended her book with a harsh critique of allotment and Oklahoma statehood. She died thirty-one years after Oklahoma became a state. Five years after Eaton's death, Rogers and Hammerstein's famous musical *Oklahoma!* opened on Broadway, turning fellow Claremore resident and Cherokee Nation citizen Lynn Riggs's play about Cherokees in Indian Territory into a celebration of Oklahoma statehood.[43] Outside of Indian Country, US citizens celebrated the statehood of Oklahoma with pride, and most did not wish to hear other perspectives. It was one thing to talk about the Trail of Tears, but to discuss allotment and Oklahoma statehood in negative terms was a recipe for censorship in white academia. It was much easier for Euro-Americans to acknowledge a supposedly inevitable tragedy that had occurred a century earlier than it was to admit to the harsh realities of recent attacks on Cherokee sovereignty and the continued strength of Cherokee community.

The poem at the end of Eaton's book eloquently points to grief at the loss that came from statehood. One line reads, "Idle the Council House, its ancient fires put out." But the loss of US recognition for the official Cherokee Nation government was certainly not the end of the Cherokee Nation, and Eaton remained a committed Cherokee nationalist. As Kirby Brown puts it in *Stoking the Fire*, Eaton and her contemporaries were "ostensibly denationalized Cherokee citizens [who] were working not simply to preserve Cherokee nationhood but to actively stoke it into a new generation."[44] In a publication by the Tulsa Indian Women's Club, Eaton noted, "For the old fire to die before the new had been kindled presaged misfortune. So Fire Keepers were appointed to watch and feed the flames from time to time, with fresh fuel, lest light and warmth not fail the clans in time of need. Desiring to preserve some embers of old tribal fires, some traditions and customs of their ancestors, the members of the Indian Women's Club [constituted] themselves Fire Keepers."[45]

Without the communities of strong Cherokee women Eaton was a part of, much of our Nation's strength and ᎣᏃᎮᏍᎩ/kanohesgi would lie dormant. But generations of Cherokee women like Eaton have continued to keep the fires burning. Eaton ended a poem she wrote for the Tulsa Indian Women's Club with a call for the Nation to "Renew your Council Fire." Perhaps she hoped that the Cherokee Nation government would once again gain recognition as the sovereign Nation it has always been. Eaton described herself as a "citizen" of the Cherokee Nation in the preface of this volume, decades after Oklahoma statehood, so she clearly recognized the continuance of the Nation even while condemning what had been lost. She died long before the re-formation of tribal government in the 1970s, but despite having lived through so many attacks on Cherokee sovereignty, she never stopped investing in strong Cherokee futures. She dedicated herself to Cherokee history and education, continuing Cherokee social structures in new and older forms. She spoke in romanticized terms of her desire to continue passing on (hi)stories to the next generation, as her grandmother had done for her: "We pride of race would cherish veneration / For ancient Knowledge, wisdom, legends, lore; / Would throw the torch each future generation / To grasp and pass, as in the days of yore." [46] Eaton's life represents one of the many ways Cherokee women chose to continue carrying the fire.

We would like to acknowledge the University of Oklahoma Press for agreeing to publish this book ninety years after declaring it "too pro-Cherokee." We particularly thank Senior Acquisitions Editor Alessandra J. Tamulevich, as well as Farina King for asking about the manuscript and prompting our meeting with the publisher. It is with great pleasure and pride that the descendants of Rachel Caroline Eaton finally present Aunt Callie's last book to the world.

Patricia Dawson
Mount Holyoke College
Great-great-great-niece of Rachel Caroline Eaton

Editors' Note

David V. Berry, Martha K. Berry,
and Patricia Dawson

This is not a new book. Dr. Rachel Caroline Eaton labored over these words more than nine decades ago, attempting to record the history of the Cherokees through statehood. When she died in 1938, her work went unpublished—until now. Since her death, many scholarly works have been published on various aspects of Cherokee history and culture. The tribe's history has been researched by scholars, examined by experts, and dissected by specialists. So, what is the value of a history of the Cherokees written so long ago? What can it add to an already weighty discussion of tribal history, culture, sovereignty, and custom? The value is this: *A History of the Cherokee Nation* conveys, as no modern-day work can, the struggles and successes of the Cherokee people—written by a Cherokee woman, a tribal citizen of the Cooweescoowee District during the final three decades of the nineteenth century, a product of Cherokee schools and Anglo universities, a firsthand observer of the turbulent years leading up to Oklahoma statehood, a witness to the effects of allotment on her own Cherokee family. The book, a reflection of the time in which it was written, is intended as a general, comprehensive history of the Cherokees from pre-contact to allotment and not a detailed analysis of any specific era. The author writes from the perspective of a Cherokee with a strong pro-Ross viewpoint, mirroring the prevailing tribal attitude of her era.

Her narrative is lively, her language colorful—some might say antiquated. We have used the author's original words and grammar. Her writing might occasionally be considered offensive by today's standards, but readers are asked to consider the time and context in which she was writing.

This book is not meant to stand alone as the only Cherokee history on a person's bookshelf. While excellently researched, documented, and presented, Dr. Eaton's findings in several cases may differ in some respects with those of other researchers. In the decades since this manuscript was written, many excellent books have been written that advance new arguments, uncover information to which she had no access, and arrive at other conclusions.

We have not attempted to rewrite her chapters to make them consistent with modern-day scholarship. To do that, we believe, would damage the historic context of the work. Her insights and perspectives, molded by the time in which she lived, have been preserved. *A History of the Cherokee Nation* by Dr. Rachel Caroline Eaton (1869–1938) is a slice of Cherokee history that she attempted to bring to the world in the 1930s. Its value today is every bit as real as it was when she lived it.

The publication of this manuscript is a result of many generations of love and labor. Rachel Caroline Eaton died before publishing this book, leaving a typed manuscript full of her handwritten editorial marks. Because of the state of the manuscript, this book has received light editing, but we have chosen to honor the historical text and not update Eaton's language.

Many years ago, David Berry began typing up the manuscript and providing light editing. From the start, he thought of it as preservation, not something that needed to be brought up to modern standards through heavy editing. Rachel Caroline Eaton was a fine writer, a great storyteller, and a historian who had worked to make sense of her time and to document those events that had brought about and reshaped the Cherokee Nation she knew.

Berry set out to capture her words and meaning accurately and to tell the story as she had intended. The manuscript had been typed on the back of stationery borrowed from the Oklahoma symbolic colors and designs woven into the texture of the token.

Adair, who for forty years was a trader among the Southern Indians and/traveled extensively through their country between 1735 and 1775, described them as "living in villages situated beside cool, sparkling streams, in which they bathed frequently, either as a religious rite, or for the purpose of seasoning the body and rendering it indifferent to exposure,"[11] they almost as impenetrable to cold as a bar of steel.[12]

Their villages lay in six main groups,[10] in addition to these main groups, there were scattered towns called the Out Towns, situated in different parts of the Cherokee Country. In was estimated in 1735 that there were sixty-four towns and villages, "populous and full of women and children,"[13] with about sixteen or seventeen thousand souls, over six thousand of whom were warriors.

The town was situated near a stream of sufficient size to furnish plenty of water for all economic needs and for the sacred rituals that played so large a part in the religious life of this tribe. Beside the stream stood the town-house which served all the purposes of a community center. There were outlying fields and gardens which were the common property of the community.

11. Adair, James. A History of the American Indians pp 224-226
12. Ibid, p 226
13. Ibid 227.

Rachel Caroline Eaton, struggling with breast cancer, finished writing *A History of the Cherokee Nation* shortly before her death on September 20, 1938. She had carefully edited the finished manuscript, in many cases inserting handwritten sections of text, attached with straight pins. In her original preface, she thanked her doctor for extending her life long enough to see the project completed. (Section 1, page 7, of the original manuscript.)

Senate. Eaton had hand-edited it heavily, correcting errors by the typist, rewriting herself, inserting footnotes as needed, crossing out whole paragraphs, then adding new thoughts in the margins or inserting segments on half-sheets pinned to the original pages.

By publishers' standards, the manuscript was too rough, and early attempts at publication were rejected partly for that reason. But the story was clear; it just needed to be scanned, polished, and moved to a digital format. As a newspaper editor, David Berry was trained to edit heavily when needed. But he believes it is often best to back off, edit with a light touch, and let the work of a good writer stand on its own. Rachel Caroline Eaton's work flowed easily, and the story came through. His editing was intentionally light, letting her tell her story as she would have in the 1930s. Berry corrected typos, grammar, and punctuation (although there was little she got wrong). He made sure her inserts, corrections, and handwritten notes went into the right places and flowed cleanly into her work. In short, he saw the manuscript as a document to be protected, a reflection of her intentions and meaning. The little "editing" he did will not stand in the way of that.

On completion of her PhD, Patricia Dawson also joined the editing process. She thought of Eaton's book as both a historical monograph and historical document and worked to keep this volume as close to the original manuscript as possible. Patricia and David worked together on editing and have corrected minor typographical errors in the original manuscript, updated some of the formatting, and done other light editing, such as the occasional punctuation change, only when necessary. For added clarity, we have also included editorial footnotes in addition to Eaton's original footnotes. In the original manuscript, there is an occasional footnote missing. Patricia Dawson included editorial footnotes in these instances, citing the sources Eaton used or noting the absence of the footnote when unable to track down the original source. Interested scholars are encouraged to consult the original sources. We have also included editorial footnotes in a few instances where modern scholarship has changed the prevailing narratives common in Eaton's time, though we do not claim to be thoroughly exhaustive. For readers unfamiliar with Cherokee history, or for those who wish to read smaller portions of Eaton's book, we have decided to include four different editor's notes throughout the manuscript to provide additional historical context.

Readers will note that Eaton's discussion of race and enslavement in the Cherokee Nation is often offensive. For example, Eaton frequently ignores or misrepresents the perspectives of Cherokee Freedmen, and in chapter 3 she claims that "the Cherokees were humane in the treatment of their bondmen, with whom there was rarely ever any intermixture of races." Cherokee enslavers made similar arguments, but the work of more recent scholars such as Tiya Miles and Fay Yarbrough has demonstrated the importance of recognizing the dark realities of the adoption of African chattel slavery.[1] Enslavement is never humane, and the Cherokee Nation still has much reconciliation work to do. Eaton used many terms prevalent at the time that are not acceptable, particularly in our contemporary context. Words and phrases such as "stock," "half-breed," and "wild tribes" are offensive, even if some Cherokees used these words a hundred years ago. Eaton sometimes exhibits prejudice toward other Native Nations, particularly ones who were historic enemies of the Cherokees.[2] Eaton also quotes others who use offensive and racist language. Because Eaton's book is a historical document, we have not changed offensive or outdated language in this text.

We have elected not to change Eaton's choices for spelling Cherokee words, but have included editorial footnotes providing modern English spellings for Cherokee words. It is much easier to spell Cherokee words using the Cherokee syllabary. Because English spellings of these words were not standardized, Cherokee words can have multiple English spellings, and these spellings have sometimes changed over time. In addition, dialectic differences often result in multiple pronunciations. Names of Cherokee individuals often have multiple spellings, and some Cherokees even had multiple names throughout their life. Rather than hide linguistic diversity, we have chosen to keep the original spellings Eaton used in her manuscript.

A salute and word of thanks is due also to Christina Berry, Martha's and Dave's daughter, who years ago created the All Things Cherokee website that deals with art, genealogy, history, and culture of the Cherokees. One page of that site saluted Rachel Caroline Eaton, Christina's second-great "Aunt Callie," and reminded the world that her final manuscript, *A History of the Cherokee Nation*, remained unpublished. That mention, we believe, prompted much of the current clamor by scholars, academics, and historians to read her work.[3]

David V. and Martha K. Berry and Patricia Dawson
December 1, 2024

Author's Original Preface
and Acknowledgments

The eminent scholar and diplomat, Dr. William E. Dodd, once said, "There is no more tragic history than that of the Cherokees. Their records are especially interesting as showing a capacity for building a culture of their own, from which they have made valuable contributions to the ethnic and economic resources of the United States."[1] Many books have been written in praise of them. They have moved through the centuries with a dignity and intelligence becoming a valiant people who loved the soil from which they sprang and strove to conserve its resources for the benefit of future generations.

After a lifelong observance of tribal institutions among the Cherokees and twenty-five years of research work in the representative libraries of the United States, the author presents this volume to the public, bespeaking for it a friendly reception.

The purpose has been to write this history of the Cherokees from the standpoint of a citizen by blood, reared in the nation, heir to its traditions, and beneficiary of its tribal institutions. I have attempted to trace the development of the political, economic, and religious influences which contributed to the formation of the Cherokee Nation, and the disintegrating forces that caused its dissolution.

The necessity for subordinating a mass of interesting topics to the main theme has precluded the discussion of a number of movements related to this phase of American History. The same general ground, up to the close of the Civil War, was covered some years ago in my thesis, "John Ross and the Cherokee Indians," which is now out of print but still in demand.[2] Some of the material found in that treatise has been incorporated into this book.

In preparation of this volume, assistance, both material and inspirational, has come to the author from many different sources. For help in checking references and for facilitating access to documentary sources in Harper Memorial Library at the University of Chicago, Miss Cora Gettys is to be thanked. For a like service I am under obligation to Miss Alma McGlenn, librarian of the Tulsa City Library; Mrs. Mary Kathryn Armstrong of the McFarlin Library at the University of Tulsa; and to Mrs. J. F. Messenbaugh, librarian in the Oklahoma Historical Society.

Mr. W. F. Ford, a former president of Northeastern State Teachers' College at Tahlequah, Oklahoma, presented the author with a copy of Tsa-La-Gi, the college annual for 1911, which has been used to some advantage in a chapter on education. Professor T. L. Ballenger, of the history department at the same institution, contributed a useful pamphlet entitled, "The Trial of Stand Watie for the Murder of James Foreman." Mrs. J. W. McSpadden, of Tahlequah; Mrs. J. C. Bushyhead and Mrs. Ellis Eaton of Claremore, have contributed the use of rare old photographs.

I am indebted to Mr. Leon C. Ross and Mr. Robert B. Ross, of Tahlequah, Oklahoma, for the free use of their collections of letters, papers, and documents, and for personal information concerning the history of the Ross family. Mr. A. S. Wyley, at one time secretary of the Cherokee Board of Education, supplied much authentic data on the subject of education. Mr. Andrew Cunningham, of Tahlequah, gave me access to the Cherokee National Records before they had been removed from Tahlequah, the Capitol of the Cherokee Nation. Mr. Mark Lee Paden, of the Male Seminary Class of 1887 and one-time secretary of the Cherokee National Board of Education, made generous loans from his rare collections in Edinburg, Texas.

Free use has been made of the John Howard Payne Manuscripts of the Ayer Collection at the Newberry Library in Chicago, which were first called to my attention by Miss Mary B. Gude, author of "Georgia and the Cherokee Indians." Other valuable sources in

Cherokee removal were found among the Indian Office Manuscript Records in Washington where government officials and employees were consistently courteous in facilitating my examination of letter books, report books, and documents on file in the Indian Office manuscript division, in 1913.

In addition to those mentioned, there are others I desire to thank for assistance rendered and encouragement offered. Among these are Robert L. Owen,[3] whose loyalty and integrity in times past inspired high ideals of patriotism among the youth of the nation; and Mr. George Washington Mayes, a veteran of the Civil War, a man of broad experience and one well versed in Cherokee lore. From his store of well-seasoned knowledge, he has generously given me rare bits of personal reminiscence, which have thrown additional light upon more than one subject.

Mrs. Alma Burge of El Reno is due thanks, gladly given, for many hours of tedious service in typing the manuscript. Mrs. Bonnie Norton, of the Oklahoma City Schools, rendered signal service by her stimulating interest in the success of my undertaking.

In acknowledging my obligations to those who have made contributions to the background of this volume of Indian history, I would not forget to mention Lucy Ward Williams, one of the last of the fireside historians of her tribe, whose enduring loyalty constrained her to repeat, hours on end, the traditions and the history of her people until they were rooted and grounded in the memory of those who were privileged to know her.[4]

It affords me special pleasure to mention Senator W. P. Morrison, Mrs. W. P. Morrison and Mrs. Stella Lee Morrison. No one has contributed more of material aid and spiritual inspiration than these three during the months I was a guest in their hospitable home. There is much I could say in praise of their generosity and magnanimity.

For his great gift of time and medical aid, I acknowledge my debt of gratitude to Dr. John Burton, physician and surgeon, whose uniform patience and kindness, no less than his scientific knowledge and skill, have been instrumental in lengthening the span of my life, thereby making possible the completion of this volume.

For benefits and courtesies innumerable received at the hands of Dr. Sophonisba Preston Breckenridge of the University of Chicago, internationally recognized for her contributions to the field of social service, I am especially grateful. Out of the crowded hours of a busy life, she has found time to read the preliminary chapters of the manuscript and to make constructive criticism as to their form and content. The author of many books, she has made suggestions that have proved helpful to one less experienced in the field of authorship.

Rachel Caroline Eaton
Claremore, Oklahoma

Editorial Commentary
for Chapters 1–6

Rachel Caroline Eaton begins her book with an introduction to Cherokee culture and a discussion of early Cherokee history before what she describes as "the constitutional period" beginning in 1827. As a strong Cherokee nationalist, Eaton's pride in her Nation clearly shows throughout her book. Eaton wrote this history for both Cherokee and non-Cherokee audiences, and she worked to dispel stereotypes Euro-Americans often believed. She gestures to old Cherokee stories as the beginning of Cherokee history, and throughout the following chapters, she demonstrates Cherokee innovation, such as Sequoyah's invention of the Cherokee syllabary.

Beginning in the late eighteenth and early nineteenth centuries, many Cherokee diplomats and intellectuals adopted the language of "progress" and "civilization" in order to convince Euro-Americans that they were "civilized" and should therefore be treated like any other sovereign nation. In the early nineteenth century, Euro-Americans who wanted to steal Cherokee land argued that the Cherokees were not "civilized" and should therefore be removed to a different part of the continent. Cherokee intellectuals, diplomats, and historians argued that while they had been "primitive" in the early years of their history, they had made "progress" and were just as "civilized" as white people. Eaton's continued use of the language of progress, while outdated, was itself a diplomatic tool to try to fight racism against Cherokees, and she clearly credits early Cherokee society as having been full of scientists, artists, agriculturalists, and intellectuals, the hallmarks of Euro-American ideas of "civilization." Readers should note the ways in which Eaton subverts Euro-American stereotypes and ideas of "progress."

As noted in the introduction, Eaton's discussion of race, enslavement, and the "civilized"/"savage" binary is often outdated and offensive. At the end of chapter 3, for instance, Eaton notes that a few Cherokees began engaging in chattel-style enslavement. Eaton describes Cherokee enslavers as "humane." Cherokee enslavers made similar arguments, but readers will note that enslavement is never humane. In addition, Eaton sometimes uses offensive and outdated language such as "primitive," "wild tribes," and "half-breed." Rachel Caroline Eaton wrote this history in the 1930s, and as it is both a historical monograph and a historical document, we have elected to keep Eaton's original language.

CHAPTER 1

The Cherokees

The native inhabitants of North America in the region lying between Hudson Bay and the Gulf of Mexico have been divided by scientists into fifty-nine main groups, classified on the basis of language affiliation. Of these the Iroquois constitutes the family of nations to which the Cherokees belong.

Ever a proud and emulative people, the Cherokees emerge from the mists which obscure their prehistoric past into the dawn of the modern era with a store of myths and legends in which they first appear upon the earth as Yûn´-wi-ya´[1] which by interpretation means The People, or Principal People. The neighboring tribes, however, knew them as Tsalagi, or Tsarigi, which, on alien tongues, became "Cherokee," a name meaning rock-dwellers, suggestive of the nature of their country.

By the end of the eighteenth century, the Cherokees had become recognized by Europeans as the most powerful and the most progressive of all North American tribes. Their domains, which at one time had extended from the eastern slopes of the Allegheny Mountains to Muscle Shoals on the Tennessee, and from the Ohio to central Georgia and Alabama, still covered a territory of fifty-three thousand square miles, half of which lay in Tennessee, a small area in North Carolina, the rest being about equally divided between Alabama and Georgia.

They were the mountaineers of the south, holding the highland barriers between the English settlements on the Atlantic seaboard and the French and Spanish garrisons on the Gulf Coast and in the Mississippi valley. Their mountain country is described by the historian, Bancroft, as the "most picturesque and salubrious region east of the Mississippi."[2]

David Brown, a young Cherokee, writing in 1822, says of his country, "Abundant springs of water are to be found everywhere. A range of lofty and majestic mountains stretch themselves across the nation, the northern part of which is hilly, while in the southern and western parts are extensive and fertile plains covered partly with tall trees through which beautiful streams of water glide. The climate is delightful and healthy, the winters are mild, and the spring clothes the ground with richest verdure. Cherokee flowers of exquisite beauty and variegated hues meet and fascinate the eye in every direction."[3]

Cradled in such surroundings, it is not strange that the people were instinctively artistic and responsive to every form of natural beauty. The song of bird and the delicate fragrance of wild flower delighted, while the massive grandeur of mountain and forest filled them with awe and admiration, often inspiring their minds to lofty flights of fancy which found expression in metaphors of rare subtlety and beauty.

Attachment to their ancestral homes was strong and sincere, deep rooted as it was in the past of ancient domestic and religious institutions. As is always the case when a primitive[4] people have dwelt for a long period of time in the same region, their legends had become localized. They were associated with mountain peak and rocky headland, with cave and spring and swiftly flowing stream.

Strong and agile, with skin of delicate texture,[5] teeth as white as milk and clear eyes of far-seeing vision, the Cherokees measured up to a high standard of physical perfection. The English traveler, Bartram, describes them as larger of stature and fairer of complexion than their southern neighbors. "In their manner and disposition they are grave and steady; dignified and circumspect in their deportment; rather slow and reserved in their conversation, yet frank, cheerful and humane; tenacious of the liberties and natural rights of man; secret, deliberate and determined in their councils; honest, just and liberal, and ready always to sacrifice every pleasure and gratification, even their blood and life itself to defend their territory and maintain their rights."[6] The men he portrays as tall and erect, moderately robust, with regular features and countenances that were open, dignified, and placid, exhibiting an air of magnanimity, superiority and rude independence; the women were tall, slender and of delicate frame, their features formed with perfect symmetry; their countenances were cheerful and friendly, and they moved with "becoming grace and dignity."[7]

They possessed a vast accumulation of practical knowledge which they applied with dexterity and discernment. With infinite accuracy and unlimited patience they fashioned tools and implements suited to their needs, made boats that were marvels of perfection, and chipped keen, symmetrical arrow heads and spear points from the hardest flint. As hunters and trappers their technique has never been surpassed, and their prowess in war still furnishes themes for song and story.

They were familiar with the medicinal properties and food values of herbs and roots, and they knew the benefits to be derived from hot and cold water. They are said to have been among the first people known to use the vapor bath. Their food, varied, wholesome and well cooked, was eaten in moderation at one main meal a day with fast and feast days to vary the monotony of civic and national life.

Houses were built of wood, each designed to suit the purpose for which it was intended. That of the Beloved Woman, Nancy Ward, of Etsauta,[8] is reputed to have been commodious and comfortably furnished. It was painted white inside and out. On the floor were rugs woven of rushes, or of buffalo hair, attractively patterned and artistically colored. There were couches of native design and workmanship over the framework of which thongs of buffalo hide or cane were woven in lattice fashion to make a mattress. On this foundation, skins, dressed so they were as soft as velvet, were draped to make a bed by night and a couch by day.[9]

No primitive people were ever more religious than the Cherokees. "Never in their most savage state did they worship the work of their own hands," wrote John Ridge, when questioned concerning the religious beliefs of his people. "They believed in a Great First Cause; in a Spirit of Good and a Spirit of Evil in constant warfare with each other, the good finally prevailing. Heaven, an open forest of shade and fruit trees, was adorned with fragrant flowers and mossy banks beside cool sparkling streams; game abounded, and there were enough feasts and dances to satisfy but not to cloy the appetite for pleasure."[10]

This happy and immortal region which was reserved for beautiful women prepared and adorned by the Great Spirit, and for men distinguished for valor, wisdom and hospitality, lay directly across the way from the land of Evil Spirits, where the wretched who had failed in life were compelled forever to exist in hunger, hostility, and darkness.[11]

An important national asset, and a valuable aid to their system of individual and group control, was the body of traditions which had grown up during past centuries and been handed down from generation to generation by the Oukah,[12] the Beloved Men of the tribe. These traditions contained creation myths dealing with the origin of the earth and its inhabitants; of fire and food; of birds and beasts and inanimate things when they talked with man as friend with friend. In them were embodied chants and charms and secret formulas, the interpretation of the wampum, and the symbols that played so large a part in national ceremonials.

The Cherokees made two divisions of their country, which they called Ayrate and Otarre,[13] one meaning low and the other high country. The language was divided accordingly into the Underhill and the Overhill dialects, which differed somewhat in enunciation and accent. Both were rich in vowel sounds. The language of a people peculiarly sensitive to environment, it reflected the undertones of wild life communing in anger or affection; gay bird calls and the cries of hunger and distress; the cadences of running water; wind notes made by swaying branches in the lowlands, or by storms that sweep the mountainsides with rain, when thunder peals from crags and cliffs and rolls to silence in the distant vales.

These First Americans were not wanting in the finer sensibilities common to superior races. In contrast to their reputation for sullen stoicism, they showed a surprising capacity for the tender emotions of love and friendship.[14] Their attachment to the soil, where the bones of their ancestors lay buried and from which they believed themselves to have sprung, was of the purest type of patriotism. Appreciation of form and color appears in their rock carvings and paintings, and in the graceful designs with which they decorated their baskets and pottery. Their bead work showed a pleasing harmony which appealed to the most refined tastes. The games they played developed strong and lithe bodies; their dances were graceful, rhythmical and replete with tribal symbolism. Every Indian was a born actor and every warrior an orator.

Agriculture was considered women's work. The mothers kept the home fires burning, planted and harvested crops, fashioned clothing and bedding from skins they dressed, taught young children things they needed to know, and cured and conserved meat the hunters brought home from the chase. They made blankets of feathers by skillfully weaving them together by the aid of hempen cord, and in the same way they made cloth for jackets and tunics that were "pleasant to wear and beautiful to see." They also wove beautiful yellow petticoats from mulberry root bark. These were tinged with red and were soft and pliable in texture. Many other kinds of cloth they wove long years before they ever saw loom and spinning wheel.[15]

The men organized hunting or war parties, manufactured weapons and boats, conducted religious ceremonials, and, since they were great traders as well as travelers, went long distances to barter their own wares for those of other regions. Their currency was beads made from shells and called wampum. These beads, woven into bands or belts, served as peace offerings between tribes and as official documents for commemorating important transactions, which were recorded in symbolic colors and designs woven into the texture of the token.

Adair, who for forty years was a trader among the Southern Indians and who traveled extensively through their country between 1735 and 1775, described them as "living in villages situated beside cool, sparkling streams, in which they bathed frequently, either as a religious rite, or for the purpose of seasoning the body and rendering it indifferent to exposure," so that they were almost as impenetrable to cold as a bar of steel.[16]

Their villages lay in six main groups,[17] in addition to which there were scattered towns called the Out Towns, situated in different parts of the Cherokee Country. It was estimated in 1735 there were sixty-four towns and villages, "populous and full of women and children,"[18] with about sixteen or seventeen thousand souls, over six thousand of whom were warriors.

The town was situated near a stream of sufficient size to furnish plenty of water for all economic needs and for the sacred rituals that played so large a part in the religious life of this tribe. Beside the stream stood the town house, which served all the purposes of a community center. There were outlying fields and gardens which were the common property of the community.

The town chief, together with a certain number of warriors renowned for prowess and sagacity, and the oldest of the Uka,[19] or wise men, managed all local affairs and represented the town at the Grand Council, which, prior to 1785,[20] was held as stated in the ancient peace town, Etsauta, or Chota, which was the Nation's "City of Refuge."

In short, the Cherokees, by virtue of their location and their adaptation to environment, had developed a splendid type of physical fitness, an artistic temperament, an indomitable spirit, and a culture that was predominantly economic and agricultural.

CHAPTER 2

Early History
of the Cherokees

Contact of the Cherokees with Europeans began as early as the middle of the sixteenth century when the daring and adventurous Spanish explorer, Hernando De Soto, marching northward from Tampa Bay and passing over "rough and high hills" arrived in the land of the Cheraqui. The Spaniards described the Indians as "a naked, lean, and unwarlike people given to hospitality to strangers."[1]

Thereafter, from time to time, the Cherokees met other Spanish explorers and English and French settlers from whom they gradually adopted such civilized arts as appealed to them. That they so long remained conservative to European ideas and appeared to disdain things alien was not owing to lack of mental acuteness. It was because their own tools and institutions were so admirably suited to their mode of life that they did not feel the need of better ones.

Firearms proved to be the exception. The Indian learned their use readily, for by them he was enabled to supply the growing demand for the furs, which were the chief article of trade with Europeans, and to hold his own with his enemies. By 1715, twelve hundred Cherokee warriors were supplied with guns, and a few years later the governor of South Carolina furnished an additional two hundred with guns and ammunition on the condition they help him in a war upon a neighboring tribe.[2]

Before the end of the seventeenth century, Virginia and South Carolina settlers began trading with the Cherokees. In 1690, Cornelius Dougherty, a Virginian of Irish descent, established himself among them and there spent the remainder of his life. Dougherty was followed by others, some of whom were not on the very best terms with the aborigines, owing chiefly to their custom of purchasing or capturing Indians to be sold as slaves to the settlements or to the West Indies; and to their general conduct toward the natives which was described as sometimes "very abuseful."[3]

Complaints of these abuses, coming from the Cherokees to Governor Nicholson of South Carolina, coupled with the jealousy of French encroachments upon English trade with the Indians, caused him to arrange a conference of chiefs to be held at Charleston in 1721. Here a treaty establishing a boundary line between the Cherokees and the settlements was agreed upon; a chief was designated as head of the Cherokee Nation in all its dealings with the colonial government; a commissioner was appointed to superintend the relation of the colony with the Cherokees; and a small cession of land was made.[4]

Nine years later, North Carolina commissioned Sir Alexander Cumings[5] to arrange a treaty of alliance with this Nation.[6] After a preliminary meeting held with the chiefs and headmen at Nequasseh[7] on the Little Tennessee River in the Cherokee country, he conveyed a committee of seven to England, where after a visit of several weeks they signed the Treaty of Dover, which bound the Cherokees to trade with no country other than England, and allowed none but Englishmen to build forts or cabins, or to plant corn among them.[8]

In 1755, a treaty and a purchase of land were again negotiated by South Carolina.[9] In 1756, North Carolina commissioned Hugh Waddell to conclude a treaty of alliance and cession, which was followed the same year by the establishment of a chain of forts in the Cherokee country. Among these, Fort Prince George was erected within gunshot of the town of Keowee on the Keowee River; Fort Monroe, 170 miles farther down the river; and Fort Loudoun on the Tennessee, at the mouth of the Tellico.[10] In 1777, Cherokee hostilities were put down with a heavy hand by the combined forces of Virginia, North Carolina and South Carolina, and a great number of their principal towns on the Tennessee were destroyed.[11]

A cession of land extorted from the Indians at this time proved to be so distasteful to the Chicamauga[12] band that they refused to assent to it.[13] Moving westward, they settled the "Five Lower Towns" on the Tennessee, among which was Lookout Mountain Town. These, with various other cessions and treaties[14] summarize the official relations of this nation with colonial governments previous to the War of Independence and the formation of the Confederation.

Charters and patents granted by England to the colonies consistently ignored the claims of the aborigines to the land, while colonial governments too often left their course to be directed by circumstances or chance. Agents and commissioners, permitted a free hand in securing cessions and arranging treaties, used bribes without scruple, shamelessly taking advantage of chiefs and headmen in negotiating agreements. These sharp practices in time bred suspicion which developed into hostility between Indians and whites.

By thus failing at the outset to adopt a definite, systematic policy of justice and humanity in dealing with the native inhabitants, the mother country and her colonies set an unsound precedent for all subsequent dealings with them.

That any amicable relation at all existed between the Indians and the English was due chiefly to the exceptional white men who dealt honorably as man to man with the natives, and to the proximity of Spaniards in Florida and Frenchmen in the Mississippi Valley and on the Gulf Coast, bidding for Indian favors. These rivals the English regarded with jealous attention, dreading not only the loss of profitable trade, but fearing the hostility of warriors who could become formidable enemies at the very back door of the settlements.

For a brief while, therefore, the colonists adopted a conciliatory policy toward the Cherokees, who, responding to their advances, formed an alliance with them against the French. In the attack upon Fort Duquesne a detachment of Cherokee warriors rendered valuable service to the English. But the contemptuous attitude of British and Colonial officers and the severe military restraint placed upon them created so much dissatisfaction that they determined to withdraw their allegiance and return home. On their return, having lost their horses in an encounter with the French, they supplied themselves with mounts from a herd found running at large on the range. The frontiersmen, who claimed the horses, regarding this as an act of horse stealing, attacked the party on its way home through the settlements, and killed forty warriors.

This and other acts of hostility and even treachery were too flagrant to be endured. Even Atta-Kulla-Kulla, the wise old peace chief, became aroused. Calling a council of war, he declared that after they should have safely conducted back to the settlements some Englishmen who were among them for the purpose of arranging a treaty, "The hatchet shall never be buried until the blood of our people shall be avenged. But let us not violate our faith by shedding the blood of those who have come among us in confidence, bearing belts of wampum to cement a perpetual friendship. Let us carry them back to the settlements and then take up the hatchet and endeavor to exterminate the whole race of them."[15]

In the bloody war which followed, villages were burned, orchards and corn fields destroyed, women and children murdered, many warriors slain, and the surviving inhabitants forced to take refuge in the caves of the mountains until peace had been restored by the humiliating Treaty of 1760.[16]

The tribesmen had not fully recovered from the effects of this struggle when they were confronted with the War of Independence. Smarting under their recent defeat at the hands of the colonists, and resenting the steady encroachment of the back-settlers upon their hunting grounds, they unhesitatingly ranged themselves on the side of England and placed their warriors at the service of King George. In the border warfare which followed, Indians and whites vied with each other in the atrocity of their acts.

Finally the Cherokees, completely vanquished, were forced to sue for peace. In 1785, by the Treaty of Hopewell, Congress was given the right to pass laws regulating trade with the nation, the Cherokees were granted the privilege of sending a delegate to Congress, and the whites were forbidden to settle upon Cherokee lands.[17]

This treaty was unsatisfactory to Indians and whites alike. The latter paid scant attention to the article forbidding them to settle on Indian lands; the natives refused to submit to the encroachments of intruders and kept them terrified by sudden raids and bloody massacres. The whites retaliated by carrying war into the very heart of the Indian country until this condition of affairs was terminated by the intervention of the federal government in 1790.

As early as 1789, General Henry Knox, secretary of war, called the attention of President Washington to the disgraceful violation of the Treaty of Hopewell, and recommended the appointment of a commission to look into the matter, and, if need be, to negotiate a more effective treaty.[18] In August of the next year the Senate passed a resolution providing for such a commission. The result was the Treaty of Holston, which, in addition to settling the boundary question, gave the federal government the exclusive right to trade with the Cherokees. To the Cherokees, it granted an annuity of one thousand dollars, promised to supply implements of husbandry, and to send four persons into the Cherokee Nation to act as interpreters.[19]

In compliance with these agreements, the federal agent, who was appointed to see that the provisions of the treaty were carried out, established an agency on the Hiwassee River near its confluence with the Tennessee, and there settled disputes arising between the whites and Cherokees, enforced intercourse laws, apportioned annuities and distributed plows, hoes, spinning wheels, cards, and looms among the Indians, instructing them in their use. Colonel Silas Dinsmore,[20] who was agent from 1796 to 1799, devoted his interest to the raising of cotton, to which some sections of the nation were especially well suited. Major Lewis succeeded him, and in turn was succeeded by R. J. Meigs. For twenty-two years, this old Revolutionary soldier, who had marched to Quebec with Arnold,[21] served as Cherokee Indian agent, rendering efficient and intelligent service to the government and to the Cherokees alike.

This new federal policy gave encouragement, impetus, and direction to the progressive spirit already abroad in the nation. Notwithstanding the half century of intermittent warfare, the

Cherokees had made considerable advancement even before the Treaty of Holston. Adair states that horses had been introduced among them early in the eighteenth century and that by 1760 they had "a prodigious number" of them and they were of "excellent" quality.[22]

The same may be said of cattle, hogs and poultry. Sevier,[23] on his expedition against the Coosa towns in 1793, allowed his army to kill three hundred beeves at Etowah and leave their carcasses rotting on the ground.[24] Benjamin Hawkins, while traveling through the Cherokee Nation three years later, met two Indian women driving ten fat cattle to the settlements to sell. Indian pork was highly esteemed by the colonists. "At the fall of the leaf," says Adair, "the woods are full of hickory nuts, acorns, chestnuts and the like, which occasions the Indian bacon to be more streaked, firm and better tasted than any we met with in the English settlements."[25]

Hunting was a lucrative occupation of the men until the end of the eighteenth century, a party of traders in 1765 taking home at one trip thirty wagon loads of furs. Colonel William Byrd of Virginia regularly for many years sent his caravans of from 50 to 100 pack horses to the Cherokee Country for the furs which they brought to his private wharf and exported to foreign markets.[26]

By their geographic position and superior numbers, the Cherokees might have held the balance of power in the south had it not been for the looseness of their tribal organization. The first attempt to weld the whole nation into closer political unity was in 1736 when Christian Priber, a French Jesuit, went to live among them. By adapting himself to their language and customs, he so won their confidence that he was able to induce them to adopt a form of government modeled after the French monarchy. According to his plan, the chief medicine man was to be emperor, Priber, himself, secretary of state, and Great Tellico, the national capitol. But when Priber was arrested by the authorities of North Carolina on the charge of being a secret emissary of the French, his scheme collapsed.[27]

It was seventy-two years afterwards that the Cherokees reorganized their government and adopted a written code of laws. In 1808 the tribal council provided for regulating parties to maintain order in the nation, named the penalty for horse stealing, and abolished the blood feud. In 1810, an act of oblivion for all past murder was passed by unanimous consent of the seven clans in Grand Council at Oostinaleh.[28] By this act punishment was taken from the clan and placed in the hands of the National Council. Thus the dawn of the new century found the Cherokees emerging from a loose tribal form of government into a coherent national system.

CHAPTER 3

A Century of Progress

At the height of their ancient tribal greatness the Cherokees had more than half a hundred towns and villages, which for administrative purposes were divided into districts or settlements called towns. The town was the political as well as the economic unit of the nation. The town's chiefs and its wise men were its representatives in the Grand Council. The head chiefs during the century immediately preceding the constitutional period, which began in 1827, were Moytoy, Atta-Kulla,[1] Oconostota, Tassel,[2] Scolacuta,[3] Inauleh,[4] Charles Hicks, and Pathkiller.

References to chief Moytoy appear in colonial records as early as 1730. In April of that year he summoned his headmen and warriors to confer with Sir Alexander Cuming, a commissioner appointed by North Carolina authorities to conclude an alliance with the Cherokees.[5] A preliminary agreement was reached at a meeting held near the headwaters of the Hiwassee River and a delegation of seven clansmen consented to accompany the English envoy to England, there to complete the negotiations. Oconostota and Atta-Kulla-Kulla were members of the party that embarked at Charleston amidst the protestation of kinsmen who, having come to see them off, were alarmed by the violence of the waves that threatened to sink the ship.[6]

On the eve of their return to America, the members of the delegation signed the Treaty of Dover, in which they obligated their nation to trade with the English, exclusively; to allow them "to make haste and build houses and plant corn from Charleston towards the towns of the Cherokee behind the mountains," and to keep their trading paths clear of Spanish and French traders, even at the cost of blood, if need be. If any negroes ran away into the woods from their English masters, the Cherokees were to apprehend them if possible and return them to the plantations from which they had run away, receiving as a reward a gun and watch coat.[7] Although this treaty was never approved by the Grand Council, the English regarded it as binding upon the Nation.[8]

Upon the death of Moytoy in 1736, Atta-Kulla-Kulla became head chief of the Cherokees. His name in English means Leaning Reed, but the white people called him Little Carpenter because of his small stature and delicate frame, and because of his expert knowledge of wood-craft. Probably no man of his time knew more about the plant and animal life of the Appalachian region than this unassuming native scientist. Unlike his nephew, Oconostota, the Little Carpenter was a pacifist whose intelligence and humanity deny the charge that there is no good Indian but a dead Indian. Yet his administration of forty-two years was troubled with almost constant warfare from which his people suffered incredible disasters that threatened the utter extinction of the tribe. Before the Revolution ended he had passed into the Darkening Land,[9] and Oconostota was chosen in his stead.

Oconostota is conceded to have been the most distinguished and the most signally honored of all Cherokees. His prowess in war was unsurpassed, his eloquence unequaled by contemporary Americans. But the great warrior was no longer a young man when, in 1786, he succeeded to the administrative leadership of his nation. Within four years of the battle of Yorktown he succumbed to the disease which had been preying on him for months and was laid to rest in the soil of his fathers. The Tassel, a younger man, succeeded to the chieftainship, which he held for scarcely three years before he was assassinated in a treacherous and brutal manner by a white back-settler.

War was narrowly averted by the election of Scolacutta, who, though no friend to the outlanders, was in favor of dealing with them through the constituted authorities of the United States, of which his old friend "Wasatuna" was president and the Great White Father of the Indians.

An incident of Scolucutta's administration was an invitation from President Washington to visit the national capitol in the summer of 1794. He was to bring with him some representative warriors and headmen, in order that all might talk together as friends and brothers over the misunderstandings that had arisen between backsettlers and Indians over boundary questions.

In response to the invitation, a delegation of seven clansmen repaired to the seat of the national government, and while there negotiated a new treaty. In addition to readjusting boundary disputes, the treaty provided for the United States to furnish the Cherokees with looms and spinning wheels and with plows, hoes, and other agricultural implements to the value of five thousand dollars. This policy marked the beginning of far-reaching changes in economic life of the people.[10]

Equal in importance with the chiefs of this era was the "Beloved Woman of Chota," Nancy Ward, about whom there are conflicting opinions and traditions. Her mother was Tame Doe, sister to Atta-Kulla-Kulla; her father, Sir Francis Ward, an Englishman of noble lineage.[11] At different periods of her life she was called "Nanne," the "Wild Rose of the Cherokees," the "Beloved Woman" and the "Priestess and Prophetess of Chota." In history, she is known as Nancy Ward, and her descendants are of the Nancy Ward stock.[12]

In recognition of her fearlessness in the face of danger and of services of a rare and special character, the Grand Council of the Nation conferred upon her the title of Ghi-ga-ou, "an honor reserved for women endowed with physical perfection and with the psychic powers required of a high priestess and mouthpiece of the Great Spirit."[13]

As Ghi-ga-ou, Nancy Ward had the privilege of sitting in the Grand Council of the nation, where a special seat was reserved for her. Hers was the power of life and death over prisoners. With the wave of a swan's wing she could free the captive bound to the stake or order the faggots to be lighted at his feet. Within the province of her authority her power was supreme.[14]

Although she could draw as true a bow as any warrior, Nancy Ward preferred peace to war and was a friend to the white people, being half Scottish herself.[15] "The white men are our brothers; the same sky is over all,"[16] was the reason she gave for befriending them in times of danger. But she never lacked loyalty to the Indians of whom she always spoke as "my people." It was not a blind clannish loyalty, however; the Beloved Woman was too fine and fearless to show petty favoritism, and far too intelligent to encourage partisan partiality.

Quick to learn and eager to teach, she introduced new customs among the Cherokees in order that they might keep abreast of the economic changes of the country. She introduced the first cattle into the Cherokee Nation and taught the women of the tribe to care for milk and to make butter. She was first among them to own slaves, which she secured from white people. With these slaves, she encouraged the cultivation of cotton in the nation at the time game had begun to grow scarce and the supply of skins had become inadequate for the needs of clothing and bedding. She also encouraged sheep raising, so that textile fibers could be supplied for the spinning wheels and looms the government had begun to furnish the Nation in lieu of money annuities.[17]

As the women gained facility in the use of the wheel and shuttle, they began to vie with each other in the amount of cloth that could be turned out in a day, and the quality and variety of colors which could be produced from the barks and roots they scoured the country to secure. New fashions in dress and household arts were thus inaugurated in the land of the Cherokees, which profoundly affected industry and set at naught some old tribal manners and customs. Nancy Ward planted the first peach trees west of the Alleghenies and made popular a certain variety of fruit which is still called the Indian Peach. A number of other beneficent innovations are attributable to her influence.

For many years, the Beloved Woman attended the Grand Council regularly and took part in its proceedings; but when the government was under a second revision in 1817 she appeared at Amohe and formally resigned her office, returned her staff with its insignia, and retired to private life at her home near Woman Killer's Ford on the Ocowee. In the year 1824, at the advanced age of one hundred and eight, she joined her illustrious contemporaries in the Land of the Setting Sun.[18]

Many Cherokees today take pride in tracing their lineage to Nancy Ward, whose memory the Daughters of the American Revolution and the State of Tennessee have so notably honored in recent years.[19]

It was during the chieftainship of Inolah,[20] who succeeded Scolacutta, that the government of the nation underwent a revision; graft had begun to corrupt some of those high in authority, causing discontent and a division of opinion among the tribesmen as they saw their domains and their supply of game rapidly diminishing. By this time also an increasing number of white people had married into the nation. It was during his chieftainship that Protestant missionaries began their beneficent work among the Cherokees.

The first English-speaking school in the nation, however, is accredited to Daniel Ross, an intermarried white citizen who had a trading post in the vicinity of Lookout Mountain. Animated by the desire to educate his large family of Cherokee children growing up around him without school advantages, this enterprising Scotch merchant applied to the Grand Council for permission to import a teacher and to open a school at his own expense. After some hesitation on the part of conservative chiefs the permission was granted and a school was opened, the services of John Barber Davis having been secured as teacher.

The experiment was successful beyond all expectation in illustrating to tribal leaders the practical advantages of having schools in their midst where their young people might learn to read and write in English, the language in which their treaties and contracts with the white people were written.[21]

John Barber Davis drilled his scholars in the rules of correct English, instilled in their youthful minds sound principles of conduct, and encouraged the habit of reading the good and useful books on their father's shelves—which constituted the first library in the Cherokee Nation.[22] Little did this Scotch school-master realize that one of his pupils was to become a great peace chief of the Cherokees.

Upon the emigration of Inolah to the Arkansas country the chieftainship passed to the grand old patriot, Path Killer, who, with superhuman energy and inspired foresight, advanced the nation to the constitutional period, which began in 1827.

With the exception of the work done by Priber and the Federal Government, no outside aid had been given the Cherokees to raise their standard of culture and no effort made to Christianize them before the end of the eighteenth century.[23]

The first mission station among the Cherokees was founded by the Moravians, a band of German Christians who had established a settlement on the Upper Yadkin about 1752. During the Indian wars, Cherokee chiefs who were hospitably received by them expressed a desire that teachers be sent to their people. Thereafter, the evangelization of the tribe had never been lost sight of by the brethren.[24]

In 1799, two missionaries from this place, hearing of Daniel Ross's School, visited the Cherokees with a view to locating a mission station among them. As a result, the next year a council was held at Tellico Agency, where after much discussion it was agreed that permission be granted the Moravians to open a school. The Rev. Abraham Steiner and Gottlieb Byham began to hold religious services at the home of James Vann, a mixed blood Cherokee of progressive ideas.

On account of various difficulties, however, the school was not opened as soon as had been agreed upon.

The Grand Council, held at Oostinaleh,[25] a few miles distant, declared that the Cherokee Nation wanted to educate its children, not to embrace a new religion, and unless the missionaries could open a school within six months they must leave the nation. With the encouragement of Agent Meigs and a few leading Cherokees the school was finally established and children of some prominent chiefs enrolled as students. In 1805, Reverend and Mrs. John Gambold took charge at Spring Place, where they remained until her death fifteen years later.[26]

In 1804 the Presbyterians followed the Moravians and established a school at Maryville, Tennessee, with the Reverend Gideon

Blackburn at its head; in 1817 the American Board of Foreign Missions founded the famous School of Brainard Mission from which Missionary Ridge took its name. A great religious revival swept the country beginning in 1818,[27] but up to this time there had been only a few conversions to the Christian faith, of which those of Catherine Brown, Margaret Vann, and Charles Hicks were the most notable.

The missionaries worked side by side with their pupils, their instruction being practical as well as theoretical, and industrial as well as religious. They, in this way, gained a very strong hold upon the natives and their influence among them for good is not easily estimated.

Until the end of the eighteenth century, intermarriage of the Cherokees with Europeans was confined chiefly to white men, but after that time several women married into the tribe. The intermarried white men were usually traders or officers at the pioneer forts, and of good English, Scotch, Irish, or Huguenot stock. By the beginning of the nineteenth century, the mixed blood population with civilized ideas was one of the dominant political forces among the Cherokees which made itself felt in the reorganization of the government from 1808 to 1827.

The opening of highways in the Indian country furnished another tremendous impetus to progress, although, like most other innovations of the white man, roads were bitterly resented by the conservative Indians who preferred their own paths or trails. Nevertheless, by 1824 treaties had been arranged[28] permitting the opening of all roads necessary for intercourse between Tennessee, Georgia, and the territory lying directly west of these states for the convenience of travelers and for commercial intercourse. Also, there were general stores and "public stops" built at intervals along the roads, which proved a source of considerable revenue to the owners, all of whom were natives. The opening of highways brought the entire nation more closely in touch with the outside world, and by stimulating trade and encouraging the accumulation of property, prepared the way for further advancement.[29]

With the opening of highways, the stimulation of trade, and the cultivation of cotton, the institution of slavery increased in favor among the mixed blood population. In 1825 there were 1,277 negro slaves[30] in the nation, and be it said to their credit, the Cherokees were humane in the treatment of their bondmen, with whom there was rarely ever any intermixture of races. By their help, agriculture and stock raising became more profitable than would have been possible with native labor alone, and more leisure and opportunity for culture were afforded Cherokee women as well as men.

CHAPTER 4

The Cherokees West

The beginning of westward emigration among the Cherokees belongs to the age of legend and tradition. The story of the "Lost Cherokees" indicates that a part of the tribe had crossed the Father of Waters at a very early time. Probably hunting parties visited the western prairies at intervals centuries before the discovery of America by Europeans. Later, wars with the settlers, discontent over land cessions, and intrusion of whites upon their domain led small detachments to move into Spanish territory where they were not molested. Such a settlement was that on the St. Francis River in the Arkansas[1] country near the present town of New Madrid, Missouri.

In 1795 the St. Francis colony was joined by a body of Chickamauga warriors led by The Bowl, town chief of Running Water, who had recently engaged in an encounter with some white men at Muscle Shoals on the Tennessee River. When it was discovered that all of the white men involved had lost their lives in the affray, the Indians, fearing that they would be turned over to the United States government for punishment, took refuge in Spanish territory and refused to return home. In time, their families joined them, thereby adding strength and numbers to the Arkansas settlement.[2]

In 1800 Spain ceded Louisiana to France and that country sold it three years later to the United States. Thus, with the Louisiana Purchase, the western fragment of the great eastern nation came under the aegis of the federal government in 1803.

An earthquake disturbed the St. Francis Valley in 1811, causing a small area to become submerged, whereupon the Indians, believing this whole region to be under the ban of the Great Spirit, removed in a body to an unoccupied tract between the White River and the Arkansas.

The policy of Indian consolidation was approved by President Jefferson, although it did not originate with him. In a confidential message to Congress on January 18, 1803, he suggested the expediency of removing the five great southern tribes beyond the Mississippi to a region set apart exclusively for their use.[3] In July of the same year, he made a rough draft of a constitutional amendment which had for its central theme the removal of all the Indian tribes of the United States to some part of the newly acquired Territory.[4] On his recommendation, an act of Congress approved March 26, 1804, provided for the organization of Louisiana into two territories, and appropriated fifteen million dollars as a preliminary step toward forwarding this project.[5] It also authorized the president to approach the tribal governments on the subject.

In 1808 when a delegation of Cherokees was preparing to visit Washington to secure an adjustment of their differences and a more equitable distribution of their annuities, the Secretary of War wrote Agent Meigs to embrace every occasion for "sounding out" the chiefs and headmen on the subject of the removal of the whole tribe.[6]

A considerable difference existed at this time between the Upper and the Lower Cherokees. The former were farmers, while the latter, who were still hunters, were beginning to feel themselves hedged in by the shrinking boundaries of their hunting grounds. Differences in occupation and domestic institutions led to a divergence of interests which resulted in discontent and even in friction, so that a considerable delegation of Upper Cherokees, which arrived in Washington in May 1808, requested that a line be drawn between their lands and those of the Lower Cherokees; that their lands be allotted to them in severalty; and that they be admitted as citizens of the United States. Their tribesmen of the south might then be permitted to hunt as long as the game lasted. In his talk with the delegation, President Jefferson encouraged removal but informed the tribesmen that citizenship could be conferred only by Congress.[7]

The next year or two, the idea of removal appears to have gained favor with both divisions of the tribe. An appropriation having been made for the purpose, a delegation, sent out to investigate the Arkansas country, returned with such favorable reports that a large number were prepared to remove at once. Jefferson went out of office, however, before anything could be done about it, and Madison did not favor removal on a large scale. Although between two and three thousand had emigrated to Arkansas before 1817, the removal was not officially countenanced, either by their own nation, or by the federal government.[8]

Following their abandonment of the St. Francis country in 1811, the western band of Cherokees occupied for a time the region between the Arkansas and the White rivers which had been ceded to the Osages in 1808. Here for a period of years they were tenants without title to their lands, much to their own inconvenience as well as the annoyance of the Osages. By the treaty of July 8, 1817, this tract was ceded to the western Cherokees in exchange for an equal amount of land on the east side of the Mississippi.[9] A year later the Osage title to the land was extinguished by the treaty of September 25, 1818.[10]

Following his departure from the St. Francis country, The Bowl located his village on the south side of the Arkansas, between Shoal and Petit Jean creeks, on land which was not included in the grant of July 1817. Instead of crossing to the north side of the river after he discovered his mistake, this chief and his followers, about sixty families in all, removed to Texas in the winter of 1818–1819, where a grant of land had been promised them by the Spanish government.[11] This band, located between the Sabine and the Neches, was joined from time to time by other tribesmen who preferred to live under Spanish rule, and became known as the Texas Cherokees.

Those who remained on the Arkansas and White rivers reorganized their settlement, divided the country into four administrative districts and designated a seat of government at Takatoka's Town. The arrival of several hundred emigrants from the ancient nation during the next few years increased the population to such an extent as to require the founding of several new settlements, thus extending the line of frontier towards the Osage villages in the Verdigris valley.

In order to keep down trouble between the two tribes, the War Department in 1817 located Fort Smith, a military post, on the Arkansas River near the southwestern corner of the Cherokee grant. Thus there came to be a Cherokee Nation West, to be distinguished from the Cherokee Nation East, and in 1818, Tahlontees-kee was chosen head chief of the western nation. Two years later, he died and was succeeded by his brother, John Jolly.

John Jolly lived on the north side of the Arkansas, near the mouth of the Illinois River. The seat of government, having been removed to Tahlonteeskee town, was three miles distant. Chief Jolly was a man of massive frame, although not tall of stature. He spoke no English, habitually wore the aboriginal dress of buckskin hunting shirt, leggings and moccasins, on his head a cloth turban, and was scrupulously punctilious in the observance of old tribal customs.[12]

In addition to the lands in Arkansas, the western nation had been granted a Perpetual Outlet West, pledged to them by the President of the United States and the Secretary of War in March 1818, and again in October 1821.[13] The Outlet was to serve as an unmolested passageway to the buffalo range and the hunting grounds of the Far West, and as a surplus for future fields and pastures as they were needed.

The Arkansas Cherokees still liked to hunt, infinitely preferring buffalo flesh and venison to pork and beef. Twice yearly they organized their hunting parties which brought home to the settlement the season's supply of wild meat and skins which played a large part in the domestic and economic life of the Indian.[14] This concession was intended also as an inducement to the Eastern Cherokees to surrender their lands in the East and remove to the Arkansas country.

These Cherokee hunting parties sometimes came in conflict with the band of Osages that had been induced by Pierre Choteau to remove from the Missouri and the Osage rivers to the Verdigris, where they would be contributory to his trading post on Grand

River.[15] By 1806, the Osages were in a state of constant warfare with the western Cherokees and all the other tribes[16] whose villages were scattered throughout this region claimed by the plains tribe. Hostilities continued with increasing rancor as offenses multiplied. When the situation became intolerable, the Cherokees appealed to Governor Clark of the Missouri Territory, complaining that "the rivers were running red with the blood of their tribesmen," and that something must be done about it else they themselves would be compelled to take the warpath in self-defense. This was in the autumn of 1817.

The following spring, the Osages made a night raid on the Cherokee settlements and drove off all their best horses, where-upon Tuh-an-tuh,[17] war chief of the Cherokees, mustered a party of several hundred warriors, reinforced by white frontiersmen, and started out to reclaim the stolen horses and to punish the offending Osages. They had no trouble in following the broad trail, which led straight to the village of Chief Claremore, "Builder of towns,"[18] now a man of many years and greatly renowned for courage. His village of Pasuga was located at the foot of a large mound on the Verdigris River. The main body of Osage fighting men was absent on a buffalo hunt, and only the oldest warriors remained behind to protect the village and prepare for the return of the hunters.

At dawn of a beautiful spring day, Tuh-an-tuh's war party made a surprise attack upon the village and put the women and children to flight in the utmost confusion. The Osage warriors made a determined stand on the rocky rim of the hill overlooking the village, but they were soon routed by the fierceness of the attack and the superior equipment of the enemy. Many were killed or wounded, and a large number were taken captive by the Cherokees.[19] Among the slain, according to Cherokee tradition, was Chief Claremore, who fell fighting bravely as he stood on the southern brow of the hill. There he was buried by the returning hunters, according to the funeral rites of the tribe, and a cairn of white limestones, heaped high above his resting-place, stood for more than half a century as a fitting monument to a great leader of a magnificent tribe of aboriginal Americans. His eldest son, by hereditary right, succeeded to the name of his father, to the chieftainship of the band, and to the blood feud of his clan.[20]

The battle of Pasuga, or Claremore Mound, which took place in Anoya,[21] the Strawberry Moon of 1818, did not end hostilities between the two tribes.

From the beginning of the western movement, communication between the Eastern and Western Cherokees was fairly active and relations for the most part were friendly. Those from the west sometimes traversed the long wilderness trail to visit friends and kindred in the east. And it was not unusual for those of the old nation to cross the Mississippi to see and judge for themselves the character of the region they were being urged to accept in exchange for their ancient domains.

The founding of the first mission station among the Arkansas Cherokees was inspired by one such pilgrimage on the part of the venerable chief, Tollunteeskee,[22] who, when visiting Georgia in 1818, met Jeremiah Evarts, treasurer of the American Board of Commissioners for Foreign Missions, at that time on a tour of inspection in the South. The aged chief besought Mr. Evarts to send someone to found a school for his people in the west, and as a result the Reverend Cephas Washburn was sent to the White River country to select a site and open a school for the Cherokees west. The missionary set out overland in 1819 and on January 1, 1821, opened a school he called Dwight Mission, in honor of the Reverend Timothy Dwight of Yale College.[23]

CHAPTER 5

The Cherokees and the Georgia Compact

During the years immediately preceding the War of 1812, the Indian question assumed unusual importance at Washington. The southern tribes, if united, were still strong enough to cause considerable trouble should they renew their allegiance to Great Britain. Disturbing reports reached the Department of War that agents of the British government were arming the Indians of the Great Lakes and the western frontier and were encouraging hostilities to the United States.[1] War with England and an uprising on the frontier at the same time appeared doubly embarrassing to a government poorly equipped for military operations of any kind.

In an effort to conciliate the Indians and to attach them as firmly as possible to the American cause, the Secretary of War instructed his agents to promote and maintain friendly relations with the natives,[2] and at the same time, he furnished them the means of carrying out this policy. Gifts to prominent chiefs, medals for services to the United States, appointments in the army, friendly interest in their tribal affairs, all tended to have the desired effect upon the southern tribes. This was especially true of the Cherokees, whose agent, Colonel Return J. Meigs, was one of the wisest and most tactful of all United States Indian Agents.

The Cherokees East, then enjoying a period of peace and tranquility, were rapidly acquiring the arts of European civilization, and consequently, they favored peace. In order to make sure of the loyalty of the Arkansas band, Agent Meigs dispatched John Ross, bearing gifts and peace talks, to the tribesmen beyond the Mississippi.

After experiencing many dangerous adventures along unfamiliar wilderness trails, the youthful envoy returned to his father's home at Ross's Landing on December 25, 1811, bringing assurances that the Cherokees West were loyal allies of the Great White Father.[3]

Thus, when the Shawnee Chief[4] made his tour through the South and, with his burning eloquence and his "almanac of red sticks," tried to fire the southern tribes to revolt, he met little encouragement from the Cherokees. A few of the mountain chiefs expressed a desire "to dance the war dance of the Indians of the Lakes and sing their song," but, thanks to the influence of progressive and influential headmen, the war spirit was quashed when the Grand Council decided there was more to lose than to gain by going to war. The Cherokees would remain neutral.[5]

In retaliation, the Red Sticks, as the war party of the Creeks was called, perpetrated outrages upon the Cherokees which aroused such indignation among the young men, already eager to take the war path, that the Council was forced to abandon its peace policy, to declare war upon the hostile Creeks, and to place its forces at the command of the federal government. Between seven hundred and eight hundred warriors under their own officers took part in the hostilities that followed, rendering noteworthy service to the American cause. In the battle of Horse Shoe Bend,[6] it was undoubtedly the bravery and daring of the Cherokee and loyal Creek forces that won the victory for General Jackson which made him a national hero and prepared the way for his election to the presidency of the United States.

This engagement took place on the Tallapoosa River near the site of the Indian Village of Tohopeka, Alabama. There the Red Sticks had thrown up a strong fortification of logs across the neck of a peninsula made by a bend in the river, and behind it about a thousand warriors with three hundred women and children had taken refuge.

Supported by the Cherokees under their own officers, Jackson was able to storm the defense. The beleaguered Muskogees[7] fought desperately but were cut down without mercy. Of the three hundred who survived in the fort, only three were men. The defenders of the

Horse Shoe were practically exterminated. Some of the Cherokees lived to rue the part they took in this inhuman massacre. "If I had known Jackson would drive us from our homes I would have killed him that day at the Horse Shoe,"[8] afterwards declared Junaluska, an able Cherokee ally of the distinguished white general.

When, in the winter of 1816, a delegation was sent to Washington to protest against the terms of the Treaty of Fort Jackson, which followed the Creek War, General Jackson, who was a member of the commission appointed by the government to arrange a treaty with the southern tribes, showed scant consideration for the loyal Creeks and Cherokees. From the former, he demanded the cession of a large tract of land called the Hickory Grounds, comprising more than half the territory of the Creek Nation, and when they demurred, he ordered them to sign the treaty or join their kinsmen who had fled to Florida.

The Cherokees, finding their domains encroached upon by the lines defining the Creek cession, protested only to discover that General John Coffee, detached by General Jackson to establish the northern boundary, had arranged a private contract with a town chief through whose village the lines ran.[9]

Of such significance was this procedure that the National Council dispatched a deputation to Washington to lay the matter before the Secretary of War. Agent Meigs accompanied them and, in spite of efforts to prejudice Secretary William Crawford against the Cherokees, he secured a satisfactory adjustment of their boundary claims in a treaty which granted also a claim of two thousand five hundred dollars for damages sustained by the Cherokees during the Creek War.[10]

General Jackson, who stubbornly opposed the terms of this treaty,[11] is said to have been greatly chagrined over the victory of the Cherokees, whose interests he had intentionally betrayed. From this time forward, he and his friends managed to secure more and more of the Indian patronage at Washington. Their influence on the Department of War leading steadily and persistently toward their ultimate aim, that of Indian consolidation west of the Mississippi.

The emissaries sent on this mission, Colonel George Lowrey, Major Walker, Major Ridge, Adjutant John Ross, and Cunnessee,[12] indicate that the Cherokees were no longer a nation to be dealt with after the fashion of former times. "These men are of cultivation and understanding. Their appearance and deportment are such as to entitle them to respect and attention,"[13] said the *National Intelligencer* in mentioning their arrival.

However, the fact that they were becoming civilized was far from gratifying to those who opposed any policy that might tend to attach the natives more firmly to the soil. Already, plans were under way to remove the five great southern tribes to the territory west of the Mississippi when, in the fall of 1816, a commission was appointed to treat with the Cherokees on the basis of their removal. At the same time, the Tennessee contingent in Congress was urging the President to free that state of Indians,[14] and Governor McMinn's agent in the nation was diligently campaigning for removal.

The Arkansas Cherokees, in a controversy with the Osages and Quapaws because no definite tract of land had been assigned to them nor was likely to be assigned without a corresponding cession in the East, appealed to the President,[15] who, relying upon reports from General Jackson assuring the administration that the Cherokees were willing to emigrate, appointed a commission instructed to meet their delegation at the agency on June 20, 1817.[16]

In May the spring Council of the Cherokees met at Amohe.[17] News of the impending negotiations had gone out and there was a large attendance. Discussions in the Council revealed strong opposition, not only to removal, but to the cession of any more land: "If the western band is not happy where they are, let them return to the eastern nation."[18] Had a sentiment for removal existed the previous year, there was no evidence of it at this time.

When the government commissioner arrived at the Agency in June, only delegates from Arkansas met them. It was three weeks before a sufficient representation could be mustered to open negotiations. The Arkansas deputation, who had everything to gain and nothing to lose, was graciously compliant, but the eastern tribesmen firmly opposed removal or a further cession of territory.

In "a talk" before the Council, General Jackson took the ground that the Cherokee delegation of 1809 had arranged with President Jefferson for an exchange of lands east of the Mississippi River for lands west of it, and that the time had now come when the exchange must be made. In order to fix the boundaries of the western country so as to prevent white people from settling within them, it was necessary for all who expected to remove at any future time to declare it now; after the bounds were marked and the lands laid off they would not otherwise be allowed to settle there.

The United States, he promised them, would provide the means of removal to those who wished to go, and to the poorer classes he would furnish implements of husbandry, arms and ammunition for hunting, and would allow them reasonable compensation for improvements. Those who preferred to remain might do so by becoming citizens of the United States. "As free men you have now to make your choice. . . . Those who [go west] go to a country belonging to the United States. . . . [There] your father, the President, can never be urged by his white children to ask their red brothers, the Cherokees, for any of the lands laid off at that place for them." As for the eastern lands, he declared that the right of occupation or hunting was the only right guaranteed to the Cherokee Nation by former treaties.[19]

The reply of the Cherokees in the form of a memorial, signed by sixty-seven chiefs, was presented by the Council to General Jackson. It stated that the great body of the Cherokees desired to remain in the land of their birth where they were rapidly advancing in civilization. They did not wish to revert to their original conditions and surroundings. They prayed, therefore, that the question of removal be pressed no farther and that they be allowed to remain peaceably in the land of their fathers.[20] Ignoring the memorial, General Jackson submitted a treaty which was signed by the Arkansas representation and by twenty-two tribesmen of minor importance in the Eastern Nation.

Forthwith, extensive preparations were started to incline the Cherokees to remove. A special agent was sent to assist Mr. Meigs, and when the work did not go fast enough to suit Governor McMinn, he himself went to the nation and canvassed for emigrants. Although bribes passed freely, and intimidation was unsparingly used[21] to get the Indians to come in and enroll for removal, the Governor of Tennessee, himself notoriously self-interested in the project, was doomed to disappointment in the final results. By the last of June, about seven hundred had enrolled and several boats were ready to descend the river for the purpose of bearing the Emigrants to the western country.[22] But the movement did not represent the sentiments of the nation as a whole.

The main body of the Cherokees was opposed to emigration, and as the summer wore away hostility towards the treaty became more and more pronounced. The Grand Council, which met in the fall, deposed and deprived of any further authority in the tribe Toochelah, the second chief, and appointed in his place Charles Hicks, a leader in the opposition. It even went so far as to pass the resolution that, "We consider ourselves a free and distinct nation, and the National Government has no polity over us, further than a friendly intercourse in trade."[23] Thus was set the earliest formulation of their opinion concerning their political status in the land of their nativity.

So active was the opposition that when a delegation of twelve Cherokees appeared at Washington in 1819,[24] Secretary Calhoun[25] entered into a new contract which effectively put an end to removal for the time being. By it the Cherokees ceded to the United States a tract of land as extensive as that to which it was entitled under the Treaty of 1817 and consented to the distribution of annuities in the proportion of two to one in favor of the eastern nation. The United States agreed to dispense with taking the census of 1817 and obligated itself to remove intruders from the Cherokee Nation.[26]

Meanwhile, Georgia, as her population increased and spread from the coast plain up the fertile river valleys, year by year pushing the line of the frontier farther and farther back into the highlands, found an ever-growing demand on the part of her citizens for the removal of the aborigines. The Creeks and Cherokees they regarded as particularly serious obstacles to progress. By 1823, demand for their removal from the state had become insistent on the ground that the federal government, in 1802, had entered into an agreement with Georgia to extinguish, for her use, the Indian title to land lying within the state as soon as it could be done on peaceable and reasonable terms.[27] A select committee, of which George R. Gilmer[28] was chairman, submitted a report to the House of Representatives on January 7, 1822, on the question whether or not the United States was keeping her part of the compact. It was the opinion of the committee that she was not.[29]

As a matter of fact, the largest Indian cessions had been obtained in other states, where, as soon as the natives relinquished their title to the land, it became part of the public domain. Acting on the report of the Gilmer committee, Congress appropriated $30,000 for the extinguishment of Indian land titles within the limits of Georgia,[30] and Secretary Calhoun at once appointed a commissioner to negotiate with the Cherokees for a cession of a part or all of their eastern land.

The Cherokee Council, when apprised of this act of Congress, passed a resolution in its autumn session "declaring unanimously and with one voice the determination to hold no more treaties" for the purpose of making cessions of lands, being resolved not to dispose of even one foot of ground. "But upon any question, not relating to a land cession," the resolution stated, "we will at all times during the session of the National Council at Echota, Newtown, receive the United States commissioners or agents with friendship and cordiality and will ever keep bright the chain of peace and friendship which links the Cherokee Nation and the government of the United States."[31]

Copies of the resolutions were sent to the Secretary of War and to the commissioners with the assurance that it would be entirely useless to put the United States to the trouble and expense of negotiating another treaty of cession. The commissioners remonstrated with the chiefs and threatened them with the indignation of the Great Father at Washington, who "would shake them off" if they persisted in their obstinacy.[32] So determined and bitter was the opposition, however, that the matter was allowed to rest until the following year, when, a vacancy having occurred at the Cherokee agency, the Secretary of War appointed Joseph McMinn, whose advocacy of removal was well known.

In spite of the Cherokee memorial of the previous year, Washington was so optimistic that aversion to cession might be "conquered by a little perseverance and judicious management,"[33] that it allowed the board of commissioners to be provided with thirty-five thousand dollars to aid them in conducting their negotiations. The War Department also instructed them to cooperate with commissioners appointed by Georgia to press claims of that state arising under former treaties.

Federal commissioners Campbell and Meriwether,[34] arriving at New Echota on October 4, 1823, found the Cherokee Council in regular session and representatives from Georgia already on the ground. Agent McMinn formally notified the Council of their arrival and was informed that the Grand Council was disposed to receive and be introduced to the Board according to the customs and ceremonies of the Cherokee Nation. Major Ridge, speaker of the Council, delivered an address of welcome and was answered by Campbell, who paid a high compliment to Cherokee civilization.

After this auspicious beginning, the federal agents showed no inclination to make haste in opening formal negotiations. Time and deliberation were essential to the judicious expenditure of the appropriation placed at their disposal and to the building up of a party in the Cherokee Nation favorable to cession. It was, therefore, somewhat to their discomfiture when they were called upon by the president of the committee two days later for a full statement of their instructions from the President of the United States relating to their business with the Cherokees.

After some hesitation on the part of the commissioners, formal negotiations finally began and, by request of the Cherokees, were conducted by both sides in writing.[35] "A novel procedure," undoubtedly it was, as Campbell observed, this "correspondence in writing conducted with a government regularly organized, composed of Indians."[36]

The negotiations are remarkable chiefly for the character of the arguments advanced by the representative of the United States, and for the straightforward manner in which the Cherokees answered them, giving the reasons why a further cession, or removal, could not be entertained by them. When the commissioners urged the plea that the white people were so cramped for land that they were driven from friends and connections to foreign lands, while the Cherokees had more land in Georgia than they needed; this was unjust; the Great Father of the universe intended the earth equally for his white and red children.

The Cherokees replied that the intentions of the Great Father they did not know, but it was quite evident that neither individuals nor nation had ever respected the principle. As for removal, the unfortunate part of the tribe which had emigrated to the west had suffered severely in the new country from sickness, wars and other calamities, and many of them would return if they could do so. Had it been their desire to go west they would have embraced opportunities formerly offered them. It was not their desire. They loved the soil which had given them birth and continued to nourish them.

Pressed further for a cession of land, since they would not consider removal, they declared that the limits of their nation were small, embracing mountains, hills, and poor lands which could never be cultivated. The Cherokees had once possessed an extensive country. In order to gratify the wishes of their neighbors, they had granted to the President cession after cession, until their limits had become circumscribed. Experience had taught them that a small grant would never satisfy the white man, therefore they had come to the unalterable determination never to part with another foot of land.[37]

As negotiations proceeded and the Cherokees remained obdurate, the talk of commissioners grew harsh and threatening. They denied the right of the Indians to the soil they inhabited, claiming that it had been forfeited by their hostilities to the United States during and after the War of the Revolution, and that the Indians were tenants at the will of the state within whose boundaries their Nation lay.[38]

Arguments, cajolery, threats, and bribery proved of no avail. The commissioners reported to the War Department the failure to consummate a treaty with the Cherokees and suggested that the prospect of securing a cession from the Creeks was more favorable.[39]

On the adjournment of Council, a Cherokee delegation, composed of John Ross, Major Ridge, George Lowrey, and Elijah Hicks, set out to Washington on horseback, and as they rode over windswept ridges and traversed forests or, at night, sat by the fire of the wayside "public stop," they never tired of discussing the questions of the day, particularly those which concerned the welfare of their own nation. For several years they had been associated together in Council, knew each other well, and trusted each other implicitly. They were all men of substance, keen and astute, and capable of holding their own in any political argument pertaining to their national affairs. Ross was doubtless the best educated of the four.

Arriving at Washington in January, they learned to their disappointment that they could not confer personally with the President, but that all business which they wished to transact with him must pass through the War Office. When they presented their credentials, they were asked if they had come to make a further cession of land.

Their answer, submitted in the form of a memorial, urged that the Cherokee Nation was laboring under peculiar disadvantages arising from the successive appropriations of Congress to hold treaties with their nation, such action tending to retard national improvement by unsettling the minds and prospects of its citizens. They repeated their determination to part with no more land, as the limits fixed by the treaty of 1819 left them territory barely adequate to their comfort and convenience, while the Cherokees were rapidly increasing in population, rendering it the duty of the nation to preserve unimpaired to posterity the lands of their ancestors. For these reasons, they asked that some other arrangement be made whereby Georgia's demand for land might be satisfied.[40]

The Secretary, in reply, laid great stress upon the Georgia compact and upon the zealous desire of the president to carry it out, "a distinct society or nation within the limits of a state being incompatible with our system."[41] He set forth in glowing terms the benefits that would accrue to the Cherokees from an exchange of their country for one beyond the annoying encroachments of civilization.

In their turn, the Cherokees pointed out that the United States was under compact to extinguish the Indian claims only on peaceable and reasonable terms; as for incompatibility with the system of the United States, the Indians were the original inhabitants of the country, and were not willing to allow the sovereignty of any state within the boundaries of their domain; they had never promised to cede their lands to the federal government, but it had guaranteed the land to them; they were not yet sufficiently civilized to cease being an independent community and become a territory or state within the Union; removal would retard their advancement in civilization since it would require time for the natives to adjust themselves to a new environment.[42]

At the suggestion of the President, copies of the correspondence were sent to the Georgia delegation in Congress and to George M. Troup, governor of the state, who held extreme state's rights views, represented the rich planter population, and who had been elected governor of Georgia with the avowed policy of ridding the state of Indian occupancy.

Georgia congressmen protested against the diplomatic courtesy shown the Indian delegates and complained that the civilizing policy of the United States tended to fasten the Indians more firmly on the soil.[43] After censuring the weak and dilatory policy of the federal government toward the Indians in the past, and accusing the white men in the Cherokee Nation of influencing them against removal, Governor Troup declared the fee simple of the lands lay in Georgia and that the Indians were tenants at her will; the state demanded the removal of these tenants, who must be given to understand that the United States was under obligation and must assist Georgia to occupy her lands even at the cost of bloodshed.

In his message March 4, 1824, President James Monroe defended his Indian policy, advocated removal beyond the Mississippi, but not by force, and expressed the opinion that the Indian title was not affected by the Georgia compact, the expression, "at the expense of the United States as long as the same can be done on reasonable terms," being full proof of the distinct understanding of both parties to the compact. The Indians had a right, he thought, to the territory, in the disposal of which they were to be considered free agents.[44]

On April 15, a select committee from the House of Representatives, of which John Forsythe was chairman, reported on this message, expressing the opinion that the guarantee of lands before 1802 granted occupancy title only, and that, if peaceable acquisition were not now possible, the Indians must be removed by force, or the United States obtain from Georgia consent to some other plan. Otherwise, the government might be put in the position of either seeing the Cherokees annihilated or defending them against United States citizens.[45]

Governor Troup was provoked to a fresh outburst of wrath by the President's message and by the discussions in Congress but when a fresh appropriation was made the last of May to extinguish Indian land titles in Georgia,[46] he quieted down for a time, confining his views on state's rights and the Indian question to the state legislature. Here, however, he hotly declared that "a state of things so unnatural and fruitful of evil as an independent government of a semi-barbarous people existing within the limits of a state could not long continue, and wise counsel must direct that relations which could not be maintained in peace, should be dissolved before an occasion should occur to break that peace."[47] In his message of 1825, the Governor recommended that the legislature adopt energetic measures for ridding the Cherokee Nation of all white people excepting only such as were necessarily employed by the United States to regulate commerce with the tribe, and that it extend the laws of Georgia over that nation.[48]

The Cherokees, however, held fast to their claim to national protection, and when Georgia attempted to send surveyors through their nation to lay out the course of a canal, the Council refused to permit it. "No individual state shall be allowed to make internal improvements within the sovereign limits of the Cherokee Nation,"[49] was resolved by the Council of 1826.

CHAPTER 6

Sequoyah and the Cherokee Alphabet

The Cherokees now earnestly addressed themselves to further national improvements. Their hopes and ambitions ran high. In a circular letter to the adjoining states in 1813, they had declared that many of their youth of both sexes "had acquired such knowledge of letters as to show the most incredulous that our mental powers are not, by nature, inferior to yours, and we look forward to a period of time when it may be said 'this artist, this mathematician, this astronomer is a Cherokee!'"[1]

There was an increasing desire among them to have their children educated. The treaty of 1819 contained a provision for a reservation of land twelve miles square to be sold by the United States, the proceeds to be invested by the President in stocks and bonds and the income applied in the manner best calculated to promote education among the Cherokees east of the Mississippi.[2] In 1822, seven Cherokee boys were being educated in a mission school at Cornwall, Connecticut. Of these, John Ridge, Elias Boudinot, and Richard Brown were to play a prominent part in the history of the nation.

In 1817, missionary activities among the southern tribes had so increased that within ten years they had eight churches and thirteen schools among the Cherokees. In these schools, which were very well attended, the children were taught not only reading, writing, and arithmetic, but the agricultural arts as well. In them, says one who visited the Cherokee Nation in 1818, "the boys take the different branches in weekly rotation; and on a Monday morning, such as are to turn out to labor, are called by naming their avocations of labor, as plough-boys, hoe-boys, axe boys, &c. to which call they answer and appear with the greatest cheerfulness and alacrity.

"The girls are taught in similar method, their occupations being suited to their sex. . . . They are instructed in the use of the needle, the arts of spinning, knitting and all household business; and it is stated, that among them are some gentle young women that would not disgrace more polished society."[3]

While progress in the academic branches was slow at first, the industrial training met with eager interest and wrought such results that village life was almost completely abandoned, the inhabitants scattering out and taking up farms. As the land was held in common, a farm was in reach of any member of the tribe, and by 1822, many families cultivated from ten to forty acres, on which they raised corn, rye, oats, wheat, and cotton. The women spun and wove their own cotton and woolen cloth and blankets, and knitted all the stockings used by their families.[4]

The mass of the Cherokees lived in houses. "It no longer remains a doubt," wrote a missionary from Brainard, Tennessee, in 1812, "whether the Indians of America can be civilized. The Cherokees have gone too far in the pleasant paths of civilization to return to the rough and unbeaten track of savage life."[5]

Political advancement kept pace with economic and educational progress. By 1820, the government was well organized and administered, having undergone considerable change since 1808. The Light Horse,[6] or regulators, provided for at that time, served their purpose well and were not disbanded until 1825, when district officers made their services no longer necessary.

In 1815 the Council provided for a standing committee whose business it was to look after claims and to adjust financial differences. This committee, appointed by the council of chiefs for two years, developed into the upper house of the legislature, while the general council became the lower house. The former body, composed of thirteen members including its president, with a clerk to record its proceedings, had the power to control and regulate financial affairs, to inspect the treasurer's books, and to acknowledge claims.[7]

The Council under the old system had been large, and the responsibility of each town chief trifling. In 1817 it had been reorganized, useless members were stricken off, and a standing body of legislators assembled in October of each year at New Echota, which was thereafter the permanent seat of government. By 1826, this body, consisting of thirty-three members, including its speaker, had power to legislate and to fill vacancies in its own body and in the national committee. The principal chief and the second chief were elected by joint ballot of both houses.

In 1820, the Council determined upon a plan to divide the nation into eight districts, in each of which was located a council house, where court was held twice yearly. District officers administered all business of a local nature. A code of laws was developed for regulating taxes, internal improvements, the payment of debts, the liquor traffic, and marriages; the franchise was limited to Cherokee citizens, and punishments were defined for crimes and misdemeanors.[8]

In order to prevent a repetition of the trouble incident to the treaty of 1817, the National Council passed a law imposing the death penalty upon any individual or group of Cherokee citizens who should undertake to sell tribal lands, further cessions to be made only by the unanimous consent of the Grand Council. In 1826, a convention of delegates met to draft a written constitution for the nation, and there was serious discussion of plans for adopting a national school system and for founding a library to be maintained by tribal funds.

Meanwhile, in 1821, a half-breed[9] Cherokee, known among his own people as Sikwayi or Sequoyah, and to the white settlers as George Guess,[10] invented a syllabary of the Cherokee language which has profoundly affected the history of this tribe. Of the father of Sequoyah little is known save that he was of Teutonic origin and had a restless, adventurous disposition, which probably accounted for his casual disappearance from home during the infancy of his son. The mother, on the contrary, was a devoted parent and an industrious and high-minded woman, who reared her gifted child according to the traditions of her ancestors and the customs of her nation.

At an early age, the boy Sequoyah showed signs of an artistic temperament, a constructive imagination, and a mind that took cognizance of everything he heard or saw.

In childhood, his small brown hands molded the clay he watched his mother using to make water jars and other vessels of household use, or he carved on wood and stone figures and designs with which he was acquainted. When he grew more skillful with experience he turned his attention to metal as a working medium, and from iron forged various useful tools and implements; from silver, fashioned and decorated with rare designs, ornaments which found favor with his own and other people. From the incomparable pipe-stone of his native highlands, he carved and polished the long-stemmed pipes, symbols of peace and friendship between the nations of the New World. By slow degrees, Sequoyah thus mounted on stepping stones of past experiences to vantage points of broader vision.

When about forty years of age, a chance conversation called his attention to the white man's ability to communicate thought by means of writing. Naturally of a contemplative turn of mind, he reflected upon the possibility of working out a system for his own people by which he could "make the leaf talk," and finally determined to attempt it. After years of patient effort, in spite of repeated failures and the discouragement and the ridicule of friends and relatives, he finally evolved a Cherokee syllabary,[11] which was so simple and so remarkably adapted to the language that, in order to read and write, it was necessary only to learn the eighty-six characters of which it was composed.[12] His daughter Ah-yo-ka[13] was his first pupil.

The masses soon recognized its possibilities for good, and in time thousands who could not speak English and had despaired of acquiring an education were learning to read and write in their own tongue. With one accord, the whole Cherokee Nation seemed to resolve itself into a great Indian academy, old and young, addressing themselves to the mastery of the system. As soon as one had learned it, he taught another. Thus, almost every fireside became a school, and every man, woman, and child, either teacher or pupil. Even at the post office, in the public houses, or by the roadside, instruction was given and received, "so that within a few months, without school or other expense of time or money, the Cherokees were able to read and write in their own language."[14]

Three years after the invention of this alphabet, a printing press was set up at New Echota by an act of the National Council, and the *Cherokee Phoenix,* a weekly paper, began to be printed in both English and Cherokee, with Elias Boudinot, recently returned from school at Cornwall, Connecticut, as editor. This enabled the most illiterate members of the tribe to read the proceedings of their government in a language they understood. Parts of the Bible were soon translated into Cherokee, and later, hymn books and textbooks. An active correspondence sprang up between the eastern and western nations, for Sequoyah, with true missionary zeal, carried his invention to Arkansas, where he took up his permanent residence in 1823.

In the fall of that year, the Cherokee Council, in recognition of his merits, awarded him a silver medal bearing a commemorative inscription in both languages. On one side of the medal was the representation of two peace pipes with stems crossed encircled by the inscription in Cherokee: "Presented to George Gist by the Cherokee National Council for his ingenuity in the invention of the Cherokee alphabet." On the reverse side, the same inscription in English surrounded a bust of the inventor.[15]

During his later years, Sequoyah, conceiving the idea of an alphabet adapted to the use of all the Indian tribes of North America, made several trips to the plains tribes with this project in mind, but, unfortunately, he did not live to see this aspiration realized.

Sequoyah was a great teacher, an experienced traveler, a born diplomat, and a man of exceptionally fine character. There are glimpses of him here and there as he worked; as he patiently endured the tongue lashings of a termagant wife, who demanded more venison for her household than he sometimes supplied; as he sat in council with his tribesmen to frame a form of government for his nation; as he went to visit the Great White Father on a mission of peace for his people.

There are shadowy visions of him as he sat in the teepees of the wild tribes[16] and talked with them of the advantages of permanent homes, of an organized form of government, of a great Indian Confederacy, of peace—always of peace—and of the futility of factional strife and of war. And there is the picture of him as he started on his last quest for the Lost Cherokees, to whom he wished to take his gift of letters and the story of the Cherokee Nation, Indian Territory, to which he hoped to lead them, but to which he, himself, never returned.

Sequoyah was the first Cherokee to attain a place in Statuary Hall in Washington. At the unveiling of his statue in 1917, one of the speakers paid this tribute to his invention: "It is one of the greatest performances ever conceived by the human intellect. . . . Sequoyah invented the only sensible alphabet ever invented."[17] Another on the same occasion remarked that "No alphabet in all the world reaches the dignity, the simplicity, and the value of the Cherokee alphabet as invented by Sequoyah," the great Redwoods named in his honor, the Sequoia gigantea, being "typical of this greatest North American Indian."[18]

"Sequoyah! Well may the great trees of California proudly bear thy name upon their lofty crests! Right royally, didst thou acquit thyself."[19]

Editorial Commentary
for Chapters 7–15

Rachel Caroline Eaton is perhaps best known for calling public attention to the Trail of Tears, but she spent a considerable amount of time discussing history before and after the forced Removal of Cherokees to the land now commonly known as Oklahoma. Eaton's work demonstrates the considerable strength Cherokees showed in resisting Removal and rebuilding the Nation in the new homelands. While Euro-Americans such as Helen Hunt Jackson emphasized tragedy and victimhood in Cherokee history, Cherokee narratives of the Trail of Tears stress survivance[1] and demonstrate the ever-present truth that the Nation continues to carry the fire no matter what adversities we face.

When the Cherokees were forcibly removed to Indian Territory, they did not arrive on empty land. As Eaton notes in chapter 4, when an earlier group of Cherokees emigrated west in 1817, they were moving onto Osage land. Eaton grew up right next to Claremore Mound, the site of a Cherokee-Osage battle that took place in 1817. Tension between the Cherokees and Osages continued for quite some time. Like many other Cherokees in the nineteenth and early twentieth centuries, Eaton adopts the Euro-American "civilized"/"savage" binary when describing Indigenous Nations like the Osage who belong to the Arkansas River valley or the Great Plains region. The following chapters contain outdated and offensive language such as "primitive," "savage," "half-breed," and "wild tribes." Rachel Caroline Eaton wrote this history in the 1930s, and as it is both a historical monograph and a historical document, we have elected to keep Eaton's original language.

CHAPTER 7

The Cherokee
Constitution of 1827

Georgia had charged, as one of its arguments for removal, that the Cherokees were a semi-barbarous people who stood in the way of state progress. As a matter of fact, they were quite as progressive as the majority of the white people of the state at that time.[1] According to a report made to the War Department by the Reverend David Brown, who traveled extensively throughout the Cherokee Nation in the fall of 1825, farming and stock raising were successfully carried on, apple and peach orchards were common, and much attention was paid to the cultivation of gardens.[2] Corn, wheat, oats, and tobacco were raised in abundance, and cotton was grown in sufficient quantities to supply their own use and to leave a considerable surplus to be shipped in boats of their own make to New Orleans. Hides and livestock sold to the neighboring states brought sufficient currency into the Nation for all its needs.[3]

There were many flourishing villages, and the numerous roads through the country had "public stops" kept by natives at convenient intervals. In the homes, cotton and woolen cloth and blankets and coverlets were woven, and stockings and gloves were knitted. There were native blacksmiths, silversmiths, stone masons, and carpenters.[4] Commercial enterprises were being extended and practically all the merchants were Cherokee citizens.

Churches and schools were increasing, and plans were being discussed for a high school, a library, and a museum to be established and maintained at the expense of the Cherokee Nation. In one district alone, there were reported to be upward of a thousand

volumes of good books, while eleven periodicals, political and religious, were taken and read. It is doubtful whether the white people
in that region could have shown a better record. Stringent laws
were passed against drunkenness and the introduction of intoxicating liquors into the nation, and indolence was frowned upon.
The government was well organized and administered, while the
revenue was in a flourishing condition.[5]

Adherence to some of their primitive[6] customs in government
had given rise to the accusation that they were uncivilized. In order
to disabuse the mind of Georgia and the whole world of this charge,
and to establish a firmer political foundation on which to build, the
Cherokees determined to establish a regular republican form of
government based on a written constitution.[7] A resolution passed
by the Grand Council in the fall of 1826 provided for a constitutional convention to be held on July 4 of the following year at New
Echota.

On July 1, accordingly, delegates to the convention were elected
from each of the eight districts into which the Nation had been
divided in 1820. Voting was conducted viva voce.[8] In some districts, interest was so keen that the election "was warm and closely
contested."[9]

The convention met and organized by electing John Ross
chairman, then proceeded to the business of drafting a form of
government. The preamble begins with, "We, the Cherokee people, constituting one of the sovereign and independent nations
of the earth, and having complete jurisdiction over its territory to
the exclusion of the authority of any other state, do ordain this
constitution."[10]

The executive branch of the government was to be composed of
a principal chief and a second chief; the legislature would consist of
a National Committee composed of two representatives from each
district, and a Council composed of three from each district, the
two branches to be styled "The General Council of the Cherokee
Nation." The judiciary followed the plan in use among the states.
White men who had married into the nation were to enjoy all the
privileges of citizenship excepting the right to hold office, and land

was to remain the common property of the nation, improvements only belonging exclusively and indefeasibly to the individual citizen. The constitution provided for religious toleration, but no minister of the gospel was eligible to the office of principal chief or to a seat in the General Council.[11]

All the provisions for a well-regulated government were laid down in much detail, and an Alabama newspaper, commenting upon it, thought the document taken as a whole was well "calculated to produce the most happy results. The success of the Cherokees will stimulate other nations to adopt a similar policy; and we may yet live to see one tribe take after another, by dropping the tomahawk, and following the example set them, rise from savage barbarity to respectability in the civilized world."[12] Three weeks later, this constitution had been submitted to the people and ratified, after which it went into effect the following year.[13]

Meanwhile, the aged Pathkiller, so long a leader of the progressive party, had died,[14] and was followed in office by the second chief, Charles R. Hicks, who outlived him less than two weeks. The government then devolved upon Major Ridge, speaker of the Council, and John Ross, president of the Committee, until the regular meeting of the Council the following fall.

Major Ridge, at this time one of the most prominent men of the tribe, was a full-blood Cherokee and undoubtedly one of the most able men the nation ever produced. Handsome and commanding in appearance, intelligent, broad-minded, and public-spirited, he was a natural leader among men.[15]

To serve the unexpired term of Pathkiller and Charles R. Hicks, in the fall of 1828 the Grand Council appointed William Hicks,[16] principal chief, and John Ross, assistant chief. Naturally, Chief Hicks wished to succeed himself at the first election to be held under the constitution. For a time it appeared that his ambition might be realized. But when the people saw how he was being courted and flattered by federal officials and Georgia propagandists, their interest in his candidacy wavered. The suspicion gained ground that he was being tampered with and that he favored removal and the sale of the country. Consequently, when the election came off, he was defeated by John Ross, the opposition candidate placed in the field at the last minute.[17]

Ross at this time was twenty-seven years of age, a prosperous merchant and a successful planter who lived in a style befitting his estate and that of his wife, Quata,[18] a woman of great beauty and charm. From Ross's Landing at the foot of Lookout Mountain, he had moved to the head of the Coosa. Here he had for neighbors, Major Ridge, who lived two miles distant on his large plantation; John Ridge, proud of his Connecticut bride and his elegant establishment on the Two Run, near Oostinahleh;[19] Major Jack Martin, treasurer of the Cherokee Nation, who had a handsome residence with carved mantel and marble hearths at Rock Springs;[20] James Vann at Spring Place; and Elias Boudinot, the editor of the *Cherokee Phoenix*, whose home was at New Echota, where his wife, the adorable Harriet Gold Boudinot, dispensed hospitality and managed her large household with true yankee efficiency. It was a pleasant neighborhood of congenial people, located in a country famed for its scenic beauty and salubrious climate.

The Cherokee Nation at this time had its own alphabet and newspaper, a code of laws, and a written constitution. What more was required of civilized people anywhere? Industry and prosperity were everywhere in evidence. Love of country and pride of nationality were never stronger, and the ambition to make of the Cherokee Nation a model Indian republic was everywhere taking form in the minds of the clansmen.

To Georgia, on the contrary, this independent republic set up with the intent to perpetuate a distinct community within her ancient and chartered limits was not to be tolerated. A resolution of the legislature on December 27, 1828 reasserted the claim that title of the Cherokees to their lands was temporary; that the Indians were tenants at the will of the state, which was at full liberty to possess herself, by any means which she might choose, of the lands in dispute and to extend over them her authority and laws. Georgia would give the federal government one more chance to rid the state of Indians, and, if this failed, the next legislature would be urged to extend the jurisdiction and laws of the state over their territory.[21]

Governor Forsyth[22] sent a copy of these resolutions to the President and included one of the "presumptuous constitutions" just adopted by the Cherokee Nation, asking what the chief executive proposed to do about the erection of an independent government within the limits of his state.[23] In March the House of Representatives took up the question and instructed the judiciary committee,[24] and later the Indian Committee,[25] to inquire into the circumstances of the new Cherokee republic and report upon the expediency of arresting its designs.

Since the War Department was negotiating a treaty with the Arkansas Cherokees, whereby their territorial limits were to be readjusted and their boundary lines permanently settled,[26] it was hoped that sufficient inducement might be held out to the Eastern Cherokees to emigrate. The Indian appropriation bill, which contained a specific grant of $50,000 for carrying into effect the compact of 1802,[27] stimulated the federal government to renewed effort and Colonel Hugh Montgomery, the Indian agent, was given orders to provide transportation, rifles, and blankets to such Cherokees as were ready to go west. To speed the project still further, confidential agents on large salaries were sent into the Cherokee Nation to induce cession or emigration.[28]

When the Grand Council convened in October 1828, it took cognizance at once of Georgia's contention, controverting it so ably as to neutralize any sentiment for removal which might have been developing among the people.[29] Colonel Montgomery, who was ordered to leave his office in charge of a sub-agent and go out among the Indians to persuade them to enroll for emigration, reported that he was convinced that the removal policy was a lost issue and that removal on a large scale, if accomplished at all, would have to be done by coercion.[30]

CHAPTER 8

The Removal Bill

In October 1828, John Ross assumed office as principal chief of the Cherokee Nation.[1] The following November, Andrew Jackson was elected president of the United States. Scarcely a month had elapsed after the results of the election became known when the Georgia legislature passed two acts intended to paralyze the new government of the Cherokees. The first added Cherokee lands to certain northwestern counties of Georgia; the second extended the laws of the state over these lands after January 1, 1830, Cherokee laws to be null and void thereafter.[2]

The Cherokees, aglow with patriotic pride and ambition, had no intention of submitting to these coercive state measures. The General Council called a special session at New Echota, passed resolutions[3] declaring the Georgia laws null and void, and framed a memorial to the President protesting the right of a state to extend its laws over the lands of the Cherokees. The memorial recalled the treaty guarantees of the government to protect the Indians in their lands; urged that the Cherokees, an innocent party, not responsible for the compact with Georgia, were compelled unjustly to suffer its consequences; called attention to the advancement of the people, due largely to their proximity to civilizing influences; insisted that the benefits to be derived from removal were purely visionary, and asked the President to protect them in their treaty rights.[4]

A delegation bearing the memorial to Washington in the winter of 1828 was unable to gain recognition from the retiring administration. Hoping against hope for greater success in dealing with an executive who proclaimed justice his cardinal doctrine, they waited to present their cause to President Jackson, attended the inaugural ceremonies, and doubtless were filled with renewed hope to hear him say on that occasion that it would be his sincere and constant desire to observe towards the Indians a just and liberal policy, and to give that humane and considerate attention to their rights and their wants, which was "consistent with the habits of our government and the feelings of the people."[5]

More than a month wore away before the delegation finally secured a hearing from the Secretary of War, and any hopes which the President's message might have aroused were dispelled by Major Eaton[6] when, on April 18, he assured them that no remedy remained for their troubles except removal. If they wanted a home they could call their own, they must go west, for there the President could guarantee the soil to them "as long as trees grow and waters run."[7] But the Cherokees contended their people had been happy and prosperous in the land of their fathers, and removal would bring retrogression and disaster upon the tribe; they did not wish to move.

But the executive mind was already made up. In May the delegation returned home, not without hope, however.[8] Before leaving Washington, they had been encouraged to believe Congress at its next session would come to their relief. An extra session of Council, called to hear the report of the delegation, therefore, drew up a memorial to the Senate and House of Representatives praying for relief and protection on the ground of treaty obligations.

But Congress was not to meet for several months, and in the interim, the President, to help along the removal project, sent a secret agent among the Cherokees and the Creeks to see what could be done in the way of securing individual acquiescence with the view to building up a party with which a treaty could be negotiated. General William Carroll, then candidate for governor of Tennessee and a man believed to have considerable influence with the Indians, was chosen for this mission, with instructions to conceal from even the chiefs his official character, and with the suggestion that presents to the amount of $2,000 be distributed to the poorer Indians, the chiefs' children and even the chiefs themselves with the objective of attaching them to his cause.[9]

General Carroll, after thorough investigation, reported to the War Department that the Cherokees were too intelligent and "too well posted on current news to be kept in ignorance of the motives and methods of those who came among them." After paying a high tribute to Cherokee civilization, the Tennessean expressed the opinion that they were encouraged by eastern newspapers to believe that the people did not support the removal, and that Congress, at the next session, would sustain them in their protests against the encroachments of Georgia.[10]

On December 8, nevertheless, the President sent a message to Congress in which he advocated Indian removal on the ground that the rights of a sovereign state were being interfered with, and stated in reply to the protest of the Cherokees against the extension of Georgia laws over them that the attempt of the Indians to establish an independent government in Georgia and Alabama would not be countenanced.[11]

Both the House and the Senate took up the question, and all through the winter the Removal Bill brought out much bitter feeling and some memorable arguments in defense of the Indians. In the Senate, it was the main topic of discussion in the committee of the whole for three weeks. Frelinghuysen of New Jersey and Sprague of Maine ably opposed it on the ground of the binding force of treaty obligations, and upon general principles of justice and humanity. Forsythe of Georgia, McKinley of Alabama, and White of Tennessee defended it on the theory of the state's right to the soil within its limits.

In the House, the fallacy of pretending to remove the Indians for their own good from a community where they had comfortable homes, cultivated fields, churches, and schools, to a wilderness where they would be surrounded by savage[12] tribes, was exposed by Storrs of New York, in a speech remarkable for its logic and forensic power. He charged the President with arrogating to himself authority never conferred upon him in presuming to deliver to Congress an opinion on state authority and for seeking to annul treaties, some of which he himself had negotiated.[13]

As these debates revealed the situation of the Indians, the indignation of the country at large was aroused, and protests poured in upon Congress. The one from Adams County, Pennsylvania, praying for the protection of the Indians is particularly worthy of notice. It declared the Cherokees were an independent nation entitled to all the rights of such, except so far as surrendered by treaty. The treaties of Hopewell and Holston had taken place before the compact with Georgia was entered into.

In this compact, Georgia had explicitly acknowledged the existence of the Indians as a nation with whom the United States were to hold treaties, and extinguish their title as soon as the same could be done on peaceable and reasonable terms, and by such acknowledgment admitted the validity of former treaties which guaranteed their existence and protection. The Treaty of Hopewell was older than the Constitution. The Constitution in declaring treaties the supreme law of the land directly recognized the right to treat with Indians; therefore, treaties, regularly negotiated with them, were as sacred as any law of the land.[14]

In spite of protests and hot debate, the Removal Bill passed in May[15] and was approved by the President. It was, in the words of Senator Benton, "one of the closest and most earnestly contested questions of the session, and was carried by an inconsiderable majority."[16]

A new complication was introduced into the Cherokee question in July 1829, when deposits of gold, found on Ward's Creek in the northwestern part of the Nation, caused the value of their land to increase enormously. Treasure seekers from the surrounding states flocked into the gold region in such numbers that within a year three thousand disorderly white men were prospecting for the precious ore on Cherokee soil. They found the business very profitable. Early in October 1830, the *New York American* reported that two hundred and thirty thousand dollars worth of gold had been received in Augusta alone during the last nine months; and that Mr. Templeton Reid was coining and stamping, at his mint in Gainesville, Georgia, one hundred dollars of gold every day.[17]

These gold diggers were intruders, operating unlawfully under an enactment of the Cherokee Nation making it illegal for anyone not a Cherokee citizen to settle or trade on their land without a permit from Cherokee officials, and under a federal intercourse law prohibiting anyone from settling or trading on Indian Territory without a special license from the proper United States authorities.[18]

The gold diggers paid no attention to either, so that a period of lawlessness prevailed in which the Cherokees who had joined eagerly in prospecting got the worst of the deal.

Governor Gilmer, always with an eye single to the interests of his state, issued a proclamation warning all persons, even Indian occupants, against trespassing upon Georgia soil, and especially from taking any gold or silver from the land.[19] The Indians, on the assumption the land was their own, disregarded the proclamation. Whereupon the Georgia authorities arrested and roughly marched them off to prison. When appealed to the United States, troops sent into the country in 1829 to quell the tumult refused to give the Indians any protection whatever on the ground that state laws were not to be interfered with.[20]

The Georgia legislature now proceeded to pass laws for the gold region.[21] And on October 29, the governor wrote to the President asking that the troops be removed, since Georgia had extended its jurisdiction over that region. This request was granted, and the troops went into winter quarters, leaving the state a free hand.[22] The Legislature next proceeded to establish a guard of sixty men, stationed at the agency to keep down disorders in the gold region, passed an act making it unlawful for the Cherokee Council to meet except for the purpose of ceding land, and fixed a penalty of four years imprisonment for Cherokee judges to hold court. The same law provided that all white persons residing in the Cherokee country on March 1, 1831, or thereafter, without a license from the governor of Georgia, should be guilty of misdemeanor, the penalty being not less than four years imprisonment; and that the governor be allowed to license those who would take an oath to support and defend the constitution and laws of Georgia and to demean themselves uprightly as citizens of the state.[23]

Further legislation followed in the next few years providing for the mapping out of the Cherokee domains into counties, and for surveying it into land lots of 160 acres each and gold lots of forty acres each, these lots to be put up and distributed among white citizens of Georgia, each receiving a ticket. While each Cherokee was allowed a reservation of 160 acres, no deed was given, and possession of it depended upon the pleasure of the state legislature.

Contests over these lottery claims were inevitable. Provision was made for those arising among white people, but a law forbidding anyone of Indian blood to bring suit or testify against a white man made it impossible for the Indian to defend his rights in any court or to resist the seizure of his homestead, or even of his dwelling house, under penalty of imprisonment at the discretion of the Georgia courts. Another law, making invalid any contract made by an Indian unless established by the testimony of two white men, practically canceled all debts due from white men to Indians.

The purpose of these measures was not far to seek. Georgia was "building fires around the Cherokees" to drive them out. White men who entered the Cherokee country in armed bands, called "poney-clubs,"[24] seized horses and cattle and drove them off, ejected families from their homes and set fire to their houses, turning the occupants out in bleak weather to seek shelter where they might. When the perpetrators were arrested and brought to trial, the cases were dismissed on the ground no Indian could testify against a white man.[25]

The indignation of the whole country was aroused as the plight of the Cherokees became known. Criticism of their treatment became uncomfortable. It had been intended that removal should be accomplished with less notoriety. In order to silence and disable them and to prevent them from employing attorneys, sending delegates to Washington, and publishing the *Cherokee Phoenix*, instructions were issued by the War Department to the Indian agent in 1830, that henceforth annuities were to be distributed among families and individuals.[26]

The annuity, it will be remembered, was a sum of money paid annually by the United States to the Cherokees in consideration of land cessions made at various times after the Treaty of Hopewell. It amounted at this time to $10,000, two-thirds of which was due to the eastern nation. Since 1819, it had been turned over to a national treasurer, elected by the tribe, and was used for the support of the government and for other national purposes.

As a per capita payment, it amounted to about forty-two cents, a sum less than the expense of a trip to the agency where it was disbursed. The Cherokees refused to receive it in this fashion and, although they voted time after time that it should be paid in the usual way to their treasurer, it was withheld and allowed to accumulate in a Nashville bank for five years,[27] while the National Council was forced to raise loans on the credit of the nation, and to issue due bills for the payment of salaries.[28] The United States commissioners used the annuities as a pretext for assembling the people for the purpose of urging removal, much to their inconvenience and annoyance.

But neither the withholding of annuities nor the encroachment upon their prerogatives by state and federal authority facilitated the object aimed at. The Cherokees, conscious of their rights and of the support of public opinion, refused to remove or even to treat for a small cession of land.

When it became evident that the object of Georgia's hostile legislation, the Removal Bill, and the President's suspension of annuities, all looked toward forcible removal, Chief Ross, acting on the suggestion of such men as Webster and Frelinghuysen, determined to appeal to the highest tribunal of the land in January 1831, and former Attorney General William Wirt and Mr. Sargeant, their attorneys, introduced a motion before the Supreme Court of the United States for an injunction to prevent the execution of the objectionable laws of Georgia. This motion was reached on the docket of the Supreme Court early in March.[29]

The bill set forth the complainant to be the Cherokee Nation of Indians, a foreign state, not owing allegiance to the United States, nor to any state of the Union, nor to any prince, potentate or any state other than their own; reviewed the various treaties between them and the United States by which their lands were guaranteed to them, treaties which the Cherokees had always faithfully observed; claimed for themselves the benefit of the clause in the Constitution declaring treaties the supreme law of the land; complained of the violation of the treaties by the state of Georgia; claimed the protection of the United States against the state, and asked the court to declare null and void the laws of Georgia which interfered with the ancient rights and privileges of the tribe.[30]

The motion for injunction was denied on the ground that the Cherokee Nation was not a foreign state in the sense of the Constitution, and therefore could not maintain an action in the courts of the United States, Chief Justice Marshall and Justice Story dissenting.

The laws of 1830 in regard to white persons residing in the Cherokee Nation were aimed at gold diggers and intermarried white men suspected of encouraging opposition to removal. But a week after the passage of the law, the whole body of missionaries in the Cherokee Nation brought themselves under its ban by holding a meeting at New Echota, where they passed resolutions exonerating themselves from the charge of meddling in Indian politics, declaring their conviction that removal of the Indians would seriously retard their progress in civilization, and that the extension of Georgia's jurisdiction would work an immense and irreparable injury.

When called upon to retract or leave the nation, they refused to do either, whereupon Dr. S. A. Worcester and J. Thompson, two ordained missionaries, and Isaac Proctor, a teacher, with others, were arrested by the Georgia Guard, chained together in pairs and were taken to headquarters, a distance of seventy or eighty miles, with considerable military display designed to impress the Indians.[31]

After a preliminary trial, the prisoners were dismissed on the ground that they were agents of the United States as dispensers of the civilization fund.[32] Governor Gilmer dissented from the opinion of the judge, and after communicating with Secretary Eaton, found that seven of the nine missionaries residing in the Cherokee Nation were supported entirely by the American Board,[33] and that only one of them, Dr. Worcester, who was postmaster at New Echota, could in any way be considered an agent of the United States.

Dr. Worcester was particularly objectionable to Georgia because of his connection with the *Cherokee Phoenix* which had published a number of articles exposing the true situation in regard to removal and the unwarranted aggression of the state, articles which appealed to the sympathy and aroused the indignation of the north and east. Dr. Worcester was at once deprived of his secular office in order that he might be made fully amenable to Georgia laws.

Thereupon, the missionaries were again arrested with great cruelty and brought before a Georgia tribunal where Dr. Worcester and Elizur Butler, refusing to accept the governor's pardon by taking an oath of citizenship, were sentenced to four years hard labor in the penitentiary where they were compelled to wear prison garb and work on the rock pile.[34] The missionaries, with Mr. Wirt as counsel, appealed to the Supreme Court which, in 1832, rendered the decision declaring unconstitutional those laws by which Georgia had extended her jurisdiction over Indian Territory, and the one under which Dr. Worcester was indicted.[35]

News of the decision reaching the Cherokees late in March was like "a shower of rain on thirsty vegetation," says Elijah Hicks.[36] The feeling of depression and uncertainty vanished like the mists before the sun. The decision was celebrated by dances and feasts.[37] The young people were merry; the older ones relieved from anxiety.

CHAPTER 9

The Treaty of New Echota

In 1828 White Path, a conservative full-blood, headed an insurrection against the new government and against the Christian religion. The movement was arrested without bloodshed and its leaders in time became reconciled to the new order of things. White Path became a member of the National Council under the constitution. A few remained irreconcilable, however, and these reactionaries eventually became the nucleus for a party favorable to emigration. William Hicks, estranged and embittered by his political defeat, joined them and with his adherents added strength to the party of defection.[1]

Benjamin F. Curry, sent by the federal government at the urgent request of Georgia to open enrolling agencies in the Cherokee Nation, lost no time in cultivating their acquaintance.[2]

Another factor was added to the problem in 1828 when Wilson Lumpkin succeeded to the governorship of Georgia with the fixed determination to force the removal of the Indians from his commonwealth. Federal and state agents cooperated and, by means of bribery and intrigue the most appalling and manipulations the most subtle, succeeded in detaching some of the noblest and most prominent citizens of the nation from their tribal allegiance, and in building up a faction favorable to removal.

Georgia had anticipated important developments from the law forbidding the Cherokees to hold assemblies within her borders. Failure of their national council to convene at the regular time was expected to annul the laws and dissolve the government of the nation, thereby leaving the Cherokee people to the will of the state. In order to avoid such a contingency, the Council in 1833 met at Chatooga,[3] Alabama, and from 1834 to 1838 at Red Clay, Tennessee.

When the question of holding the next national election presented itself in 1835 at a popular convention called for the purpose of determining upon emergency measures, it was decided to continue in office the officials last elected, "the same being the people's choice."[4] Until elections could be held regularly under the constitution, all vacancies were to be filled by the principal chief subject to the approval of the national senate.

Meanwhile, the sentiment for removal grew by what it fed upon. The men who continued to associate with state and government agents created a bad impression upon the masses so that they soon became ostracized by the mass of Cherokee people. John Ridge was impeached by the council on complaints from his own district on the ground that he no longer represented the wishes of his constituents.[5] Major Ridge and David Vann were next charged with advancing policies contrary to the will of the majority. All three resigned. In 1832 Elias Boudinot relinquished the editorship of the *Cherokee Phoenix* and joined the Ridges and Vann in organizing the minority, which had a sufficient following by 1835 to form a treaty party with William Hicks as principal and John McIntosh, assistant chief.[6] A legislature was appointed, and steps were taken to supplant the existing government.[7]

Dissension soon arose in their ranks, however, and a number of the insurgents emigrated to the Indian Territory. Those who remained, however, came out boldly against the existing government and worked openly for removal. Major Ridge, his son John Ridge, and Elias Boudinot, being their most astute leaders, headed this faction which came to be called the Ridge Party.

Of Major Ridge and Elias Boudinot some account has been given. John Ridge, handsome, brilliant, ambitious and well-educated for that time, was a young man of distinction at home and abroad.[8] After returning from school at Cornwall, Connecticut, with his New England bride he entered with ardor and enthusiasm into the political and social life of the tribe. His superior wealth, his distinguished appearance, enhanced by his good taste in dress, and his eloquence in address all combined to give him the reputation of being the most promising young man of the nation.[9] Undoubtedly all were sincere, high-minded tribesmen who, seeing the futility of opposing the will of a government stronger than their own, were willing to take the chance of doing ill that good might come of it. And so before it had been fairly launched, this little Indian republic called the Cherokee Nation found its very existence threatened by sinister forces from within and without.

The motives that prompted them were not altogether selfish and personal. Some of them at least were undoubtedly high-minded farsighted men who, honestly convinced that their people could never be restored to peace and happiness in the east, and seeing the futility of further resisting the federal government, took what appealed to them as the only way out of the unbearable situation.

No one appreciated this situation more keenly than did the captain of the small craft of state. With every faculty alert, he bent all his energy to the task of quelling the mutiny on board while weathering the tempest steadily growing darker and fiercer without, threatening to overwhelm him and his people in shipwreck and ruin. Sustained by his Christian optimism, John Ross kept a clear head and a steady hand, firmly believing that the justice of the Cherokee cause would finally triumph and that a quiet harbor would yet be reached if domestic peace and harmony could be restored and forbearance and patience maintained towards the disturbing elements.

Appealing to his people, as well as to a higher power than his own or theirs, he issued a proclamation recommending July nineteenth,[10] as a day of fasting and prayer throughout the Cherokee Nation. The proclamation declared, "We have need to go to the Ruler of the Universe in this day of deep affliction. We have been too long trusting to an arm of flesh which has proved to be but a broken reed," and whether the time of tribulation and sorrow through which they were passing was caused by the wanton depravity and wickedness of man, or by the unsearchable and mysterious will of a wise Providence, it equally became them as a rational and Christian community humbly to bow in prayer for guidance.[11]

The majority of the tribe responded, and on the day appointed, age and youth, middle age and childhood, repaired to ancient meeting grounds, to convenient groves and dwellings, and fasted and prayed. The occasion was profoundly dignified and impressive. Ross knelt and prayed with his people and arose to resume his duties refreshed in spirit and entrenched in the hearts of his tribesmen, whose abiding faith in him was to stand the test of intrigue and calumny to the end of his long and stormy career.

Chief Ross, heading a delegation, spent the following winter in Washington, bringing to bear every influence at his command upon the President and Congress to furnish some relief to the Cherokees. But the only suggestion offered was removal. Finally, in a communication dated January 28, 1833, Ross assured the President that, notwithstanding the various perplexities his people had experienced, they were yet unshaken in their objection to removal. They had no assurance that removal would not be followed in a few years by consequences no less fatal than those which they were then suffering.[12] He then suggested that the government satisfy those Georgians who had taken possession of Cherokee land under the lottery drawing by assigning them unoccupied lands in other territories.

Secretary Cass[13] replied he could not foresee any cause for fearing removal would be injurious either in its immediate or remote consequences. A mild climate, a fertile soil, an inviting and extensive country, a government of their own, adequate protection against other Indians and against United States citizens, pecuniary means for removal, all were offered them.

He could not see the subject in the melancholy light in which the Cherokees had presented it. Only by removal could they find a safe retreat for themselves since as long as any remained in Georgia they were subject to the laws of that state, "surrounded by [white] settlements and exposed to all those evils which had always attended the Indian race when placed in immediate contact with a white population. It was only by removing [that they could] expect to avoid the fate which had already swept away so many Indian tribes."[14]

Ross replied that, in this scheme for Indian removal, he could see more of expediency and policy to get rid of the Cherokee than to perpetuate their race upon any permanent fundamental principle. If the doctrine that they could not exist contiguous to a white population should prevail and they should be compelled to remove west of the states and territories of the republic, what was to prevent a similar removal of them from that place for the same reason?[15]

The delegation again returned home in March without having secured any promise of relief or any encouragement whatever. Before leaving Washington, however, Chief Ross agreed to submit to the Council a proposition for the United States to pay the Cherokees $2,500,000 for their land if they would remove at their own expense. In consequence of this agreement, Benjamin F. Curry was appointed to represent the interests of the government at the meeting of Council called for the purpose of receiving the report of the delegation. Major Curry left no stone unturned in his zeal to secure a treaty of cession. But his crass method in dealing with the Indians disgusted them and rendered all his efforts of diplomacy futile. The Council refused to accept the president's terms and adjourned after having appointed another delegation to Washington.[16]

Deprived of their annuity funds, the country disorganized politically and economically, the Cherokees were in a sad state of duress.[17] But they could no longer look for relief from Washington. Meanwhile, the factional fight grew more bitter day by day as fresh recruits were added to the Treaty Party.

To add to the confusion, the Georgia Legislature had passed an act granting to fortunate drawers of lots the lands occupied by the improvements of those Indians who had accepted reservations under former treaties. This act included the improvements of all who had enrolled for emigration and, after having accepted payment for improvements, had remained in the nation.[18] The next year a law granting possession of these lots was a signal for worse depredations than any formerly committed. Some of the best Cherokee homesteads were seized, livestock confiscated, and owners ejected from their homes. Among these was Charles Hicks, who was forced to vacate his pleasant and comfortable residence in the dead of winter and move his family to Tennessee, where they found shelter in an old sugar camp.[19] Mr. Martin,[20] the Cherokee treasurer, received notice from the state agent, Colonel William Bishop, on January 20 that he must prepare to give possession of his premises within the next thirty days or suffer the penalty of law.[21] His carved mantels and marble hearths were part of the prize that fell to another fortunate Georgian.

Other cases there are to show that in her determination to cleanse her soil of the aborigines, the state and her citizens were prepared to go any length, though all the while strenuously disavowing any selfish or sinister motives toward the Indians.[22] Outrages were perpetrated upon the poor as well as upon the prosperous. The suffering and destitution of these helpless victims was pitiful to see, yet they remained unshaken in their determination to remain on the soil of their fathers.

When the fall Council in 1833 took up the discussion of the advantage to be gained by surrendering their tribal autonomy and becoming citizens of the United States, a memorial was drawn up, in which, after asserting that they would never voluntarily give up their homes, the Cherokees consented to satisfy Georgia by ceding part of their land on condition that the federal government protect them in the remainder until a definite time to be fixed by the United States, after which they should become citizens of the United States.[23] But removal was the only remedy offered in the reply from Washington.

Meanwhile, there had appeared at the National Capital three Cherokees representing the faction favoring removal. The leader suggested to the Commissioner of Indian Affairs that, if authorized to do so, they would return to the Cherokee Nation and bring back a delegation with whom a treaty could be effected for the cession of the whole or a part of the Cherokee Nation. It was agreed that if a treaty should be concluded the United States would bear the expenses of the delegation. The plan met with approval.[24]

Returning to the Cherokee Nation, this delegation assembled about two dozen of the treaty faction at the agency and succeeded in organizing the Treaty Party with William Hicks as principal chief and John McIntosh, second chief. A legislature was chosen and a full quota of officers appointed. This rival government now only awaited the psychological moment to supplant the constituted authority of the Nation.

Excitement among the people ran high when the regular session of the national council met at Red Clay in October. The disposition of President Jackson to recognize the "set of unauthorized individuals calling themselves the Treaty Party"[25] spread consternation throughout the nation among the main body of the tribe now beginning to be recognized as the National Party. A delegation was appointed to Washington with instructions to circumvent the proposed treaty at all costs. If a new treaty was unavoidable, let it be made with the constituted authorities of the nation. Thus, during the winter of 1835, two opposing delegations, one headed by Chief Ross and the other by Major Ridge, watched each other apprehensively from their headquarters in Washington.

The Secretary of War first recognized the Ross delegation by offering them practically the same terms as those which had been recently rejected by the Cherokee Council. When this proposition was declined, he turned to the Treaty faction and commissioned the Reverend J. F. Schermerhorn to negotiate with this party. The National delegation protested against the recognition of the Ridges as authorized agents of the Cherokee government, themselves offering to submit a tentative proposition for a treaty. The offer was accepted and Commissioner Schermerhorn was instructed to suspend negotiations for a period of two weeks.[26]

At the end of that time, Chief Ross tendered an offer to cede to the United States twenty million acres of Cherokee lands for twenty million dollars, the proposition being contingent on the consent of the Cherokee people. The administration refused to consider this offer on the ground that the price was exorbitant, and charged Chief Ross with trying to defeat the policy of the government by interposing unnecessary delays.[27]

In an effort to clear himself of this charge of filibustering, John Ross suggested that the Senate set the price, the question to be referred for ultimate decision to a vote of the people themselves.

The offer was eagerly accepted, and a statement of all the facts in the case, set forth in the form of a memorial, was sent to the Senate Committee on Indian Affairs whose chairman was Senator King of Georgia. In less than a week, the Secretary of War informed the Cherokees that, in the opinion of the Senate, their lands were worth no more than five million dollars.[28] On that basis he invited the delegation to negotiate, but John Ross declined to do so.[29]

The government now returned to the Ridge Party, and on February 8 negotiated an agreement fixing the price for their lands at fifty cents an acre. The Senate ratified the agreement on March 14, with the express stipulation that it be approved by the Cherokee people in full council assembled before it became binding on either party.

The ratification of the treaty by the Cherokees was a matter of deep concern to the advocates of removal. The President himself took an active interest in bringing it about, and to this end issued an address to the Cherokees calling them friends and brothers, inviting them to a calm consideration of their condition and prospects, and urging upon them the benefits that would accrue to their nation from the ratification of the treaty and their removal to the western country.[30] A copy of his address was delivered to the Cherokees by Commissioner Schermerhorn when he repaired to the nation for the purpose of completing the negotiation.[31]

With much at stake, the treaty men hastened home two weeks in advance of their opponents and with the assistance of federal and state agents undertook to secure control of the government and the purse strings of the nation, while Major Benjamin Curry, agent for the Cherokees, was holding up the annuities with the intention of using them to advantage in furthering their designs. To that end, he circulated the notice of a meeting to be held at the head of the Coosa River on the first Monday in May to determine the manner in which the annuities should be paid.[32]

The treaty adherents called a meeting for the same time and place to explain what had been done by them in Washington, but in spite of Major Curry's threat that he would pay the annuities to the person selected at that place to receive it, even if there were only four in attendance, fewer than one hundred were present and twenty-five or thirty of these were Cherokees, chiefly emigrants, the rest being Georgians. No vote was attempted. Major Curry merely posted notice of another meeting to be held at the same place on July 20 for the purpose of determining in what manner the annuities should be paid.[33]

Upon his arrival from Washington, Chief Ross found his family dispossessed, the homestead having been drawn in the Georgia land lottery and everywhere the people were anxious and perplexed by reports of a treaty which had ceded away all their land.[34] In order to explain to them what had actually transpired in Washington, he issued a call for a council to meet at Red Clay, at which there was a large attendance. A vote taken on the treaty and on the manner of paying the annuities revealed that the Indians had changed their minds on neither issue.

Immediately upon the adjournment of council, Chief Ross went to the agency to inquire about the payment of the annuities. While in Washington he had been informed that the money was in the hands of Lieutenant Bateman, ready to be disbursed as soon as the Cherokees had fully decided the manner in which the money should be paid. Bateman informed him that a vote would have to be taken at a meeting to be held in July. The money would then be paid even though only ten persons were present to receive it.[35]

John Ross was still at the home of his brother in the vicinity of the Agency when Mr. Schermerhorn arrived to be the guest of John Ridge during his sojourn in the nation. In an interview with the Principal Chief, the commissioner expressed a desire to meet the leading men of the tribe, saying, "I would deem myself extremely fortunate if I could in any way be the means of bringing together, and to a general close, by treaty, the unhappy difficulties existing between you and the United States." But when Chief Ross declared his willingness to arrange such a meeting to be held at Red Clay, the envoy hesitated, consulted Major Curry, and declined since he would be meeting them on July 20 at Ridge's.[36]

It had now become perfectly obvious that both the commissioner and the agent intended to make use of the annuities to force acceptance of the treaty. The time set was inconvenient. The Indians, but lately returned from the council, were occupied in making their crops. Nevertheless, swift runners went up and down the nation summoning the people to a meeting that would take place within ten days of the notice and at a distance of one hundred or more miles for many of them. Moreover, they were compelled to gather and prepare provisions for the journey. In spite of all hindrances, the people turned out by hundreds and voted: two thousand two hundred and twenty-five in favor of paying the annuities according to law to the national treasurer, and a hundred and fourteen in favor of paying them per capita, as federal agents advised.

During the summer and fall of 1835, Curry and Schermerhorn exhausted every available device to secure consent to a treaty, going so far as to importune the legislatures of Tennessee and Alabama to pass laws prohibiting Cherokees, ejected from their possessions in Georgia, from taking up residence in those states, Curry openly alleging it to be the policy of the United States to make the situation so miserable as to drive the Indians into a treaty or abandonment of the country.[37] Indians were arrested and thrown into jail on the slightest excuse or none at all, held without trial and dismissed without explanation at the pleasure of the Georgia Guard.[38]

For the express purpose of depleting the population of the eastern nation and weakening its government, thereby rendering it more amenable to the state and federal policy, Agent Curry now redoubled his efforts in the direction of enrollment, halting at no methods to secure individual consent, or semblance of consent, to emigrate. To this end he allowed whiskey to be brought into the Cherokee Country and used freely among the Indians, although their own laws forbade it, exercised the coarsest kind of intrigue among the more ignorant and helpless and, where everything else failed, used force in securing enrollment.

As evidence in this indictment there is the incident of Atahlah Anosta, a full blood, who, while under the influence of liquor, was induced to enroll against the wishes of his wife and children. When the time came for him to leave for Arkansas, he absconded. A guard, sent to fetch him, arrested his wife and children and drove them through a cold rain to the agency where they were detained under guard until the woman agreed to emigrate.

There is also a story of Sconatachee, an Indian over eighty years of age, whose consent to register had been secured during a fit of drunkenness into which he had been inveigled by Curry's accomplices. When he failed to appear at the time the emigrants were collecting, Curry, with an interpreter, went after him. The Indian refused to accompany him, whereupon Curry drew a revolver and tried to drive the old fellow to the agency. Failing in his attempt at coercion, the agent later sent a sufficient force to overpower and tie him hand and foot, and thus the white-haired chief of a once mighty race was hauled in a wagon to the agency like a hog to market.[39]

But neither these measures nor others which the federal officials had yet been able to devise seemed to incline the Indians to emigrate nor to render them more friendly to a treaty. The commissioner, convinced he was making a poor headway, finally wrote the Secretary of War suggesting that a treaty be concluded with a part of the nation only, should one with the whole be found impracticable. In reply, he was advised that if a treaty could not be concluded upon fair and open terms he must abandon the effort and leave the nation to the consequences of its own stubbornness.[40] Mr. Schermerhorn, now face to face with the fact that he must bring the Cherokees to terms very soon or lose favor with the President, began to plan his course of action regardless of instructions, confident that a successful treaty would meet with executive approval, and no questions asked.

As time for the October Council drew near, the Indians seemed to consider the meeting of great importance, and the popular attendance bade fair to be unusually large. When Council convened, Mr. Schermerhorn and Major Curry were on hand. Their hopes ran high, if their correspondence at this time can be credited, their intention being to create a division in the National Party, thereby weakening it to the advantage of the Ridge faction and the proposed treaty.[41] They were doomed to failure, however, for the unexpected again happened. The two factions got together, as they had been trying to do since July, had agreed to bury in oblivion all unkindly feelings and to act unitedly in arranging with the United States a new treaty for the Nation.[42] As a result, the Schermerhorn treaty was unanimously rejected by the Council, the Ridges and Boudinot using their influence against it.[43]

The astonished commissioner, in reporting the affair to the Secretary of War, acknowledged his disappointment in the unadvised and unexpected course taken by the Ridges, explaining it on the ground that they had become discouraged in contending with the power of Ross; he thought perhaps some consideration of personal safety may have had its influence also. "But," he piously observed, "the Lord is able to overrule all things for good."[44]

His chief hope in accomplishing a treaty now lay in the fear on the part of the Indians of Georgia legislation. Alabama and Tennessee, he thought, would pass some wholesome laws to quicken their movements.[45] In order that he might have assurance of executive approval of steps already taken, and support in occupying higher ground, Mr. Schermerhorn sent Major Curry on to Washington "with private dispatches of a confidential nature to the president and secretary of war, part of which were verbal."[46]

In the glow of good feeling which attended the reconciliation, the Council passed a resolution providing for a committee of twenty members to be chosen from both parties with power to arrange a treaty with the commissioner in the Cherokee Nation or at Washington.[47] John Ridge and Elias Boudinot were both members of this committee. Upon consulting Mr. Schermerhorn and finding he had no authority to treat with them upon any other basis than that of the agreement just rejected, the committee prepared to set out for Washington.

But, unfortunately, trouble was again brewing among the newly reconciled parties. The Treaty men began to think they were not sufficiently recognized on the committee and that due consideration had not been shown them by the Council. These and other grievances of a personal nature added fuel to the smoldering embers of factional enmity, which were soon fanned into a blaze by assiduous federal and state agents. Accusations and recriminations

became the order of the day, and resignations of the Ridge men
from the committee naturally followed. First John Ridge resigned,
then Boudinot, and they were soon won back to their former alliance with Mr. Schermerhorn.

On the eve of the departure for Washington, Mr. Ross was seized
by the Georgia Guard on the plea that he was a white man residing in the Indian country, and conducted across the Georgia line,
where he was held for some time, but was finally released without
trial or explanation.[48] All his private correspondence, as well as the
proceedings of Council, were seized at the same time and searched
for incriminating evidence which would justify his removal from
the chieftainship. With their leader out of the way, it was thought
the Indians would be more amenable to reason.

At the same time, John Howard Payne, who as the guest of
Ross was in the nation for the purpose of collecting historical and
ethnological material relating to the tribe, was seized and all his
manuscripts rifled. A few weeks before this, the *Cherokee Phoenix* had
been suppressed and its plant seized and carried off by the Georgia
Guard at the instigation of Major Curry, who saw that it was thereafter run in the interest of removal.[49]

Before leaving Red Clay in October, Mr. Schermerhorn had
posted on the walls of the council house, notice of a meeting to be
held at New Echota the third week in December for the purpose
of agreeing to the terms of a treaty. The notice was accompanied
by the threat that those who failed to attend would be counted as
assenting to any treaty that might be made, and the promise that
all who should attend would be subsisted at government expense.

Threats and promises alike proved of little avail, and when the
proceedings opened, there were present not more than three hundred Indians, men, women and children. Of these a goodly number were emigrants, and none of them were principal officers of the
Cherokee Nation. Major Curry, who had returned from Washington, evidently with the assurance of executive support, proceeded
to carry things with a high hand, openly threatening anyone who
had come there to oppose a treaty agreement.[50] At Mr. Schermerhorn's suggestion, a committee of twenty was selected from among

those present to confer with him as to details of a treaty. The ballot showed seventy-nine in favor and seven against.[51] A delegation of thirteen was appointed to accompany the commissioner to Washington for the purpose of urging the ratification of the treaty. It was clothed with power to assent to any alterations made necessary by the president or the Senate. Mr., Schermerhorn notified the Secretary of War of his success, exulting in the belief that John Ross was at last prostrate, the power of the nation having been taken from him as well as the money.[52]

The treaty required the Cherokee Nation to cede to the United States all its remaining territory east of the Mississippi River for the sum of four million five hundred dollars and a common joint interest in the country occupied by the Western Cherokees. The Cherokees were to be paid for their improvements and removed and subsisted for a year at the expense of the United States, and the removal was to take place within two years of the ratification of the treaty. Provision was made for the payment of debts owed by the Indians out of money coming to them from the treaty; for the re-establishment of missions in the west; for pensions to the Cherokees wounded in the services of the government in the War of 1812 and the Creek war; for permission to establish such military posts and roads in the new country for the use of the United States as should be deemed necessary; for satisfying Osage claims in the western territory; and for bringing about a friendly understanding between the two tribes.

In addition to these items, the treaty arranged for the commutation of all annuities into a permanent national fund, the interest to be placed at the disposal of the officers of the Cherokee Nation and by them disbursed according to the will of their own people, for the care of schools and an orphan asylum, and for general national purposes.[53] It was signed by J. F. Schermerhorn and William Carroll as commissioners of the United States, and by the committee of twenty on the part of the Treaty Party, prominent among whom were Major Ridge and Elias Boudinot.

The main body of the nation, amazed and indignant, stood ready to contest the treaty. Second Chief Lowrey called a meeting of the Grand Council at Red Clay in January, and although the weather was bitterly cold and stormy, and smallpox had broken out in one district, over four hundred persons were present. Those who were detained sent in their ballots by friends and neighbors.[54] A resolution denouncing the methods used by the commissioners and declaring the treaty null and void was signed "by upwards of twelve thousand Cherokees" and forwarded to Washington.[55]

This protest, along with one signed by three thousand two hundred and fifty residing in North Carolina, was presented to Congress by the Ross delegation, as it was still believed the National Legislature would not stand for the methods used when the facts in the case became known.[56]

In spite of the strenuous opposition against ratification, the treaty passed the Senate by a majority of one vote and was promptly signed and proclaimed by the President on May 23, 1836.[57]

The treaty allowed the nation two years in which to remove, and no time was lost by the administration in taking preliminary steps to carry it into execution. To Governor Lumpkin of Georgia and Governor Carroll of Tennessee, who had been instrumental in bringing it about, was given the authority to supervise and direct the execution of the treaty, while Benjamin F. Curry was made superintendent of removal. The details of graft, which crop out in the correspondence of the time, as they appear in the official records, indicate that the removal of the Indians provided many a fat job for friends of the administration. Many a political debt was paid with the capital furnished by the sale of the Cherokee Nation East.[58]

CHAPTER 10

Opposition to the Treaty

Chief Ross remained in Washington until after the treaty passed the Senate, hoping that either sentiment against it or some technicality might defeat it. Seeking an interview with President Jackson, he was bluntly informed the Executive had ceased to recognize any existing government among the Eastern Cherokees.

On March 26 he wrote home advising his people to ignore the treaty but to remain quiet.[1] A copy of this letter falling into the hands of his enemies was exploited as evidence of the chief's intention to resist the treaty and called forth bitter denunciation from federal and state officials, who persisted in asserting that the majority of the Cherokees were in favor of removal and that all the trouble was due to Ross's efforts to arouse them to resistance.[2]

Rumors of a brewing insurrection, supported by an anonymous letter warning white men in the Cherokee country of a plan to attack and drive them from the nation, alarmed the administration and horrified the neighboring states. "When white men fight for home and country they are lauded as the noblest of patriots. Indians doing the same thing are stigmatized as savages. What a fortunate and convenient excuse the doctrine of manifest destiny has proved."[3]

But, as a matter of fact, the Indians had no intention of resorting to arms, as they attempted to prove by a meeting of representatives of the mountain districts held at Hiwassee in the summer of 1836, where they drew up resolutions stating the condition of their people and showing the futility of armed resistance. They had no military system, they said, no military supplies. The scalping knife and tomahawk had been buried half a century, while the love of war and the practice of it had become obsolete. A number of their old men still survived who had spilled their blood and had seen their brothers fall beside the Chief Magistrate of the United States; but their young men had never known war, had never heard the war whoop, nor "viewed the pitiless carnage" of battle which "wrings with hopeless agony the hearts of mothers, sisters and friends."[4]

This protest, with others of like tenor from different parts of the Cherokee country, failed to restore public confidence, and General Wool[5] with an army of seven thousand men was sent late in July to overawe the Indians and to "frown down opposition to the treaty."[6] In two meetings held soon after his arrival in North Carolina, where dwelt the most conservative members of the tribe, he found the people peaceably but firmly opposed to the treaty.

When they evaded the question of whether they would remove willingly, he issued the ultimatum of peace or war, remove or fight. When they expressed the wish to consult their principal chief, the privilege was denied them on the ground that Ross had led them astray from their interests and happiness too long by his pernicious counsels. General Wool, they were told, was hereafter the proper person to advise them.

No decisive action having been taken when the meetings broke up, he sent out and overtook the chiefs, held them prisoners overnight and released them only after they had promised to obey the treaty and send their young men in to surrender their arms.[7] He reported to the Secretary of War that nineteen-twentieths, if not ninety-nine out of every hundred of the North Carolina Cherokees were opposed to the treaty and would not comply with it unless compelled to do so by military measures, and asked that additional troops be sent to his assistance.[8]

President Jackson's second term was now nearing its close, and the Cherokees, encouraged by friends in Congress, entertained some expectation of relief from the next administration. In the summer of 1836, Ross had written a friend that if Henry Clay and Mr. Frelinghuysen[9] were elected it would be a godsend to the country at large as well as to the poor Indian.[10] Cherishing this forlorn hope, the Indians held on and removal came almost to a standstill.

Announcements posted throughout the Cherokee Nation that a handsome steamboat stood ready to transport them in ease and luxury to the new country aroused no enthusiasm. Published addresses, describing in the most alluring terms all the advantages the Cherokees could secure by removal, and offering inducements the most enticing, made no impression. Spurious documents, attempting to prove that Chief Ross himself had consented to remove, were unheeded. Complaints went up to Washington again and again that the Cherokees "would not come in."[11]

The Council of 1836 adopted resolutions denouncing the motives of the United States commissioner in making the treaty, declaring the treaty null and void, and asserting that it could never in justice be enforced upon the nation.[12] In a memorial to the president praying for an impartial statement of the negotiations of the treaty, they piteously invoked the "God of truth to tear away every disguise and concealment from their case, the God of justice to guide the President's determination, and the God of mercy to stay the hand of their brothers uplifted for their destruction."[13]

A copy of this memorial and the resolutions transmitted to the Secretary of War by General Wool so enraged President Jackson that he expressed surprise that an officer in the army should have received or transmitted a paper so disrespectful to the executive, to the Senate and to the American people; declared his settled determination that the treaty should be carried out without modification and with all consistent dispatch; and directed that, after a copy of the letter should have been transmitted to Ross, no further communication by word of mouth or writing should be held with him concerning the treaty. It was further directed that no council should be permitted to assemble to discuss the treaty.[14]

But the Cherokees, far from convinced, kept up a vigorous campaign against the spurious treaty. In order to enlist the help of their western tribesmen and unite the efforts of the two nations, the Council of this year had appointed a delegation, of which Ross was a member, to visit the western nation. The United States agents had no intimation of this action until the delegation had already set out for the west. Major Curry, furious at being circumvented, notified the commissioner of Indian affairs, who sent strict orders to Fort Gibson to have the principal chief arrested if he should appear there and begin inciting the Indians to opposition.[15]

With rare tact and diplomacy, Chief Ross paid a friendly visit to ex-governor Montford Stokes at the agency of Bayou Menard and completely disarmed the agent to the western Cherokees with his amiable, quiet manner,[16] won over the chief, John Jolly, obtained the promise of the western nation to oppose the treaty, and secured the appointment of a delegation to Washington to protest against it. This done, he and his party quietly departed and returned home, having eluded and outwitted the United States authorities, much to their anger and chagrin.[17]

Having secured the cooperation of the western nation, he saw to it that the delegation went on to Washington, where on March 16 they addressed a communication to the President asking for a hearing, requesting that their claims be investigated, the rightful authorities dealt with, and the results of the investigation submitted to the Cherokee Nation.[18] The Secretary of War replied that the treaty of New Echota had been ratified constitutionally, but that any measures suggested by them would receive candid examination if consistent with the treaty.[19] President Van Buren granted the delegation an interview, treated them politely, even cordially, but told them frankly that nothing could be done to alter or amend the treaty.

Meanwhile, the condition of the Indians had been growing steadily worse. General Wool describes the whole scene in the Cherokee country as heartrending and such a one as he would be glad to get rid of as soon as circumstances would permit. The white men were hovering like vultures watching to pounce upon their prey and strip them of everything they possessed. He predicted that ninety-nine out of every one hundred would go penniless to the west.[20] "I am surprised," he said, "that the Cherokees have not risen in their might and destroyed every resident white man in the country."[21]

General Dunlap, in command of the East Tennessee troops called out to quell the rumored insurrection in 1836, soon found that the Indians, not the whites, needed protection, and that by furnishing it he excited the hatred of the lawless rabble which had long played the part of tyrants. He finally decided he would "never dishonor the Tennessee arms in a servile service by aiding in carrying into execution at the point of the bayonet a treaty made by a lean minority against the will and authority of the Cherokee people." Disbanding his brigade, he went home in disgust.[22]

Even the members of the Treaty Party, to whom the government was deeply indebted, did not go scatheless to the west. Returning from Washington after the final arrangements of the treaty had been completed, they found their plantations taken and suits instituted against them for back rents on their own farms. They were in danger day and night from disorderly bands that flogged Indian men, women, and children with hickories and clubs, even constables and justices of the peace being concerned in the mistreatment. Major Ridge, in a letter to the President, declared that unless given protection by the United States, the Indians would carry nothing with them to their new homes but the scars of the lash on their backs.[23]

Through all their afflictions and tribulations, however, the Indians remained so consistently opposed to emigration that not one of them who attended the meeting called by General Wool in January 1837 would receive rations or clothes from the United States for fear they might compromise themselves, preferring rather to live upon roots and the sap of trees. Thousands of them had no other food for weeks.[24]

John Mason, sent in July 1837 as a confidential agent of the War Department to investigate conditions among the Indians, was convinced that opposition to the treaty was unanimous, irreconcilable, and sincere. The Cherokees claimed that they did not make the treaty and it could not bind them, that it was made by a few unauthorized individuals, and the nation was not a party to it.

With all his influence with them, and Mason believed the mass of the nation, especially the mountain Indians, would stand or fall with their chief,[25] Ross could not stem the tide of sentiment against removal. If he had advised the Cherokees at this time to acknowledge the treaty, he would have forfeited their confidence and probably his life.[26] His influence was constantly exerted to preserve peace, the reports of his enemies to the contrary notwithstanding.

Opposition to the treaty was sincere and sprang from a love of country, and was not a political game played by Ross to maintain his ascendancy in the tribe. When Colonel Lindsay, who succeeded General Wool, was given authority in the summer of 1837 to arrest Ross and turn him over to the civil authorities if he did anything further to encourage the Cherokees in their hostilities to removal, he sought in vain for some excuse to ignore his instructions.[27]

Regardless of threats, a council was called for July 31, to which Mr. Mason was dispatched with instructions to traverse and correct any misstatements that might be made by John Ross and his followers, and if need be to prohibit the assembling of the Council.[28] Chief Ross met these trying situations with a calm dignity and strength of purpose that could but inspire with confidence the minds of the harassed multitude of Indians, who came to rely upon him with a respect and affection akin to reverence. At his humble home in Tennessee he dispensed what hospitality his means afforded to high and low without discrimination, and to the poor full-bloods who were reduced to desperate straits, he was a brother in adversity.

To the white men, however, whose plans and schemes he had so often thwarted, Ross appeared in an entirely different character. Major Curry regarded him with hatred beyond expression and treated him with a contempt that bespoke poor breeding. The agent's attempts, through dark and devious courses, to alienate the Indians from their leader were notorious, and his methods of dealing with the aborigines were without a trace of honor, so that he was cordially hated and thoroughly feared by them. Congressman Peyton of Tennessee denounced him and Schermerhorn in the House in 1836 as "the two worst agents that could have been selected in all God's creation."[29]

The Major's death in December 1836 caused a feeling of relief throughout the Cherokee Nation. It was the opinion of General Wool that if Curry had lived long enough he would have been killed by the Indians.[30] Nathan Smith, who succeeded him, was a man of honor and integrity who finally overcame much of the prejudice which he at first entertained towards the Cherokees.

Governor Lumpkin naturally had no love for the Indians who encumbered the soil. He saw no good in them. All his racial antipathy seems to have become concentrated against Mr. Ross, whose character he assailed, whose motives he misrepresented, and whose acts and conduct he distorted for the purpose of discrediting him before the world. The Georgian arrogantly refused to recognize the chieftainship of Chief Ross and urged the government to do so, not on the ground of justice but of policy, acknowledging that if Ross and his party were recognized, the validity of the treaty could be called into question.[31]

He even went so far as to say that Mr. Ross ought to be "put in strings and banished from the country; that, although a large slaveholder, he was well qualified to fill a prominent place amongst the New England abolitionists, or in the Republic of Hayti," and that to one of these places he wished to see him emigrate. He considered Ross the soul and spirit of the opposition. To the Georgian, this Scotch Indian was a "subtle and sagacious man" who, under the guise of an unassuming deportment, concealed an unsurpassed arrogance, and by his dignified, reserved manner, "acquired credit for talents and wisdom which he never possessed."[32]

Fearing some change of Indian policy from the Van Buren administration, Mr. Lumpkin hastened to redouble his energies in fortifying the mind of the new administration against the stratagems of the wily chief. Writing the Secretary of War in the summer of 1837, he warned him that Mr. Ross was the master spirit of opposition to the execution of the treaty, on whose movements he would keep a watchful eye so far as circumstances would allow, for he was a reserved, obscure, and wary politician.[33] It is not strange therefore that the President became increasingly reluctant to hold intercourse with Ross and his party.

Pressure for removal under the supervision of Mr. Lumpkin[34] became more constant and uniform, but when the end of the year approached without any indication of an intention on the part of the Indians to go west, the United States commissioners and agents issued a proclamation[35] stating that, according to the treaty, they now had only five months in which to remove. They were not to be deceived by the hope that a longer time would be given them.

The treaty, the proclamation declared, would be executed without change or alteration and another day beyond the time named[36] would not be allowed to them. They were warned to rely no longer upon John Ross and his friends, who had been misleading them and subjecting them to pecuniary losses. The executive had declined all further intercourse with Ross, and an end had been put to all negotiations upon the subject of the treaty.[37]

To this the Cherokee delegation, then in Washington, replied in a memorial that the New Echota Treaty was an outrage on the primary rules of national intercourse, as well as of the known laws and usages of the Cherokee Nation. It was therefore destitute of any binding force upon them. "For adhering to the principles on which your great empire is founded, and on which it has advanced to its present elevation and glory, are we to be despoiled of all we hold dear on earth?" they asked. "Are we to be hunted through the mountains like wild beasts, and our women and our children, our aged, our sick, to be dragged from their homes like culprits and packed on board loathsome boats for transportation to a sickly clime?"[38]

Cherokee removal and the New Echota Treaty called forth strong remonstrance from some of the greatest statesmen of the country, who denounced the policy of the administration in vigorous terms. Webster and Everett of Massachusetts, Frelinghuysen of New Jersey, Sprague of Maine, Storrs of New York, Crockett of Tennessee, and Clay of Kentucky protested strongly against it. It became almost a party question, the Democrats supporting Jackson, the Whigs condemning him.

Henry Clay considered that the chief magistrate had inflicted a deep wound on the American people.[39] Webster remarked in the Senate in May 1837 that there was a growing feeling that great wrong had been done the Cherokees by the Treaty of New Echota.[40] "Speeches in Congress," says Benton, "were characterized by a depth and bitterness of feeling such as have never been excelled on the slavery question."[41] Calhoun of Tennessee did not regard the New Echota Treaty as a binding contract at all, since only about twenty persons out of eighteen thousand assented to it.[42]

Henry A. Wise declared it was not a bona fide treaty. The Cherokee Nation had never agreed to it and now almost unanimously protested against it. The whole proceedings in relation to the negotiations, he declared to be "a fraud upon the Indians."[43] Schermerhorn, he stigmatized as a "raw head and bloody bones" to the ignorant Indians while their chiefs were at Washington, and he had made what he called a treaty with a very small portion of the tribe.

Henry A. Wise, in a speech in the House, paid high tribute to John Ross as the man who swam the river at the battle of Horse Shoe Bend, and at risk of his life brought away the canoes which enabled Jackson's forces to gain victory over the Creeks. "And now he is turned out of his dwelling by a Georgia Guard and his property all given over to others. This is the faith of a Christian nation. John Ross is known to many members of the House to be an honest, intelligent man, worthy to sit in the councils of the Nation, let alone the councils of an Indian tribe."[44] His objection to the treaty, Wise considered an honest one, and declared that Ross, the Indian chief from Georgia, would at any time compare favorably in intellect and moral honesty with Forsyth, a member of Van Buren's cabinet, from the same state.[45]

A memorial of the Cherokee delegation in the winter of 1838 was laid on the table of the Senate by a vote of 36 to 16, and others from citizens of New York, Pennsylvania, Massachusetts, and New Jersey, requesting an inquiry into the validity of the New Echota Treaty, met a similar fate in the House. Discussions of these memorials brought out expressions of sympathy for the Indians but took no practical course for their relief.

CHAPTER 11

Compulsory Removal

Throughout the winter and spring of 1838, Chief Ross continued protesting against the validity of the treaty, remonstrating against its execution, and seeking to secure a more favorable one made with the legally constituted authorities of the Nation. "We will not recognize the forgery palmed off upon the world as a treaty by a knot of unauthorized individuals," he declared, "nor stir one step with reference to that false paper."[1]

And yet, although it was the wish of the Cherokees to remain on "the soil of their ancestors inherited from the common Father of us all," they were at length, under the necessity of circumstances, ready to go west if the federal government would pay them for their land far less than it asked for the wildest of its own. Removal by compulsion, he pointed out, would prove more expensive than a new treaty, and, aside from the question of the faith of nations, the federal government could well afford to do itself and the Indians the justice for which they were pleading. He was supported by memorials and petitions from various parts of the country, particularly from Pennsylvania and Massachusetts, praying for a repeal of the Schermerhorn treaty on the ground that it did not represent the will of the majority of the Cherokee people.

The friends of removal in general, and Mr. Lumpkin in particular, met these protests and petitions with arguments supporting their contention. The idea of submitting a treaty to an Indian People, to be decided upon "the broadest basis of democracy," was scoffed at by the senator, who maintained that "It ought to be sufficient to satisfy the wise and good everywhere that the treaty was negotiated on behalf of the Cherokees by the most enlightened and patriotic

Indian men who ever negotiated a treaty, and that it secured to the whole people more signal advantages than were ever before secured to an Indian people by treaty entered into with this government."[2]

As evidences of the superior advantages to be gained by removal, he read to the Senate a letter from John Ridge, who had already emigrated to the west, picturing in the most alluring terms the beauties of the western nation, the richness of the soil, the healthfulness of the climate, and all the other natural advantages which, in his judgment, far surpassed those of the eastern country.[3] Why the Cherokees refused to emigrate to a land where such superior opportunities and resources awaited them was beyond comprehension, and he was of the opinion that people of such poor discernment should be treated "as minors and orphans, and other persons who are incompetent to take charge of their own rights."[4]

So alert were the advocates of removal, and so strong their determination to carry out their Indian policy, that all efforts to secure the abrogation of the treaty were contravened and thwarted at every point.

As for the mass of the Cherokee people, two years of threats and promises had failed to bring them to admit the validity of the treaty or to show any inclination to emigrate of their own accord. The failure of their delegation to secure the repeal of the treaty did not weaken their determination to stand on their rights. Even the threats of fresh troops, sent into the country to put down opposition, failed to terrify them into submission or frighten them into abandoning such haunts as had been spared them on account of the inaccessible nature of the country, and to which they stubbornly clung, unsubdued yet unresisting.

When it had become perfectly evident that removal could be accomplished only by sheer brute force, protests from the country at large became so vehement that the administration began to look for a way to satisfy public sentiment without antagonizing the states concerned. As a result, the president early in May proposed a compromise to extend the time of removal two years.[5] This suggestion met with such strong opposition from Governor Gilmer that the treaty was allowed to take its course.[6]

As a result of pressure brought to bear by executive authority, between the adoption of the New Echota Treaty and January 1838, about two thousand Cherokees had emigrated, more than thirteen thousand remaining in the Cherokee Nation East. In the spring of 1838, the president, convinced that they would not remove without compulsion, dispatched General Winfield Scott to their country to take command of the troops already there, and to collect an additional force comprising a regiment each of artillery and infantry, and six companies of volunteers, a sufficient force unquestionably to overawe the disarmed, starving natives and compel submission.[7] In case he found it necessary, however, the future hero of the Mexican War was authorized to call upon the governors of the neighboring states for voluntary militia.

General Scott, from his headquarters at New Echota, issued a proclamation announcing that the President had sent him with a powerful army to cause the Cherokees, in obedience to the treaty of 1835, to join their brethren beyond the Mississippi, and before another moon had passed every man, woman, and child must be on the way to the west.[8]

In order to carry out instructions to remove the Indians at any cost, General Scott began enrolling and collecting them at such a rate and in such a manner as to work the greatest hardship upon them. Stockade forts were built at convenient places and squads of soldiers were sent into the surrounding country with guns, bayonets, swords, and pistols to search every cave and chasm of the mountainside for the natives, who were driven at the point of the bayonet and the muzzle of the musket to one of the concentration camps.

Accounts are given of such cruelty and inhumanity, perpetrated upon the helpless victims, as seem impossible to have occurred in a civilized country. Mr. James Mooney, after having talked with some of the Cherokees who had experienced this reign of terror in the Allegheny Mountains, gives the following account of it: "Families at dinner were startled by the sudden gleam of bayonets in the doorway and rose up to be driven with blows and oaths along the weary miles of trail that led to the stockade.

"Men were seized in their fields, or going along the road; women were taken from their wheels and children from their play. In many cases, on turning for one last look as they crossed the ridge, they saw their homes in flames, fired by the lawless rabble that followed on the heels of the soldiers to loot and pillage. So keen were these outlaws on the scent that in some instances they were driving off the cattle and other stock of the Indians almost before the soldiers had fairly started their owners in the other direction,"[9] and before nightfall, ghoulish thieves were searching Indian graves for the silver pendants and other valuables deposited by the natives with their dead.

In order to take the Indians completely by surprise and prevent all possibility of escape, the soldiers were ordered to approach and surround the houses as noiselessly as possible. One aged full blood, finding himself so surrounded, calmly called his household of children and grandchildren about him, and kneeling prayed with them in their own language, while the soldiers looked on in shamefaced astonishment. Upon rising from their devotions, they were warned by their captors to make no needless preparations but to be off at once. Thus they were hurried away, each one carrying such possessions as he could quickly lay hands on, even the little children grasping in their hands or hugging to their hearts some childish treasure.

Those who attempted to escape were shot down like criminals. The story is told of a deaf boy, who upon seeing the soldiers approach, became panic stricken and started to run away. When he failed to respond to the order to halt, a musket was leveled at his back, and he fell to the ground mortally wounded.[10]

Those who were utterly unable to travel, the helpless cripples, the aged, and the mortally ill, were left in remote cabins to die of starvation and neglect. Children were separated from parents, who in some cases never saw them again nor knew what fate befell their little ones. A few women and children, warned of the coming of the soldiers, fled to inaccessible mountain fastnesses and hid in caves to perish of starvation, while their men-folk were hunted and trapped like wild beasts.

Old men, delicate women, and little children were driven like cattle[11] until strength failed them and they fell fainting by the roadside. When brutal kicks and saber thrusts failed to rouse them to further effort they were loaded into wagons and hauled over rough mountain roads to stockades; or, where wagons were wanting, left to recover or die as they might, while friends and family, pricked on by the bayonet, were not permitted to minister to them.[12]

At night, sick and well were forced to lie upon the bare ground in the open with no protection from the weather and to herd together for warmth like beasts. Not infrequently death relieved them from their suffering before the journey's end. In such cases the soldiers were considered quite humane who tarried long enough to dig for a grave a shallow trench by the roadside, and to fling a few shovel-fulls of earth over these lifeless bodies.

Submission was the rule among the Indians, but there were occasional exceptions, as in the case of Tsali, an old man who, with his wife, a brother, and three sons, with their families, were surrounded, taken captive by the soldiers, and started on foot towards one of the stockades. Tsali's wife, a frail and delicate woman unable to keep up with the others, was prodded on by the bayonets of the soldiers until the old man, goaded to desperation by the sight of this brutality and his wife's suffering, suggested to the others that they make a dash for liberty.

As the conversation was carried on in the Cherokee language, the soldiers did not understand it, and when each warrior suddenly leaped upon the nearest white man the surprise was so complete that one soldier was killed, while the rest fled in confusion. The Indians escaped to the mountains where they were joined by some of their tribesmen who had either escaped from the stockades or had succeeded in eluding the soldiers.

Among them was an Indian named Euchela,[13] who, with a hundred followers, belonged to this class of outlaws. Having failed in every attempt to take the fugitives by force, General Scott determined to employ conciliation. Colonel W. H. Thomas, a trader well known to the Indians, was sent to make overtures to Euchela and his band, promising that if they would surrender Tsali and his family, they would be permitted to remain in Carolina and be at peace until their case could be adjusted by the federal government.

"I cannot be at peace," Euchela declared, "because it is now a whole year that your soldiers have hunted me like a wild deer. I have suffered more than I can bear. I had a wife and a little child, a bright-eyed boy, and because I would not become your slave they were left to starve upon the mountains and I buried them with my own hands at midnight."[14] Finally, however, he was induced to accept the overtures of General Scott, and summoning his warriors with a whoop, he laid the proposition before them. After much discussion and deliberation, they all agreed to the offer.

Tsali heard of this compromise and knowing his fate was sealed, came in voluntarily with his brother and his two eldest sons and surrendered. They were tried by court-martial and sentenced to be shot. Bound to the tree where he was to be executed, the old man, at his own request was permitted to speak, "I am not afraid to die; O, no, I want to die, for my heart is very heavy, heavier than lead."

Turning to Euchela he continued, "But, Euchela, there is one favor I wish to ask at your hands. You know I have a little boy who was lost among the mountains. I want you to find that boy if he is not dead and tell him that the last words of his father were that he must never go beyond the Father of Waters,[15] but die in the land of his birth. It is sweet to die in one's native land and be buried by the margin of one's native streams."[16]

When he had finished speaking the bandages were placed over his eyes and the execution proceeded. Some delay having occurred in the arrangement, he uncovered his eyes to see a dozen of his tribesmen in the very act of firing. Calmly and deliberately he replaced the cloth and the next instant his spirit had entered the Darkening Land.

General Scott had commanded that a dozen Cherokee prisoners be compelled to do the shooting in order to impress upon the Indians the helplessness of their situation. Tsali's youngest son, Wasituna, was eventually pardoned because of his youth, and allowed to remain in North Carolina, thus fulfilling his father's wish that he might die in the land of his birth.[17]

Conditions in the stockades were in keeping with the whole policy of forcible eviction. Musty corn meal and fat salt pork or rank bacon were the only provision furnished by removal officers who had let the contracts for furnishing subsistence at war prices. This was the time of year, too, when the natives were accustomed to fresh fruits and vegetables in abundance, but the women asked in vain for permission to go out and gather wild berries, onions, and greens for their families. There was no milk even for the little children. Old and young, sick and well, were compelled to eat the stale rations doled out to them by their captors.

Colonel Z. A. Zile, of the Georgia Militia, in describing to Mr. Mooney this chapter of Cherokee history in which he himself participated, said, "I fought through the Civil War and have seen men shot to pieces and slaughtered by the thousands, but the Cherokee removal was the cruelest work I ever knew."[18]

CHAPTER 12

The Trail of Tears

When a sufficient number had been gathered into stockades the work of removal commenced. Early in June several parties, aggregating about five hundred, were brought down to the Old Agency at Calhoun, Georgia, to Ross's Landing, now Chattanooga, and to Gunter's Landing at Guntersville, Alabama, where they were forced into filthy boats and sent down the Tennessee River.

In one instance so many were crowded into a ramshackle steamer that it threatened to sink. A part of the passengers were then hastily and indiscriminately unloaded, thus separating children from parents and husbands from wives. They were not reunited until months afterwards, when they met in the West.[1] In some instances, they never saw each other again.

These boats were sent down the Tennessee to Muscle Shoals, where a transfer was made before the journey could continue to Little Rock. There a second landing was made and in the heat of summer the emigrants were compelled to await the convenience of removal agents, sometimes for weeks, before they could continue to Indian Territory. Much sickness and suffering resulted and many deaths were reported.

From first to last the forcible removal of the Cherokees was strangely bungled. Contracts had been let to incompetent persons who neglected to provide adequate means of transportation, particularly wagons for the land route, sufficient rations for the emigrants, and provender for the horses. They also failed to establish depots of supplies along the way, a very important oversight when it is remembered that much of the country through which they were to pass was sparsely populated and in the frontier stage.

A drought lasting from May until October rendered travel by land impracticable as it was estimated that for many marches in succession, food supplies were not available, and for a company of a hundred there was not even a scanty supply of water. Up to June a shortage of boats had made it impossible to send off a large number by water,[2] and by that time the Hiwassee and the Tennessee had almost ceased to be navigable. It was also reported that the Arkansas River was very low.

This was the state of affairs on July 23 when the Cherokee Council proposed to General Scott that the whole business of emigrating be taken over by the nation. The condition of the people, they reasoned, was such that all dispute as to the time of emigrating had been set at rest; since they were under the absolute control of the commanding general; all inducements to prolong their stay in the Cherokee Nation East had been removed; and that although attachment to the home of their fathers remained unimpaired, their wishes now were to depart as early as might be consistent with safety.[3]

General Scott granted the request on condition that the Council be held responsible for the good behavior of the Indians in the camp and on the march and that the first detachment should have started by the first of September, the last not later than October 20. The Council was to take entire control of all departments, provide all necessary means of travel and subsistence, and employ all assistance in transportation. The sum of sixty dollars a head was allowed for the expense of moving each man, woman, and child.

The situation of the captives improved immediately. The military was removed, the Georgia Guard forced to retire, and the white doctors were dismissed. The people, permitted to scatter out freely and to seek better locations for camps, found their condition much more endurable than it had been under martial law. They naturally regarded as a godsend the change in arrangement for removal, for they felt that their interests would now be safeguarded by their chiefs and councilors, who had stood by them through the severest of temptations, and who had refused to betray them for fear or favor.[4]

Left to themselves, the Cherokee officials set about organizing their forces in an orderly and systematic manner. By resolution of Council they made Chief Ross superintendent agent of emigration, and entrusted the entire management of removal to a committee of their own selection.[5] This committee organized the people along the line of kinship and of family ties, where it was possible, dividing them into thirteen detachments comprised of as nearly equal numbers as was practicable. Over each detachment were placed two men well qualified to manage that particular group of emigrants. After a thorough investigation had been made of the different routes, each division was to proceed over the one selected by its leaders.[6]

Late in August 1838 the Council and people, assembling for a final meeting at Aquohe Camp, two miles south of the Hiwassee River, passed a resolution declaring that, never having consented to the sale of their country either themselves or through their representatives, the original ownership still rested in the Cherokee Nation, whose title to the lands, described by the boundaries of 1819, was still unimpaired and absolute; that the United States was responsible for all losses and damages in enforcing the pretended treaty; they had never relinquished their national sovereignty, therefore the moral and political relations existing among their citizens towards each other and towards the body politic could not be changed by their forcible expulsion; and finally, they pronounced their laws and constitution in full force, to remain so until the general welfare rendered a modification expedient.[7] This action bound anew the people into a body politic which went, not as individuals or groups, but as a nation, into exile.

As September approached, every effort was made by leaders and people to keep their promise to General Wool that the first detachment should be under way by September 1. Notwithstanding the continuance of the drought and the great amount of sickness among them, it was determined that a company should be ready to start on the last day of August from the camp located about twelve miles south of the agency in Tennessee.[8] The plan was to get a part of the company in motion on August twenty-eighth, the remainder to follow the next day and come up while they were crossing the Tennessee River, which was twenty-five miles distant.

At noon everything was in readiness to start. Wagons and teams were stretched in a line along the road through the dense forest. Groups gathered around the wagons or lingered about sick friends or relatives who were to be left behind. The temporary shacks, covered with rough boards or bark, which had served as their only shelter during the past weeks, had been given to the flames and were now crackling and falling into glowing heaps of embers here and there on the camp ground. The day was bright and beautiful; not a cloud dimmed the blue above. Yet a gloomy thoughtfulness shadowed the faces of the people. "In all the bustle of preparation there was a silence and stillness of voice which betrayed the sadness of heart."[9]

When at last the signal was given to start, Going Snake, a white-haired chief of four score years, mounted his faithful pony and took his place at the head of the column, followed by a cavalcade of younger men. Just as the procession was on the point of being set in motion, a clap of thunder smote the stillness and a dark spiral cloud was seen rising above the western horizon. Peal after peal rent the air and reverberated among the mountain peaks like the voice of some mighty, offended deity, while overhead the sun still shone in an unclouded sky. Not a drop of rain fell. The cloud presently dissolved and the thunder died away in the distance, but the scene was not one to be easily forgotten by a people always keenly alive to natural phenomena to which they often attached divine significance.[10] Was it an augury of good or of ill? Did it portend happier times or worse to come? Only time could tell.

In consequence of the sickness which still prevailed in the camps and the drought which rendered travel distressing beyond description, General Scott called a halt and ordered emigration suspended for several weeks.[11] Not until winter approached was the last detachment ready to set out for the west.

This party, under the personal direction of the principal chief, left Rattlesnake Springs, near Charleston, Tennessee, on October 31. Crossing to the north side of the Hiwassee at the ferry above

Gunstocker Creek, the procession continued down along the river. The sick, the old people and the children rode in the wagons,[12] which carried the provisions, bedding, cooking utensils, and such other household goods as had been spared. The rest proceeded on foot or on horseback.

The march was conducted with the order of an army; a detachment of officers, heading the procession, was followed by the wagons, while the horsemen and those on foot brought up the rear, or when the road permitted, flanked the procession. Crossing the Tennessee River near the mouth of the Hiwassee,[13] the procession passed through Tennessee by way of McMinnville and Nashville and thence through Kentucky to Hopkinsville, where a halt was made to bury Whitepath,[14] who had fallen victim to illness and exposure.

They buried the venerable chieftain, veteran of many wars with the white men, by the roadside and built over his grave a wooden box in lieu of a more enduring and fitting monument to his long and loyal service to his people. At the head and foot they placed poles bearing black streamers as a signal to those coming on behind, in order that they might not pass by without noting the last resting place of their revered clansman. Moving on, they crossed the Ohio near the mouth of the Cumberland, and thence passed through southern Illinois to Cape Girardeau.

A severe winter had set in before the last detachment reached the Mississippi. The river was choked with floating ice, crossing was dangerous, and they were compelled to await the clearing of the current. The weather was intensely cold, and hundreds of sick and dying filled the wagons or lay upon the frozen ground with only an armful of grass or leaves for bed and a sheet or blanket to protect them from the cutting blast. The hardships through which they had passed during the last few months had reduced their vitality, while homesickness and mental depression so preyed upon their minds as to render them an easy prey to disease from which they could not rally. Hundreds never lived to cross the Father of Waters, and their bodies were left to molder in alien soil.

When finally the last detachment was able to cross the river and continue the journey, they found it necessary to take the northern route through central Missouri by way of Springfield and Southwest City, because those who had preceded them, going through the southern part of the state to Fort Smith, had killed off the game upon which they depended largely for subsistence. It was March before they reached their destination. More than four thousand had perished on the way; among them was the wife of Chief Ross.

Thus passing from ancestral fields, "broad set between the hills," to trackless wilds unknown, the pilgrim train went west along a weary way beset with pain and death. And ever as they went, their bruised and bleeding feet transformed into a nation's highway the toilsome road that had been to them "A Trail of Tears."

Time passed, but the Cherokees never forgot the loved ones they had buried beside the way. Three score years had come and gone and one old man still lived who remembered as if it had been yesterday the details of that fateful journey. And this is the story which he told in his own broken English to one of his questioning tribesmen:

Long time now I have live. Strange thing I have seen. Much dangers I have pass through. Few year, now, and I be seen no more. All my peoples now gone; no brother, no sister, no close kin.

Peoples ask some times to tell most terrible thing I remember. They know I was soldier in Mexican War; also in Civil War, and think I tell about great fights with cannon and musket, but what I tell about is what is call Removal of Cherokees from Old Nation. That was long time—fifty year ago. It is now 1889 when I tell peoples what keep asking for something strange and terrible.

When removal is made I am young man, born at foot of Lookout Mountain in 1819. My father, he was soldier in Cherokee regiment and he made much fight at Talladega, at Horse Shoe Bend, on Tallapoosa River, March 1814— great fight my father make. He is call captain by great white general what got to be president—Jackson was his name. Most everybody say if Cherokee regiment ain't been there and make fight Creeks win big battle.

Log house of my father was in great valley. Close by was deep river and great mountain stand high up in skies. Council House not far away. Much Cherokee live in valley. Raise plenty to eat and want no trouble with anybody. Cherokees quit fighting with white peoples after war with Red Coats from country beyond big water. They settle down and want live in peace and be friend with ever body.

Few year they live that way and then much talk is made how new president is much in favor to send all Cherokees west to far country beyond BIG RIVER. Cherokee don't think much be done. They say they help President when he was fight Creeks at Talladega and he must be friend.

Time pass by. News come president he say: 'Cherokees, go west!' They won't go. Say, 'Stay and maybe-so things will be better.' Not so, but worse. More time pass, then big prison pens is built and Cherokees is put in them—what won't get up and go. Two thousand soldier with cannon and with musket come and guard Cherokees and drive them on like cattle, like hog, prodding with musket. At head of file ride great big man on fine horse called General Scott—*Big* man on *Fine* horse! He say he don't want shoot Indian but he must be quiet and not try and make troubles on trail.

Cool weather arrive. Big march far west is made. Long time Indian travel new country, O, so far! Road, o so full of thorns! Peoples feel bad when leave Old Nation. Womens cry and make sad wail. Childrens cry. Mens cry, and all look like when friend die. But say nothing; just keep on going west.

Days pass and peoples die very much. My father—now old man—fought with Jackson at The Horse Shoe, walk along and all of sudden fall down in snow—can't get up. One day he live in covered wagon and then is dead. We bury him close by trail and go on. A week pass and one day my mother cry out and fall over and speak no more. We bury her and go on. Three week pass by and two brothers is sick, then three sisters; all die, one each day, and all are gone. We bury them beside the trail. Others die every day, so we go on. We bury and march. Soon some more is dead. We bury and go on. Looks like maybe we all be dead before new Indian country is reach, but all time march on. All time is cry made from wagons where is old peoples and childrens—all day, all night is cry and moan.

Time pass; maybe so fifty years. Long time I am live in hills of new country and much good peoples what lives close by me say, "why not some time laugh?" Look like I never smile in lifetime. No man has laugh left after he's made long march from old country. Most times I am keep thinking of old Nation; of how big mountain look in spring time when birds sing and Cherokees go on long hunt down deep river. Then come picture of march on long trail towards setting sun and seem like I hear moan and cry of old peoples and childrens.

Guess, maybe-so when new land is reach in skies where all my peoples is meet me, I shall make joyous laugh, I think. Maybe-so, too, I shall know why Cherokees must leave old nation and go west.

The story of the Indian, dispossessed, expatriated, and exploited by his white brothers, is one of the cruelest chapters in American history. His virtues, unacknowledged, his vices, magnified, his contributions to the culture of the New World, ignored, the First American too long has been looked upon as only:

A savage! Let him bleed and eat his heart and swiftly go;
Our strength's our right. The tale is old! E'en so.
The panther footed, lithesome Indian brave
We thought not worth our while to try to save,
But welcomed hither hordes of king-crushed souls,
The worn out serfs who cringed to lords for doles;
We gave an eagle race the grave as bed;
Only our fields yet bear his sign, the arrow head.[15]

CHAPTER 13

The Constitution of 1839

Detachment after detachment, the exiled nation, moving by painful stages toward the west, arrived during the winter and spring of 1839 and went into camps selected by scouts sent ahead to prepare for their coming. There they nursed their sick, recruited their strength, and looked about them on a bleak and unfamiliar landscape. The party under the command of Reverend Jesse Bushyhead located near Westville, in the eastern part of the nation and its camp was called by a Cherokee name meaning Bread Town.[1] Hildebrand's detachment at the end of the journey stopped at Chisholm's Spring on Beattie's Prairie, a mile west of Maysville, Arkansas, where "These people, being transplanted from a warm climate, and having to live in open tents in January, and to suffer the blizzards of that country in winter, died in hosts. There were between fifty and a hundred of them buried in my father's grave yard," is told in her memoirs by one who, as a young girl, saw this party of desolated full-bloods as they arrived in the winter of 1839.[2]

The last detachment to leave the ancient nation and the last to reach the new was conducted by John Ross,[3] who made an encampment on the Illinois River within a few miles of Park Hill mission, where Dr. Worcester and Elias Boudinot were already engaged in their work of translation and publication. The Illinois Camp Ground was centrally and conveniently located for emigrant headquarters and a disbursing center for the newcomers during the year following removal.

There had been two parties in the eastern nation. There were now three in the western: the Old Settlers, or Cherokees West; the Ridge, or Treaty Party; and the Ross, or National Party. The Treaty men had preceded the Emigrants to the Indian Territory, located homesteads, cultivated the friendship of the leading western chiefs, and established amicable relations with the border towns of Arkansas as a measure of social and political security. Wealthy, resourceful, and high in the favor of government officials, they had entrenched themselves on the frontier in an apparently impregnable position, and with the commandant at Fort Gibson as an ally, they were ready to receive their tribesmen from beyond the Father of Waters—preferably as friends, as enemies if need be.

The establishment of the Cherokee Nation West had not been without design on the part of the government, which had nurtured and neglected it by turns. The tenure of this little frontier colony of civilized Indians for many years had been a precarious one. The tract of land granted them by the Treaty of 1817 had been claimed by the Osages until the title of the plains tribe was finally quieted by the Treaty of 1825. Delay in surveying the boundary lines and taking the census, and the withholding of annuities until the census had been taken in the hope that the whole tribe might be induced to emigrate, all tended to create a feeling of insecurity and to retard progress.

There was also a movement on the part of Arkansas to get rid of her Indians, and when a delegation of western chiefs was sent to Washington in the winter of 1828 to urge the settlement of their boundary claims, so much pressure was brought to bear upon them by the War Department as to practically force the exchange of their grant of 1817 for a tract of seven million acres in the Indian Territory. Upon their return home, the chiefs who negotiated the treaty barely escaped execution when it became known what they had done. The council pronounced them guilty of fraud and treason and declared the cession null and void. Before it could be prevented, however, Congress had ratified the treaty, after which protest was of no avail. Thus, "hardly ten years after they had cleared their fields in Arkansas, the western Cherokees were forced to abandon their claims and plantations and move once more into the wilderness."[4]

Some progress, even under such discouraging conditions, had been made as early as 1819 when Thomas Nuttall, the well-known traveler and naturalist, paid them a visit on the Arkansas. Their farms then were well fenced and stocked with cattle and "their houses were decently furnished, a few of them even handsomely and conveniently."[5] On January 1, 1822, Dwight Mission, opened at the earnest solicitation of Tollunteeskee, had given them their first school.[6]

The civil affairs of the Cherokees West had been confused and disturbed not only because of the indifferent policy of the federal government, but by the constant arrival of emigrant parties from the old nation. Their first chief, The Bowl, had been summarily succeeded in 1813 by Takatoka, and he, five years later, was forced to give place to Tollunteeskee, who had recently arrived at the head of a large band of emigrants.[7] Then, Tollunteeskee had died in 1820 and his nephew, John Jolly, succeeded him.

In a reorganization of the government in 1824, the nation was divided into four districts, from each of which two councilors, elected to serve for a term of twelve months, were to constitute the National Committee. "Accordingly, the people met in their respective districts and selected their eight members, who convened at John Smith's on Piney, September 11, 1824," and there organized themselves into a committee. Colonel Walter Webber was elected to preside as chairman of the Committee and David Brown as clerk."[8] A resolution was adopted providing that the executive department of the government consist of a First Chief, a Second Chief and a Third, or minor Chief, to be appointed for a term of four years and to receive annual salaries, the first and second chiefs, a hundred dollars each, and the third, sixty dollars. Thereafter the council was to convene annually the first Monday in October at Tahlonteeskee[9] Council House, near the mouth of the Illinois River.

In the fall of 1838, John Jolly died, having served as principal chief for eighteen years. John Brown, first assistant chief, whose term of office was due to expire in October of the following year, became the nominal head of the government.[10] The general condition of the country was unsettled and confusing with parties of emigrants arriving at intervals, ill and travel worn. Doubt and uncertainty prevailed among the Old Settlers since they had no assurance of protection from the government against their eastern kinsmen, who were arriving in such multitudes as to outnumber them two to one. The leading men, encouraged and supported by the Treaty Party and remembering how a large party of emigrants twenty years previously had proved to be usurpers, determined to keep the reins of government in their own hands as long as possible.

To this end, John Brown, repenting of his resignation of the previous year, called an extra session of the council whose eight members unanimously concurred in the appointment of John Brown as principal chief for the unexpired term; John Looney was made first assistant chief, and John Rogers second assistant chief of the Western Cherokees.

In response to a request from the National Council of the eastern nation, soon after the arrival of the Ross detachment at the Illinois Camp Ground, Chief Brown called a meeting for the purpose of bringing about a union and consolidation of the two nations. The convention which met on June 14 was attended by chiefs and councilors from both nations and by representatives of the Treaty Party besides. After a formal reception given by the western to the eastern chiefs, the two councils convened separately, the Old Settlers, behind closed doors, communication between the two bodies being conducted in writing.

The Old Settlers opened negotiations by demanding of the nationalists a formal statement of their wishes in regard to the proposed union. In reply, the nationalists requested that the adjustment of relations be left to a joint committee composed of equal numbers from both sides together with the principal and assistant chiefs of both nations. The Western Council refused to accede, declaring that they considered the two nations already virtually united. Had not the newcomers accepted the welcome of the western chiefs by taking their hands in friendship? This act they regarded as acceptance of them as rulers. The government and laws of the Cherokees from the east could not be admitted in the west. Therefore, since two governments were not to be tolerated in the same region, the newcomers must accept the organization which they found already in operation when they arrived.

On the contrary, the emigrants denied that the two peoples were already united and that the chiefs of the minority had any right from prior residence in a place set apart for emigrant Cherokees generally to claim allegiance to themselves and their laws from a body of newcomers so greatly outnumbering them. They reminded them that prior to removal it had been proclaimed and had been understood by Cherokees on both sides of the Mississippi that the nationalists had not relinquished a single law, but had emigrated in their national character with all the attributes which had belonged to them from time immemorial as a distinct community. But for all that, notwithstanding they constituted so large a majority, they had not come to make any but just and equitable demands.[11]

Upon receipt of this communication, the Old Settler council on June 20 adjourned without further notice and informed the people that "the meeting was broken up."[12] Dissatisfied in the outcome of this joint council, the people of all factions resolved themselves into a popular assembly in which they declared that since their representatives had failed to accomplish a plan of union, a national convention should meet on July 1 at the Illinois Camp Ground to "recast the government upon a system applicable to their present conditions, a government that provided equally for the peace and happiness of the whole people."[13]

The assembly, before adjourning, sent an express to notify General Arbuckle, Commandant at Fort Gibson, of their failure to effect a union and of their determination to hold another convention in July; also to request that no disbursements of moneys due the eastern nation, nor any other business of a public character affecting their rights, be made or transacted by the government agent or with any other Cherokee authority until a reunion of the people should have been effected.[14]

While negotiations were still in progress and before the Old Settlers had delivered their ultimatum, the Treaty men had abruptly left the ground, but not before their conduct had aggravated the old grievances beyond forbearance. Feeling against them ran high, and threats were heard on all sides that it was not yet too late for them to pay the penalty reserved for traitors and murderers of women and children.

Heretofore, out of deference to the wishes of Chief Ross, it is said the death penalty imposed by the law against selling Cherokee land had been held in abeyance. Conditions had now taken such a turn that it was determined to proceed to its execution without his knowledge. Pursuant to a secret agreement, three hundred clansmen banded themselves together, pledged to stand by each other to the last extremity. Of the three hundred, forty were chosen by lot to execute secretly and at once the plan agreed upon. All were disguised and acted with such dispatch and precision that within twenty-four hours they had put to death Major Ridge, John Ridge, and Elias Boudinot.[15]

The blow, long deferred, had fallen with a heavy hand. The fact that the executioners were of the National Party and that Boudinot was done to death within two miles of Chief Ross's home, lent color to the story that John Ross himself had instigated the execution. News of the affair, reaching the remotest corner of the nation, precipitated a panic. Great excitement prevailed. Treaty men, who regarded their friends and associates as martyrs to a good cause, vowed that the price of their lives should be paid with the blood of John Ross.[16]

A party of Old Settlers and Treaty men took refuge at Fort Gibson where they sought the protection of the garrison and their friend, the commandant, of whose sentiments they felt sure. As a fair and impartial mediator, General Arbuckle could have done a great deal towards arranging a compromise between the warring factions, ninety percent of whose people desired nothing so much as peace and unity under a strong and efficient government. In an effort to bring about peace, he would have had the cooperation of the agent for the Cherokees, the honorable Montford Stokes, former governor of North Carolina, who from the agency on the Bayou Menard, assured all factions of his desire to do everything in his power, without partiality to anyone, to prevent further effusion of blood.[17]

But General Arbuckle was a man of war, not peace, who had served General Jackson as an aide in the War of 1812. In 1824, on the recommendation of the hero of New Orleans, he had been commissioned by the Secretary of War to locate a military post in aid of Indian removal near the Three Forks of the Arkansas. Pursuant to these instructions, he founded Fort Gibson, where he remained in command for a number of years.

Long before the emigrants arrived, he had cultivated friendly relations with Old Settlers, and later with Treaty men, and consequently was more or less prejudiced against the nationalists, whose coming he had expected to cause trouble in the country which his garrison was designed to tranquilize. After June 22, General Arbuckle openly espoused the cause of the Treaty Party and sent a dispatch to Washington apprising the administration of the Ridge-Boudinot tragedy.

The messenger returned in twenty-four days with orders from the government to defend the Treaty Party, support the Old Settlers, take care of such Cherokees as might manifest a hostile disposition, and demand the apprehension of the assassins. Acting on these instructions, General Arbuckle informed the western chiefs they would be recognized as the only legitimate authority in the Cherokee Nation, and advised Chief Brown to hold on to his authority, by no means to give it up. As he would be sustained by the military, the people would be compelled to submit.[18]

When, therefore, the time came for the meeting at the Illinois Camp Ground on July 1, the factions appeared farther apart than ever before. Partisan feeling ran high among the parties and threats of reprisals from the Treaty leaders, who really feared for their lives, kept popular anticipation keyed to a high pitch. There was a large attendance, nevertheless, and Old Settlers, as well as emigrants, participated in the gathering. The aged Sequoyah was present and used all his influence for peace and harmony. A delegation, sent to assure the Fort Gibson group that the meeting was a peaceable one, and to invite them to join in the work there in progress, was met with cold aloofness.[19]

Having passed resolutions looking towards the immediate demands of the situation and providing for a constitutional convention which was to meet at Tahlequah in September, the delegates adjourned in an orderly fashion, Thus impressing the people favorably, so that there developed an increasing confidence in the National Party as the only one capable of establishing a new government on sound political principles adequate to the needs of the united people.

From September the sixth to the tenth, the convention met at Tahlequah and formulated a constitution which provided for a government divided into legislative, executive and judicial branches. The legislative branch was styled the National Council, each member of which, before taking his seat of office, was required to take an oath to conduct himself for the best interests and prosperity of the nation and to support and defend the constitution.

The supreme executive power was vested in a principal chief, who should be elected by the qualified electors of the nation for a period of four years; and an assistant chief, likewise elected by the people for a term of four years. They were required to "attend at the seat of government" when the National Council was in session. There was to be an executive council of five members appointed by the National Council, which, with the assistant chief, constituted an advisory board subject to the call of the principal chief. The treasurer of the nation, before entering upon his duties, was required to give bond for the faithful discharge of his duties.

The judicial power was vested in a Supreme Court and such circuit and inferior courts as the National Council should ordain and establish. A sheriff for each district was to be elected by the people for a term of two years and no person who denied the existence of a supreme being was permitted to hold office under the government. The National Council was to convene annually on the first Monday in October.[20]

At the election in which the constitution was submitted to the people for adoption, officers for the new government were elected. John Ross was chosen principal chief and Joseph Vann, a former chief of the Cherokees west, assistant chief. In the executive council and in the two legislative bodies, the western Cherokees had a slight advantage in numbers, both the speaker of the Council, William Shorey Coody, and the president of the national committee, Young Wolf, being western Cherokees. When the First Monday in October arrived, the Cherokee Nation, Indian Territory, was ready for its initial session of the National Council.[21]

The Council in October appointed a delegation to Washington for the purpose of securing the payment of moneys due the nation. Meanwhile, the Fort Gibson group of Old Settlers had called a convention of their own which repudiated all that their opponents had done and dispatched a delegation to the national capital to protest against the recognition of the rival government. Thus with two contending parties, each claiming to represent the nation, all efforts to secure recognition were frustrated by the opposition. Weeks and months of delay ensued with all the tribal money held up and no funds available for conducting the nation's government.[22]

This sort of thing could not last always. Everybody knew that the Cherokees had money invested for them by the government with interest coming due semi-annually, so that even negligent and dilatory administration officials eventually had to recognize their responsibility for devising some measure of relief. The Secretary of War through the Commissioner of Indian Affairs at last instructed Agent Stokes to call a meeting and settle by popular vote the question as to which of the rival governments should prevail.[23]

A convention called by the Indian Agent in compliance with this ruling, voted unanimously in favor of the Act of Union and the Tahlequah Constitution. Captain Page, who was present to represent the government, sent to Washington a certified copy of the votes cast showing that all those present were in favor of the Act of Union.[24]

Still the Fort Gibson faction, including General Arbuckle, was dissatisfied, claiming that the convention had not been conducted legitimately and asking the Secretary of War for another convention to frame a new constitution.[25] The request was granted and General Arbuckle was authorized to dissolve both rival governments and to call a third constitutional convention, over which he himself should preside, at Fort Gibson on July 25, 1841, each faction being authorized to send a deputation of twenty-five or thirty.

The plan pleased neither party. The National Council, nevertheless, took the trouble to appoint a full delegation, which appeared at Fort Gibson with a copy of their Act of Union and Constitution, so that it was apparent from the start that the advantage was theirs, as Chief Rogers, head of the Old Settler delegation, had no well-defined plan to offer. General Arbuckle finally had to acknowledge defeat, advising the Old Settlers to accept the plan of government submitted by their opponents on the condition that the agreement eventually should be referred back to the people for their final approval.[26]

Although there was never any subsequent action on the part of the Western Cherokees concerning the compact, which was signed by twelve from the eastern nation and eleven from the western, the federal government regarded it as binding, and for all practical purpose recognized the government organized under the Tahlequah Constitution and Act of Union as that of the Cherokee Nation, Indian Territory.

CHAPTER 14

The Cherokee Nation,
Indian Territory

The seat of government for the nation organized under the Constitution of 1839 was located at Tahlequah, a short distance from the Illinois Camp Ground and less than a "Sabbath day's journey" from Park Hill Mission. It was centrally situated in a sheltered valley well supplied with water which, issuing from hillside springs formed a brook that flows over a rocky bed to join the Illinois River. Wolf's Spring was a favorite resort for councilors and towns people who had the habit of walking down for a draft of the clear, cold water at sunset.

In this pleasant valley a council ground was laid off in the form of a square whose corners were as accurately drawn as if surveyor's instruments had been used in plotting the lines. A shed was built within its inclosure to shelter the first session of the National Council. Later two log houses were constructed for the accommodation of the legislative bodies, and for the executive and judicial departments.

The first Council under the Constitution of 1839 was held from September nineteenth to October twelfth of that year. In quick succession, it passed acts for punishing criminal and other offenses; for regulating arbitration; for prohibiting the sale of ardent spirits; for granting permission to found new mission stations; and for other measures necessary to a well-organized government.[1] The country was divided, as in the ancient nation, into eight districts for the convenience of apportioning representation and for greater ease in administering the judicial and the fiscal affairs of the several sections.[2]

These districts bore the significant names of Flint, Skin Bayou, Going Snake, Saline, Illinois, Canadian, Delaware, and Tahlequah.

According to the compromise of 1841, in the interest of unity and harmony, one third of the officers elected under the new constitution resigned and Chief Rogers, representing the Old Settler government, appointed Western Cherokees to fill the unexpired term with the distinct understanding that thereafter each candidate, regardless of party affiliation, was to take his own chance at election. Thereafter, when council convened each year, the new officers appeared and took their places after having taken the oath of allegiance to the constitution and laws of the nation.

The delegation to Washington the previous winter returned home in October bringing news that was far from heartening.[3] The unsettled condition of the country and the conflicting claims of rival parties had given the administration an excuse for delay in remitting the semi-annual interest payments to the treasurer of the nation, and for evading the obligation imposed upon the government by the late treaty, while the delphic vagueness of the document became embarrassing to the administration when the Cherokees called for an accounting.

Even the Senate, which body had approved the agreement, could shed no light upon it, nor was the President nor the Secretary of War able to reconcile its contradictory statements as to whether the expense of removal should be subtracted from the five million to be paid for the lands of the old nation, or whether it should be borne by the United States. In Article eight the federal government made itself plainly liable for the expense of removal, and by Article fifteen this same item, together with the charge for subsistence, is enumerated with other expenses to be taken out of the amount paid the Cherokees for their eastern lands. Supplemental articles to the treaty, which had been found necessary to give character to the original document before it could even pass the Senate, cleared up some points, but on others, rendered the confusion more confounding.

To add to the complication, the Old Settlers now claimed that, if they were to be forced to share their country with the newcomers, they should share with them in the per capita payment which was to be made of all the moneys remaining from the sale of the eastern lands after expenses were paid. Also, the Treaty men claimed that, since they had been allowed only twenty dollars per capita for removal while the Emigrants had been promised three times as much, they should be reimbursed for the difference.

These conflicting claims added to complication already existing, and the Van Buren administration, now nearing its close, took no definite step towards reducing it to order and harmony. The delegations to Washington in the winter of 1840–1841 appealed in vain for a final interpretation of the treaty and a complete execution of all its terms. But the Indians and all their troubles were too remote to cut any figure in the present political situation, and the future was not yet to be reckoned with. With the Cherokees safe beyond the Mississippi, the President and Congress had been glad to free their minds of them. It seemed well-nigh impossible to attract any intelligent attention at this time, and their affairs had to drift on into the next administration.

With the accession of the Whigs, who had loudly denounced Jackson's force policy, high hopes for relief were entertained by the Cherokees. Yet weeks passed into months before the Indians succeeded in gaining the ear of the executive. Finally in September President Tyler addressed to the delegation a letter in which he deplored the injustice they had suffered at the hands of the federal government and promised that, as far as lay in his power to prevent it, no Cherokee should ever again petition in vain for justice.

He had carefully read the various treaties, he said, wherein he found promises of friendship on one side, and of protection and guardian-care on the other. He had read Washington's address to the delegation of the nation as it was inscribed in the silver-bound book presented to them at Philadelphia, wherein he found a record of the mutual obligations existing between his government and that of the Cherokee Nation. He also had read the talk made by Jefferson and inscribed upon a parchment and surrounded by an endless chain of gold. "Let us keep that chain bright and unbroken," he enjoined them; "In its preservation consists our mutual happiness."

A new treaty was then promised, giving them indemnity for all their wrongs, establishing upon a permanent basis the political relations between them and the United States, and guaranteeing their lands in fee simple. In closing, President Tyler prophesied that a new sun would soon dawn upon the Cherokee people, in whose brightness their permanent happiness and true glory might be read by the whole world. "And I shall rejoice to have been the President under whose auspices these great and happy results shall have been produced."[4]

With a view to carrying out his promise, the president instructed the Cherokee agent to procure all the information possible upon the subject of the injustice done the members of the tribe, to the end that amends might be made them as far as possible. The secretary of war, acting upon this report, prepared the draft of a new treaty, which proved to be so far from satisfactory to all parties that the attempt at adjustment came to naught.[5]

Meanwhile, the possibilities suggested by Tyler's letter had been working sad havoc among the newly reconciled parties at home. Should investigation prove that large sums of money to be paid per capita were rightfully due the tribe, would members of all parties share and share alike, or would the Emigrants claim, and by their superior numbers and political strength, secure the lion's share? These questions began to agitate the minds of the opposing factions. Lawyers, sensing the possibility for gain to themselves in these contesting claims, began to revive old grievances, which soon produced a repetition of all the old party wrangling and bitterness. Old Settlers and Treaty men put forward separate claims, conflicting with those of the emigrants. Some of the Western Cherokees, with whom the Ridge men made common cause, attempted to reestablish their government at the mouth of the Illinois River. The Cherokee National authorities tried to suppress the movement on the ground of treason and the opposition, angry and resentful, appealed to Washington to have a certain section of the nation set apart for them, complaining that they could not live in peace and harmony with the Ross government. The administration, at a loss to know what to do, took refuge in inaction.

The Cherokee Council, having failed in the attempt to restore harmony and unity at home, dispatched a delegation to Washington in the winter of 1843–44, for the purpose of arranging a new treaty. Armed once more with President Tyler's letter, they presented to the Secretary of War a statement of the salient points on which they desired to negotiate a new agreement. Representatives of the other two factions[6] were also present and their hostility to the Ross party convinced the President that the cause of turbulence in the tribe must be investigated and responsibility for it fixed before a new treaty could be considered.

Charges had been brought against the dominant party, claiming that grievous oppressions were practiced by it, insomuch that they were not allowed to enjoy life, liberty, and the pursuit of happiness, and that the act of union was never authorized or sanctioned by the legal representatives of the people. The Nationalists contended, on the contrary, that the Western Cherokees and the Treaty Party enjoyed the same degree of security and the same fullness of rights enjoyed by any other part of the nation, and countercharged that the alleged dissatisfaction was confined to a few restless spirits whose motto was "rule or ruin."[7]

Unable to reconcile these contradictions, President Tyler appointed a commission to inquire into the disturbances and the grievances of the weaker parties. This commission,[8] arriving at Fort Gibson in the early winter, issued a proclamation stating its business with the Cherokees and inviting them to come in and register any complaints which they might have against the party in power. Conferences held at different points were well attended, over nine hundred being present at one meeting. A thorough investigation was made, lasting several weeks.

Based on this investigation, the commission reported that, after an impartial examination of the facts in the case, the committee was thoroughly convinced that the authority for the proceedings on either side at Fort Gibson in July 1840 was adequate since the representatives of the Western Cherokees who had attended and taken part in the deliberations were regarded by both Eastern and Western Cherokees as authorized agents; that the stipulations in regard to office were at once carried out, and many of those now denying the validity of the compact had taken office under it, and consequently had taken the required oath; and while the proceedings were never referred back to the people, there was probably never any intention that they should be so referred. At any rate, the reason that they were not referred seemed to have been not the fault of the Ross party.

The commission further reported that the complaint of oppression against the Ross party since the passage of the Act of Union was unfounded and that no life had been endangered by them, except in the administration of wholesome laws, but there was great danger to life from frequent and stealthy incursions of a desperate gang of bandit half-breeds,[9] notorious in the nation as wanton murderers, house burners and horse thieves, but whose fraternity was not of the dominant party; among the mass of the people there was no discontent, the bitterness and hostility to the dominant party being confined to a few. The commission concluded its report by recommending a new treaty on the basis of President Tyler's letter.[10]

It would seem there was no occasion for further delay, but that the time for action had arrived. Justice to all parties demanded it. When the report reached the President, however, the country had just emerged from the throes of another presidential election, resulting this time in the final overthrow of the Whigs. Tyler, with an eye single to the annexation of Texas, was willing to leave the much-vexed Cherokee question to the tender mercies of his successor,[11] who, during the first months of his administration, was too seriously involved in important foreign relations and domestic troubles to pay any attention to Indian affairs.

Seeing no probability of adjustment, a group of Old Settlers and Treaty men resolved in the fall of 1845 to ask the United States to provide them a home in the Texas country upon the relinquishment of all their interests in the Cherokee Nation, or to assign a section of the Cherokee Nation to them with the privilege of adopting their own form of government and living under it without molestation.[12] In reply, the Commissioner of Indian Affairs sent to President Polk a report approving the plea.

Influenced by this report, the President recommended to Congress that, as there was no probability of the different parties being able to ever live together in peace and harmony, the well-being of the whole tribe required that the factions should be separated and live under different governments as distinct tribes.[13]

The National Party resented this recommendation and vigorously objected to any federal interference with their internal affairs, particularly to having their country divided and the authority of the United States courts extended over them,[14] regarding it as a distinct violation of the article in the New Echota Treaty,[15] which promised the Indians protection in the laws which they should make, providing only that these laws be not inconsistent with those of the United States.

The situation in the summer of 1846 became so acute that a commission was appointed with power to examine into the causes of the controversies and to adjust them if possible.[16] As a measure of precaution, a memorandum of agreement was drawn up which bound all parties to abide absolutely by the decision of the commission and to sign such agreement as should be necessary to insure the execution of a treaty. The result was the conclusion of a treaty on August 6, 1846.[17]

This treaty states that "The lands now occupied by the Cherokee Nation should be secured to the whole Cherokee people for their common use and benefit," the United States to issue a patent for the said land which, in case the Cherokees became extinct or abandoned the country, should revert to the United States; it was agreed that difficulties and party differences should cease; a general amnesty for all offenses was declared; laws were to be passed for the equal protection of all; all armed police or military organizations were to be disbanded and the laws executed by civil powers. The United States agreed to reimburse the Cherokees for all sums unjustly deducted from the five million dollars under the treaty of 1835, and to distribute what remained of that amount according to the treaty.

As to the claims of the Old Settlers to sole ownership of the lands of the western nation, it was decided they had no exclusive title against the eastern Cherokees, who, by the Treaty of 1835, had acquired a common interest in the western lands. On the other hand, the Old Settlers were to be given one-third interest in what remained of the five million dollars received for the eastern land, to be paid per capita.

The Treaty Party was to be indemnified to the amount of $115,000.[18] The sum of $2,000 was allowed for the printing presses seized by the Georgia Guard in 1835, and $5,000 was to be equally divided among those who had been deprived of their arms by General Scott.[19] The treaty left the Senate to decide whether the amount of subsistence was to be chargeable to the treaty fund, whether interest should be allowed, and at what rate and from what time. A clause also provided that the treaty should not take away from the Cherokees still living in the east their right to citizenship in the Cherokee Nation.[20]

The elucidation of the Treaty of New Echota was not the work of days or weeks, but of months and years. After two years' study and deliberation, Commissioner Medill expressed it as his opinion that the five million dollars was in full for the entire cession of the eastern land, and that nothing more should be paid for removal, subsistence or for any other purpose.[21] Against this interpretation the Cherokees entered a vigorous protest, and disagreement and contention on the part of both sides delayed a settlement.[22]

The question in all its perplexity drifted on for another couple of years. It was not until August 1850 that the Senate Committee, to which the treaty had been referred, reached a decision. Their decision upheld the claim of the Cherokees that the charge for subsisting the emigrants during, and a year after removal, ought to be borne by the United States, and that the expense of removal agents was not rightfully chargeable to the Cherokees, but should be borne by the federal government. Their award for these items, however, was very conservative, and far from what the Cherokees had a right to expect.

After the amount of the award had been fixed, there was further delay in securing the necessary appropriation by Congress. The last item was provided for by an act of February 27, 1851,[23] and was done with the requirement that it should be in full settlement for all claims and demands of the Cherokee Nation against the United States under any treaty theretofore made by them. Instructions were finally issued in September to John Drennan, Superintendent of the Southern Division, to proceed without delay to make the payment. Thus Georgia had been in full possession of the eastern lands of the tribe for thirteen years before the Cherokees received compensation.

Neither the Old Settlers nor the Emigrants were satisfied with the award of the Senate. The former received what was paid to them under protest, lest their acceptance of it should be so construed as to prevent them in the future from pressing claims they considered just, but which were not admitted by the treaty. Before accepting the money and complying with conditions prescribed by Congress, the National Council registered its disapproval by a set of resolutions solemnly protesting against the injustice its people had suffered through the treaties of 1835 and 1846, copies of which they sent to both Houses of Congress.

The per capita payment brought a short period of personal prosperity, which showed itself in improved farms and farming implements, better buildings, and larger herds of cattle and horses. The Cherokee government, with no revenue other than the income derived from the funds invested in government bonds, and with the heavy expenses incurred by the establishment and maintenance of government and a school system, saw the national debt increase year by year until it assumed disturbing proportions. The district schools began to languish for lack of funds, and the high schools, in which they had taken such pride, were finally closed for the same reason.

To add to the perplexity of the Cherokees, there swept over the Southwest in the summer of 1854 a blasting south wind accompanied by a drought which blighted the promising crops, parched the vegetation, and caused a partial water famine. Taken utterly by surprise, the people were unprepared for such a crisis and before the end of the year, many of them had been reduced to destitution amounting almost to starvation. This was the situation in the fall of 1854 when they sent a delegation to Washington for the purpose of arranging the sale of some of their surplus detached lands as a measure of relief from the burden of their public debt, and to replenish their exhausted school fund. A large part of the winter was spent in fruitless negotiations, and the delegation was at last forced to return home empty handed.[24]

The only point gained was the removal of the garrison at Fort Gibson, which was not actually accomplished, however, until three years later. In 1857 Chief Ross in his message to the National Council in 1857 authorized the site of the abandoned fort to be laid off into town lots and sold to Cherokee citizens. The sale of the lots netted the nation the sum of $20,000.

CHAPTER 15

The Cherokee National School System

Those who, by reason of seasoned strength and perfect health, survived the ordeals of that long, long, journey from the fastness of the Allegheny Mountains to the wilderness of the Indian Territory were fortunate, indeed, to find harborage for a season in the concentration camps provided for their protection until they could locate permanent homesteads.

As an aid to readjustment, the government at its own expense was to subsist the emigrants for a year after their arrival, but rations, apportioned irregularly by fraudulent contractors, were sometimes of such inferior quality as to be unfit for use. In order to supply themselves with the game all Indians prize so highly, they were compelled to resort to the primitive bow and arrow, the blow gun and the fishing spear, or gig, because the guns taken from them in Georgia had been neither returned nor paid for.

But for the kindness of Old Settlers, the emigrants would have fared ill indeed during their first few years in the new country. Regardless of political feuds and personal differences, the western received the eastern tribesmen with kindness and hospitality; gave them material aid in selecting the best locations, in fencing fields, and in plowing and planting against the time of the harvest moon. Nor did they forget to warn the mountain clansmen of the deadly malaria that lurked in the heavy cane brakes of the marshes.

The virgin soil was admirably adapted to agriculture on a large scale, uplands as well as valleys producing larger crops than the Georgia and Tennessee fields had ever yielded. The prairie grass and the wild cane furnished abundant forage for any number of livestock to subsist upon the year around without care or cost. Game was plentiful and wild fruits and nuts flourished in their season.

As had always been the usage, the land was held as the common property of the nation, the improvements alone belonging to the individual. Intermarried white men and women, called citizens by adoption, had all the rights and privileges of citizens by blood except that of holding office under the government. Non-citizens residing in the nation were required by law to pay taxes, either as common laborers or as merchants who paid an excise duty on all goods sold in the nation.

Instead of collecting in towns and villages according to the ancient custom, the Cherokees now settled in neighborhoods because they were better adapted to a strictly agricultural mode of life. Park Hill was one of the most densely populated of these districts.

Slavery was an established institution among the Cherokees West as early as 1819. Chief John Jolly, who had an extensive plantation near the mouth of the Illinois River in 1830, owned a large number of slaves whose cabins in the background of his estate resembled a small village. The emigrants who owned them brought colored servants with them to perform the heavy work incident to pioneer life. Only a few full bloods, however, had adapted themselves to the institution.

During a period of four years, the nation lived in constant fear of an uprising of the wild tribes[1] on the frontier, such as the one that had threatened to annihilate the emigrants in 1839. Finally the Cherokees determined to make a supreme effort to remove this menace to their safety and peace of mind by forming a league of friendship with as many of the plainsmen as they could induce to join them in a grand peace council. "Swift runners were sent with the pipe and tobacco" to tribes as far west as the Rocky Mountains, inviting them to Tahlequah where they were requested to take part in a series of friendly talks with a view to forming a league of perpetual peace and friendship among Indian nations.

Of the thirty-six tribes invited, twenty-three sent deputations which began to arrive on June 5 and continued to come in until a great concourse of Indians had assembled at the little inland village and overflowed into the surrounding country where their encampments presented a picturesque spectacle of Indian life and culture.

In a large building with unenclosed sides, the deputations assembled for the opening session presided over by Chief John Ross of the Cherokee Nation. The delegates took their places on the rows of benches reserved for them, the Delawares appropriating front seats or places of honor reserved for the "grandfathers of all Indians."

Conferences were conducted from day to day with the aid of expert interpreters; many inspiring addresses were delivered; the pipe of peace was smoked; and the interpretation of the wampum was rendered by the venerable Major Lowrey, the only man then living who understood its mysteries.[2]

Around the "Great Council Fire at Tahlequah" on July 3, a compact was entered into by the tribes represented, pledging them to perpetual peace and friendship with each other.[3] The visitors then mounted their ponies and, well pleased with their hosts, their neighbors and themselves, rode away toward the setting sun, and the Cherokees returned to their affairs with a feeling of security they had not known before since their arrival.

After the Georgia laws had rendered their residence in that state intolerable and after the building at Brainard Mission in Tennessee had been destroyed by fire, the missionaries had removed to the Cherokee Nation west. Those who accompanied the eastern nation into exile joined their brethren already on the field engaging in religious and educational work among the Cherokees west, so that by 1840 there were several mission stations and a number of religious organizations in active operation in the new nation in Indian Territory.

The first mission station in this region was located on Grand River about fifty miles from Fort Gibson, founded in 1821 under the auspices of the United Foreign Missionary Society by Epaphras Chapman and Job Vail. "It had been planted there for work among the Osages who had settlements in the Verdigris Valley." In 1823 there were fourteen instructors and seven families at this post, and the improvements and equipment were appraised at twenty-four thousand dollars.[4]

Four miles distant from Union Mission were the extensive fields of Hopefield, an agricultural school designed to teach the Osages the advantages of a settled over a roving life and to redeem them from the influence of Catholic priests and French traders. Although, in the beginning, Union and Hopefield had been dedicated to work among the Osages, children from other tribes were admitted also. Of the total enrollment for ten years as reported in 1832, only seventy-one of the one hundred fifty-four Indian children admitted were Osages. Fifty-four were Creeks, and twenty-nine, Cherokees.[5]

When, under the treaty of 1828, the Cherokees West removed from the Arkansas country to Indian Territory, Dwight Mission was transferred to a location on Sallisaw Creek about twelve miles from its confluence with the Arkansas River. A new plant was established and the school was founded on the Lancastrian plan as the first had been. The buildings at Dwight were of hewn logs and arranged to face an oval recreation ground sheltered by native trees, which were in time gradually replaced by those of less rugged growth. There were houses for the mission force, dormitories for girls and for boys, school rooms, a dining room and kitchen, and a guest house for the visitors who came often to the mission. Parents were particularly welcome, their presence indicating an active interest in the progress of their children and the welfare of the missionaries.

The founder of the mission, Reverend Cephas Washburn, who had led his mission force to its new location on the Sallisaw, remained there as superintendent until 1841, when at his own request he was relieved of his duties. The teachers were Miss Ellen Stetson and Miss Esther Smith; the supervisor of buildings and farm was James Orr; and the steward, Jacob Hitchcock.

With the arrival of the emigrants, there came to Dwight from Brainard, Dr. Elizur Butler, who had suffered imprisonment in the State Penitentiary of Georgia for residing in the Cherokee Nation without a permit from Georgia, and with him were two missionaries from Brainard, D. S. Buttrick and William Potter. There came also a large number of children from emigrant families, so the mission was filled to capacity, more room was required, and additional teachers were needed. Branch schools also had opened at the forks of the Illinois, later called Elm Springs, and on Mulberry Creek, fifteen miles north of Dwight at a place called Fairfield Mission.

In the spring of 1835, there came from the Cherokee Nation East, Dr. S. A. Worcester, whose unparalleled services to full-bloods set him apart as a unique figure among missionaries to Indians. Upon his release from prison in 1833, he became convinced he should be handicapped as long as he remained in Georgia or Tennessee. Eager to be at work again, he determined to go west where he could carry on unmolested. Physician and educator as well as preacher, he was interested in every phase of Cherokee development and had consecrated his life and all his talents to the problem of bringing knowledge and Christianity within the range of those Cherokees who did not understand the English language.

In order that he might better accomplish his object, he planned to prepare textbooks on different subjects using the Sequoyah script. At one time, he began the arrangement and translation of a geography which he was compelled to put aside because it took too much time from his work on the Bible. A grammar and a dictionary, which were in a forward state of preparation when he left Georgia, were lost with all the rest of his effects when the steamboat on which he was going west sank in the Arkansas River. Many tracts, pamphlets, and sermons were printed in Cherokee and distributed gratis to those who wished them.

Imbued with the desire to continue this work, Dr. Butler sought safety and seclusion beyond the Georgia pale by retiring with his little hand press and a few necessary articles of equipment to the frontier mission settlement on Grand River. Here he remained for a year and more, converting the mission post into a publishing plant that turned out a number of things of some account at that time. While here, he assembled a large part of the material used in the first edition of the *Cherokee Almanac*.

On December 2, Dr. Worcester removed his effects to Park Hill Mission, over which he had been appointed superintendent, and there began his work on a much larger scale. First, with the aid of Elias Boudinot, and later with that of the young Cherokee preacher Stephen Foreman, a graduate of Princeton, Dr. Worcester published in the Sequoyah script a large number of tracts, hymns and leaflets. In addition to these, he translated and published in Cherokee the New Testament, Genesis, Exodus, portions of Psalms, Proverbs and Isaiah; also the Catechism, a Cherokee primer, a tract on marriage, a tract on temperance, an address on temperance, *The Discipline of the Methodist Church, The Constitution and Laws of the Cherokee Nation, The Dairyman's Daughter, The Swiss Peasant, The One Thing Needful, The Negro Servant,* and *Poor Sarah,* a romance written by Elias Boudinot.

In 1836 he got out the first edition of the *Cherokee Almanac,* a clever little publication somewhat similar to Benjamin Franklin's *Poor Richard's Almanac.* It was computed for the meridian of Fort Gibson and contained an assortment of interesting local information, proverbs, scriptural precepts and medical first aids. It was published annually from 1836 to 1861 at the expense of the American Board,[6] and its two dozen slim volumes constitute a valuable source of local history.

Park Hill was the largest mission station in the Cherokee Nation. At one time it boasted a book bindery, a blacksmith shop, a grist mill, a church, and a school building. There were residences for the missionaries, and there were barns and stables belonging to a large farm operated by the mission force. To all intents and purposes, Park Hill before the Civil War was a self-sustaining community of a superior type to be seen nowhere else in Indian Territory or in any of the adjacent states.

Among the several smaller mission schools was Baptist Mission, founded by Reverend Jesse Bushyhead upon his arrival from beyond the Mississippi in 1839 at the head of one of the emigrant companies for which he established an encampment on the site of the present community of Baptist near the Arkansas line. The Reverend Evan Jones attached himself to Baptist Mission, and by cooperating with the founder, he helped make this a school of high standard patronized largely by the full bloods of the eastern section of the nation.[7]

Associated with Worcester, Butler, Buttrick, and Jones were several native interpreters and preachers of ability and superior education, and with Bushyhead were Kaneedah,[8] who was the first native Baptist preacher among the Cherokees, and Aganoyah, his friend and associate.

The Moravians established a school on Beatie's Prairie[9] in 1840, but removed it to Spring Creek, after which they called it New Spring Place. One of the native teachers in that school was James Ward, a descendent of Nancy Ward,[10] the Beloved Woman of the Cherokees, and a native preacher was Karselowy, a splendid type of the Christian Indian. The Moravians were never able to build such a school in the new country as their Oothcalogy[11] had been in Georgia, located as it had been in the vicinity of the Nation's Capitol, New Echota. Their church and missions near Tahlequah, though, were ably administered and appeared to be flourishing.

Among native Presbyterian missionaries, Stephen Foreman was the most eloquent preacher and indefatigable worker in the nation after removal. In 1843, the year of the Great June Council at Tahlequah, he was noticeable among the large number of distinguished Indians who were in attendance. Upon the death of Elias Boudinot, Stephen Foreman became assistant to Dr. Worcester in his work of translation and much of Dr. Worcester's success in later years was due to the cooperation of this young Cherokee who was highly regarded not only for his work of translation but as the most eloquent native Presbyterian preacher.[12]

The Methodists had built their first mission in the eastern nation as late as 1824, their policy being different from that of the other denominations, in that they did not rely so much upon schools as upon house-to-house visitations made by their circuit riders, and upon revival meetings held at intervals in the various communities. Almost no attention was given to academic training and but little to primary schools. Their farthest outpost was in the Big Bend of the Arkansas River in the Cherokee Outlet, where a full-blood church, located near the northern boundary of the Cherokee Nation, belonged to the circuit assigned to a young evangelist named McIntosh.[13]

Another organization was the Cherokee Bible Society organized at Tahlequah in 1841 for the dissemination of the sacred scriptures in both the English and the Cherokee languages. "Free from sectarianism this society was designed to unite Christians of all denominations in the good work of circulating the Bible." Some of its prominent members were John Thorn, John W. Stapler, Thomas Pegg, David Carter, James V. Hildebrand, John T. Foster, Riley Keys, and John C. Cunningham. Stephen Foreman was its secretary and Edwin Archer, printer at Park Hill, was its corresponding secretary.[14]

In 1836 the Cherokee Temperance Society was organized for the purpose of discouraging the use of the intoxicating liquor which had a demoralizing effect upon all Indians addicted to its use. Women as well as men were members of the society and after the war there was organized a Woman's Christian Temperance Union which carried on actively until the dissolution of tribal government, when it merged with the state organization.

By 1841, Sunday schools were in operation throughout the nation, each church and mission station having a well-attended school to which parents with their children went on the Sabbath to study the scriptures diligently, for in them they thought they had found eternal life. In a large number of these Sabbath Schools only the Cherokee language was spoken.

The missionaries were the "Torch Bearers" to the Cherokees,[15] leading the way into the high road of Christian civilization and preparing the Indians themselves to take the lead in the forward march. During a period of forty years, the mission stations served as training grounds and experiment stations where promising boys and girls were taught the arts and sciences, Christian living, and educated in the elementary branches preparatory to entrance into higher institutions of learning. The missionaries were cultured Christian men and women whose one purpose in life was to instill in the minds of the Cherokees right principles of living and thinking.

From the beginning, chiefs and headmen had encouraged the work of the missionaries with a definite project in view. In 1819, when a cession of land was made in Alabama and Tennessee, they had reserved the proceeds of a tract twelve miles square as a nucleus for a national school fund.[16]

Article 10 of the New Echota Treaty provided that the President of the United States should invest "in good interest-bearing stocks the following sums for the benefit of the Cherokee people, the interest thereon only to be expended: $200,000 in addition to their present annuities, for a general national fund; $50,000 for an orphans' fund; $150,000 in addition to the existing school fund for a permanent national school fund; the disbursement of the interest on the foregoing funds to be subject to examination and any misapplications thereof to be corrected by the President of the United States."[17]

By 1825, the Cherokees were considering plans for a national school system supported and conducted by themselves. The lack of sufficient funds to maintain it and the increasing demands for the removal of Indians from the states prevented them from realizing such a project, but did not cause them to abandon it, as this clause in the Constitution of 1839 indicates: "Religion, morality and knowledge, being necessary to the good government, the preservation of liberty, and the happiness of mankind, schools and the means of education shall forever be encouraged in this Nation."

Three weeks later, the National Council passed an act providing that "All facilities and means for the promotion of education by the establishment of schools and the diffusion of general intelligence among the people shall be afforded by legislation commensurate with the importance of such objects, and the extent and condition of the public finances; and all schools which may be and are now in operation in this nation, shall be subject to such supervision and control of the National Council as may be provided."

The act stated that in future all missionary schools should be established and maintained only by permission of the National Council; and that a committee of three persons should be appointed to mature and prepare a system of education by schools and to report to the Principal Chief before the next annual meeting of the council. The committee was also to visit all the schools in the nation, examine the plan on which they were conducted, and the improvement of the pupils, and to return a report to be submitted to the National Council by the Principal Chief.[18] Thereafter, all missionary schools were authorized by the Cherokee National Council and amenable to its laws.

The unsettled condition of the nation after removal caused the semi-annual interest payments to be withheld for a time, resulting in financial embarrassment in all departments of the government. It was two years, therefore, before an act was passed providing for a superintendent of education and eleven public schools, and for an appropriation for their maintenance. Teachers received a salary of thirty dollars a month, and orphans attending schools had their expenses defrayed. Seven additional schools were authorized in 1843, bringing the number up to eighteen.

Stephen Foreman was the first superintendent of education. Under his direction, the schools got off to a good start. In 1860 there were thirty-two primary schools in the nation with an enrollment of fifteen hundred, all children of Cherokee citizens. Only two of the teachers were non-citizens. The influence of the missionaries was to be seen in the character of the teachers employed, many of whom had received their education at the missions. All were required to be well qualified for their work.[19] The subjects taught were geography, history, and the Testament, in addition to reading, writing, and arithmetic.[20] An examining board of three members, to pass on the qualifications of teachers, was created in 1849.[21]

Five years after the primary school system had been founded, an act of Council provided for the establishment of two high schools. The Park Hill Seminary for girls was built four miles southeast, and the Male Seminary, one mile west of Tahlequah. They were built of brick[22] on the same architectural plan, were two stories high with basement, and were located within walking distance of Park Hill Mission, Sehon Chapel,[23] Rose Cottage, the Murrell Mansion, and the Illinois River. On the west, a prairie opened toward the setting sun and manifold adventures.

The cornerstones were laid by Chief Ross on June 21, 1847, and the structures were completed three years later. The male seminary was opened on May 6, 1851, and the Female Seminary on the day following. Each accommodated about a hundred students at a nominal charge for room, board, and laundry. Free textbooks were furnished to all students.[24] Miss Sarah Worcester and Miss Ellen Whitmire, both educated at Mount Holyoke, were engaged as the first teachers at Park Hill Seminary, and Miss E. Jane Ross, also educated at Mount Holyoke, was later added to the faculty. Miss Ross was a Cherokee, endowed with charming manners and a benevolent disposition.

The character of the schools was academic rather than vocational, the course of study for the high schools including geography, botany, arithmetic, English, geometry, history, Latin, Greek, and such subjects as Watt's Improvement of the Mind, and Paley's Natural Theology and Intellectual Philosophy. Thirty minutes a day were devoted to the study of the Bible. No attention was given to industrial training except that each girl or boy was assigned by turns to some special duty in the general economic scheme of the household.

Although lack of funds had made it necessary to close the seminaries in 1857, sixty-two young women and a slightly smaller number of young men had been graduated before the Civil War. Not a few parents sent their sons and daughters to the states to finish their education in institutions of higher learning. For two decades, chiefs and headmen had bent their energies to the task of raising the standard of literacy among all classes, not realizing that they were founding the first public school system west of the Mississippi.

The success of the experiment was due in part to the character of the leaders of thought in the nation during these years. Principal and assistant chiefs and councilors possessed a remarkably clear vision of their national need, and with singleness of purpose set themselves the task of ministering to that need. They appointed as superintendents men of talent and education, distinguished for their ability. They drafted such laws as were needed for their guidance and support. Stephen Foreman served only two years and was followed by David Carter, and he by James Madison Payne. In 1847 Walter Scott Adair was appointed and served for four years. After him came W. A. Duncan, another minister of the gospel. Henry Dodson Reese was superintendent for six years and Charles Holt Campbell was the last superintendent of education before the Civil War.

Rachel Caroline Eaton studies in her room at McCollough Cottage, Drury College, Springfield, Missouri. She received a bachelor's degree from Drury in 1895. (Family photo collection.)

"The old homeplace" in Sageeyah, Cooweescoowee District, Cherokee Nation, was where Rachel Caroline Eaton grew up. The home, built by her father George Washington Eaton around 1880, was part of a large ranch stretching to the slopes of Claremore Mound. The family's holdings were diminished by allotment, and the home burned to the ground on Christmas Day, 1942. (Family photo collection.)

The Cherokee Female Seminary opened in 1851 at Park Hill, Indian Territory. It was a boarding school and offered students a quality high school education. Rachel Caroline Eaton was in her senior year when the building burned on Easter Sunday, 1887. (Courtesy of the Northeastern State University Archives and Special Collections.)

A fire destroyed the Cherokee Female Seminary in Park Hill on Easter Sunday 1887 during Rachel Caroline Eaton's senior year. She received her diploma that year along with the men of the Cherokee Male Seminary. (Courtesy of the Northeastern State University Archives and Special Collections.)

Rachel Caroline Eaton taught at the rebuilt Cherokee Female Seminary in Tahlequah, Indian Territory, from 1896 to 1897. Handwritten on the back: "Miss Eaton—Our most beloved instructor." (Courtesy of the Northeastern State University Archives and Special Collections.)

Cherokee National Seminary faculty, 1896–97. The new Cherokee Female Seminary, which replaced the original structure that burned, was relocated from Park Hill to Tahlequah, Indian Territory, and opened on August 26, 1889. The faculty members during the fall 1896 and spring 1897 semesters were Miss Florence Wilson, principal; Mrs. Eugenia Thompson, fifth assistant; Miss Nell Taylor and Miss Cora McNair, music teachers; Miss Oklahoma Spradling, third assistant; Miss Rachel Caroline Eaton, first assistant; Miss Sarah Jane "Bluie" Adair, second assistant; and Miss Lelia Morgan, fourth assistant. (Courtesy of the Northeastern State University Archives and Special Collections.)

The Cherokee Male Seminary football team, 1898: Seated from left are William Meeks, Henry Dameron, Harold Hough (infant son of the coach), Joel Merritt Eaton (younger brother of Rachel Caroline Eaton), and William Harris. Kneeling from left: James Sanders, T. P. Roach, Joe Ross, George Cox, and Richard Parris. Standing from left: George Russell, Larken Sevenstar, Prof. J. G. Hough (coach), Casper Lipe, B. A. Mills, R. A. Ballard, Joe Sevier, and Wallace Thornton. (Courtesy of the Northeastern State University Archives and Special Collections.)

The Pocahontas Club was founded June 29, 1899, by young women of Native American descent from the Oowala community north of Claremore, Indian Territory. Pictured are the original members, posing at Kephart Springs in 1903. Top row from left: Ada Foreman, Lettie Starr, and Flora Foreman. Middle row from left: Trixie Dannenberg, Bess Schrimsher, Nancy Eva "Nannie" Lipe, Cora Hicks, Lola Vann Lipe, Bessie Barrett, Gazelle Lane, and Mary Starr. Front row from left: Mary McClellan, Ida Collins, Juliette Melvina Schrimsher, Zoe Bullette, and Martha "Mattie" Eaton (Rachel Caroline Eaton's sister). Will Rogers and Emmett Starr were among the young men invited into the club as honorary members. (Family photo collection.)

Sequoyah's cabin near Akins, Oklahoma, as it appeared on September 14, 1934, a century after the creator of a Cherokee written language died in Mexico. The cabin, built in 1829, was acquired two years after Rachel Caroline Eaton's visit by the Oklahoma Historical Society, and a shelter was built over it in 1936 by the Works Progress Administration. The cabin, now part of Sequoyah's Cabin Museum, is owned by the Cherokee Nation and on the National Register of Historic Places. (Photo taken by Rachel Caroline Eaton. Family photo collection.)

The Eatons and Schrimshers were part of the Claremore social scene. Clockwise from top left: Rachel Caroline "Callie" Eaton, Bessie Schrimsher, Martha Pauline "Mattie" Eaton (Callie's sister), and Juliette Schrimsher. Photo was probably taken in 1901 during the first Street Fair in Claremore, Indian Territory. (Family photo collection.)

Rachel Caroline Eaton visits what the Eaton and York families called "the Old Homeplace" in Sageeyah, Claremore, Oklahoma, in 1925. She sits in a chair that belonged to her grandmother, Lucy (Ward) Williams, who came west on the Trail of Tears in 1834. (Photo of Rachel Caroline Eaton taken by Penelope Allen, 1925. Penelope Allen Collection, MS 2033, University of Tennessee, Knoxville Libraries.)

Home of James Ward Jr., brother of Rachel C. Eaton's grandmother Lucy (Ward) Williams. Following the Trail of Tears, James Ward Jr. became a Moravian missionary at New Springplace Mission near Oaks, Indian Territory. He was slain by pro-Union "Pin" Indians outside his home in 1862 during the Civil War. (Family photo collection.)

Cherokee Female Seminary, class of 1897–98. Taken on the porch of the new seminary. Rachel Caroline Eaton stands in the back on the far right. (Courtesy of the Northeastern State University Archives and Special Collections.)

Editorial Commentary
for Chapters 16–21

The following chapters trace the events leading up to the Civil War, the destruction that took place during that conflict, and the rebuilding of the Cherokee Nation. The West was a major front of the Civil War, one that is often ignored in many academic histories. As the United States attempted to grab more Indigenous land, the North and the South had competing visions for the West, and arguments erupted over whether enslavement in new states and territories would be legal, leading to the Civil War. The United States continued to grab more land during the Civil War and Reconstruction, and the Union and Confederate forces fought each other as well as Indigenous Nations during the war. As Rachel Caroline Eaton notes, Principal Chief John Ross tried to remain neutral at the beginning of the war, but he was eventually pressured into siding with the Confederacy. There were Cherokees who fought on both sides of the war, and heavy fighting took place on Cherokee land. Many homes and communities were destroyed, and some Cherokees who supported the Union were forced to flee to Kansas, while others who supported the Confederacy fled to Texas and Arkansas. Cherokee Confederate General Stand Watie was the last general to surrender in the Civil War.[1]

The Cherokee Nation has a strong Afro-Indigenous community, one whose history too often gets ignored. Some Cherokees had begun enslaving people before Removal. Chattel-style enslavement gradually increased in the Nation during the first half of the nineteenth century, and there were varying beliefs and practices regarding enslavement and abolition. The Keetoowahs, or "Pin Indians," were traditionalists, as well as abolitionists, who supported John Ross's attempts to remain neutral. Many of them fought against the Confederacy during the war, and later refused to participate in allotment. Black Cherokees actively created community, sought freedom, and worked to secure Cherokee citizenship. As Eaton notes, the Treaty of 1866 granted citizenship to Cherokee Freedmen, Black Cherokees in the Nation who were formerly enslaved or free, and their descendants. While Eaton discusses varying perspectives among many Cherokees, she often ignores or misrepresents perspectives of Black Cherokees. Some Cherokees fought against Black Cherokee citizenship, and since 1866, Black Cherokees have continued to fight for recognition of citizenship and equality within the Cherokee community.

While Eaton appears to support Cherokee Freedmen's citizenship, she sometimes uses outdated and prejudiced language in her discussions of Cherokee Freedmen's history. In addition, she sometimes uses outdated and offensive language such as "wild tribes," "half-breed," and "blanket Indians" to describe Indigenous people, particularly those who were not from the Five Tribes, or the Cherokee, Choctaw, Chickasaw, Seminole, and Muscogee nations. Rachel Caroline Eaton wrote this history in the 1930s, and as it is both a historical monograph and a historical document, we have elected to keep Eaton's original language.

CHAPTER 16

Secession

The period between 1840 and 1860 was one of transition in which the Cherokees, virtually free from federal and state interference, adapted themselves to a new environment, converting a wilderness into homesteads and waste places into cultivated fields. So successful were they in their enterprises that the federal government in 1859 proposed to allot the tribal lands on the ground that such an act would tend to affect favorably the progress of the country. But the Cherokees, preferring their own system of land holding, objected strenuously to such a change.

Although handicapped by financial troubles over their invested funds, by floods and droughts and internal conflict, they had made such progress within twenty years that their agent could say that: "From their general mode of living the Cherokees will compare favorably with their white neighbors."[1] Their population was estimated at twenty thousand native Cherokees, one thousand whites and four thousand negroes. And then, apparently out of a clear sky, the Civil War was upon them in all its devastating fury.

The issues involved in the presidential election of 1860 were of vital interest to the Five Civilized Tribes of Indian Territory, many of whose citizens were slaveholders, allied socially and economically with the people and institutions of the south.

Indian superintendents and agents in the territory during the Buchanan administration had been southern and pro-slavery. Firmly believing in the institution as of divine origin and an economic blessing to both master and slave, they were intolerant of abolition sentiments to the point of forbidding the teaching of them among the Indians. Missionaries and school teachers who were especially zealous in spreading antislavery propaganda were summarily sent from the Territory. Due to the influence of Northern missionaries, the Cherokees, although slave holders, with the exception of the conservative full bloods, were less inclined to secession than the people of the other Five Civilized Tribes.

With the excitement incident to the election of 1860, the old factional feud among the Cherokees flared up anew with all its original rancor. Leaders of the Treaty Party and other anti-Ross mixed blood and intermarried white men aligned themselves with the South and organized the secret fraternity called Knights of the Golden Circle, with Stand Watie as their moving spirit. The opposition, composed largely of full bloods, joined a society known as the Keetoowahs, an ancient tribal order revived and reorganized for the purpose of maintaining neutrality in the Cherokee Nation. John Ross was the acknowledged head of this party.

The election of Lincoln and the secession of the southern states were watched with interest by both factions. What would be the policy of the new administration towards the Five Tribes? Within six weeks of the inauguration, this question was answered by the Secretary of War when he ordered all the federal troops stationed in the Indian Territory to withdraw to Kansas, thus abandoning the loyal Indians whom they were obligated to protect and leaving forts Washita, Cobb, and Arbuckle to be occupied without opposition by Confederate forces.

The Confederacy adopted a different policy. The strategic importance of the Indian Territory as a buffer against the wild tribes[2] and as a source of subsistence during the war was early recognized by the Confederate Department of War. From the very outset of the conflict, even before the organization of the Confederacy, preliminary steps had been taken to secure the sympathy and cooperation of the tribes of the Southwest. Federal agents among the Five Civilized Tribes and Elias Rector, the head of the Southern Superintendency, began in early winter of 1861 to take an active part in fortifying the minds of the Indians against the incoming administration, and arousing sympathy for the Southern cause. Douglas H. Cooper, agent of the Choctaws and Chickasaws, an appointee of

President Buchanan, took advantage of the remoteness of his situation to work openly for secession.

As a result, the Chickasaw legislature, on January 5, issued a call for an intertribal council to meet, should a political separation between the North and the South take place,[3] a suggestion which was received with favor by all except the Cherokees. Chief Ross objected to the plan on the ground that the controversy between the North and the South was strictly a white man's quarrel and no concern of the Indians. He was overruled, however, and the council was called for February 17.

Without waiting to see what its neighbors would do, the Choctaw Council on February 7 declared for the Confederacy on the ground that their national interests bound its people indissolubly in every way to the destiny of their neighbors of the South.[4] When the intertribal council met ten days later at the Creek Agency, neither the Choctaws nor the Chickasaws were represented. The Cherokee, Creek, and Seminole delegations discussed the situation at length and decided simply to do nothing, but to keep quiet and comply with their treaty obligations. Mutual expressions of good feeling were given and promises exchanged that whatever exigencies of the future might arise, bound by a common destiny, they would act in concert for the greatest good of all.[5]

The action of the council was watched with the keenest interest by Arkansas, no section of the South being more vitally concerned with the sentiment of the Five Civilized Tribes at this crisis, as the Cherokee and Choctaw Nations hemmed in her entire western border. The action of the Choctaws had been gratifying. The cooperation of the Cherokees must be secured at all cost.

More than three months before the state seceded from the Union, Governor Rector wrote to Chief Ross, calling attention to the fact that the Cherokees, in their institutions, productions, latitude and natural sympathies, were allied to the common brotherhood of slaveholding states, and assuring him that it was an established fact that the Indian country was looked upon by the incoming administration "as a fruitful field ripe for the harvest of abolitionists, free-soilers and Northern mountebanks." He proposed to give the

Cherokees protection in their exposed condition and to assume the monetary obligations of the federal government to them if they would join the South in the defense of her firesides, its honor, and its institutions.[6]

Chief Ross replied, expressing the regret and the solicitude of the Cherokees for the unhappy relations existing between the two sections of the country and hoping for the restoration of peace and harmony, at the same time declaring the loyalty of his people to the federal government. The Cherokees, he reasoned, having placed themselves under the protection of the United States, were bound to enter into no treaty with any foreign power, neither with any individual nor citizen of any state. The faith of the United States, he reasoned, was solemnly pledged to protect them in their land titles and all their individual rights and interests of person and property. The Cherokees were inviolably allied with the United States in war and were friends in peace. While their institutions, locality, and natural sympathy were unequivocally with the slaveholding states, and the social and commercial intercourse between the Cherokee Nation and Arkansas were of great importance to his people, these interests must be subordinated to the higher one of his nation's honor.[7]

Not satisfied with his reply, citizens of western Arkansas and the commandant at Fort Smith demanded to know on what ground he stood, as they preferred an open enemy to a doubtful friend.[8]

To them he replied that the Cherokees would take no part in the trouble. Weak, defenseless, and scattered over a large section of country in the pursuit of agricultural life, without hostility to any state, and with friendly feeling to all, they hoped to be allowed to remain neutral. Being fully aware of the defenseless condition of the Cherokees, their friends would surely not expect them to destroy their national and individual rights and bring around their hearthstones the horrors and desolation of a civil war prematurely and unnecessarily. "I am—the Cherokees are your friends," he assured them, "but we do not wish to be brought into the feud between yourselves and your Northern brethren. Our wish is for peace—peace with you and peace at home."[9]

In March 1861 the Confederate Provisional Congress created a Bureau of Indian Affairs and attached it to the War Department.[10] David L. Hubbard, of Alabama, was placed at its head, with instructions to repair immediately to the Indian country where he would make known to all the tribes the desire of the Confederate states to protect and defend them against the rapacious and avaricious designs of their common enemy, whose real intention was to emancipate their slaves and rob them of their lands.[11]

Illness having prevented Mr. Hubbard from carrying out his intention of going in person to the Indian Territory, he wrote to Chief Ross and, in addition to his instructions, reminded him that nearly all the funds of the Cherokees, representing their annuities and school funds, were invested in southern securities, which debts were already forfeited unless the Cherokees joined the Confederacy.

To this, Chief Ross's answer was that if the institutions, locality, and long years of neighborly deportment and intercourse did not suffice to assure the Confederacy of the friendship of the Cherokees, no instrument of mere parchment could do so. "We have no cause to doubt the entire good faith with which you would treat the Cherokee people, but neither have we any cause to make war against the United States, or to believe that our treaties will not be fulfilled and respected. At all events a decent regard to good faith demands that we should not be the first to violate them." [12]

It was not the business of the Cherokees, he thought, to determine the character of the conflict going on in the states. It was their duty to keep themselves free from entanglements, and afford no ground to either party to interfere with their rights. As to the question of whether the Cherokees would receive kinder treatment at the hands of the South than could be expected from the North, he remarked significantly that the settled policy of acquiring Indian lands had always been a favorite one with both sections, and but few Indians north or south pressed their feet upon the soil of their fathers.

Meanwhile, as previously stated, in April all the federal troops were withdrawn from Indian Territory,[13] which was immediately occupied by the Confederacy and formed into the Military District of Indian Territory under the command of Benjamin F. McCulloch. With a regiment from each of the states of Arkansas, Louisiana, and Texas, and with instructions to raise additional regiments among the Five Tribes to be attached to his command, he prepared to establish headquarters at some suitable place in the Cherokee Nation.

The Knights of the Golden Circle, in full sympathy with the plan, determined upon a strategic movement to raise the rebel flag over the capitol at Tahlequah, guarding their intentions with profound secrecy.[14] Great was their discomfiture, therefore, when they arrived on the appointed day to find themselves checkmated by a band of grim-visaged fullbloods gathered from all parts of the Cherokee Nation to thwart their designs.[15]

Chief Ross, fearing the demoralizing effect upon the tribe of the Tahlequah incident and the plan for establishing Confederate headquarters in the Cherokee Nation, issued a proclamation on May 17 counseling the people to cultivate peace and harmony among themselves and to observe, in good faith, strict neutrality toward the states threatening Civil War.[16] McCulloch, thus finding his designs firmly opposed by Chief Ross, whom he was as yet unwilling to antagonize, changed plans and began mustering his forces at Fort Smith, just over the Arkansas line.[17]

It was at this stage of the rebellion that the picturesque figure of Albert Pike appeared upon the scene of the conflict in which he was to play a more or less important part. A Bostonian by birth, he had studied law at Harvard, taught school in New England, experienced exciting adventures in New Mexico, and finally settled down in Arkansas, where he became an avowed friend and an advocate of the Red Man. When the Civil War came on, he declared for secession, offered his services to the Confederacy in effecting alliances with the wild tribes of the Southwest,[18] and was commissioned by the Richmond government to negotiate treaties with all the Indians of the Indian Territory.

Commissioner Pike set out at once, stopping on the way for an interview with General McCulloch at Fort Smith. Here a party of Cherokees representing the Knights of the Golden Circle called upon him to find out whether the Confederate states would protect them against Mr. Ross and the Pin Indians[19] if they should organize and take up arms for the South.[20] He assured them of Confederate protection and arranged to meet with them and their friends at the Creek Agency two days after a conference which he expected to have with Chief Ross and General McCulloch at Park Hill.[21]

Arriving at Park Hill somewhat in advance of his attendants, General Pike awaited General McCulloch, who presently joined him, and negotiations for a treaty of alliance were formally opened. Chief Ross took a firm stand, repeating his determination to remain neutral and pleading that it would be a cruel thing for the Confederacy to force a weak and defenseless people into a quarrel not their own. While frankly admitting all their sentiments and feelings were on the side of the South, he declared that he could not permit his people to become involved in any way if he could prevent it.

They were unable to shake the purpose of the old Chief by force of argument or clever strategy, and the conference came to a close with the promise of General McCulloch to respect the neutrality of the Cherokees and to refrain from placing troops in their nation unless it should become necessary in order to expel a federal force or to protect the Southern Cherokees.[22]

Doubtless General McCulloch made the promise in good faith. A few days later he wrote Ross again assuring him of his intention of respecting the agreement of neutrality, but now insisting that all Cherokees who were in favor of joining the Confederacy should be allowed to organize into military companies as Home Guards for the purpose of defending themselves in case of an invasion from the North.[23]

Unwilling to be drawn into a scheme which would virtually commit him to the Confederacy without any of the advantages of a formal treaty, Mr. Ross replied that he could not give his consent to such a plan. It would not only violate Cherokee neutrality but would place in their midst a band of organized and armed men not authorized by Cherokee laws, and not amenable to them.[24]

Out of patience with what he considered the irritating obstinacy of Mr. Ross, General McCulloch began collecting troops at

Sculleyville, in the northern part of the Choctaw Nation near the Cherokee line with the avowed purpose of intimidating the Loyal Cherokees and forcing them to abandon their position of neutrality.

General Pike, on leaving Park Hill, pressed on to the Creek Agency and thence to the west where he succeeded in arranging treaties with the Choctaw and Chickasaw Nations and with various bands of western Indians.[25] While the Confederate commissioner made his way westward arranging treaties with the Indians, and while the marshaling of forces on the borders went forward with dispatch, the position of the Cherokees grew daily more precarious. The Creeks and the majority of the Seminoles still remained faithful to their agreement of the previous winter, but the federal government gave no assurance of sending them aid and protection.

Realizing that something must be done quickly, Chief Ross, with the support of Hopothleyohola,[26] leader of the loyal Creeks, sent out a call for an intertribal council to be held near Antelope Hills, in the extreme western part of Indian Territory. The purpose was to weld the western tribes into an independent Indian Confederacy with strength enough to command respectful attention from both sections before General Pike could arrange treaties with them. The council was held and the representatives entered willingly into the proposed compact, but the ultimate purpose of the plan was defeated by General Pike, who, having received intimation of it, succeeded in securing an agreement with a faction of the Creeks while their representatives were in council at Antelope Hills.[27]

The failure of the Indian Confederacy, the neglect of the loyal Indians by the federal government, and the concentration of Confederate forces on their border had caused the loyal Cherokees disappointment and alarm. Then came news of the Battle of Wilson's Creek and the defeat of the Union forces. McCulloch's army was marched back to the borders of the Cherokee Nation and the Cherokees were compelled to decide at once whether they would take up arms for the North or the South.

Faced with this alternative, Chief Ross called his Council together on August 21, 1861, for the purpose of taking under consideration the difficulties and dangers surrounding their nation and to determine upon the best course of action. A call was sent out summoning the Nation to a conference at Tahlequah. About four thousand Cherokee citizens responded. The southern party turned out in full force. Agent Crawford took a prominent part in the meeting, painting in glowing colors the advantages to be gained by secession.[28]

Chief Ross in his message, after having justified his previous policy of neutrality on the ground of good faith and expediency, declared that the Cherokees had at last come to the parting of the ways. Neutrality was no longer possible. Since they had been deserted by the federal government, the Cherokees owed no further allegiance to it. There was no longer any reason to doubt that the Union could not defend them, and there was no cause for hesitation as to the course the nation should pursue.

Two days before the convention, however, Chief Ross had declared that he would rather die than become a party to the rebellion. The U.S. Indian agent, E. H. Carruth, had this to say of his defection: "The convention had been called for the sole purpose of reconciling differences between the Watie party and the full-blood Indians. Stand Watie had raised a regiment and been accepted into the rebel service. Mr. Ross did all in his power to prevent a collision among the Cherokees, and the convention of August 21 was intended to harmonize the conflicting elements" in the Cherokee Nation and prevent fratricidal strife.[29]

Just at this junction, he learned that McCulloch and Stand Watie were to unite and overrun the Cherokee country, McCulloch having assured Watie he would crush out the Union element of the tribe. McCulloch was then at Camp Walker, near Maysville, Arkansas, with 14,000 men and expecting reinforcements. The danger was imminent; Ross wished to avert it and did so in the only possible way.[30]

However that may be, the convention unanimously adopted a resolution to abandon relations with the federal government and to form an alliance with the Confederacy if the latter would guarantee to them the payment of an amount equal to their invested funds.

A messenger was forthwith dispatched to General Pike, apprising him of the action of the convention and inviting him to return to the Cherokee Nation for the purpose of arranging a treaty with their government. He was met at Fort Gibson by Colonel Drew's regiment of home guards, composed chiefly of full-bloods and Pins, which had been raised by order of the National Council and was conducted ceremoniously to Park Hill where a treaty was arranged.

The treaty provided that the Confederate States, having accepted a protectorate over the Cherokee Nation, would never desert it, but that they would maintain unbroken the ties created by the identity of interests and institutions, and strengthened and made perpetual by this treaty. The Confederate States bound themselves to pay the Cherokees the sum of two hundred and fifty thousand dollars upon the ratification of the treaty, to continue the annuities they had formerly received from the United States, and to indemnify them for all losses which they might suffer as a result of abrogating their treaties with the United States.

The Cherokees on their part agreed to furnish all their able-bodied men to the Confederate States for military service against the United States, with the stipulation that their forces should not be required to march outside their own country without their own consent.[31] A regiment of Home Guards under Colonel John Drew was now placed at the service of the Confederacy, and a second regiment was recruited and placed under the command of Colonel Stand Watie.

CHAPTER 17

The Civil War

Since the Cherokees were the first to violate the compact of neutrality entered into at the Creek Agency and at the Antelope Hills Conference, it now became incumbent upon them to explain to their allies the reasons for their shift of allegiance. For this purpose John Ross sent a circular letter to the various tribes, giving the causes which had impelled the Cherokee Nation to join the Confederacy and suggesting the advisability of a similar course for the other tribes.[1]

One of these letters he dispatched to Opothleyohola, leader of the Upper Creeks, who had supported the Cherokee chief in his stand for neutrality. The loyal Creek chief returned the letter with a few words written across the back, asking if John Ross could be the author. This sharp thrust at his constancy was not lost on the Cherokee. Post haste he sent a special delegation headed by the second chief, Joseph Vann, on a mission of peace to the Creeks. To Opothleyohola he extended a special invitation to visit the Cherokee National Council, then in session. But the old warrior would not receive the delegation nor have any dealings with its members. His mind was made up to remain loyal to the Union and he would not talk of changing.

Filled with resentment towards their former allies, the Creeks made a raid on Cherokee stock and ravaged their farms. To avoid reprisals from the Cherokees and then in an effort to avoid intimidation at the hands of the Secession Creeks, Opothleyohola withdrew with his loyal Muskogees and a band of Seminoles to a point on the Deep Fork of the Canadian River, where there rallied to his standard about two thousand warriors, a large number of women and children, and nearly three hundred negroes.

Upon finding his position threatened by a secession army of Indians and Texas Rangers, the old chief decided to retreat to safer ground, hoping to escape attack until federal aid could come from Kansas. On November 5, the strange procession started up the valley of the Arkansas. Near the mouth of the Cimarron, the Confederates overtook and attacked their rear guard, but the refugees escaped across the Arkansas River and thence to Bird Creek where they entrenched themselves in a bend of the creek at a place called Chusto Tahlasseh, situated ten miles from the Creek Village of Tulsey Town.[2]

Here they were attacked but again escaped by night, this time to the hills of Chustenahla. That Colonel Cooper[3] did not follow them immediately was due to the defection of a large part of Colonel Drew's[4] Cherokee regiment, which deserted on the eve of the battle. They had no objection to killing yankees, they said, but shooting their old neighbors, the Creeks, was a different matter.

The fear of further desertion caused Cooper to return to Fort Gibson for reinforcements, so that the third attack was not made until December 26.[5] The weather was then cold and stormy with a blizzard blowing from the northwest. The women and children stood shivering behind a barricade of wagons until their defense was stormed by Colonel James McIntosh[6] and his Texas Rangers, who forced them to seek safety in flight over snow-covered ground and in the face of a blinding blizzard. Many fell by the wayside. The survivors, heading northward, finally reached Walnut Creek, Kansas, where they camped on the bleak prairie for the remainder of the winter.

The winter of 1861 and 1862 was a bitter one for these Indian refugees.[7] Loyal bands from the Five Tribes with detachments from other tribes kept arriving until the number aggregated more than six thousand, camped along the southern border of the state. Half naked and nearly starved, they presented a sorry sight to the kindhearted white pioneers.[8] The attempt of the federal authorities to relieve them tended only to furnish opportunity for peculation to government agents and state politicians. There appeared to be no means of relief for the Indians as long as they remained in Kansas.

The only hope lay in their return to Indian Territory, now occupied by Confederate troops. Before the Indians could go back in safety, the country would need to be cleared of the enemy and reoccupied by federal forces, which, at this time, were so much needed in other regions of military activity.[9]

While political intrigues were sacrificing the Union Indians in Kansas,[10] General Curtis[11] was marching his troops across Missouri to avenge the defeat of Lyon and Wilson's Creek[12] and of recovering Union strongholds in Arkansas and Indian Territory. Confederate forces west of the Mississippi under command of Major General Earl Van Dorn were concentrated in northwest Arkansas to oppose him. They consisted of Sterling Price's volunteer troops, chiefly from Missouri, McCulloch's regulars, and several regiments of Indians under General Albert Pike. The opposing armies met near Fayetteville, Arkansas early in March and two engagements took place, one at Pea Ridge, and the other at Elk Horn Tavern. The result was a defeat for the Confederacy, due in part to a lack of cooperation among commanding generals. Both were bloody battles in which Indians on one side were pitted against Germans on the other.[13]

After these defeats, the white Confederate troops were drawn off toward the east, where they were needed to stay the march of the Union army, steadily advancing down the eastern side of the Mississippi River. Colonel Drew's Cherokee regiment went into camp at the mouth of the Illinois River in the Cherokee Nation. Colonel Watie's Cherokees were sent on a raiding expedition into southwest Missouri. General Pike established headquarters in the Choctaw Nation at Fort McCulloch.[14]

At length, after various delays, the Lane expedition[15] had been organized and ready to march southward into Indian Territory. Leaving Humbolt, Kansas, in the latter part of June it crossed the southern border of the state five thousand strong. The advance guard was led by Colonel Weer,[16] who, upon entering the Indian country, offered to make terms with the Cherokees on condition that they return to their former allegiance. They declined the offer, saying that a treaty had already been entered into with the

Confederacy, the reasons for which were too well known to Colonel Weer to require recapitulation.[17]

The country was now in a defenseless condition, and a letter was sent post haste to General Hindman,[18] in command of the Trans-Mississippi District since the death of McCulloch at Pea Ridge, calling on him for protection against the invading army. He at once ordered General Pike northward to join the Cherokee regiments in the vicinity of Fort Gibson. Pike, whose forces were inadequately equipped,[19] sulked in his tent, ignoring the order. After it had been repeated several times, Pike resigned, and Douglas H. Cooper was put in command.

Cooper moved northward too late to prevent a Confederate defeat at Locust Grove, where a small command of Cherokee troops and a battalion of Missourians, under Col. J. J. Clarkson, were routed and their supplies captured. Of more consequence than the loss of the supply train was the effect of the misadventure upon Colonel Drew's fullblood warriors, who, with the exception of a small force under Captain Pickens Benge, deserted to the enemy. It was the second time defection had decimated Colonel Drew's ranks. Repairing to Cabin Creek, whither the captured train had been sent for safety, the deserting allies helped to fill up the lines in the Second Indian Home Guard regiment.[20]

Following the engagement at Locust Grove, Colonel Weer moved his army southward in two detachments and established headquarters on Grand River, about sixteen miles above Fort Gibson. From this place he sent a message to John Ross by Dr. Gilpatrick under a flag of truce. Chief Ross refused to receive the emissary or to consider his request for an interview, reminding Colonel Weer that the Cherokee Nation had entered into an alliance with the Confederacy.[21]

Meanwhile time pressed, and there was need for haste; supplies were running low, and a strong Confederate force at Fort Davis was threatening every movement made by the army of invasion. On July 14, Colonel Weer, as an emergency measure, sent out two detachments, one led by Major W. T. Campbell, who was to go to the neighborhood of Fort Gibson, the other under Captain H. S. Greeno, instructed to repair to Tahlequah and Park Hill.

Captain Greeno arrived at Tahlequah the evening of the fourteenth and the following day moved his command to the vicinity of Park Hill, where he found two hundred Cherokees awaiting an opportunity to join the Union. Among them were Colonel W. P. Ross and Major Thomas Pegg, who, while debating whether they should respond to an order just received from Colonel Cooper to report for duty at Fort Davis, the two officers, were arrested and sent to headquarters.

The war clouds were now gathering thick and fast about the gray-haired chief[22] of the Cherokees. A few days before this, Colonel Cooper, in the name of President Davis, had commanded him to issue a proclamation calling on every able-bodied Cherokee man between the ages of eighteen and thirty-five to enlist in the Confederate military service. Following on the heels of this demand, and probably because of it, the Pin Indians rose in rebellion and compelled their chief, at the end of a halter, to declare for neutrality. To comply with the demand of Colonel Cooper meant death at the hands of his own tribesmen. To ignore it was to put himself at the mercy of the Confederate commander. While debating what was best for him to do, he was arrested by Captain Greeno and placed on parole; thus the confusion of issues rendered the danger of his position and that of the nation insupportable.

With the Confederate army in retreat, the federal forces in control of the Cherokee Nation, and his own government in anarchy, Chief Ross found himself compelled to act quickly. The Confederacy had proved itself no more faithful to treaty obligations than had the federal government. Good faith no longer bound him to either. Expediency pointed to a renewal of relations with the Union while there was yet a shadow of chance to save his nation from utter disruption. When Colonel Weer again approached him on the subject, he yielded, and as the Cherokee Nation was no longer a safe place for him, he accepted the offer of a Union escort to Fort Gibson and thence to Fort Scott, Kansas. With the national archives and what valuables could be loaded into two ox wagons he left the country.[23]

The success of the first Union invasion proved to be temporary. At this time, a small, well-organized force could have held the country easily, but inefficiency and lack of harmony among the commanding officers led to mutiny and insubordination on the part of the soldiers. Delay resulted, giving the Confederate Indians under Cooper and Stand Watie time to join forces with white troops under General Rains. When the combined commands moved northward, the Union army retreated towards Kansas, leaving the Cherokee country once more in the hands of the Confederacy. Tahlequah was occupied by the victorious southern Cherokees, a convention was held, resolutions were passed deposing Chief John Ross from office, and Stand Watie, now a military hero, was named to succeed him.

The triumphant army was not content to enjoy the fruits of its victory with moderation and mercy. Summary vengeance was wreaked upon the families of loyal Cherokees. Women, children, and old men, driven out of doors at midnight, were forced to seek protection by following the trail of the retreating Union army in the light of their burning homesteads. Beautiful Rose Cottage, after it had been sacked and denuded of whatever of value could be carried away, was given to the flames, and the council ground strewn with the ashes of the ravaged capital.

The success of the Confederate army was short-lived. Within a few weeks, the federal forces having rallied for a second invasion of Indian Territory, marched back into Indian Territory, this time under command of Brigadier General James G. Blunt, who defeated Cooper at Fort Wayne on Beatie's Prairie in the Cherokee Nation, and, with the assistance of Colonel W. A. Phillips, drove the Confederate Army south across the Arkansas River. Fort Gibson was retaken in April, and from that time until the end of the war remained the base of Union operations in Indian Territory.

When the fortunes of war had again wrested the eastern part of the Cherokee Nation from the hands of the Confederacy and it appeared that the federal army had come to stay, the loyal Cherokees met in Council at Camp John Ross on Cowskin Prairie in February 1863, Thomas Pegg acting as principal chief, and repudiated the alliance with the Confederate States, renewed allegiance to the Union, abolished slavery and involuntary servitude in the Cherokee Nation, and passed a law confiscating the property of all

Cherokee citizens who were enemies of the Union. John Ross was reelected principal chief, and Lewis Downing was made assistant chief. The party of secession had already met at Webber's Falls and organized a provisional Cherokee Nation South, with Stand Watie as principal Chief.

From the Spring of 1863 to the declaration of peace, the Union army controlled the Indian Territory north of the Arkansas River, and succeeded in driving the Confederates farther south until it defeated them at Oktaha, in the battle of Honey Springs in July 1863. After this, the war developed into a series of raids and counter raids with the country around Fort Gibson, the debatable ground contested by both armies.

Fort Gibson had entered upon a new era of its history in April 1863, when Colonel W. A. Phillips took possession of the little town and made it his headquarters and base of supplies. As the original fortifications had been abandoned by the United States before the war, a new site was chosen on higher ground. Here fortifications were constructed, and all necessary equipment installed. The loyal refugees found protection in the vicinity of the fort, where they endeavored to cultivate small patches of corn and vegetables and tend the cattle and horses which belonged to the garrison; but they dared not venture any distance from the guns of the fortress if they valued their lives at all.

Supplies of food, clothing, medicine, and ammunition for the garrison and for these Indian dependents were brought from Fort Scott, Kansas, in wagon trains under the protection of military escorts. From the time the cortege left Hudson Crossing, in the northeastern corner of the Cherokee Nation, until it entered the garrison gates, it was in constant peril from Confederate foraging parties, scouting along the Military Road that followed the Grand River valley as far south as the Fort Gibson crossing.

The capture of such a train, worth a small fortune to the federal government, was of much greater value to the isolated army post, situated a hundred sixty miles from its base of supplies. To the hard-pressed Southerners, it was a consummation devoutly desired and finally artfully achieved when, in September 1864, General

Stand Watie captured a train of three hundred wagons and a great number of horses and mules, camped for the night at Cabin Creek crossing, a few miles south of the present town of Vinita.[24] The elated victors escaped with their booty across the Verdigris and the Arkansas to enjoy the fruits of a victory which more than compensated them for the loss of Clarkson's train at Locust Grove two years previously.

The Battle of Cabin Creek was the last engagement of any consequence on Cherokee soil. After the Union forces had driven the Confederate troops beyond the Arkansas River, the few Southern sympathizers left in the Cherokee Nation received scant consideration or protection from the army of occupation. Marauding bands of Kansas Jayhawkers terrorized the women and children and murdered men in cold blood. Cattle rustlers drove off all the livestock that had escaped the foraging parties of the Union and Confederate armies. The resources of the natives were exhausted, their economic system was in confusion, their lives were constantly threatened by lawless Indians and ruffian whites from beyond the border.

What was left for them to do but to follow the retreating Southern army and seek sanctuary where they were most likely to find it? A large number camped for the remainder of the war near the Red River among the hospitable Choctaws and Chickasaws. Others went into Texas and there threw themselves upon the hospitality of the kindly Texans, who were themselves none too well-off with their able-bodied men in the army and their economic system disorganized. These exiles, like those in Kansas, suffered untold hardship and privations which decimated their numbers but did not dim their loyalty to a losing cause.

Probably no part of the United States suffered such havoc as did Indian Territory during this crisis. After the besom of war had swept the country north, east, and south, hardly a building was left standing, nor a fence intact. The country presented a tragic picture of blackened chimneys rising from charred homesteads, idle fields overgrown with weeds and brambles, and of a population reduced to the very verge of despondency, their once charming little nation racked by the bitter hatred of party factionalism. Thus did the Red

Man help to pay the price of freedom for the Black, and the story is not yet half told.

When finally, peace was declared, the southern refugees were left in destitute circumstances a long way from home, nor could they hope to better their condition while they remained in exile. Those who had returned from the north in the spring of 1863 were faring little better with a country overrun by Kansas cattle rustlers and jay hawkers. In the summer of 1865, the Cherokee National Council met at Tahlequah with Colonel Lewis Downing, the assistant Chief, acting as principal chief in the absence of John Ross, who was detained in the east.

There on the Council Ground, among the ruins of their public buildings, they met day after day to deliberate on the condition to which the war had reduced government and people, and to pass measures for restoring a state of security in which to rebuild their desolated country.

With a view to stabilizing and composing their tribal affairs, thereby precluding all occasion for federal interference, the Cherokee National Council on July 14, 1865, passed a set of resolutions restoring citizenship to those who would agree to take an oath of fidelity to the constitution and laws of the Cherokee Nation within a certain limited time. Exception was made of those who held military commissions above the rank of captain, after March 1, 1865; of those who held office in the government of the Cherokee Nation South; of all who had violated their parole as prisoners of war; and of all inter-married white citizens who had joined in the rebellion.[25]

This proffer of the olive branch to the main body of the Southern Cherokees was ignored in the expectation of securing better terms from the Peace Commission, which was to meet at Fort Smith in September. Their leaders were already preparing to secure the segregation of Canadian District as a separate political unit, where they believed greater harmony would prevail; they were also promising to secure, if possible, a part of the tribal funds to assist the exiles in returning home. Such aid would have been a godsend, especially to those stranded in Texas and compelled to live on the bounty of friends and relatives.

CHAPTER 18

The Fort Smith
Peace Council

Had Lincoln lived, some things would have been different after the war. Had Lincoln lived, the Indians might have been spared some of the rigors of reconstruction that were dealt out to loyal and rebel alike by the hands of his friends.[1] But six days after Lee's surrender at Appomattox, Lincoln died, and his reconstruction policy, falling from lifeless hands, was cast aside for one of sterner measures.

Under abnormal war conditions, those disintegrating forces which had been working for years to undermine the unity and integrity of Indian Territory gained in volume and strength. The fierce factional jealousies which rent the nation in twain at the first clash of arms, had emboldened gigantic railroad corporations and land syndicates to reach possessive hands toward the rich Indian country as it lay prostrate under the feet of trampling armies.

During the entire period of the war, Congress had devoted a great deal of attention to the Indian question. As early as February 1863, the Senate Committee on Indian Affairs had prepared a fairly well-formulated plan for the reconstruction of the Indian Territory. Its scope was sufficiently comprehensive to embrace the Indians of Kansas, in fact, all the tribes east of the Rocky Mountains.[2]

In his annual report for 1864, W. P. Dole, the commissioner of Indian affairs, recommended that "in the process of reconstruction the Southern Tribes should be made to provide room for other Indians."[3] Already, on March 19, this policy had been suggested to the military authorities in a letter from Colonel W. A. Phillips, then commandant at Fort Gibson, the occasion being a convention held by the Choctaws at New Hope the preceding March with a view of profiting by the President's Amnesty Proclamation. They had appointed a provisional governor for their nation and a delegate to Washington.

Colonel Phillips, upon hearing of this, forwarded a protest to the War Department, stating the tribe was still in a state of rebellion, and advising that no terms be made until a more secure basis of readjustment had been reached. The suggestion was added that the situation furnished a good excuse for reducing the great Indian domains to mere reserves and for opening up land for settlement, an opportunity which the country could ill afford to neglect.

Presumably, this procedure was proposed as a war measure designed for the punishment of tribes in rebellion. Yet no one realized more fully than Colonel Phillips must have done that it would operate with equal severity upon the loyal Indians, who, even then, were risking their lives in defense of the Union.

By February 1865, a plan sponsored by the Senate Committee on Indian Affairs, of which Senator James Harlan, of Iowa, was Chairman, was ready to be submitted to Congress. On March 2, it passed the Senate after heated discussion. As the session of the Thirty-Eighth Congress ended on March 3, the bill was never considered in the House. Its policy, compounded of several different projects, had been blended and harmonized to conserve every interest in the country save that of the Indian.

The Harlan Bill provided for the removal of all Indian tribes between the Mississippi River and the Rocky Mountains to the Indian Territory; for the organization of Indian Territory under a territorial form of government; and for the appointment by the President of a governor and a secretary. The tribal governments were to be continued but no determining voice was to be given to the Indians in the proposed territorial reorganization.

Chief Ross, who was in Washington at the time the bill was before the Senate, opposed it on the ground that the location of the wild tribes[4] in proximity to the civilized Indians would prove detrimental to both. Other objectionable features of the measure he mentioned also, and in so doing offended the author of the bill, who, on May 15, 1865, became the new Secretary of the Interior under the appointment of President Johnson. With the Department of Indian Affairs under his supervision, the new cabinet officer was in the best position possible to carry out the measures prescribed by his bill.

John Ross was not the only Indian who was troubled over the turn affairs had taken. Word had been passed that the Department of the Interior was inclined to exact the last farthing in retribution for their disloyalty; that the treaty rights of the Indians were considered abrogated; and in the renewal of friendly relations the tribes would be completely at the mercy of the United States in consequence of their part in the rebellion.[5]

The citizens of the Five Tribes, having much to lose in that case, were particularly uneasy and desirous of renewing their treaty relations on the best terms they could secure. As a step towards that end, a Grand Council of all the southern Indians was called to meet at Camp Napoleon, Chattahomah, on May 24, 1865.[6] Representatives of fifteen tribes are reported to have been present. A solemn league of peace and friendship was entered into, resolutions were drawn up expressing their purpose and wishes, and delegates from each of the tribes were authorized to go to Washington to confer with the federal government on the subject of new treaties.

Apprised of this meeting and its purpose and deeming it better policy to treat with the tribe in their own country, the President appointed a commission to meet their representatives at some place in the Indian Territory,[7] probably at Fort Gibson. Accordingly, a call went out for a Grand Council to convene in September, not at Fort Gibson, however, as was suggested at first, but at Fort Smith, Arkansas, to suit the convenience of the Commissioners.

A notable gathering it proved to be. The federal government was represented by D. N. Cooley, Commissioner of Indian Affairs; Elijah Sells, Superintendent of Indian Affairs for the Southern Superintendency; Thomas Wistar, a prominent Quaker of Pennsylvania; Major-General W. S. Harney, of the United States Army; and Colonel Ely S. Parker, a Seneca Indian, who had served as a member of General Grant's staff during the war.[8]

Milton W. Reynolds, present as a reporter for the *New York Tribune*, declared that the delegates of the Indian tribes were no less brilliant and conspicuous than the representatives of the federal government, but if the truth were told, so far as power of expression, knowledge of Indian treaties, and real oratory were concerned, the Indians had a decided advantage.

The National Council in extraordinary session at Tahlequah during August 1865 had appointed as a commission to represent the Nation, Lieutenant-Colonel Lewis Downing, assistant chief of the nation; Captain Thomas Pegg, Captain Smith Christie, and H. D. Reese, all veterans of the Union Army.[9] The Grand Council of all the Confederate Indians which was then in progress at Armstrong Academy, prevented the Southern delegations from arriving in time for the early sessions.

But there was on hand a large aggregation of lawyers and lobbyists from Kansas, who had come for the purpose of demanding that room be made in the Indian Territory for the Indians then living in Kansas and other states. There were also representatives of certain railroad corporations wishing to extend their lines through the Indian Territory on the land grant subsidy plan.

The meeting was called to order by D. N. Cooley, Commissioner of Indian Affairs, and prayer was offered by Colonel Lewis Downing of the Cherokee delegation, after which Commissioner Cooley stated the purpose of the meeting, first informing the Indians that their treaties had all been forfeited, but that those who had remained loyal would be protected in their rights.

Since the majority of them had violated their treaty obligations by entering into diplomatic relations with the Confederacy, they had forfeited all annuities and interests in lands in the Indian Territory. However, the long-suffering President was willing to hear his erring children in extenuation of their crime and to make treaties with such nations as were willing to be at peace among themselves and with the United States, he assured them.

There were certain general terms on which their relations might be restored. The opposing factions of each tribe must enter into a treaty of amity and peace among themselves, between each other as tribes, and with the United States; the tribes settled in the Indian country should bind themselves, at the call of the United States authorities, to assist in keeping peace among the wild tribes of the plains; slavery should be abolished and measures taken to incorporate the slaves into the several tribes on an equal footing with the original members, or they should be otherwise suitably provided for by them; slavery or involuntary servitude should never again exist in any tribe or nation except in the punishment of crime; a part of the lands hitherto owned and occupied by the Indians were required to be set apart for the friendly Indians then living in Kansas and elsewhere on such terms as might be agreed upon or fixed by the government; and a territorial form of government would be extended over the Indian Territory by act of Congress.

The opening days were devoted to submitting credentials and explaining the limitations placed upon their delegations by instructions from their tribal governments, the loyal Cherokees embracing this occasion to decry the charge that they were rebels in consequence of the treaty they had been forced to sign with the Confederacy.

Mr. Cooley, speaking in behalf of the Secretary of the Interior, peremptorily informed them they had been guilty of open defection from the Union, and if they expected any leniency for their great crime, let them show it by repudiating John Ross, who had led them astray; then if they wished to remove the stigmas and inabilities placed upon them by a few renegades, they could do so by submitting to terms proposed by the government.[10]

Unmoved by the blatant truculence of the Commissioner of Indian Affairs, the Cherokee delegation refused to sign any agreement until their loyalty to the Union had been recognized unequivocally. Moreover, they objected to the proposed treaty on the ground that it would not be to the best interests of the emancipated negro, nor of the Indian, to incorporate the former into the tribe on an equal footing with their masters. They objected also to consolidating all the tribes of Indian Territory under one government because of the many incongruous and irreconcilable members, which no power on earth could bring into a semblance of assimilation.

Reese, the secretary of the Cherokee delegation and its spokes-
man, stood his ground firmly against all attempts to move him, his
delegation supporting him as a unit.[11] They would sign no preliminary agreement with the federal government until their loyalty to
the Union had been recognized in a manner satisfactory to themselves, and from that pronouncement they would not yield a single
point.

Meanwhile plots against the venerable John Ross had been mul-
tiplying behind closed doors and thickening under cover of darkness.[12] His reputation for political sagacity was well known. Knowing
he could not be bent to their will, the agents of corporate interests
determined to break him. Detained in the East by the death of his
wife and son, Ross did not reach Fort Smith until the afternoon of
the thirteenth, when exhausted and ill, he joined the loyal Cherokee encampment on the opposite side of the river from the Council
ground. The next day he appeared in the assembly hall with his
colleagues.[13]

Meanwhile, representatives of the Confederate Cherokees had
presented themselves and been seated with E. C. Boudinot, the most
conspicuous figure of the convention, as their chairman. Already
it had become apparent that the old factional feuds still rankled
and that there was little prospect of an early compromise between
the rival groups. Aggravated by the Confiscation Act passed by the
Cowskin Prairie Council in 1863, and embittered by their unsuccessful venture in aid of secession, the Southern contingent had gone
to Fort Smith with the avowed purpose of disrupting the Cherokee
Nation or reinstating their followers on their own terms.

The Southern Cherokees were still living in destitution in Texas
or in the Choctaw Nation, unable to return home with the confiscation laws still in effect. Their representatives had demanded
that the obnoxious measures be repealed and their people rein-
stated. This, the loyal contingent refused to promise, claiming that
its members had no power to bind their council by any agreement.
For this John Ross was blamed. As soon as his presence was known,
he became the target of the vitriolic invectives of Colonel Boudinot
who, with utter irrelevance, hastened to launch a scurrilous attack

upon the probity and honor of his ancient enemy. This proceeding the chairman of the convention not only condoned but seized upon as the opening for the announcement that he "refused in any way or manner to recognize Ross as chief of the Cherokees," giving as his reasons that Ross was disposed to breed discord among his own people; that he did not represent the will and wishes of the loyal Cherokees; that he had tried to persuade the Creeks of Opothleyohola's faction to desert the Union; and that he was regarded by the commissioners as an enemy to the United States.[14]

Chief Ross himself tried to answer these charges, denying them as openly as they had been made. But Commissioner Cooley, in a manner so unfair and insulting as to proclaim his own unfitness for public office, refused to listen to him. This aroused the venerable chieftain's colleagues to remonstrate in a written protest, stating that the act of the Commissioner was based on erroneous information; that Mr. Ross was not the pretended chief of the Cherokees but was their chief in law and in fact, having been duly elected to that position by the qualified voters in accordance with the provisions of the constitution; that for the past three years he had been the authorized delegate to Washington and the recognized head of the Cherokee Nation.

There had been no action on his part during this time which impugned his loyalty to the United States or his fidelity to the Cherokee Nation; and as to his course in the Civil War, he had remained loyal long after the tribes and states in his vicinity had abjured their allegiance to the Union, and after all protection had been withdrawn by the United States, yielding to the Confederacy only when further resistance threatened the entire destruction of his people.[15]

Discussions followed in which Colonel Boudinot figured conspicuously in the presence of men of high financial standing and corporate interest, who stood ready to reward the man who could help them. The consideration accorded the handsome, vivacious Cherokee by the federal commissioner tended to widen the breach between the two factions and to create a lack of confidence on the part of the loyal Cherokees in the real purpose of the Peace Commission. The restoration of friendly relations appeared yet a long way off, and all hope of reaching an agreement at this time was abandoned.

The National delegation consistently refused to enter into any negotiations for land cessions until their Council should appoint a delegation clothed with the proper authority to treat. Consequently, the Fort Smith Peace Council adjourned after arrangements had been made for a preliminary treaty of peace and amity as a basis for future action, and an agreement had been made on the part of the Cherokees to send a delegation with full power to treat at Washington, probably in December.[16]

CHAPTER 19

"That Dark Treaty"

The report of Secretary Harlan in December following the Fort Smith Peace Council indicates the trend arguments were to take in the impending negotiations with the Indians for new treaties. "Civilized and powerful tribes residing within the Indian Territory," he charged, had "united early in the year of 1861 with the Indians of the prairies for hostile operations against the United States.

"In flagrant violation of treaties and in the absence of any just ground of complaint the Indians had entered into an alliance with the Confederacy and organized troops who fought side by side with the rebel soldiers. The perfidious conduct of those Indians in making war upon the United States had been visited with the severest retribution in having their lands laid waste, property destroyed, and the inhabitants reduced from a prosperous condition to such extreme destitution, that thousands of them must inevitably perish during the present winter, unless timely provision can be made by this government for their relief."[1]

On the contrary, Superintendent Coffin in 1863 had been of the opinion that, "if the government, at the time of the breaking out of the rebellion had promptly offered to the various tribes in the Indian Territory the protection provided for in existing treaty stipulations,—that they would all have remained loyal."[2] But instead of doing that, the government had withdrawn from the vicinity of the Indian Territory all the Union forces, and thus had left the Indians at the mercy of the enemy. Thus, the alienation of the larger or smaller fractions of the tribes had been the result.[3]

In compliance with the preliminary agreement at Fort Smith the previous September, the National Council in October had appointed a delegation of seven, all of whom had served in the Union army, and by special act had made Chief Ross the chairman of the delegation, with instructions to his colleagues that they were not to proceed with negotiations until his rank and prestige had been recognized.[4]

Stand Watie, principal chief of the Southern Cherokees, named E. C. Boudinot, W. P. Adair, Richard Fields, J. A. Scales, and Saladin Watie, his son, to represent the Southern Party. Chief Watie, himself, remained in the Indian Territory, holding himself in readiness to organize the Cherokee Nation South as soon as the way was clear. The delegation was joined in Washington in the spring of 1866 by John Rollin Ridge, son of John Ridge and grandson of Major Ridge, whose reputation as poet added luster to this group of brilliant Southern tribesmen distinguished for discernment and political adroitness.

Smarting under their failure to gain control of the tribal government and to secure the repeal of the drastic confiscation measures directed against them by the party in power, they were prepared to prosecute their claim to the uttermost farthing, and in this determination they received encouragement from Washington in the assurance that Congress would appropriate funds for their expenses, including fees for legal counsel.

But with their people torn between hope and despair, firesides desolated, fields laid waste, mills dismantled, schools and churches but a memory, and their council ground sown with ashes, they should have seen that this was no time for party recriminations, diplomatic intrigue, and dispiriting delay. Yet when the rival delegations met the Commissioner of Indian Affairs in Washington, the preliminary discussions presaged troublesome negotiations long drawn out. Both sides had engaged strong legal counsel and the arguments presented were ably conducted. Draft after draft of a treaty was submitted only to be rejected for one reason or another.

From the beginning, the National delegation contended that reconstruction measures did not apply to the loyal Cherokees, many of whom had sacrificed their lives in defense of the Union. The arguments made and explanations offered at Fort Smith were again reviewed and stressed, and again the Commissioner of Indian Affairs scouted them. As soon as the loyal delegates would agree to repudiate John Ross, the government was ready to treat with them, but not before, he assured them.

When the seven as a unit steadfastly refused to proceed without the recognition of Chief Ross, Mr. Cooley turned to the opposition, who, claiming that it would be unsafe for them to return to the Cherokee Nation with the Ross party in control of the government and the confiscation laws in force, demanded, as the only hope for their peace and well-being, a division of the lands and annuities in proportion to the number in each party.[5]

Against this demand a determined stand was taken by the opposition, who had consistently objected to any scheme that threatened their national integrity. They now proposed instead that the Canadian District be set aside for a period of two years for the exclusive occupation of the Southern Cherokees pending a final settlement of their differences. This proposition was unacceptable to the opposition because of the limited area of the district and for other obvious reasons.

Passed now weeks and months of delay and confusion while each rival faction vied with the other in efforts to secure favorable action from a government whose agents were ever intent on pitting faction against faction in order to confuse issues in the public mind and to wear down resistance to measures long prearranged for the acquisition of lands on which to locate Kansas tribes; for the gift of free homesteads to Cherokee freedmen; and for the grant of right of way to certain railroads.

Despairing of an agreement with the loyal Cherokees, whose obduracy he attributed to John Ross, the Commissioner of Indian Affairs finally decided to break the stubborn old chief whose official character he had contemptuously refused to recognize. To this end he brought charges of malfeasance against Ross, claiming that large sums of money had been paid over to his brother, Lewis, the treasurer of the nation, which had never been accounted for. This payment had been made by the Confederate government through its emissary, Albert Pike, and in agreement with the Confederate treaty Pike had negotiated at Park Hill in 1861. But when proof positive was offered of Ross's innocence, Commissioner Cooley did not choose to hear the evidence, the press having already published the story at his instigation. His own delegation, however, stood by the failing chieftain to the end, and when he became too ill to attend conferences, they gathered at his bedside to listen to his counsel.[6]

At length, the general public became aware of what was in progress when Horace Greeley gave wide publicity in his paper, the *New York Tribune*, to a memorial from the Cherokee National Council demanding recognition of their principal chief. Thereupon the Secretary of the American Baptist Home Missionary Society wrote Secretary Seward on May 16 that he hoped the President would favor the loyal Cherokees in the matter of the treaty, as they were believed to represent the great body of the nation. At the same time he expressed "great fear that the Confederate faction were sacrificing the interests of their nation to the interests of speculators."[7]

Undeterred by all these protests and criticisms, the Department of the Interior drove right on to its objective with ruthless determination. Urged to do so, the Ridge Party decided to treat on the terms dictated by the government, and on June 16 submitted the draft of a treaty to the Secretary of the Interior, from whose office it never reached Congress. But no matter. It contained the main measures desired by the government to whip into line the National delegates, who themselves were not unprepared.[8]

Depressed though they were by the loss of the veteran, Captain Pegg, who had died of worry and anxiety in April, and the illness of John Ross, whose days were numbered, this delegation had spent hours on end trying to prepare an agreement that would meet the coercive demands of the government and at the same time save their own nation some vestige of integrity and autonomy. And there was now need for haste. John Ross had become desperately ill, for the obloquy that had been heaped upon his venerable head was preying on his mind, and his devoted daughters were beseeching the President to vindicate his honor that he might go in peace.[9]

Four weeks after the Southern delegation reported their treaty, the National contingent negotiated their agreement, known as the Treaty of 1866. Among its articles were those providing for the repudiation of the alliance with the Confederacy and amnesty for all past offenses. It agreed to repeal the confiscation laws against the Confederate Cherokees and granted them permission to settle in Canadian District under certain conditions and with certain privileges, pending the final settlement of the controversy. It secured to the nation the right to control and regulate its trade and maintain its own system of taxation, and it granted the right of use and occupancy to every denomination or society which had erected buildings for religious or educational purposes on lands belonging to the nation.

Provision was made for a federal court to be established in the Indian Territory with jurisdiction over United States citizens. Cherokee freedmen were granted the right of citizenship; and to all free colored persons who were in the nation at the commencement of the rebellion and to their descendants were given all the rights of Cherokees by blood.

The Cherokee Nation agreed to grant a right of way to one railroad through the Nation from north to south and one from east to west; and consent was given for the establishment of a general inter-tribal council for the Indian Territory to be presided over by a governor to be designated by the Secretary of the Interior and a secretary elected by the council. To the United States was granted the right to settle friendly Indians within the Cherokee dominion on unoccupied lands east as well as those west of the ninety-sixth meridian.

The Cherokee Nation ceded in trust to the United States the Neutral Lands, a tract located in Kansas, to be paid for at the rate of a dollar and a quarter an acre, the Secretary of the Interior to be authorized to pay the reasonable costs and expenses of the delegates of the Southern Cherokees out of the proceeds of these sales to an amount not exceeding twenty-eight thousand dollars.[10]

The Cherokee National Council, or any duly appointed delegation thereof, was granted the privilege of appointing an agent to examine the accounts of the nation with the government of the United States. All funds then due the nation from the sale of lands by the United States were to be invested in registered stocks, and the interest, paid semi-annually, was to be applied to the maintenance of schools, government and orphans. Of this general fund thirty-five percent was to be applied to the schools, fifty to the government and fifteen to the orphan fund.

In addition to the last named fund, all unclaimed arrears for service of Cherokees in the regiments of United States volunteers, which remained unclaimed for a period of two years after the ratification of the treaty, should be applied to the foundation and support of an asylum from the education of orphan children.

The United States guaranteed to the Cherokees the quiet and peaceable possession of their country, and protection against interruption or intrusion from all unauthorized citizens of the United States, who might attempt to settle on their lands or reside in their territory. The sum of ten thousand dollars was to be paid by the United States as the expenses of the delegates and representatives of the Cherokees invited by the government to visit Washington for the purpose of making this treaty. It was to be paid only upon the ratification of the treaty.

The treaty was proclaimed on August 11, six days after John Ross had died vindicated, his rank and prestige at last recognized in the words of the treaty: "John Ross, principal chief of the Cherokees, being too ill to join these negotiations." Convinced that his end was near, the commissioner, at the suggestion of the Secretary of the Interior, repealed the decree of the previous year deposing him from the chieftainship of the Cherokees on the ground that the reason which had rendered this action necessary no longer existed.[11] These are the main points of the agreement, to this day called among the Cherokees "That Dark Treaty."

CHAPTER 20

Rebuilding the Broken Walls:
The Homes

Both factions felt themselves cheated by the treaty of 1866. The Loyal Cherokees had expected something better at the hands of a government they had sacrificed their life blood to defend. The Confederate Cherokees on their part had received assurance from their delegates to Washington that an appropriation would be set aside from the tribal funds to aid their destitute families in returning home.

Disappointed in their hopes and expectations, the Southern refugees finally found their way back home as best they could, some in ox-wagons, a few in run-down carriages, others on horseback, and a large number afoot. The pathos of these returning exiles, the salt of the earth in any community where they chanced to sojourn, was as heart-rending as that of the long procession that had dragged its weary way in the path of the northern army on the return from Kansas in 1863. Footsore and destitute, they were happy to stand once more on their own soil.

Undismayed by the desolation that met the eye on every side, they wasted no time in weak complainings. Everybody set to work with a will to reclaim fields and to rebuild houses. The work was hard at first, with so much to be done and so little with which to do it. Very few returned with any household goods, farming implements or livestock of any kind.[1] The occasional saw or butcher knife was regarded as a treasure to be entrusted only to reliable hands.

"Money in those early days," a Confederate veteran was once heard to remark, "was as scarce as hen's teeth." A system of barter took care of the bulk of transactions between neighbors, the paper money or script issued by the national government being, in fact, the chief medium of exchange in use for some time.

The scarcity of tools and implements, a handicap at first, was overcome in part by a will to work that was infectious. Those who before the war had depended upon their slaves for menial tasks and exhausting toil were now compelled to earn their bread by the sweat of their own brow—not an insufferable hardship since everybody else was doing the same thing and appearing to like it.

Fortunately, material for rebuilding was not far to seek; the forest, practically intact, offered an abundance of timber for all uses. The prairies and canebrakes gave pasturage for what little livestock the Kansas bushwhackers and cattle rustlers had left; swift water courses provided power for mills, springs of crystal clearness held healing in their cool depths, and smiling skies raised their dome above a soil so rich it needed but "to be tickled with a hoe to laugh with a harvest." All nature appeared to be welcoming the exiles home.

Reverting to ancient tribal custom in clearing fields and building houses, they helped each other, the whole community pooling their labor so effectively as to perform a task in a day or two that unaided effort would have required a much longer time to accomplish. Log rollings and house raisings were extremely popular for their social contacts as well as for their economic advantages. Entire families turned out, the men to haul up the logs and raise the walls, the women to prepare the noon-day meal[2] and the children to fetch and carry as directed. Thus everybody became constructive minded, forgetting past afflictions in cooperative rehabilitation.

Those first lean years did not last long. The Indians are a resilient race, else already they would have passed into oblivion, forgotten as their traditions and native culture have become. Like Truth, "crushed to earth they rise again," if perchance any ground is left on which "to press their feet."

Snapshots, as it were, sent from the Indian Agent in his annual report to Washington during those years, reveal the people going about purposefully and soberly, mending their broken walls. In 1867 this laconic sentence tells a pleasant story: "Peace and quiet in the Cherokee Nation, and good crops."[3] And again: "Health good. No epidemics."[4] This was in 1869. Previously there had been an epidemic of cholera at Fort Gibson that had caused many fatalities.

Various meetings had been held the preceding winter, attended by delegates from both factions, and a better feeling and a more perfect understanding had been arrived at. Several tribes in Kansas were to become merged in the citizenship of the Cherokee Nation almost immediately.[5] There was a ripple of excitement at Fort Gibson in 1870 over the report that the Osages again were about to become neighbors to the Cherokees.[6]

After five years of peace, "rehabilitation has made considerable headway." There were at this time three thousand seven hundred ninety-two houses, chiefly of logs, "many of them double-log houses, a thousand of them nice;"[7] some, a story and a half high with stone chimneys whose workmanship showed skill beyond ordinary stone-masonry. A few of these houses were weatherboarded. The population was estimated at eighteen thousand. The number of dwellings increased to four thousand in a later report, after which the people were regarded as having become adequately housed. The problem remaining concerned improvement in the quality and appearance of the buildings and grounds rather than in their number.

To the enumeration of their material achievements is appended the following tribute, proffered with no thought of its ever coming to their attention: "The Cherokees, perhaps of all the Indian tribes, great or small, are first in general intelligence, in the acquisition of wealth, in the knowledge of the useful arts and in social and moral progress. The evidences of a real and substantial advancement in these respects are too clear to be questioned; and it is the more remarkable from the fact that a few years since they were as a people almost ruined by the ravages of the Civil War. . . . Poverty is the only thing that interferes with their success."[8] The war animosities had died down and they were living side by side in peace.

The treaty gave the Southern Cherokees two years in which to decide whether or not they wanted to locate in a body in Canadian District which, however, was to remain an integral part of the Cherokee Nation, under its constitution and laws. Long before the expiration of that time, the people, taking council of their own wisdom, had repossessed old homesteads or found new locations better to their liking. Whereupon, political leaders were compelled to fall in line with an intelligent citizenship that knew its own mind.

And some of the more adventurous, farsighted of the younger generation, loading a minimum of household goods into wagons, trekked with their little families westward into the spacious, sparsely settled reaches of Coo-wee-scoo-wee, the nation's frontier district, which offered the attraction of boundless prairie and rich pasture lands for the herds that soon came to graze on the tall grass growing in such abundance as to appear inexhaustible. There developed here in time the broad wheat fields that filled the nation's granaries, from which countless bushels of food and feed stuffs found their way into distant markets. The proceeds from these agricultural products put more coffee, sugar, and Louisiana molasses on the tables of the enterprising pioneers.

The expansion of the range cattle industry, with its accompanying ranch life and annual "round-ups" began here a new era in Cherokee history, an era in which legends, traditions, and folk tales, woven into the very warp and woof of the district's background, portray a culture as vivid and colorful and at the same time as orderly and legitimate, as any to be found in the chronicles of the New World.

There were busy scenes, cast in the wide open spaces where everybody worked hard all day and, dead tired at night, slept in serene security behind unbarred doors, to be up before daybreak and off for another round of toil that was redeemed by endless adventures and substantial compensations. In these hives of industry, no drones were tolerated. Even the children had their allotted chores, in the performance of which they considered themselves a real part of the system. Thus they learned to do necessary things by doing them, and to become good citizens by obeying implicitly the simple rules of a household.

In the building of the family fortune, the women had a very definite place. Cherokee women had the reputation of being not only industrious but good managers, with an eye for beauty as well as utility. They made fine gardens, not forgetting to plant roses, four-o-clocks, and morning glories as well as beans and cabbages. Their comfortable houses were furnished with taste; they had books, magazines and musical instruments; and their larders were stocked with bacon, potatoes, and choice preserves at a time when that region that now boasts the state capitol was a howling wilderness, peopled by squatters and by blanket Indians.[9]

Meanwhile, an agricultural society had been organized for the purpose of stimulating interest in the improvement in quality and output of commodities. "The large and magnificent herds of cattle have disappeared from our prairies," one laments, "and the accumulation of forty years, vanished into nothingness. But the grass still grows and water runs, inviting and urging our people to untiring efforts to renew their herds of cattle, horses, hogs, sheep and goats. Markets will soon be brought to our very doors by the extension of railroads, the increase of travel through the Territory, and the teeming population that moves with restless activity around our borders. The people who have homes and cultivated fields and orchards are more secure from intrusion and aggression than those who have no fixed residence or abiding place."[10]

The Agricultural Society held its first fair at Tahlequah in October 1870, and although there was not a large show of stock, grain, vegetables, or textiles, there was manifested considerable interest, evidenced by the numbers of competitors for premiums. The cattle were good and some of the saddle horses, fine. The exhibit of vegetables was gratifying and of cereals there was much to be said in praise.

In the ladies' department were exhibits of needlecraft and fabrics from the looms of the nation, showing a lively interest in household arts; and there was even a collection of paintings to grace the exhibit.[11]

Three years later, the Grand Council of Indian Territory organized an Indian International Fair, held at Muskogee, Creek Nation, in which all the tribes in Indian Territory were invited to participate. Substantial premiums were provided, and the neighboring states, especially Arkansas, were invited to come over and see for themselves that Indians were not hopelessly given over to impeding progress. The plains Indians were in attendance and full blood choirs sang in their native tongue. There were veterans' reunions, a temperance meeting, and a Sunday School Convention.[12] This Indian International Fair became an established institution which lasted a number of years.

Associated with economic rehabilitation were cultural and religious revivals. Churches were rebuilt, Sunday Schools started, and the Baptist Association returned to the custom of holding its annual camp-meetings, which were widely attended by members of that denomination and others.

Temperance societies were particularly active and much could be said for the manner in which they helped to counteract the baleful influence of bootleggers from over the border, operating to undermine the morale of the people even within hailing distance of the federal garrison at Fort Gibson.

One of the most active leaders in the temperance movement in the Cherokee Nation was Mrs. E. Jane Stapler, daughter of that staunch old patriot, Elijah Hicks. Mrs. Stapler, who was called the "Mother of the Presbyterian Church" at Tahlequah, was a half-breed[13] Cherokee, who as a child attended Dwight Mission, finishing her education at Mt. Holyoke. In 1871 she organized the first Sunday School in Tahlequah and served it as superintendent for twenty-one years.

At the celebration of the Golden Anniversary of that church, this tribute was paid to "Aunt Jane's" memory: "When I look backward down the sixty years of my recollection I see Aunt Jane Stapler on her errands of aid to the unfortunate, ministry to the sick, and prayers and consolation to the bereaved. I see myself as a little boy carrying a lantern, accompanying her through the dark night on her missions."[14]

Behind the low white picket fence across the street from the Council Ground, her pleasant home was open to high and low alike. Among many noted guests who enjoyed her hospitality was her friend and co-worker, Frances Willard.

Associated with Mrs. Stapler in every good work was Mrs. Eliza Alberty, sister of Chief Dennis W. Bushyhead, and daughter of the native missionary, Reverend Jesse Bushyhead. She was a member of the Baptist Church and an active social worker. At the National Hotel, her home for many years, she dispensed hospitality to many distinguished guests who visited the territory before statehood. "Aunt Eliza" had a way with young people that was inimitable, particularly with the boys and girls from the seminaries, whom she sometimes entertained over the weekend. She invariably sent them back to work healed of home-sickness and renewed in courage and ambition. That historic hostelry was a national institution under her management, for Mrs. Alberty was a diplomat of rare charm and tact as well as a successful business woman.

Another well-remembered Cherokee woman was Mrs. Narcissa Chisholm Owen. Born in the Cherokee Nation West, educated at Dwight and in Virginia, where she married Colonel Owen and lived until her sons were educated, Mrs. Owen had enjoyed the experiences of broader contacts than most of her tribal contemporaries. When she returned to the Cherokee Nation in the early eighties to take a place on the faculty of the Park Hill Seminary, where she taught music, she was easily the most distinguished woman in the nation. As an example of all that was admirable and worthy of emulation "Auntie Owen" exercised a greater influence upon the personality of Cherokee girls than any teacher of her time.

This handsome daughter of a chief of the Cherokee Nation West was not only a musician but an artist of note, whose studio in the Corcoran Art Gallery in Washington for a time was a favorite gathering place for Cherokees visiting the national capitol. And there is a volume of Memoirs from her pen which is much prized for its contribution to Cherokee history. Of the many talented and devoted women of this nation, none have exercised a more wholesome influence upon the ideals and aspirations of Cherokee womanhood of the nineteenth century or have been cherished with a deeper affection than these three: Mrs. E. Jane Stapler, Mrs. Eliza Missouri Alberty and Mrs. Narcissa Owen.

Born travelers as well as shrewd traders, the Cherokees were ever given to making pilgrimages to see what other peoples were doing and thinking that would benefit them to know. With the return of prosperity an increasing number of progressive tribes-men were enabled to broaden their experience and knowledge by travel. When, on May 10, 1876, the Centennial Exposition was inaugurated at Philadelphia by President Grant, several prominent Cherokee citizens attended. In their party was Ed D. Hicks, a youth of sixteen, who saw there for the first time a telephone which Alexander Graham Bell had on exhibition. This new invention interested the youth strangely, and upon his return home he determined to fathom its mysteries. After ten years of intensive study, Mr. Hicks was prepared to give to his nation the advantages of the first telephone system introduced into the Indian Territory himself, installing the long-distance line from Tahlequah to Muskogee.[15]

CHAPTER 21

Rebuilding the Broken Walls: The Nation

While the people had been engaged in the economic, religious, and social rehabilitation of the nation, their officials were grappling with the political questions of reconstruction. The death of John Ross at so critical a time had complicated the task. Those who had been accustomed to his leadership in times of doubt and uncertainty were overwhelmed with confusion by "that Dark Treaty," scarcely a stipulation of which did not give offense to a proud and independent people, whose internal and foreign policies were to be adversely affected by it for all time to come.

The appointment of a successor to Chief John Ross devolved upon the National Council, which on November 19, 1866, chose William Potter Ross to complete the unexpired term. Although a comparatively young man, the new chief was an eminent lawyer, a distinguished educator and a statesman thoroughly familiar with national affairs.

The assistant chief, Colonel Lewis Downing, was a veteran of the Union Army, a Baptist preacher of power, and a friend to the full bloods, with whom he classed himself.[1] This "fighting parson" and uncompromising abolitionist had no use for negroes, either as slaves or as freedmen, and the thought of having them planted on the soil of his beloved nation was so far from agreeable that he never became reconciled to the treaty.

In his first message to the National Council, delivered in the presence of a large concourse of people assembled on the Capitol grounds, Chief Ross reminded them that the war was over. "Let the

Cherokee people remember that all their interest and hopes lie in union of sentiment and action. However profitable to others, strife is fatal to ourselves." For the benefit of the Confederate Cherokees who lacked the means of returning home, he recommended an extension of the time allowed by the existing law governing abandoned improvements;[2] stressed the need of giving immediate attention to schools and to war orphans; and warned nation and individual against all untoward words and acts that might lead to the loss of tribal autonomy.

In regard to the late treaty, he assured them that, whatever their opinion might be as to the justice and wisdom of some of its stipulations, their duty was to comply with all its terms in good faith, since it was the very best their delegation had been able to secure. By this course alone was it possible to render harmless those articles that required changes in the constitution, changes which, he feared, contained germs of discord and strife.

This message, well though it was meant, did not register agreeably with the multitude, who would have preferred hearing the treaty denounced outright as an unqualified outrage, particularly those promises guaranteeing freedmen and free negroes, who had been living in the nation prior to the war, full rights of citizenship with the Cherokees themselves, than which no other demand upon them gave greater offense.

In spite of his plea for precaution, feeling against the negroes ran high until it became so pronounced that the freedmen finally appealed to Washington asking for protection and for a separate tract of land of their own,[3] a policy which some far-sighted patriots advocated. Colonel Downing favored it,[4] and the federal government appointed a commission to go to Fort Smith, Arkansas for the purpose of conducting an investigation. But little ever came of the movement except the assurance from Washington that freedmen would be secured in their treaty rights.

Thus reassured and encouraged, the malcontents grew more amenable to public opinion, more docile; the noisy self-conscious and aggressive leaders at length withdrawing to remote, unoccupied areas of land to form segregated negro settlements,[5] where they could sit under their own vines and fig trees, enjoying the social contacts so dear to black folk; and where they found satisfaction in their separate schools, their churches, and their biennial visits from native political aspirants seeking the "colored vote."[6]

While the freedman question was being thus adjudicated and other reconstruction measures were receiving the serious attention of the Government at Tahlequah, the Cherokee secession problem automatically solved itself. The treaty had allowed the northern and southern factions two years in which to compound their differences, reserving to the President of the United States the right to interfere in event of internecine strife.[7] Long before the allotted time had expired, the southern refugees had settled the question by returning to their old homesteads and repossessing such improvements as had escaped the ravages of war. In no time at all they were thoroughly absorbed in the familiar tasks of building and planting on soil endeared to them by former associations, while their leaders concentrated their constructive genius upon the problems of national readjustment and reorganization.[8]

Permitting no grass to grow under their feet, this Southern group made tactful overtures to some members of the opposition with the result that during the winter of 1867 various meetings, held to discuss the treaty, were attended by delegates from both factions. "A free interchange of opinions was given relative to the matter of the differences that divided them, plans of union were discussed and a better feeling and more perfect understanding resulted."[9] Such was the report to the office of Indian Affairs that year.

About this time an estrangement began to develop between the first and second chiefs over real or fancied disagreements on reconstruction policies. This coolness eventually led to a split in the National Party, fostered, it has been said, by John B. Jones, the missionary, who wielded a powerful influence over the full bloods who were predominantly Baptist in faith. The *entente cordiale* growing out of the winter meetings made possible a coalition of the Downing adherents and the Southern faction to form a People's Party in time for the election. The ticket was headed by Assistant Chief Downing, himself, with James Vann, a former Confederate officer, as his running mate. Both candidates were elected.

The People's Party thereupon changed its name to the Downing Party. One of the most significant features in connection with the election was the peaceful character of the campaign. No blood was shed, no disorder inflamed the people's minds to acts of violence. Without outside assistance from anywhere,[10] the Cherokee people had handled a delicate political readjustment in accordance with their own conception of democracy, and with characteristic adaptiveness the parties at once began to take council together on measures of pressing importance.

Thus the unity and integrity of the Cherokee Nation were preserved, and a sense of harmony the people had not known for many years came at length to pervade the country. Now and then, to be sure, came little political differences that were soon composed, after which everybody went on working shoulder to shoulder for the good of the nation. With disparagement to no one and credit to all, it may be said in all sincerity that the compromise, with Lewis Downing as principal chief of the nation, was a happy one for all concerned; his leadership being largely non-partisan, was religious as well as political among a people, many of whom associated religion with politics somewhat as they had done in ancient times.

While the people were prosperous and busy, they were also uneasy because of the persistent efforts of Congress to extend a territorial form of government over Indian Territory. Their agent, John B. Jones, at length registered a protest against the activity on the part of those senators and congressmen at Washington who spent entire nights canvassing ways and means of cleverly putting through this measure, regardless of the welfare or wishes of the tribes concerned.[11]

"It is a matter of such vital interest to them that the whole nation is most profoundly moved on the subject," he said. "Masses of people, including the most intelligent and patriotic, oppose it. One of the strongest motives which can be brought to bear upon the wild tribes[12] to induce them to adopt civilization would be for the civilized Indians to be able to point to their own condition of elevation and comfort and to testify that the people and government of the United States fulfill all obligations to the civilized tribes and secure them in their rights and immunities."[13]

This constant threat from the outside, hanging over them like the sword of Damocles, tended to draw the people closer together as a common danger often tends to concentrate attention on problems of defense and to create a spirit of unity and cooperation too often lacking among American aborigines. By 1871, "Civil War animosities had died down and both factions were living side by side in peace and friendship."[14]

Chief Downing was reelected in August of that year, and upon his death a few months later the National Council elected William P. Ross to complete the unexpired term. It was during this administration that the first decade of peace drew to a close. The Cherokees could now say that, as far as they were able to do so, they had conformed in all good faith to the terms of "the Dark Treaty," but how, in the name of outraged justice, had the other contracting party discharged its obligations, they frequently asked.

The settlement of friendly tribes within Cherokee borders began in 1867 with the coming of the Delawares, who, having disposed of their reservation in the vicinity of West Port, Kansas, the Delawares paid into the treasury of the Cherokee Nation a sum agreed upon by both parties. These "Grandfathers of all Indians" then moved down across the Kansas border to found homes on unoccupied lands in the northern part of the Cherokee Nation. Thenceforward they became merged with the Cherokees as citizens of the nation.[15] The Shawnees followed the Delawares, and in 1872 came the Osages, who had secured a reservation in the eastern extremity of the Cherokee Outlet. Some smaller tribes settled on reservations in the northeastern corner of the Cherokee Nation, each under its own tribal management.[16]

Among the last arrivals was a band of their own Cherokee tribesmen from North Carolina, who came on the "MK and T Railroad to Choteau in good railroad cars." Detraining there, they camped on the prairie while messengers, dispatched to Tahlequah, notified the "chiefs and headmen" of their arrival and brought back official recognition of the band as citizens of the nation.[17]

In addition to the friendly Indians came also some white intruders who had been such a source of annoyance before the war. Of these there were two classes: One, spuriously claiming Cherokee blood,[18] filed claims for citizenship and, while their cases were pending, "squatted" on desirable lands which they monopolized indefinitely without paying rent or taxes; the other class came in, boldly and brazenly defying authority, while they waited for Grant or Cleveland or Roosevelt to do as much for them as Jackson had done for their grandfathers. Both classes complained bitterly that their children were denied admission to the free schools of the nation.

Washington furnished no relief from this intolerable situation, notwithstanding its guarantee of protection "against interruption or intrusion from all unauthorized citizens of the United States."[19] The more aggressive and affluent among them organized, employed counsel, and prepared to push their cases actively. Claims that had been disallowed by the Cherokee Citizenship Court were appealed to United States authority on the ground of unjust discrimination. The result was a conflict between Cherokee officials and the federal agents who were under obligations to remove them. Instead of removing them, they frequently issued certificates to those whose titles had been denied, authorizing them to hold the lands now in their possession until a final settlement had been reached.[20]

Within fifteen years after the war closed there were in the Cherokee Nation five hundred and thirty-one families whose claims to citizenship had been denied by the Cherokee Court, and two hundred fifty-three claimants whose cases had not been tried.[21] All remained in the nation to complicate enormously the enforcement of law and order, with the neighboring states looking on and complaining of disorderliness among the natives. So harassed became the Cherokees at last that they cried out in desperation, "We are willing that the wild tribes of the plains be settled on our lands, but we emphatically object to the settlement of wild white men from the states among us."[22]

All the while they were building, plowing, planting orchards, improving the quality of their livestock, launching new enterprises and sending their children to school, the people kept a watchful eye on Tahlequah, whence came much of the inspiration and the direction of all progress. And there are interesting data showing with what energy and intelligence the leaders of the nation had thrown themselves into the work of rehabilitation.

There were acts providing for schools and the care of orphan children, for repairing the office of the *Cherokee Advocate* and the two national high schools, for enclosing the public square with a substantial fence, and for building a brick council house two stories high on the Council Ground, a spacious colonial structure, provided with suitable committee rooms, senate chamber, council hall, executive offices, and library, at a cost of $22,000.

Appropriations were made also to found an orphan asylum and a home for the deaf, dumb, blind, and insane of the nation. Nor did they neglect to provide a jail for the punishment and reformation of criminals, behind which, in the jail yard, stood a scaffold for the execution of murderers and confirmed horse thieves.[23] Feeling for the enforcement of law was strong and crime was no more prevalent than in the adjoining states.[24]

Thus it had required little more than a decade to reconstruct their government, to place the Cherokees under shelter, to restore harmony, to settle tribes from Kansas within their borders, to greet tolerantly the arrival of a railroad, to clear and plant thousands of acres of land, to set out orchards, to increase their flocks and herds, and to put a little money in their pockets.

Editorial Commentary for Chapters 22–30

Rachel Caroline Eaton lived through the history she describes in the following pages. This section will perhaps be most interesting to readers, as it contains information not discussed in her previous book, *John Ross and the Cherokee Indians*, which ends with a chapter on Reconstruction. Eaton grew up in the Cherokee Nation with a strong sense of community and kinship, values that remain clear in her descriptions of the history her community experienced during her lifetime. In the aftermath of the Civil War, Cherokees began rebuilding their nation and invested in institutions like the Cherokee Female Seminary, which Eaton herself attended and later taught at. In the late eighteenth and early nineteenth centuries, Cherokees faced new threats to land and sovereignty with railroads, allotment, land grabs, Oklahoma statehood, and the end of US recognition of the Cherokee Nation government. Today, we still have some of our allotment land in our family, but much of it was sold within my (Patricia Dawson's) lifetime. For Eaton, who lived most of her life before Oklahoma statehood, the attack on Cherokee sovereignty was devastating, which she poetically attests to at the end of her book. But she still called herself a citizen of the Cherokee Nation even after the United States attempted to dissolve the Nation's government. Today, the US government recognizes the Cherokee Nation government, and in 2020 the US Supreme Court ruled in *McGirt v. Oklahoma* that Cherokee land in Oklahoma is a reservation.

Cherokee Freedmen continued to face many challenges at this time, even as they invested in community alongside other Cherokees. Many Indigenous Nations have strong Afro-Indigenous communities, including the Cherokee Nation. Cherokee Freedmen were formerly enslaved or descendants of enslaved Black Cherokees. As Eaton notes in earlier chapters, the Treaty of 1866 granted Cherokee citizenship to Cherokee Freedmen. Cherokee Freedmen were enrolled on a separate roll on the Dawes Rolls but were considered citizens of the Nation. In the 1980s, the Cherokee Nation claimed that Cherokee Freedmen were no longer citizens, demonstrating racial prejudice and resulting in a decades-long crisis where Cherokee Freedmen continued to fight the Cherokee Nation government for citizenship. In 2017, the US District Court ruled in *Cherokee Nation v. Nash* that Cherokee Freedmen have citizenship, but the Cherokee Nation still has much work to do toward ensuring equity. While Eaton appears to support Cherokee Freedmen's citizenship, she sometimes uses outdated and prejudiced language in her discussions of Cherokee Freedmen's history.

Readers should note that there is an instance in chapter 26 on p. 238 where the author quotes a racist man who uses the reprehensible N-word. Eaton herself sometimes uses what is now outdated and offensive language such as "half-breed," and "wild tribes." Eaton wrote this history in the 1930s, and as it is both a historical monograph and a historical document, we have elected to keep the original language.

CHAPTER 22

The Restoration
of Schools

In addition to disrupting the political and economic life of the
Cherokees, the Civil War had completely effaced their schools. In
advancing the people at home and giving them prestige abroad,
their public school system, the first of its kind west of the Mississippi,[1] had proved to be an asset too valuable in the past to be
neglected in the future. Consequently, in the plans for national
rehabilitation, much attention was given to education. Chief William P. Ross, in his message to the National Council in the fall
of 1866, recommended that immediate attention be given to the
restoration of schools, and to the care of orphans, "whose number
the war had increased as it had lessened the ability of their friends
to care for them."[2]

The following March, thirty-two primary schools were opened,
at each of which five orphans might be educated at a cost not to
exceed thirty dollars a month for board and clothing. An appropriation of $8,200.00 was made by the National Council for the main-
tenance of these schools, including the cost of textbooks.[3]

Additional schools were established from time to time, as there
was need for them and as funds became available, until in 1887
there were one hundred of these little seats of learning placed here
and there throughout the nation wherever they were required. The
enrollment was upwards of four thousand and the average attendance something less than sixty percent.[4]

For each primary school there was a local board of three members appointed by the superintendent of education. This board had

general supervision of the school with the responsibility of providing a suitable building, properly furnished by the community.

The National Council appointed the superintendent of education, who selected the teachers, was responsible for the purchase of textbooks and necessary stationery for the schools, and for the equitable distribution of supplies. It was his duty to visit the schools at stated intervals and inspect them, in order that he might make a report to the National Council each year. He also held teachers' examinations and passed on the qualifications of all employees of the seminaries and the orphan asylum. In later years, a national board of education, of three members, replaced the superintendent of education.

Teachers were appointed with regard to moral and physical, no less than intellectual fitness. Everything else being equal, preference was given to Cherokee citizens. A few non-citizens were always employed, however, especially in the faculties of the seminaries. Of the one hundred and three primary teachers for the school year ending June 1887, eighty-nine were natives, thirty-three speaking both languages: Eight of these had received their education at the Cherokee Orphan Asylum, thirty-two at the Male and Female Seminaries, two at Worcester Academy, and three at Baptist University. From these figures it will be seen that the Cherokees themselves were engaged in educating, as rapidly as could be expected, a sufficient number of their own citizens to supply their schools with instructors.[5]

Ten years after the first schools were opened, the Indian agent reported to his chief in Washington that the Cherokees were provided with ample advantages for the education of all their children, even up to a degree of advancement equal to that furnished by ordinary colleges in the states; the common day schools were kept open ten months[6] in the year; their two high schools had commodious and well-furnished buildings designed after the best style of architecture and equipped with furniture and fixtures of the latest and best manufacture. "Strangers visiting the nation for the first time," he said, "were surprised to meet so many well-educated people."[7]

A few years later, Dr. T. A. Bland, the general agent for the National Indian Defense Association, who had spent several months visiting the different tribes of the Indian Territory, said in his report: "There is not in the Cherokee Nation an Indian, man, woman, boy or girl, of sound mind, fifteen years of age, or over who cannot read and write."[8] Twenty years before statehood, therefore, there was no illiteracy in the Cherokee Nation among the natives. What ignorance existed must be ascribed to the freedmen blacks and the noncitizen whites, both alien races. At the time disintegrating forces, operating from without, began to lay possessive hands on this noble little experiment in civilized Indian culture, it was a model of its kind never surpassed by any tribe or nation.

While the primary school system was developing, the seminaries, due to lack of funds, were compelled to wait several years for their turn. Fortunately, the two substantial brick buildings, though badly damaged,[9] had been spared demolition by the opposing armies during the war. By means of an appropriation made by the National Council in 1872, the buildings were repaired and enlarged;[10] to each of the old structures, which were two-story and of brick, was added a three-story annex which increased the dimensions to one hundred eighty-five feet in length and one hundred nine in breadth.

Set in spacious grounds, the buildings never failed to surprise and charm all who saw them. For dignity and simplicity of architecture, they were said to resemble the Greek Parthenon, while verandahs, supported by stately columns surmounted by Greek Doric capitals, produced an effect of classic beauty that harmonized admirably with the background of natural scenery, which served as a perfect setting for these two crown jewels of the nation.

The Park Hill Seminary was opened in 1872 with Miss Ella Noyes of Mount Holyoke as principal.[11] Since the nation was still short of school funds and so many orphans were in crying need of attention, it was decided to use the Male Seminary buildings and grounds as a temporary refuge for these desolated war victims. On March 28, 1872, Reverend W. A. Duncan, the superintendent, and S. S. Stephens, the principal, at the head of fifty-four children, entered that stately edifice, which must have appeared a veritable "House of many mansions" to the homeless children, and with an appropriate ceremony, opened the Cherokee Orphan Asylum.[12]

Up to this time, orphans had been cared for by relatives or by religious institutions. Hence-forward, between the ages of nine and sixteen they were fed, clothed, and educated in a Christian home provided for them by "Mother Nation, who was always more than kind to her children."[13]

In 1875 the institution was removed to a permanent location at Grand Saline[14] near the site of the historic Choteau trading post. There the plantation of Lewis Ross, one time "Prince of Indian merchants," had been converted into a model farm, and the three-story mansion, remodeled and enlarged to accommodate the orphanage.[15]

The spirit of this institution set it apart as an illustration of what an Indian nation can do when it sets its hand to a task. For twenty-eight years, during sixteen of which Reverend Joseph Thompson served as superintendent, there was never an act of violence committed by an inmate nor a complaint of ill-treatment by the students against the faculty. It was a large, well-ordered family from which a goodly number went forth to achieve distinction, and none to careers of violence or shame.[16]

After the removal of the orphans, the Male Seminary was again occupied by the boys. The course of study was revised and modernized[17] to give the seminary proper a four year course in English, history, mathematics, foreign languages, science, philosophy and the Bible. In addition to these, music, drawing and physical training were given some attention.

Life within these institutions was regulated strictly by a daily schedule prepared by the faculty and approved by the superintendent of education. A "rising bell" each morning signaled the time for everyone to get up and dress for the day, and an hour was spent in the study hall before breakfast; an hour and a half devoted to breakfast and detail duty brought the day up to half-past eight and chapel. Recitations began at nine and closed at four, with an hour's intermission at noon. When the weather permitted, outdoor recreation was required before supper, which was served at six. There was study hall again in the evening, after which followed the first, and then the second, retiring bell with lights out for the night at half past nine. Attendance in the Sunday School, conducted in the institution, was required of all students.[18]

The social life of the schools was given some attention. From time to time, entertainments and receptions were held, but the most important social event of the school year, next to commencement, was the annual May Day picnic. It was held on the anniversary of the founding of the seminaries, at the historic Illinois Camp Ground, which, with its large spring of excellent water, grounds shaded by primeval forest trees, and its clear swift little river, was an ideal location for such gatherings.

The students and faculties of both seminaries and citizens of the surrounding country attended. For the young people there were games and boating, and for all there were the happiest of greetings and much merry chatter. To crown all came the noonday feast, when an abundance of very fine barbecued beef, prepared in true Indian fashion, was served with other delectable viands on a long table at which notables of the nation rubbed elbows with future notables in friendly fashion.

These social contacts and wholesome outdoor recreation had a definite place in the greater national scheme, cultivating, as they did, a wide acquaintance among young people in different sections of the nation and cementing friendships that have been known to last a lifetime.

In these and other ways the schools helped to foster a spirit of cooperation among the men and women busily engaged in rebuilding the broken walls while their girls and boys were being prepared to fill positions of usefulness and honor in the national polity. The quality and character of the classroom instruction under competent instructors, close association in boarding school with homogeneous groups in familiar and wholly agreeable environment, produced a type of educated Indian well-calculated to advance the standard of the nation in which he expected to make his home and fortune.

Much might be said of the teachers who sent out from the fostering walls of these institutions hundreds of young people inspired with lofty ideals of democracy and loyal Christian citizenship. Some of them were native Cherokees and a few men and women were from the states, selected with careful regard to qualifications. A volume could be written about these teachers alone, but little would be gained by singling out a few for special mention, gratifying though it would be to name them. Suffice it to say that they were men and women distinguished for culture and refinement whose names are enshrined in the hearts of those who have survived the passing years.

The Park Hill Seminary was destroyed by fire on April 10, 1887.[19] This was a total loss to the nation as the insurance had expired a day or two before the catastrophe. But Chief Bushyhead, never a man to waste a moment in weak regret, called a special session of the National Council, which convened in May and made an appropriation of sixty thousand dollars for a new building.[20]

The following November, the corner stone was laid, the veteran educator and statesman, William Potter Ross, making the chief address. In May 1889 the new building was dedicated,[21] not on the old site at Park Hill, but on a new one adjoining the city of Tahlequah, the most favorable location that could have been found anywhere in the Southwest.

A relatively small proportion of the nation's young people ever reached the seminaries, but the mass of the population had the primary schools brought to their very doors. The level of literacy, therefore, depended in more ways than one on the rural institutions. In order to raise the standard of instruction in these rural schools by improving the qualification of teachers, a normal training school was introduced on the recommendation of the Board of Education in 1886–87. Citizens of the nation were privileged to attend free of tuition, but at their own cost of board and room; and non-citizens were admitted on payment of a reasonable tuition fee.[22]

In compliance with the Treaty of 1866, fourteen separate primary schools had been provided by the Cherokee Nation for the children of freedmen.[23] In addition to primary schools, there was a colored high school situated four miles north of Tahlequah. Appointment of students on the basis of competitive examinations was made every two years. When attendance dropped below the average of twenty-five, the school was to be discontinued. The course of study was arranged primarily for the purpose of training teachers for the primary colored schools.[24]

The only classes of people within its boundaries for whose children the Cherokee Nation did not provide some sort of free school facilities were the non-citizens—white and black—intruders, and railroad and federal employees. To neither of these classes did the nation owe any obligations whatever, as they were under federal jurisdiction and acknowledged no allegiance to the country in which they were sojourning.

The white licensed renters, operating under a legal permit from the Cherokee Nation, constituted a different class. Having placed themselves under the laws of the nation, pledged to good behavior and constantly under the surveillance of the citizens who stood good for them month after month, the renters were privileged to send their children to the primary schools by paying a nominal tuition fee, provided such schools had room to accommodate them.

In the larger towns, subscription schools were maintained at the expense of the patrons and independent of national control. Each of these local systems served as a nucleus for a larger organization after the Curtis Act went into effect.

Supplementary to the Cherokee National school system and in complete accord with its policies were missions of the various denominations. The missionaries, who had been forced to flee during the War of the Rebellion, returned with the cessation of hostilities. On their arrival, they were compelled to reestablish their missions, whose buildings and equipment had been destroyed. With a fine optimism and courage, each and every one set about the task of reconstruction, the Moravians and the Baptists taking the lead, with other denominations following. When schools had been re-established and churches restored, the work of propagating the gospel went forward with renewed zeal. Reconstruction without the aid of the missionaries would have lacked something of the fine Christian fortitude and forbearance that characterized it.[25]

The reconstruction period found the Cherokees more school-minded than they had ever been before. Parents who had been deprived of the advantages of education coveted them for their children. Experiences gained during the war in which the entire citizenship of the nation had been forced into contact with white people, either with the shifting, swarming, acquisitive hordes of the North or the static particularists of the South, had furnished them food for thought and direction for action. All the people of the nation had been places and had seen things, some of which were worth adapting to their own needs.

Following the trend of the times, the Cherokees in 1870 organized an agricultural society with the intention of developing the natural resources of the nation on a scientific basis. As an aid to training their young men they conceived the idea of an agricultural high school which they planned to found at Tahlequah with the view to securing for a location the building and grounds from the Baptist school at that place. John B. Jones, the agent for the Cherokees and a man well qualified to appraise their needs, presented in his report to the Commissioner of Indian Affairs in 1871 the recommendation that federal aid be given for such a school. The plan was not approved at Washington. However, it was destined to live in the minds of the people and to reappear in a more ambitious scheme some years later.

An event of more than ordinary interest during the period of the eighties was the Inter-tribal Educational Convention, held at Muskogee in September 1884. Delegates representing each of the Five Civilized Tribes were in attendance. A permanent organization was effected and a full quota of officers elected. The Cherokees, who were astute politicians and who could always be trusted to carry off their share of the honors, secured the election of Reverend W. A. Duncan, a veteran Cherokee educator, as president. Robert L. Owen, a young man recently graduated from Washington and Lee University, in Virginia, was made treasurer. Miss Alice Robertson, of the Creek Nation, was chosen secretary of the association, and Miss Ada Archer, a member of the Park Hill Seminary faculty, vice president for the Cherokee Nation. Each nation was entitled to a vice president.

The organization started a movement to secure an industrial and mechanical training school for Indians, similar to the Indian Training School at Carlisle, Pennsylvania. The convention sent a resolution to Congress petitioning that the military post at Fort Gibson be abandoned and the buildings donated to the uses of the proposed school.[26] The project was doomed to failure from the beginning, owing chiefly to the seeming inability of tribal leaders to carry out any cooperative plan requiring sustained agreement and unity of action.

Another worthy project entertained by the Cherokees was a national library and museum to be maintained at the expense of the nation. The plan had its inception as far back as 1825, if not farther. How much the missionaries had to do with it is not known. Major Lowrey and the venerable Path Killer were certainly behind it, both being interested in preserving relics of their ancient arts and science and their tribal lore and legends. All too soon, Georgia put a ban on this ambitious project by sending the people into exile after confiscating their printing press and council house with all the tribal archives.

The idea of a public library persisting, outlived the men whose brain conceived it. In those lean years after the war, there was no money, and with the return of prosperity came many new demands on the national treasury, and fewer incentives to build enduringly, any new enterprise. When the time came for the dissolution of the tribal government, a valiant effort was made by a few devoted men and women under the leadership of Mrs. Eliza Alberty to have the Cherokee Council House reserved for the use of a library and museum, for the maintenance of which Congress was to be asked to make an appropriation.

Much that was valuable historically could have been preserved in that way and made available to students of history who seek for it in vain today. As a museum the plan held intriguing possibilities at the time interest was most active. Northeastern State Teachers

College and the Carnegie Library at Tahlequah, have done something towards carrying out this idea.

The dissolution of the tribal government was brought about by the passage of the Curtis Act and the subsequent measure called the Cherokee Allotment Agreement.[27] The Cherokee Nation under their operation lost the control of its school system when the United States government took over the tribal funds, which thereafter were to be disbursed by the Secretary of the Interior through federal agents.

In 1899 Mr. John D. Benedict, of Illinois, took charge as Superintendent of Education for the Five Tribes, with Mr. Benjamin S. Coppock as Supervisor for the Cherokee Nation. The federal policy was to consolidate the schools of the Five Civilized Tribes into one organic whole, which, by the aid of congressional appropriation, "would shape toward a workable system for an organization of county and state schools."[28]

The two Seminaries continued to operate for two years after the dissolution of the nation. In the summer of 1909, "as the time was approaching for winding up all tribal affairs,"[29] the Female Seminary and its beautiful grounds were sold to the state for a Normal Training School. In September the two high schools were combined, continuing their courses at the Male Seminary until March 20th. On that date, the historic building was destroyed by fire. Thus ended the Cherokee National Male and Female Seminaries, the primary schools having already passed into the system outlined in the Curtis Act.[30]

As long as the Cherokees maintained exclusive control of their schools there was no illiteracy among them. Those who did not speak English could both read and write in their own language. With the passage of the Curtis Act and the subsequent merging of their schools with the state system, that region of Oklahoma which once constituted the Cherokee Nation lost something rare and fine in native culture and civilized Indian institutional achievements.

Only within recent years have government officials and educators begun to admit that a wise and beneficent United States government has made a mistake, and that it would do well to go a long way back and begin all over again with the Indian question, letting the Indians themselves act as leaders and guides in the training of their young people, with the government furnishing only material support and assistance. As a race, Indians are endowed with the ability to impart as well as to acquire knowledge, and the fact has long been recognized that the Cherokees were ever their own best teachers.

CHAPTER 23

The Railroads and the Okmulgee Constitution

The Fort Smith Peace Council had adjourned in September 1865. On the following December 12, James H. Lane, senator from Kansas, introduced a bill in the United States Senate for the organization of the Indian Territory.[1] On March 17, 1870, Senator Rice of Arkansas proposed a bill to establish the Territory of Oklahoma.[2] Between these two events more than a dozen similar measures were brought before Congress under one name or another, but all looking towards a territorial form of government for the Indian Territory.[3] Among them were three bills for its organization as the territory of Lincoln.[4] None of these bills, however, provided for the type of territorial organization contemplated by Secretary Harlan in 1865.

During the four years from 1866 to 1870, the Cherokee Nation had scrupulously conformed to treaty stipulations. The constitution had been amended to meet the changes prescribed; citizenship had been conferred upon Cherokee freedmen, and schools provided for their children; factional differences had composed and some Kansas tribes had been located on the nation's domain. Three main events of the next few years were the coming of railroads, the meetings of the inter-tribal council and the establishment of federal courts.

The Treaty of 1866, which was ratified by Congress on July 27, granted the right of way to two railroads across the Cherokee Nation, one from north to south, and the other from east to west. Their charters, issued by Congress on July 26 and 27, entitled each to a land-grant subsidy on the condition that the Indian lands ever became public domain.[5]

The Missouri, Kansas and Texas railroad reached the Cherokee Nation in June 1870, and in 1872 was completed to Preston, Texas. Railroad officials now could ride triumphantly through the "Beautiful Indian Territory," appraise its resources and prepare to launch the next project on their program.[6]

The road from east to west, chartered as the Atlantic and Pacific, after crossing the Grand River in May 1872, was extended to a junction with the Missouri, Kansas and Texas, at Vinita,[7] a distance of thirty-six miles. Here construction stopped when it became apparent that the Indian title would not be extinguished, nor the land opened to settlement.[8] It was ten years before the road reached the Arkansas River.[9]

The advantages afforded by these railroads were not underestimated by the Cherokees who had occasion to use them. Agriculture and the range cattle industry, receiving new impetus, launched more ambitious programs as markets were made accessible by rapid transit. Train loads of livestock and grain, shipped to Kansas City, St. Louis, and Chicago, found a ready market, and the money and commodities for which they were exchanged brought unaccustomed luxuries into many homes that had been reduced to extremity by the war. Gradually the people began to travel more by train and found it pleasant as well as stimulating.

Unfortunately, railroad building through the Indian Territory was attended by some disadvantages to its people. When their work was completed, the construction gangs moved on, leaving behind them tracts of land denuded of timber that had taken several lifetimes to produce. Such a loss was viewed with consternation by this tribe of builders and conservationists who regarded the forests as reserves to be utilized thriftily for shelter for themselves and refuge for the wildlife that harbored there. The wanton extermination of game by officials, as well as by workmen, and especially by irresponsible travelers from the states, who were too often "careless with fire,"[10] was almost as appalling to the Cherokees as was the senseless slaughter of the buffalo to the wild tribes.[11] There is no question of the disintegrating influence of the railroads on the Indian Territory.

All the while the South was being reconstructed under a carpet-bag regime and the North revolutionized by gigantic financial enterprises, the government had done nothing about article twelve of the Dark Treaty. Four years had now elapsed and still the Secretary of the Interior had not called the general council agreed upon in 1866, although Congress had entertained measure after measure for the reorganization of Indian Territory under one plan or another, and railroads were actively seeking a change that would validate their provisional land-grant subsidies.

The treaty provided that the Secretary of the Interior should fix the time and place of meeting of the council, whose sessions were limited to a period of thirty days. Each tribe was entitled to representation in proportion to its population, and Congress was empowered to appropriate a sufficient fund to cover the expenses of the meeting, including the per diem and the mileage of the delegates.

The function of this council was "to legislate upon matters pertaining to the intercourse and relations of the tribes and nations of Indians and the colonies of freedmen residing in Indian Territory; the arrest and extradition of criminals escaping from one tribe to another; the administration of justice between the citizens of the Indian Territory and aliens from the states; and the common defense of the different nations of the Territory."[12]

When on March 17, 1870, Senator Benjamin F. Rice, of Arkansas, introduced a bill for the organization of the territory under the name of Oklahoma Territory, and the bill had been reported favorably out of committee, the Indians determined to take the initiative themselves by calling for an intertribal council.

On September 27, and again on December 5, the first meeting of the Grand Council convened at Okmulgee,[13] and a permanent organization was effected with Enoch Hoag, the superintendent of the Southern Superintendency, presiding. Delegates from the Five Civilized Tribes and several of the wild tribes were present.

One of the first acts of the convention was to pass a resolution calling for a memorial to be sent to the President and to Congress protesting against any legislation that would impair the obligations of existing treaty guarantees; against the sale or grant of lands to railroads or corporations chartered for the purpose of constructing such roads, other than those already chartered by treaty; objecting to the creation of a territorial form of government over them other than that of the General Council; and requesting that the people be organized under a government of their own choice, republican in form, with its powers clearly defined, and with full guarantees given for all the powers, rights, and privileges reserved to them in their treaties.[14]

In the midst of these deliberations there arrived at Okmulgee four distinguished agents of the government. On the afternoon of the thirteenth, the president of the convention introduced the "Honorable Eli. S. Parker, Commissioner of Indian Affairs, who delivered an address setting forth his views as to the wishes and expectations of the Government and of friends of the Indians throughout the United States regarding the General Council of Indian Territory," with suggestions as to the best modes of legislation to meet those expectations. He also expressed words of cheer and encouragement in this great and important undertaking.[15]

Three members of the Board of Indian Commissioners, "Messrs. Campbell, Lang and Farwell," were present also. These were men prominent in civil life, whom the President had appointed in 1869 to cooperate in an advisory capacity with the Department of the Interior in managing the Indians; this was among their first visits to the Indian Territory, and they were well pleased with conditions as they found them among the Five Tribes.[16]

On December 16, the committees on constitution reported Articles of Confederation which, after discussion and amendment, were ratified by the General Council, after which it was submitted to each of the tribal governments for adoption. The Chickasaw legislature, the first to act, rejected the Okmulgee Constitution because it provided for proportional, instead of equal representation.[17] The Creek Nation was the only nation that ratified it.

Interest in the adoption of the plan was affected by the President's objection to it on the ground that it did not give Congress the right to pass upon the legislative acts of the council. Although James H. Harlan, as chairman of the Senate Committee on Indian Affairs, twice reported bills for the ratification of the Okmulgee Constitution, it was never considered by Congress.

The General Council for the Indian Territory continued to meet for a number of years. According to the records of the Department of Indian Affairs for 1875,[18] it had not passed a single act of legislation, yet it had cost the United States sixty-six thousand, five hundred dollars. The previous year, the Secretary of the Interior had complained that the council was failing to accomplish its purpose of preparing the Indians for a territorial form of government, and that the Okmulgee Constitution did not give the United States any part in the proposed Indian organization.[19]

Nevertheless, the Indians of the Five Civilized Tribes were not indifferent nor idle during the years following the first meeting of the General Council. Convinced that the cooperation of the wild tribes, which had become their neighbors under the treaty of 1866, was essential to a confederation of all the tribes of Indian Territory, they arranged a peace council at Wichita Agency in May 1871 for the Arapahos, Cheyennes, Comanches, and for the Kiawas,[20] who were on the warpath against white hide hunters engaged in killing off their precious buffalo herds. The object was to secure attendance upon the sessions of the General Council in the hope that the civilized Indians might induce them to abandon the raiding parties, which were bringing reproach upon all the Indians of the Southwest, and to settle down to peaceable and industrious lives.[21]

But the Kiawas, to whom danger and excitement were as the breath of life, were not responsive, even when a second meeting was called, this time at Fort Cobb, in 1872, and representatives from the Civilized tribes addressed them eloquently on the advantages of settled life as compared to the insecurity of a roving existence.[22] All their reasoning was lost upon the bands which could not be induced to "turn into the bright path of peace." Deprived of their semi-annual buffalo hunts, they continued to satisfy their craving for adventure with wild raids into Texas. Time was required for them to readjust their point of view and to learn wisdom of experience, as they did eventually.

The Indian International Fair, chartered by the General Council in 1873 and held at Muskogee, helped to bring about a community of interests between the wild and the civilized tribes. Although invited and even urged to attend, at first they were slow to respond, not understanding exactly what was expected of them. Eventually, however, no one was more enthusiastic than the Pawnees, Arapahoes, and Kiawahs in entering exhibits of their handicraft, for which special prizes were provided for their benefit.[23] In 1876 fifteen tribes were represented.

The proceedings of the intertribal council during December of 1870 had been followed with interest by the friends of the railroads who objected to the organization of Indian Territory by the Indians themselves. With their own reasons for doing so, the Kansas contingent in Congress[24] had an act inserted in the Indian Appropriations Bill of March 3,1871, which decreed that no Indian nation or tribe should hereafter be acknowledged as an independent nation with which the United States might contract by treaty; but that all contracts with such tribes should be called agreements instead of treaties.[25]

The reasons for this change, as explained by the Secretary of the Interior, were to bring under the immediate control of Congress the diplomatic, as well as the commercial intercourse with the Indians in order to simplify and expedite such diplomatic negotiations as might, from time to time, become necessary in safeguarding their rights.[26]

By the treaty of 1835, the Cherokees were entitled to a delegate in the House of Representatives whenever Congress should make provision therefore. This provision was never made by Congress, but each year the National Council appropriated the expense of a delegation to Washington as each of the other civilized tribes was accustomed to do. Not infrequently these tribal delegations acted conjointly when questions of common concern were pending.

It happened in 1873, that when an especially radical Oklahoma bill[27] was before the House Committee on Territories, the Creek and Cherokee delegations combined to defeat it.[28] The obvious intention of the measure was to break down Indian autonomy in the interest of railroads under the pretense that a contest was on between civilization and savagery.

Both Creek and Cherokees were represented by able native advocates who advanced the charges that railroads were being built in advance of the demands of business and because it was a speculation to build them; and that the animus of no small part of the surrounding country came from the desire to convince Congress that Indian lands were something that could be taken with impunity whenever they became sufficiently valuable to tempt cupidity. They vigorously denied that no adequate government machinery existed in the nations of the Five Tribes; that immense herds of Texas cattle were stopped at the border[29] and not permitted to cross to market; "and that a savage Indian, with war paint and tomahawk, stood guard at the gateway of civilization."

On the contrary: "Not only have our own people exported large herds of cattle to your markets, but every year hundreds of thousands of Texas cattle are driven peaceably through our country. During the emigrant season, hundreds of emigrant-teams crowd the highways, and a murder or a robbery against them has hardly been known. In all cases between white men and Indians the jurisdiction by law and treaty is in the courts of the United States. It was provided by treaty that a distinct United States Court for the Indian Territory should be created, and we have petitioned you earnestly for its immediate creation. If it has not been so far created, the fault is yours, not ours."[30]

Since before the Civil War, there had been a crying need for a federal system of courts to deal with the large non-citizen population in the Indian Territory, over which the courts of the Five Civilized Tribes had no jurisdiction.[31] Again and again, the attention of the government had been called to this need and to the stipulation in the treaty of 1866 calling for such a system, but it took Congress twenty-three years to get round to this piece of much-needed legislation.

At the earnest solicitation of the Indians, and on the urgent rec-ommendation of the Indian agents among the Five Civilized Tribes, a United States Court was at last established at Muskogee in 1889.[32] Thereafter justice was more equitably administered in the Indian Territory over an ever increasing outland population. No longer did Indian witnesses have to make the long and expensive trip to Fort Smith as witnesses, nor unfortunate liquor-loving Cherokees, having become embroiled in a drunken quarrel with a designing white man, have to be hauled off to Fort Smith for trial. Thereafter, in cases where an Indian became embroiled with a United States citizen, he stood his trial in his own territory where his friends and tribesmen heard the testimony.

United States marshals and other federal agents located at Muskogee, Creek Nation, learned after a time to appreciate the good qualities of Indians and to even cultivate the friendship of a few. Thereafter, for a decade, a very different attitude from that of former years was taken towards the nation.[33]

CHAPTER 24

The Perpetual Outlet West

For more than a decade after the Civil War, the federal policy followed the Harlan Plan of concentrating Indians in the Indian Territory.[1] During that time, a number of tribes and fragments of tribes were located on reservations carved from lands which had been surrendered in 1866 by the Five Civilized Tribes for that purpose. In 1879, however, Congress determined that no more Indians should be removed to this region for colonization,[2] since other uses for the unoccupied lands had made their appearance.[3] The most powerful factor in bringing about this change was the railroads, which, for financial reasons, preferred to see the unassigned land settled by white men rather than by Indians, whose picturesque towns and villages were not designed to aid the corporations in paying dividends.

The Atlantic and Pacific railroad, later chartered as the St. Louis and San Francisco, the line most vitally interested in white settlement, had a right of way through the Indian Territory with the track laid to Vinita, Cherokee Nation, in the early seventies. But there was no use trying to extend its thirty-six miles of completed road through the Territory until there was a sufficient number of white settlers to support the enterprise and make it profitable.

As a matter of fact, this ambitious project was practically on the verge of bankruptcy when, on March 22, 1878, an attorney for the company appeared before a Senate investigating committee to testify regarding its financial status. "We could not build the road through a desolation of 400 or 600 miles," he averred. "The government would not give us the land we supposed they would, and the result has been that many of our people have been ruined."[4]

It was primarily in the interests of the Atlantic and Pacific and the people who were about to be ruined by its failure that the Boomer Movement was launched in 1879 by Elias Cornelius Boudinot.[5] The ulterior object of the movement was to accomplish by indirect methods what Congress had failed to do by direct ones in bringing about a territorial form of government for the Indian Territory, the allotment of lands in severalty, and the opening of surplus Indian lands to white settlement. Its immediate purpose was to call attention to the unassigned lands in the western part of the territory, to create a popular demand for their immediate availability, and to sound out the attitude of the government regarding their status.

In 1879, Colonel E. C. Boudinot was employed as clerk in the House Committee on Private Land Claims, which position gave him access to the files of the Commissioner of the General Land Office. At the same time, David L. Payne was assistant doorkeeper in the House of Representatives. Payne had lived in Kansas and had fought Indians on the plains with Custer in the winter of 1868–69.[6]

As if in reply to a Senate inquiry of the previous year regarding unoccupied lands in the Indian Territory, there appeared in the *Chicago Times* of February 17, 1879,[7] an article over the signature of Elias C. Boudinot. The article stated that the lands referred to were located in the western part of the Territory, that they had been ceded to the United States in 1866 by the Choctaw, Chickasaw, Creek, and Seminole for the purpose of settling friendly tribes upon them, and that they did not include the Cherokee Outlet.[8] A large part of this cession had not been assigned at the time Congress abandoned its policy of Indian consolidation.

Colonel Boudinot, appearing to quote from the last annual report of the Commissioner of the General Land Office, stated that the unoccupied portion of the ceded lands constituted an area of about thirteen million acres. This area, being free from Indian occupancy or title, was at present an integral part of the public domain, and as such belonged to the public without encumbrance.

In addition to the article published in the Chicago paper, the author composed a circular letter in which he gave a detailed account of the legal status of the lands in question; claiming that, since the United States possessed "an absolute and unembarrassed title to every acre" of the thirteen million, the tract was already available to white settlement. The land was the richest on the continent, was well adapted to the production of corn, wheat, and other cereals, and was unsurpassed for grazing purposes.

To supplement the letter, he prepared a "plain and accurate map," showing the location and extent of the region and indicating railroads that furnished the nearest approaches to it. He also marked the important stations on each road and computed the distance of each from the district in question.

Without doubt, the railroads had some part in the agitation that followed the appearance of this article in the *Chicago Times*, a paper reputed to be "in the pay of the railroads." The regional press gave wide publicity to it, a Kansas City paper printing a great deal of news designed to arouse interest in the Indian Territory. At any rate, the invasion that followed has the appearance of a carefully arranged plan of considerable proportions.

Before frost was out of the ground in Kansas, the mania for Indian lands was urging large numbers of people to drop whatever pursuits they were engaged in and join the mobilization camps that sprang up along the border. By April, these people were threatening to invade the Cherokee Nation from camps located at Baxter Springs and Coffeyville.[9] Farther west, spurred on by the newspapers and the telegraph companies, they had already crossed the line and were galloping over the cattle ranges of the Strip in the direction of the unassigned lands. Following those on horseback came wagonloads of men, women and children on their way to the vicinity of the Sac and Fox Agency, where they expected to stake out homesteads.[10]

There was much excitement in the border towns where businessmen hoped to profit by the movement, and among the ranchmen whose peaceful herds had been stampeded by the invaders as they passed through, spreading the report that the Outlet itself was to be opened to white settlement at an early date.

The invasion continued to threaten the Cherokee Nation, causing such perturbation among its citizens, and alarm to officials, that some thought was entertained of calling a special session of the National Council. A report brought back from the Strip by the revenue collector so increased the agitation that a telegram was dispatched to Washington apprising the President of the prevailing anxiety and asking for federal intervention against the lawless hordes of aliens threatening the security of Cherokee citizens.[11]

Ready action on the part of President Hayes in calling on the War Department[12] to quell the disturbance and remove the squatters at the point of the bayonet, if necessary, turned aside further incursions at the border, so that by May, General John Pope, who had been sent with a detachment of soldiers to clear the Indian Territory of "too-sooners" reported they were quietly returning to Kansas whence they had come.[13] It was his opinion that the whole movement had been launched for the purpose of testing the attitude of the government on the question of forcing the opening of Indian lands to white settlement.

While the invasion was in full swing, a representative from Missouri had reported to Congress a resolution of his state legislature calling for a better organization of the Indian Territory. On the same day, he introduced a new bill for the organization of the Territory of Oklahoma.[14] Thus it might be inferred that a certain amount of cooperation, discreetly managed, had supported the movement in Congress. That its collapse was not regarded as an utter failure is significant.

1879 stands out as an eventful date in the annals of the Cherokees. Not only does it mark the beginning of the Boomer Movement, which drove the entering wedge into the heart of the Indian Territory, but it introduced the modern era of politics and industry into the Cherokee Nation. The administration of Oochalata, the last full blood principal chief of the nation, came to a close in November of that year. D. W. Bushyhead succeeded him, with W. P. Adair as assistant chief. The Outlet came into prominence during that year, and for more than ten years was a dominating factor in the economic and political life of the nation.

Hitherto, infrequent mention has been made of the Outlet, commonly called the Strip, for the reason that it had played an inconspicuous part in the history of the nation before the treaty of

1866. Its origin, however, dates back to a much earlier time, when an executive agreement, made in March 1818 and reaffirmed in October 1821, granted to the Cherokees a Perpetual Outlet West. In 1828 the grant, again reaffirmed, was embodied in the Cherokee treaty of that year. In the New Echota Treaty of 1835 it was made still more specific, and three years later a patent was issued by the government which covered all the lands ceded to the Cherokees, including the Outlet. Thereafter the Cherokee Nation held these lands as it held those of the nation, in fee simple, guaranteed by a patent from the United States government.

In 1866, the nation sold the Cherokee Neutral lands in Kansas to the United States, but it did not sell the Outlet.[15] It only agreed to allow the government to settle friendly Indians thereon in reservations. The reservations were limited to one hundred and sixty acres for each member of the tribe and were to be paid for to the Cherokees at a price agreed upon by the contracting parties. In the event no agreement could be reached by them, the President of the United States had the right to fix the price.

Originally, the Outlet extended from the ninety-sixth to the one hundredth meridian, a distance of two hundred and twenty miles, approximately. From north to south it was sixty miles, and the area was something over six million acres. If, as was afterwards claimed by the federal government, it had regarded the grant as an easement or a passageway to the buffalo ranges and hunting grounds of the far West, the Cherokees had not so understood it. On the contrary, they looked upon it as part of their domain, to be kept as a national reserve for the use of future generations of a virile race always demanding plenty of elbow room. Until the growing population should create a demand for more homes and cultivated lands, the nation expected to conserve the Outlet for a game preserve and a national playground for its citizens.

Until after the Civil War when the Osages secured from the Cherokees a grant of land at the eastern extremity of the Strip, no barriers separated it from the lands east of the ninety-sixth meridian. From time to time thereafter, however, other tribes—the Kaw, the Tonkawa, the Otoe, the Ponca, and the Missouri tribes—secured reservations west of the Osage nation in compliance with treaty stipulations.

Through these peaceable reservations, the Cherokees were careful to reserve the right of passage to their hinterland, where they continued to hunt and exchange amenities with the wild tribes,[16] whose warriors restlessly patrolled the plains, uneasy and rebellious over changing conditions and modes of living.

Since 1846 and even before that time, there had been a gradual drift of Cherokee tribesmen from the older centers of population, swarming westward as had been their habit when outlanders crowded upon their borders causing the margin of subsistence to narrow, when hunting grounds became depleted and cattle ranges became circumscribed, or when political or religious variances arose among them. Even before the Civil War, there had been isolated communities on Candy's Creek and Hominy and as far west as the Big Bend of the Arkansas, where a little Methodist Church there on the frontier had for its first minister in 1855 Elowie or Elijah Butler, who with William McIntosh was in charge of the circuit when the Civil War called them into service.

For administrative purposes, the Strip was attached to Coo-wee-scoo-wee District when it was organized in 1857.[17] The Sheriff of this district made periodic rounds for the purpose of collecting revenues from the droves of Texas cattle passing through from the plains of Texas to the stock yards of Kansas, and to see that squatters and outlaws did not harbor there.

From border to border, the Outlet was rich in natural resources. Its soil was suited to agriculture and stock raising, occupations for which the Cherokees have a natural aptitude. It had quantities of wood and stone; a wealth of mineral deposits. Its prairies and woodlands, that abounded in wild life, were the haunts of the buffalo until hide-hunters had converted its ranges into shambles and strewn them with the ghastly carcasses of these, the noblest wild beasts of the western continent.

For more than half a century, however, it did not occur to the Cherokees to value their Perpetual Outlet West in terms of money. Its priceless worth to them lay in its charm of beauty and mystery;

in its great open spaces, unspoiled by the hand of man. To them it was a region of romance where almost anything might happen, and where many incredible things did happen; where Spanish explorers, in the dim, distant past, had hidden gold beside some path they were never able to retrace; or had discovered rich lodes of ore which they concealed when ready to pass on; for so the legends ran.

Naturally such idyllic conditions could not continue indefinitely. When Kansas began to be settled by a thrusting, aggressive throng of white men whose evaluation of the soil differs from that of the Indian, the Strip lost much of its isolation and something of its magic charm. Too many buffalo trails and Indian traces threaded its length and breadth for it to remain unnoted and untenanted by ubiquitous outlanders for whom Indian lands always held a peculiar fascination.

One of those dim trails, which the plains tribes had been wont to travel for centuries, was worn into a well-marked wagon road by the retreating federal soldiers in the spring of 1861 when, leaving the Five Tribes to their fate, they withdrew from the garrisons of the Indian Territory to the security of northern Kansas, led thither by Black Beaver, a well-known Delaware guide.[18]

Four years later, the fading tracks of this road were retraced by another celebrated Indian scout and frontiersman whose name was Jesse Chisholm, an enterprising Cherokee trader whose wagon tracks became a famous highway, known as the Chisholm Trail.

The Chisholm Trail cut across the Strip about midway of its length. In 1867, the town of Abilene was located as a shipping point on the Kansas and Pacific Railway a few miles above the southern boundary of the state. Over this trail, and others, hundreds of pilgrim herds of Texas cattle trailed their picturesque accouterments across the Outlet's sixty miles of emerald landscape, pausing as they went, sometimes for days or even months, to rest and feed and gain in flesh before continuing their journey to the stockyards that made Kansas famous for a season.[19]

At first, the Cherokee Nation, busy with its problems of reconstruction, permitted these herds to pass unchallenged, appearing to take no cognizance of them. After a time, however, the presence of the drovers and their livestock was taken into account in a law passed by the National Council, levying a drovers tax on every head of cattle that crossed their border.

At first, the tax was hard to collect and was often evaded. Ranchmen in southern Kansas who bought the Texas longhorns to fatten for market sometimes drove their herds into the Strip in order to avoid paying taxes on them in the state, and afterwards drove them back across the line to evade the revenue officer from the nation. Not infrequently, a drover refused outright to pay, claiming that there was no law to compel him to do so.

In order to obviate this leakage, the National Council in 1878 passed an act requiring all ranchmen who held cattle on its lands to secure written permits from the nation to pasture their stock on the range. For a number of years, Cherokee citizens had been locating claims there, which they called head-rights, and inclosing large areas of grazing lands which they rented to non-citizen ranchmen on terms advantageous to both parties.

In 1880, the attorney general ruled that the Cherokee Nation had no right to settle its citizens on the Outlet, but two years later, when a controversy arose between some ranchmen and an oil company over the possession of the range, the Secretary of the Interior, after a thorough canvass of the situation, ordered that the ranchmen might remain so long as they made satisfactory arrangements with the Cherokee national authorities. Thereafter, these men proceeded with greater assurance to acquire grazing privileges from individual Cherokees and from the nation.

Thus, in a few years there developed a gigantic livestock industry in which the Cherokee Nation became financially concerned. Its six million acres of "the best grazing land on earth" were ideally located and conditioned to become the center of a range cattle business organized on an extensive scale. The ground, clear of obstructions, was ready to be laid out in pastures convenient to the railroads to which there was safe and easy access.

By 1880, cattlemen were fencing large pastures here and paying the nation for grazing privileges at the rate of forty cents a year per head for grown cattle and twenty-five cents for young stock. In 1883, there were three hundred thousand head of cattle in the Outlet, two thirds of which were there by permission of Cherokee authorities, the grazing tax the previous year amounting to $42,000. A hundred thousand, belonging to citizens of Kansas ranged there, on which no tax was paid.[20]

A system of graziers' license was adopted stating the number and kind of cattle the ranchmen were entitled to pasture. For purposes of protection, the men who used these pastures formed an organization which three years later was incorporated as the Cherokee Strip Live Stock Association, chartered under the laws of Kansas for a period of forty years.[21]

In order to secure permanence and stability for its project, the corporation applied to the Cherokee Nation for a long-time lease of the entire Outlet. At a special meeting of the National Council, called by Chief Bushyhead in May, an act was passed which went into effect on October 1, 1883, granting the association a lease for a term of five years in consideration of one hundred thousand dollars a year, payable semi-annually, payments to be made in April and October. Failure to remit automatically canceled the agreement.[22]

The negotiation of the lease had attracted a good deal of outside attention to the Cherokee Nation, partly from the fact that two members of the association, Major Andrew Drum and Colonel Charles Eldred, who had gone to Tahlequah to represent the interests of the cattlemen, had engaged as counsel a prominent citizen of the Nation, who was accused of "practicing influence" in behalf of his clients. Rumors of graft and corruption on the part of the association in securing the lease led to a congressional investigation in 1884–85. Nothing of an unsavory nature was uncovered, however, although it was admitted that a considerable amount of money had changed hands at the Cherokee capitol during the spring and summer of 1884.[23]

While the investigation appeared to have failed in its purpose, it did reveal that the organization from the start was a going concern, doing a thriving business in a large way. It would, therefore, bear wary watching by those who, themselves, had designs on the Strip. Moreover, it had stirred up political jealousies between the two parties in the nation and started future trouble for the Cherokees as well as for the super-cattlemen's association.

CHAPTER 25

Cherokee Outlet Agreement

The first lease of the Cherokee Strip Live Stock Association ran from 1883 to 1888. D. W. Bushyhead was reelected principal chief in 1883, and Rabbit Bunch, assistant chief. Two years after this election, a New York land syndicate proposed to buy the entire Outlet, at three dollars an acre.[1] The offer could not be taken under consideration without the consent of Congress, but the Cherokee Strip Live Stock Association, fearing that its costly project was in jeopardy, dispatched a committee to Tahlequah to secure a renewal of their lease for another five years. Their lack of success tended to renew the talk of bribery and corruption which was to figure conspicuously in the campaign of 1887, in which Joel B. Mayes was elected principal chief over Rabbit Bunch.

One of the first acts of Chief Mayes was to veto a bill for renewing the lease of the Outlet for another five years at one hundred twenty-five thousand dollars a year, a price which he considered entirely too low. By dint of finesse and determination, he succeeded in securing a new contract at the unprecedented rate of two hundred thousand dollars,[2] a victory which greatly enhanced his prestige with all classes and parties, but at an enormous cost to the association and, in the long run, to the Cherokee Nation.

The influence of the Cherokee Strip Live Stock Association upon the nation had been noticeable from the beginning. Not only the officials, but the entire population experienced an impulse to move forward purposefully. Contact with an organization of super-cattlemen gave to native ranchmen a new angle on stock-raising and advanced ideas of thrift and cooperation in marketing. Personal contact with commission merchants and occasional trips to the large shipping centers opened new vistas and furnished fresh incentives to increase their enterprises.

Incidentally, the association directed toward the nation the attention of other livestock associations,[3] and of land speculators whose lobbyists brought to the hospitable little inland capitol sharper estimates of money value, together with a fuller realization of the prestige material wealth reflects upon men and their families.

The income from the Strip, called by the Cherokees "grass money," filled a depleted treasury and restored the national scrip from forty cents on the dollar to a hundred. The need of better banking facilities led to the founding of several banks in the Cherokee Nation, and during this period the Cherokees got the reputation of being the wealthiest Indians in the United States, which was unfortunate for individuals and nation alike, it being a well accredited fact that it caused the Cherokees to become again the victims of Anglo Saxon covetousness. In the last analysis, the operations of the Cherokee Strip Live Stock Association tended to hasten the loss of the Strip and the dissolution of tribal government.

In March 1889, Congress passed a bill creating a commission to treat with the tribes of the Indian Territory for their surplus lands, with the Cherokees in particular for the Outlet at a dollar and a quarter an acre.[4] This was the noted Springer Commission, usually referred to as the Cherokee Commission, of which General Lucius Fairchild became the chairman. Without waiting for the Cherokee National Council to convene, the commissioner hastened to Chief Mayes with an offer to purchase the entire Outlet at the price stipulated by Congress. The offer was declined on the ground that the principal chief lacked constitutional authority to negotiate the sale of tribal lands.[5]

In November, General Fairchild repaired to Tahlequah in time to be on hand when the National Council convened. When informed by the commission, appointed by the National Council to conduct the negotiation, that the Cherokee people were unalterably opposed to ceding another foot of land; that already this tribe had all but beggared itself with trying to meet the demands of the government; and that the Outlet was a good investment which the nation could ill afford to sacrifice even at the price of three dollars an acre, General Fairchild, unconvinced, produced a letter from the Secretary of the Interior to prove to them that opposition to the government would be futile.

The letter reviewed the entire history of the grazing industry on the Outlet, going back to 1880 when he had found in a ruling of the Attorney General that the Cherokee Nation had no right to settle its citizens on these lands, that right having been relinquished by the nation in the Treaty of 1866.[6] In 1881 the Secretary of the Interior had denied the right of the government to approve the leases issued by the Cherokee Nation to the ranchmen on the Strip.

From these premises, the letter advanced to the ground that the title of the Cherokees to the lands in question was shadowy and precarious;[7] that the grant of the Outlet was in the nature of an easement, or passage right.[8] Should the United States find its own title superior, it had a right to take the lands, and would, in fact, take them "when the circumstances of the American people should require it." The offer of the United States to pay the Cherokees a dollar and a quarter an acre for the entire tract, he believed to be a munificent one under the circumstances, considering that their title even to its use was liable to be defeated.

Waxing militant, Secretary Noble attacked the Cherokee Strip Live Stock Association, charging them with designs to rival and defeat the government, thereby acting in defiance of law and against public interest. Such unpatriotic intentions and actions justified the government, beyond question, in laying hands on those pretended lessees and removing them and their property no later than June 1, 1890.

No one had a greater familiarity with Congressional legislation and executive rulings than the Cherokees themselves, and no one a clearer understanding of their treaty guarantees. Consequently, they reasoned cogently: "What if Judge Brewer had said in the Circuit Court that the Indians had only the right of passage?"[9] Secretary Cass had ruled that the entire property of this tract of six million acres was for their unconditional use.[10]They called to mind also that President Jackson in 1835 had mentioned their nation west of the Mississippi as covering an area of thirteen million, eight hundred thousand acres. Without the Outlet there were only seven million. If the Strip had been granted as an easement no mention of that understanding had been made in 1866 when the Cherokees gave the United States permission to colonize friendly Indians there.[11]

Unable to refute these claims or to negotiate an agreement, General Fairchild left the conference in a huff and went back to Washington where he reported that the Cherokees were an obdurate people, incapable of sound judgments. Thereupon President Harrison, in his message to Congress, again denounced the cattlemen for obstructing the plans of the government and declared that the United States, under treaties with the Cherokees, had certain rights to the lands of the Outlet. Those rights would not be used oppressively, he assured Congress; "But it cannot be allowed that those who by sufferance, occupy these lands, shall interpose to defeat the wise and beneficent purpose of the government."[12] He could not but believe that the advantageous character of the offer made by the United States to the Cherokee Nation for a full release of these lands, as compared with other suggestions now made to them, would yet obtain a favorable consideration.

When this pronouncement did not bring the Cherokees to terms, President Harrison on February 17, 1890, issued a proclamation warning the cattlemen that they would no longer be permitted to occupy the Outlet,[13] a ruling which not only rendered the Strip valueless to the Cherokee Nation, but indicated the government was prepared to use actual coercion if necessary. The Cherokees had no recourse.[14] Bowing to the inevitable, they permitted the National Council to appoint a commission to negotiate an agreement to sell the Outlet for $8,595,736.12.

The negotiations were conducted by three commissioners on the part of the government,[15] and seven on the part of the Cherokee Nation.[16] These ten commissioners drew up a contract in which the Cherokee Nation agreed to cede its lands west of the ninety-sixth meridian to the United States at a dollar and a quarter an acre, in return for which the government promised to remove the intruders from the Cherokee Nation immediately upon demand of the Principal Chief. All their goods were to be removed with them at federal expense in order that there would be no excuse for their returning.

In addition, the United States promised to render an account of all moneys due to the Cherokees from the sale of their lands in the past, beginning with the treaty of 1817. The Cherokees were granted the privilege of entering suit against the government in the Court of Claims, "with the right of appeal to the Supreme Court of the United States by either party for any alleged or declared amounts of money promised but withheld by the United States."[17]

The total area of land thus ceded amounted to six million, twenty-two thousand, seven hundred and fifty-four acres. From this amount, certain deductions were to be made. "Head-rights" of eighty acres each were allowed to seventy Cherokee citizens who had been residing on the Strip and had improvements on the land prior to November 1, 1891.

The agreement, approved by the National Council on December 19, 1891, was ratified by the citizens of the nation in an election held on January 4, 1892. Having been revised by Congress, it was signed by the Secretary of the Interior on the part of the government on May 17, 1893.[18] On September 16 of that year, the lands were opened to white settlement. By that time, more than two years had elapsed since the ranchmen's cattle had been driven from the range.

The proceeds from the sale of the Strip finally became available to the Cherokee Nation under the condition that the freedmen and the Delaware and Shawnee Indians, who had been admitted to citizenship under the Treaty of 1866, should not be unjustly or illegally discriminated against, Congress reserving the right to safeguard the welfare of these two classes of people. The Strip money was at length disbursed per capita in the summer of 1894, almost a year after the government had sold the lands to homesteaders at a handsome profit.[19]

By that time, an accumulation of protests had been filed by claimants whose names were not on the citizenship rolls of the Cherokee Nation. The great majority of these claimants were rank intruders, without the shadow of right to their claims, yet their vociferous clamors had to be heard by a paternal government pledged to secure its own citizens in their privilege of participating in the proceeds.[20]

A number of these claimants professed to be intermarried freedmen who had been unable to establish their claims in the Cherokee Citizenship Court.[21] The friendly Indians likewise became uneasy concerning their status, and filed claims against the nation for a stipulated apportionment of the proceeds, far beyond their just rights.[22]

For the purpose of protecting these three classes the government set aside a sufficient reserve pending final adjustment of their claims by the United States. After the required deductions had been made, the money was apportioned per capita to those whose names were on the roll approved by the Cherokee Citizenship Court.[23]

The arbitrary rulings of the government during the period from 1889 to 1891 ruined the Cherokee Strip Live Stock Association and ended a noble experiment in cattle culture and wholesale marketing, unique in the history of the industry. The association failed to meet its obligation to the Cherokees for the last payment on the lease. Probably the "super cattlemen" could not pay. In an attempt to bring them to terms, Chief Mayes, representing the Cherokee Nation, took the case into the courts of Kansas and lost the suit.

For a brief season, the Strip had been a valuable financial asset to the Cherokees. Its forced cession deprived them of large amounts of revenue, which they had come to depend upon. It also reduced the capital stock of the nation by the sum of twenty million dollars, thereby lowering its financial rating so abruptly as to complicate payment of the nation's outstanding warrants, which amounted to several hundred thousand dollars.

Wall Street brokers who held a hundred and twenty-five thousand dollars worth became uneasy and called upon the government to protect their investments. One of the consequences of the sale, therefore, was an act passed by Congress in 1893, creating the Commission to the Five Civilized Tribes.

CHAPTER 26

The Dawes Commission

The organization of Oklahoma Territory and the consummation of the Cherokee Outlet transfer had the effect of quickening the trend of the governmental policy towards a stronger control of Indian affairs. Unmistakable evidence of this tendency appears in a Senate Committee report of December 1892, in which it was declared, "the anomalous conditions of the separate independent Indian governments in the United States must soon, in the nature of things, cease," the purpose of the government now being to make all the Indians citizens.[1]

A few weeks later, the joint delegation from the Five Tribes, then in Washington, notified their tribal officials that they were being told, even by those who had formerly been their friends and advocates, that Congress had the legal right to take away from the Indians their political independence. Moreover, the Supreme Court of the United States had ruled that Indian treaties could be abrogated by Congress.[2]

On the heels of this message came another, bringing news that Congress had passed an act[3] providing for the appointment of a Commission to the Five Civilized Tribes, authorized to negotiate with them for the extinguishment of their land titles, either by the cession of all or a part thereof, to the United States, or by the allotment and division of these lands among the citizens of the tribal nations; and to secure the consent of these nations to the dissolution of tribal governments, preparatory to the ultimate creation of a state embracing the lands within the Indian Territory.[4]

In November 1893, President Grover Cleveland appointed the members of the commission of which Senator Dawes of

Massachusetts[5] was named chairman. Because of his prominence, the commission became known as the Dawes Commission. The two ranking members were Meredith H. Kidd of Indiana and Archibald McKennon of Arkansas. In December, the commissioners held a preliminary meeting in Washington, D.C., where instructions and a large amount of data were furnished them by the Secretary of the Interior. Early the following year they arrived in the Indian Territory, where temporary headquarters were established at Muskogee, a station on the Missouri, Kansas and Texas railroad.

From this coign of vantage, formal credentials and copies of instructions from the Secretary of the Interior were dispatched to each of the Five Tribes, in addition to which a circular letter was released to the press. *The Purcell Register*, whose editor, W. H. Walker, a non-citizen and an avowed advocate of the dissolution of the tribal governments, seized upon it eagerly. Other papers devoted space to the text of the letter and to editorial comments on its startling pronouncements. Under the caption of "An Address Embodying Advice and Warning to the Citizens of the Five Civilized Tribes," the letter enumerated many wrongs to be righted by the commissioners. "Believe us," they urged, "when we tell you the present anomalous condition existing in the five tribes cannot last."[6]

The reason given practically amounted to an indictment. In the first place, the expenses of the judiciary were becoming too burdensome; the United States should not be expected to endure them longer. Yet crime was all too prevalent, the larger unsettled districts affording harbor and refuge for criminals, making it well nigh impossible for officers to perform their duty. Trials in the Indian courts were a farce, and justice was a byword, according to reports that had reached the commission in Washington.[7]

The public moneys, it was charged, as they filtered through the hands of tribal officials, were absorbed so that nothing ever reached the poor and penniless.[8] Twenty thousand children, both white and Indian, were growing to maturity without the opportunity of obtaining a common school education or the advantages of religious instruction. This was something else the United States government could no longer tolerate. It was neither wise nor humane, and it was a matter of the gravest concern to every friend of the Indian who desired to see him happy and prosperous and on the way to a higher civilization.

While conditions in the rural districts were deplorable, those in the towns were worse, or at least equally bad. There was no provision for levying taxes with which to run the schools and provide modern improvements and legal protection for the white citizens. Populous towns had grown up along the railroads without having been surveyed and platted; large and valuable buildings had been erected by non-citizens on tribal land, for which no title could be secured by the enterprising white men who had invested thousands of dollars only to become tenants at will of Indians who owned the lots. This situation was insufferable and dangerous. Something must be done immediately to adjust the equities growing out of a complication that any time might become insupportable. Since there were several times as many white people as Indians in the Territory at this time, the implication was ominous.[9]

Another evil complained of was the monopoly of the best lands by a few half-breeds[10] and intermarried white citizens. So great was this monopoly among the Cherokees, the most wealthy and progressive of the Five Tribes, that one hundred persons among the Cherokees were reported to have appropriated fully one-half of the best land. They had fenced, under the laws and usages of the tribal government, tracts ten times their share, while the diffident and retiring full bloods, crowded back among the wooded, stony hills, were compelled to wring a sorry existence out of a few sterile acres so far removed from progressive influences as to make schools impossible. Thus advancement in civilization was being shamefully and even dangerously impeded.

In order to purge the Nation of this unparalleled corruption, to correct glaring inequalities, to eliminate waste and inefficiency, and to discharge the government's obligation to the weak and oppressed of Indian Territory, the commission announced its intention of allotting the lands among the citizens of the Five Civilized Tribes so that each individual should hold his share in severalty; to dissolve the tribal governments and to organize a territorial form of government over Indian Territory, or annex it to Oklahoma Territory. Finally the assurance was given that the complaints above enumerated had come from the various tribes by non-citizens of the highest character.[11]

The speciousness of these charges was too obvious to escape the challenge of the Indians themselves, who remembered Senator Dawes' allotment hobby of old. Several years previous to this time, he had made a tour of inspection through the Indian Territory, at which time he visited the Cherokee Nation and checked up on its school system, which he commended with some show of enthusiasm at that time, declaring that it would compare favorably with the schools of the adjacent states.

The accusation concerning lawlessness among the Indians had obviously come from the Governor of Arkansas, who had written a letter to the President in December 1893, in which he claimed there was reason to suspect that a very large percentage of the bank and train robberies which took place west of the Alleghenies and east of the Rocky Mountains were organized, or at least originated, in Indian Territory. These criminals he believed to be rapidly converting Indian Territory into a school of crime, of which the young Cherokee, Henry Starr, was a principal teacher.

Such spurious accusations, obviously based on propaganda and disseminated from the very border of the nation, were not permitted to pass unquestioned. When the letter came to his attention, Chief Harris, of the Cherokee Nation, wrote to Judge Isaac C. Parker, of Fort Smith, inquiring of him what percentage of the crime committed in the Territory was attributable to Indians.

Judge Parker's reply, published in such newspapers as the *Atoka Indian Citizen* in March, stated that he had been holding federal court at Fort Smith for sixteen years and during that time, in his judgment, the number of Indians who had been charged with high crimes compared with United States citizens, was about ten percent. For minor offenses, such as introducing liquor into the Indian country, it was about fifteen or possibly twenty percent.

There had never been any trouble to speak of growing out of crime committed by Indians. The vast majority of real crime was attributable to persons "who have refuge in that country from another state or territory of the union." The trouble had always arisen from the failure of the government to carry out its obligations to the Indians; obligations which required that intruders be removed from Indian Territory. Had that been done from the beginning, the amount of crime in the Indian country would not have been as great as it had been in any western state. "The influence of this class of refugee criminals in their country is most pernicious upon the Indians. They are not there, however, by any fault of the Indians. They are there because the government has permitted them to be and remain there. It would not do to say the laws are not enforced in the Indian Country. They are more vigorously enforced there by the courts of the United States and by the Indian courts than they are in any western state."[12]

Ignoring Judge Parker's testimony, the Commissioners steadily held to their course of instructions. They had been delegated not to investigate facts but to carry out a policy already determined upon by the powerful Indian Ring in Washington, working in the interest of great corporations. On February nineteenth, an inter-tribal council of delegates from the Five Nations met the Dawes Commission at Checota and for nine days listened attentively to Senator Dawes and his colleagues explain their mission, enumerate the many evils of the system of government and land-holding within the nations, and state the intention of a benign government to rectify those evils by instituting a system of its own over the Indian Territory.

On the tenth day of the sessions, the Indians submitted their reply in the form of a memorial in which they expressed unalterable opposition to a change in their land tenure or in their tribal autonomy, and the earnest desire to be left undisturbed in all their social, economic, and political customs and usages.[13] From the stand thus taken, the tribal commissioners, supported by their Indian constituencies, remained adamant to all arguments or appeals on the part of the federal emissaries.

Throughout the summer and early autumn, the Commissioners brought to bear upon their project all the authority and resourcefulness at their command, not only among the Indians but among the non-citizens, hundreds of whom availed themselves of every opportunity to pour into the ears of the Commissioners the stories of their grievances at the hands of tribal citizens who "formed a cast that monopolized, not only the lands, but the schools and the local governments, so far as the latter existed."[14]

Among the complainants were members of the Cherokee Citizenship Association, an organization constituted of rank intruders, and founded by an outlander by the name of Jeff Watts[15] about the time the "Strip Money" was beginning to enrich the treasury of the Cherokee Nation. Mr. Watts, then a man of middle age, had never claimed Indian blood until it occurred to him that to be a Cherokee citizen might have its advantages. Whereupon he began "to feel like an Indian" and, crossing the line somewhere in the vicinity of Fort Smith, squatted on a rich tract of Cherokee land, and invited his numerous relations to join him. About seventy of them did so.

The Cherokee authorities repudiated Mr. Watts' claim and asked the government to eject him and his associates. This was never done. Watts, meanwhile, organized his Citizenship Association and built up a tidy fortune by charging a five dollar initiation fee and a dollar and a quarter a month membership dues to anyone who wished to join, "Arkansas niggers[16] and all."[17]

The Dawes Commission made no discrimination against intruders, who along with other outsiders, received a great deal of attention. The Indians observed it with amusement and commented upon it among themselves with their inimitable sarcasm. It had been understood at first, they said, that Senator Dawes and his commission had come to treat with the Indians, but judging from appearances their real business was with the non-citizens, white and black.

On November 20th the commission submitted its first report to the Department of Interior. The Indians, it stated, had refused to treat with the Commission on the basis of allotment of lands and the dissolution of tribal governments, and that they had been encouraged to do so by messages received from their delegations in Washington assuring them that no steps would be taken by the federal government towards the reorganization of the Indian

Territory in opposition to the wishes of the Indians themselves. In the opinion of the Commission, a change was absolutely necessary, the monopoly of lands by a few of the more powerful and enterprising adopted citizens and those of mixed descent having absolved the government of its treaty promises.[18]

A joint delegation of the Five Tribes,[19] sent to Washington during the fall and winter of 1894–95 to represent the interests of the Indians and to counteract the misrepresentations that were being disseminated in Washington concerning conditions in the Indian Territory, submitted to Congress a memorial entitled "An Appeal to Justice" in which they explained the origin and operation of their present tribal customs. Their system of holding lands in common instead of in severalty, they explained, had come down to these tribes from time immemorial. Their ancestors had found it good and commended it to their descendants, who were accustomed to it, finding it suitable to their present needs. Lands in common meant perpetual homes for them and their descendants, while allotment of land in severalty meant certain loss of homes and ultimate pauperism to their race.

In their opinion, the charge of monopoly in land had been grossly misunderstood. "When our lands were patented to us by the United States, we were guaranteed the right of local self-government. Having plenty of land at that time, our law making power had thought it wise to allow a citizen to enclose and cultivate as much of the public domain as he might desire, so long as he did not interfere with, or encroach upon the possessions of another citizen." Their legislatures, at any time it seemed advisable, could limit the holdings of any citizen. That would never become necessary, however, if the United States would remove the intruders in agreement with treaty obligations.

It had been said that the governments of the Five Tribes were corrupt and their officials marked by venality. They replied that perfection in government was not to be found in any nation, and that for the time and opportunity afforded the Indians they had made wonderful progress in good government. "It must be remembered that but a short time has elapsed since our country was a wilderness and the people uneducated and untrained to the methods of civil government."

On the other hand the people of the United States had had more than a hundred years in which to perfect their system, with a constituency of a very high order of civilization to begin with. "And we dare say you find work yet to do." With all their drawbacks, they believed themselves to have made progress. Their laws, schools, churches and institutions for orphans and unfortunates, they believed would compare favorably with those of other territories and with the younger states.

The charge of lawlessness they denied unequivocally. The large majority of their citizens were as orderly and law-abiding as those in the surrounding states. The crimes committed on Indian soil were those of white men, citizens of the United States, intruders who should have been removed long ago in accordance with treaty agreements.

In closing, the memorial entreated the government to keep faith with their people; to give them time to think and consider this great and serious question. "Should we ever become citizens of the United States, we want to be able to honor the flag, the laws, the institutions and the people of our adopted country. We want the hearts of our people and those of their descendants to feel free from the sting of real or fancied wrongs."[20] They wanted to share in the feeling of pride that swells the breast of every true patriot when he sees his country's flag floating on high.

But to this appeal there was no response. The Commissioners, having returned to Washington in the autumn, remained there in close touch with Congress and the Department of the Interior during the winter. By the Civil Service Appropriation Act of March 2, 1895, their number was increased to five,[21] and fresh blood was infused into the body by the appointment of two new members. Mr. Kidd was removed; several charges having been filed against him.[22]

There was some talk of Senator Dawes resigning in the spring of 1895. More and more his advancing years incapacitated him for active service in a country lacking many of the modern conveniences indispensable to the venerable statesman. Henceforth he gave little active attention to the work of the Commission, although he was retained as nominal chairman in order that he might influence public opinion in the east where he had a wide reputation as an authority on the Indian question.

The other members of the Commission returned to the Indian Territory in May. There was a rumor that "the Secretary of the Interior was coming on from Washington to help them," and that he would visit Tahlequah about May 8. The rumor created quite a ripple of interest among all classes of citizens; Secretary Hoke Smith was not only a man of importance because of his high office in the government, but because he was a native of Georgia, where once they had built fires around the Cherokees to "smoke them out."

Thus far the Five Civilized Tribes had opposed creation of a solid front of resistance to the federal policy in the belief that their combined resistive powers would serve them better than separate negotiations. With the intention of fostering this spirit of harmony and cooperation, the Cherokee Nation sent an invitation to each of the Five Tribes inviting them to a meeting to be held at Fort Gibson on May 20.[23] Extensive preparations were made for the entertainment of the delegations, and great effort was put forth to make a success of the meeting. When the day arrived, the Choctaws were conspicuous by their absence,[24] and since no binding agreement could be reached without unanimous consent of the Five Tribes, the assembly adjourned to meet at Eufaula on June 26. The Eufaula meeting in its two-day session was more successful.[25] It unanimously adopted resolutions reasserting all the objections to a change in their system of land tenure and in their form of government, and prayed to be left undisturbed in their treaty rights.

All efforts toward negotiations having failed, the Dawes Commission, upon adjourning for the summer, repaired to Washington and there maintained an office in order to keep in touch with the Secretary of the Interior and the Department of Indian Affairs. Convinced that nothing could be gained by reasoning and persuasion, the Commission recommended that the government assume at once the political control of Indian Territory for the reasons that the tribal governments were wholly inefficient, absolutely unreliable, and so notoriously unsound as to absolve the government from all treaty obligations to the Indians.

Specifically, the citizenship rolls of the Cherokee Nation were assailed on the ground that they were said to be in such a chaotic condition as to defeat the enforcement of United States criminal laws in that nation. For personal and political reasons, many persons who had always been recognized as Cherokee citizens, it was charged, had been stricken from the legal rolls by the Cherokee citizenship commission and placed on the intruder list. The Dawes Commission recommended, therefore, that these rolls be taken over by the federal government in preparation for allotment, that a territorial form of government be given Indian Territory, and that the jurisdiction of the United States courts be extended over the Five Tribes.[26]

What, may be asked, was the motive for singling out the Cherokee rolls for special mention? The answer is to be found in section two of the Cherokee Outlet Agreement in which the United States obligated itself to remove immediately upon request of the Principal Chief all intruders from the Cherokee Nation.[27] Congress later, however, extended the time to January 1, 1896, the government having neither removed intruders nor made appropriation for so doing, in spite of repeated requests for their removal. Instead it had permitted others to cross the border and to squat on Cherokee soil with the expectation of being permitted to remain indefinitely.

Some of these, having tried to register claims to Cherokee citizenship, had demanded a share in the "Strip Payment" in 1894. Failing in this, they appealed to Congress and were given an extension of time to dispose of their improvements. Needless to say they were never removed. When Chief Harris went to Washington in the summer of 1895 to urge that the agreement be kept and that the intruders be removed, he was answered by incriminating charges against Cherokee national officials for trying to defraud their own citizens of participation in tribal moneys.

On June 10, 1896, Congress passed an act enlarging the powers of the Dawes Commission by authorizing it to proceed at once to hear and determine all the applications for citizenship in any one of the Five Nations. The purpose of this act, it was stated, was to prepare the way for the United States to establish a government in the Indian Territory "which would rectify the many inequalities and discriminations now existing in said territory and afford needful protection of the lives and property of all citizens and residents thereof."[28]

This was the answer to the appeal of the harassed Cherokees for protection under treaty promises. The federal government, having assumed citizenship jurisdiction in the Indian Territory, had established an excuse for not trying to remove the intruders, and at the same time had deprived the nation of a vital function of government, that of determining the membership of its own body politic. The Cherokee Citizenship Commission, which had been in operation since 1879, was to be discontinued, [29] having been rendered inoperative by this measure.

Congress appropriated, on March 2, 1895, thirty thousand dollars for the maintenance of the Dawes Commission for one year. Expenses were mounting from year to year. In 1896 they were increased to forty thousand, and the next year to forty-five thousand dollars.[30] The price of "Manifest Destiny" came dearer far than had been expected; but Uncle Sam, having set his hand to the plow, would not look backward, "though the plow share cut through the flower of life to its fountain; though it passed o'er the graves of the dead and the hearts of the living."[31]

The Dawes Commission soon found it had indeed taken on a big assignment. The preparation of the citizenship rolls was a herculean task which lengthened its life and increased the cost of maintaining the Commission. The compilation of the rolls required an army of clerks, stenographers, and attorneys. It was estimated that six thousand government employees from the states found lucrative jobs in the Indian Territory during a part of the time this work was under way. A separate set of rolls had to be made for the Cherokee freedmen, over which there was sufficient litigation to furnish to alien lawyers large contingent fees payable in terms of land.

Additional hordes of foreign adventurers who had never claimed citizenship in the Indian Territory now rushed in, claiming to be

Indians. Aided and abetted by unscrupulous claim agents and shyster lawyers, they registered as citizens, trusting that their records would not be too scrupulously investigated. It was said of them: "These court claimants do not look like Indians, they do not act like Indians, they have none of the attributes of the Indians. They are white adventurers from the surrounding states, and any intelligent and impartial jury would so declare them."[32]

The effect of the citizenship measure upon the headquarters of the commission was revolutionary in character. The enlarged corps of assistants, among whom were a few women clerks and stenographers, introduced an innovation at Muskogee. Arriving with their suitcases, they soon transformed Muskogee, a small railroad station, into a populous boom town with modern conveniences. So many lucrative positions were awarded favorite sons of influential fathers in the older states as to create comment. One of the leading papers was moved to say that Congress was rapidly converting carpetbags into wardrobe trunks in the Indian Territory.

A large number of non-citizens who were neither government employees nor claimants to citizenship were attracted to the Territory by its vast resources and its promise of future opportunities. Among them were ambitious young men and women from the older states, Kansas, Arkansas, Missouri and even far-away Georgia and New Jersey and Ohio, who, discouraged by finding all the desirable offices preempted by older men at home, packed their grips and set out on the great adventure of achieving fame and fortune among the Indians of whom they had many erroneous notions. A number of these adventurers were idealistically fine; many were merely ambitious to get on in the world, while a few were actually bad.

Originally the Dawes Commission had been clothed with negotiatory powers only. The measure of June 10, 1896, enlarged its powers by giving to it the judicial authority to pass upon the citizenship of the Five Tribes. From this time forward, the Commission worked under different conditions,[33] its prestige increasing in proportion to its power. During 1897, it was able to make agreements with the Choctaws, Chickasaws, and the Seminoles, which furnished the opening for which it had been maneuvering. On June 7, 1897, an act of Congress gave the United States Courts jurisdiction in all civil and criminal cases after January 1, 1898. This act provided also that laws thereafter enacted by the tribal legislatures should not become effective until approved by the President.[34]

The Cherokees protested and refused to treat with the commissioners. Their old treaties, they reiterated, guaranteed to them their domains as long as grass grows and water flows. If the government could repudiate these old and sacred treaties, what would it profit them to enter into new agreements.[35]

CHAPTER 27

Chiefs and Headmen
Under the Dark Treaty

Of the nine principal chiefs of the Cherokees after the Civil War, only Colonel Lewis Downing, Oochalata, and Bushyhead approached the native type in either appearance or personality. All of these spoke the Cherokee language fluently, even eloquently, when addressing full blood audiences, and the English when occasion demanded it. Chief Downing, a descendant of an English Revolutionary soldier, was himself a warrior of renown before he became head peace chief of the nation. Several times he served as a delegate to Washington, and once returned with an eastern bride, for whom he built a home at Tahlequah. He was reelected in 1871 and died the next year. William Potter Ross was elected to serve his unexpired term.

By reason of his enunciation and address, Chief William Potter Ross might easily have been taken for a high-bred Englishman, although his serene composure and his kindly tact under trying circumstances bespoke his Indian ancestry. Scholar, diplomat, and educator, he could have achieved distinction in any country. He chose rather to consecrate his talents to the development of the institutions of his own nation along broad constitutional principles. A foe to ignorance, he advocated such a national school system as would give every Cherokee child the opportunity of securing, free of cost, a liberal education that would enhance his usefulness and increase his capacity for enjoyment, thereby raising the standard of Cherokee citizenship.

He was succeeded in office by Oochalata, who, upon entering politics as senator from Delaware District in 1867 had adopted the name of Charles Thompson, for political reasons, as he, himself, explained. Chief Thompson was the son of a full blood father and a white mother who spoke the Cherokee language from preference. He enlisted during the War[1] with the Indian Home Guards, with whom he spent several months in Kansas where he had observed and learned many things in campaigns outside his own country. During his administration, the restoration of the nation was completed, and at its close a new epoch began. In 1879 he was defeated by Dennis Wolf Bushyhead, when David Rowe, the assistant Chief, was succeeded by William Penn Adair.[2]

Chief Bushyhead was a son of the native missionary, Reverend Jesse Bushyhead, the chief justice of the nation at his death in 1844, and one of the charter members of the National Party. As a young man his son, Dennis Wolf Bushyhead, the future chief of the Cherokees, had gone during the gold rush to California, where he remained until 1868, thereby escaping the civil disturbances which had divided the nation into rival camps for four long harrowing years.

Upon his return, young Bushyhead threw himself into the work of rehabilitation with such energy and enthusiasm as to win universal approval of his conduct and executive ability. He served in several positions of trust in the government of the nation before his election as principal chief by the National Party whose confidence in thus honoring him he justified by giving the nation eight years of unprecedented prosperity at home and much prestige abroad.[3] His salary of two thousand dollars was larger than the office had formerly paid,[4] but since it enabled him to reside at Tahlequah,[5] the people were well content.

To have him do so was advantageous in several respects. When emergencies arose, it was no longer necessary to summon the head of the nation from a distance; should distinguished visitors arrive by stage coach,[6] his doors were open and he, himself, stood ready to receive their calls. His home was situated on an eminence overlooking the Council House. Shielded by indigenous oaks which stand for constancy and strength,[7] the two-story structure, imposing and well-ordered in appearance, served for eight years as the nation's executive mansion, lending distinction to the little inland capital at a time when the people still gathered at sundown to drink water from Wolf's Spring near the foot of the hill beyond the Council Ground.

The period of the eighties constitutes the silver era of Cherokee history, for it was during that time that the Strip came suddenly into prominence, and the income from its grazing lands mounted from a few hundred dollars to two hundred thousand a year, all within a period of ten years. This gave the people a season of prosperity which amounted almost to opulence.

It was also an era of internal tranquility. Nature, having bound up the wounds of war, was busily intent on restoring the population to its wonted strength[8] and virility, while the fostering earth, aided by industry, gave to a long suffering people bread for stones, sweet waters for bitter, laughter for tears, beauty for ashes, and life for death.

In the ten years between 1879 and 1889, the Cherokee school system reached its zenith; newspapers, periodicals, and current literature gained in circulation with a reading public which was interested in a variety of subjects, including science and invention; and a greater number of Cherokee citizens visited the states to see what new conveniences they might acquire for themselves, and what improvements make in national conditions.

Among those who attended the Centennial Exposition in 1876 was a sixteen-year-old Cherokee boy, E. D. Hicks, who, while there, saw for the first time a telephone. "I studied that phone religiously. I could not get the idea off my mind. Voices carried over a piece of wire seemed uncanny to me," he said in reminiscence fifty years later. Upon his return home, he read everything he could find on the subject and questioned everybody who had seen or used a telephone. In 1866, young Hicks organized a company at Tahlequah to finance the construction of a line to Muskogee through Fort Gibson. He himself superintended the stringing of the wire which was attached to trees or rough poles by means of brackets made as they went. When the job was completed, the Cherokees had the first telephone system in Indian Territory, and one of the first west of St. Louis.[9]

Always the great event of November was the Chief's Message, which if the weather permitted, was delivered out of doors on the Council Ground where a great concourse of people assembled. Among them were many full bloods, for whose benefit an experienced interpreter stood beside the speaker to translate his message, sentence by sentence, into the Cherokee Language.

As a rule, some of the advanced students from each of the seminaries attended out of respect, it was said, to Mother Nation, whose messenger the great chief was; whose agent, the National Council; and whose "swift runners" were the officials who helped to enforce the laws. Thus ingeniously the wise ones of the tribe endeavored to inculcate a spirit of wholesome respect for constituted authority and to inspire a patriotism that transcended factional partisanship and clannish exclusiveness.

Beginning with 1879, the revenues from the Outlet wrought political, no less than economic and social changes in the nation. The authority of the principal chief was augmented, his duties became more onerous, and his tenure of office more precarious. Content with having given the nation eight years of efficient service, Chief Bushyhead declined to become a candidate for a third term. Whereupon Rabbit Bunch was named standard bearer for the National Party in 1887, the main issue being the renewal of the lease to the Cherokee Strip Live Stock Association.

Bunch's opponent was the Confederate veteran, Judge Joel Bryant Mayes. A man of education and broad experience, of fine physique and dignified presence, Judge Mayes inspired even his enemies with admiration, for he was known to be a statesman of high rank as well as a patriot ready to sacrifice his life for his country. Ever a pioneer in spirit, he chose the wind-swept prairies for his familiar haunts as he pursued the occupation of farming and stock raising in the Grand River valley.

Rabbit Bunch, also a Civil War veteran, but on the Union side, was an equally prosperous farmer and stock man, and an influential citizen in his neighborhood where he dispensed hospitality after the tradition of his ancestors. He was a zealous Christian, and a pillar in the community church of which he was a member. Also, he was a gifted orator with an inimitable manner, for which he had an enviable reputation among his constituents. His experience as assistant chief and as a delegate to Washington more than once, together with his long service in the National Council, recommended him as a strong candidate for the highest office of the nation.

Due to the fact that the election of 1887 was one of more than ordinary interest,[10] the campaign was conducted with careful regard to the minutest detail of organization, and as election day approached, excitement ran high. Although voting was conducted viva voce[11] by means of an original system of checks and balances which should have precluded all suspicion of corrupting the ballot, the national partisans challenged the election, charging fraud, when the returns showed a small majority in favor the Downing candidate.[12] This threw the contest into the Senate where the Nationals were in the majority. There resulted a fierce conflict in which guns are said to have figured menacingly.

In the end the Downing candidate was seated with some show of violence on the part of his supporters, who broke into the executive office and installed him triumphantly in the face of all opposition. Almost at once, however, the discord died away[13] and party leaders turned their attention to other interests, relegating their political rivalry to oblivion as was their custom, never dreaming that their partisan recriminations reverberating through the halls of Congress would return to plague the nation in days to come.

Samuel Smith, who spoke English reluctantly, although he understood the language perfectly, had been elected assistant chief without protest and therefore was acceptable to all factions. In the background of this administration, he moved quietly, devoid of all rancor and clannish particularism. Aware of his own distinguished position in the nation, he never presumed upon it, nor sought publicity through the press whose very silence speaks goldenly of his poise and self-restraint. Only now and then are there glimpses of him going about his official duties on the Council Ground, or attending the annual camp meeting of his denomination, or transacting the business of a successful man of affairs. The assistant chief was not a candidate for reelection in 1891, preferring to represent his district in the Senate, where he belonged to the conservatives until the dissolution of tribal government.

Principal Chief Mayes was elected for a second term on August 5, 1891. Four months later, while the sale of the Strip was still pending, he succumbed to a sudden attack of illness, leaving the nation to mourn a great loss. Thus another native patriot became a martyr to the blighting theory of "Manifest Destiny," and the lengthening shadows of the "Dark Treaty" fell more and more threateningly athwart the land of the Cherokees. Four days before the passing of Chief Mayes, the recently elected assistant chief, Henry Chambers, had been carried away by a virulent epidemic of influenza.[14] It thus became the duty of the National Council to fill two vacancies within a week. Colonel Johnson Harris was elected to the former office, and Stephen Teehee, the latter.

Chief Harris was a citizen noted for his versatility and resourcefulness. He took his duties, as his honors, seriously, devoting all his time and energy to the tasks bequeathed to him by his predecessor.

Stephen Teehee, a Baptist minister and judge of the circuit court, spoke both English and Cherokee. He had an unusual capacity for observation and reflection and always had a good reason for what he did. Also, he was regarded by his contemporaries as a "serious, honorable and cautious" patriot.[15] During their administration, which was an eventful one, the Dawes Commission arrived in the Territory and began warning the citizens of the intolerable corruption then existing among the officials of the Five Tribes. This was amazing, though far from convincing news to the Indians themselves, who had the utmost confidence in the men they had chosen to represent them.

Chief Harris was not a candidate for reelection in 1895. Instead, he himself headed a delegation to Washington[16] to urge the removal of the offending aliens who were crowding into the nation in ever increasing numbers, scoffing at the idea of having to obey the laws of Indians, thus becoming a law unto themselves, emboldened to take this high ground of independence by a provision which had been included in the Indian appropriation bill specifying that intruders could not be disturbed until January 1 of the ensuing year.[17]

In 1895, George Washington Swimmer was elected assistant, and Samuel Houston Mayes, principal chief of the nation. Swimmer was a full-blood, a farmer and merchant and a practical businessman who represented the conservative element of the tribe as Rabbit Bunch, Samuel Smith, and Stephen Teehee had been doing for the past several years. The Swimmer was unobtrusive and reserved in manner, but dependable and always ready to cooperate for the best interests of the nation.

Chief S. H. Mayes was a brother of Joel B. Mayes, whom he resembled in many ways, having inherited many of the family and tribal traits of his ancestors. Under the most trying circumstances, he never appeared perturbed, but was alert and resourceful in performing the duties pertaining to his office. The four years of his administration were eventful ones in the history of the nation.

In 1899 he was succeeded by Thomas Mitchell Buffington, who was reputed at Washington to hold advanced views on allotment. The mass of the people, nevertheless, regarded him as a true patriot whose inherent honesty could never be corrupted by corporation bribes nor betrayed by insinuating flattery.

The last chiefs of the nation were William Charles Rogers and David McNair Faulkner. Chief Faulkner had been politically active in the Downing Party for a number of years. As a senator from his district, he had acquired a reputation for political acumen beyond the ordinary, by reason of which he wielded a considerable influence in his party and in the nation.

William Charles Rogers, a man of destiny, elected in August 1903, was the last principal chief of the Cherokee Nation, as his grandfather, John Rogers, had been the last chief of the Cherokee Nation West.

As a competent ranchman and merchant, W. C. Rogers was well and favorably known. Although he had represented his district more than once in the Cherokee Senate, he was not inclined to seek political favors. Thus, for many years the merchant and cattleman lived an active and orderly life as lived many a good tribesman of his acquaintance. It was J. George Wright, the Indian Inspector who unintentionally transformed him into a national hero and raised him to the highest office of the Cherokee people. But let Inspector Wright relate the story as he reported it to the Secretary of the Interior in his forthright manner:

> W.C. Rogers of Talala[18] had his store closed in June, 1900 for non-payment of the merchant tax of one fourth of one percent on all goods introduced and offered for sale by him. Rogers refused to pay the tax and declared himself opposed to the collection of revenues by officers of the United States government. An attempt to force Rogers to pay his tax engendered considerable feeling among Cherokee merchants throughout the nation, and a fund was raised among these citizen merchants to prosecute the case in the courts, the amount of which was $500, a sum in excess of what the taxes of the contributors would have been had they been sufficiently patriotic to have paid the taxes for their own people without contest.
>
> They secured from the Hon. Joseph A. Gill, Judge of the United States Court, a temporary restraining order preventing officers of the Government from interfering with the business of Rogers in this matter, which order was made perpetual on the following September, after long arguments at Vinita. The court found that the officers of the United States had no authority to enforce collections of merchandise tax from Cherokee citizens. The non-citizen merchant tax does not include many of the large merchants.[19]

Inspector Wright had been located in the Indian Territory by the Curtis Act for the purpose of conducting the governments of the Five Tribes and paying off their indebtedness while the Dawes Commission completed enrollment and allotment in preparation for the dissolution of tribal autonomy.

As a national hero, Chief Rogers bore his honors modestly and discharged his duties well. He served as the nominal head of the nation until his death in 1919. In a little mission churchyard near Skiatook, "where his bones lie buried," stands a plain monument which tells a few simple facts about his life as the "Last Chief of the Cherokee Nation, Indian Territory:"

> From the Land of the Setting Sun these and other great Cherokees ever reach loving lands to comfort us whose faltering feet still press the soil, whose failing eyes still view the scenes they loved so well.

CHAPTER 28

The Keetoowah

The arrival of the Dawes Commission in 1894 quickened the interest for a time without creating an acute sense of apprehension among the Indians. Great and small, they pursued their accustomed ways, performing their daily tasks with the utmost outward serenity. Underneath this stoic calm, however, there smoldered a deep resentment of the indignities offered them by the ever-increasing throngs of aliens, many of whom showed arrogant contempt for the full-blood Indians, who as a group were actively alert to all that went on within their nation and the Territory, having vital interest at stake and their own methods of finding things out.

The *Cherokee Advocate* they scanned with care for information that concerned them. The little country churches, the rural post offices and country stores conducted by citizens of the nation were favorite meeting places. Here topics of interest were discussed in characteristic Indian fashion by a few who stood apart, or squatted on their heels with no apparent haste to be about their business. There was likely to be little conversation but in the long periods of listening silences pregnant with meaning, thoughts were exchanged with scarcely any need of spoken words.[1] The Indians were ever a psychic people.

By nature the Cherokees were a religious people, sincere and loyal in the devotion to their adopted faith. A great many were Baptists; but there were also Methodist, Moravian, and Presbyterian churches among them. But not all full bloods, nor those of mixed descent, had abjured the faith of their fathers and turned Christian.

Always there has been a creditable minority who practiced the rituals and believed in the principles taught by the ancient religion handed down by the priesthood from time immemorial. This was true even after the removal had separated the tribes from the crystal waters of their hallowed streams, beside which had stood the town houses consecrated to the devotional, as well as secular uses.

The ancient rituals and sacred formulas used by the Keetoowah or ancient order of priesthood, recorded in manuscripts in the Sequoyah script, had been carried by those Emigrants, who wished to perpetuate their native faiths in the new nation.

Those who clung to this pagan faith practiced it in secret for a time. After 1850, however, with the arrival of belated emigrants from the mountains of North Carolina, the cult gained in numbers and in confidence. New members were initiated into its mysteries, and with a priest whom they called Red Bird Smith as leader, the Keetoowah Society was formed with a constantly increasing membership of conservative full bloods.

In 1859 the Reverend Evan Jones, a radical abolitionist and a man of extraordinary adaptability, seized upon the idea of using this pagan group as the nucleus for a secret order, which he organized to oppose slavery among the Cherokees. Membership of the new organization included Christians with those of pagan faith. The new order adopted a constitution and by-laws, signs and pass words, and an emblem made of two ordinary pins crossed on the lapel of the coat or hunting shirt.

Upon the outbreak of war this organization opposed the secession of the Cherokee Nation and was thus pitted against the Knights of the Golden Circle, who joined the Confederacy. More than six thousand Keetoowah warriors, computed to be two-thirds of the fighting strength of the Cherokee Nation, saw active service in the federal army from 1862 to the end of the war.

The line of cleavage between the Christians and pagans had become so marked during those long hard months of camp and campaign life in the states, as to make a division advisable, even before peace came. In the main the evangelical group followed Colonel Lewis Downing into his party in 1867, while the conservatives adhered to the National Party, rekindled the fires, and practiced their rituals in secret with an actively interested membership, predominantly full blood.

In the excitement incident to the opening of Oklahoma Territory in 1889 and the agitation over the sale of the Strip, which followed, the two organizations reunited under a constitution that was wholly political in character, and they were thus functioning when the Dawes Commission arrived in the winter of 1894 to "wind up the affairs of the Five Tribes by allotting their lands and dissolving tribal governments."[2]

The Keetoowah society, as a unit, was against these measures—passively at first—because they believed themselves to be protected in their tenure by treaty guarantees such as that of 1828 in which they read: "The anxious desire of the government of the United States is to secure the Cherokee Nation of Indians a permanent home which shall, under the most solemn guarantee of the United States, be and remain forever a home that shall never in all future time be embarrassed by having extended around it the lines or placed over it the jurisdiction of a territory or state."[3]

By 1895, the opposition had become active and determined as the importunity of the federal Commission began to irk them. They held special meetings, sent scouts throughout the nation to find out everything possible regarding the intention of the commission and the sentiment of the Cherokee people in the various localities, and lent encouragement to the opposition in every way known to them. Because of the alertness of the non-Christian Keetoowahs and because of their secret activities, they were called Nighthawks. Their ultimate aim was to see that the people be kept thoroughly and correctly informed in order that when the right time came they might go to the polls and vote down obnoxious measures.

Following the advice of the inter-tribal council of June 1896,[4] the Cherokee Nation appointed a commission of eight, clothed with authority to confer with the Dawes Commission, but not to bind the Cherokees to an agreement until it had been approved by the people.[5] The members of the commission were: D. W. Bushyhead, chairman, C. V. Rogers, DeKinney Waters, Robin Pan, Adam Lacy, W. A. Duncan, R. B. Ross, and S. H. Mayes. It was agreed that the

Cherokee Commission should meet the Dawes Commission early in January, but when that time came, the federal emissaries were out of the country, having gone to Washington for the holidays, and remained there until after the inauguration of President McKinley.

While the Cherokee Commission awaited their return, the Keetoowahs raised funds by personal subscription and sent to Washington a delegation of their own number, including their best interpreter.[6] Their purpose, as they said, was to correct the impression prevailing in Congress that the chiefs and headmen were responsible for the full-blood opposition to allotment and the dissolution of tribal government. This pilgrimage had caused a congressional investigation to be made of the work and methods of the federal Commission, which came near putting an end to its existence before it could muster sufficient support to quash the charges that had been made against it.

Immediately upon their return, the Dawes commissioners went to Atoka, Choctaw Nation, where they negotiated an agreement with the Choctaws and Chickasaws on April 23. Ten days later, they finally reached Tahlequah, where a short conference was held in which they proposed the allotment of the whole Cherokee Nation, but before any action had been taken a peremptory order came from the Department of the Interior to reserve from allotment one hundred and fifty-seven thousand acres for the Delawares, thereby creating a situation which rendered it impossible for the Cherokees' Commission to continue negotiations in conformity with its instructions.

The conference, therefore, adjourned to meet in June at Fort Gibson, where the Dawes Commission had established headquarters. A few days later, the Missouri, Kansas, and Texas railroad served notice of a claim to eight hundred thousand acres based on their provisional land grant charter. These two notices put a new face on the entire question of Cherokee allotment, creating such a storm of opposition as had not been witnessed before.

Thoroughly convinced that the Delawares, the railroads, and the intruders were in league to deprive them of their lands, "the poor benighted full bloods, thrust back into the stony, wooded hills,"[7] now became so enraged that the glories of the long-abandoned war path again flamed red on the horizon, menacing alike their own and government agents who persisted in foisting a new agreement upon the nation.

The Cherokee Commission arrived at Fort Gibson on June 8. The following day, Congress passed an act giving "the United States Courts exclusive jurisdiction over all persons and over all matters civil and criminal within the Indian Territory after January 1, 1898,"[8] provided that, in the meantime, the Five Civilized Tribes did not make an agreement that would satisfy and be ratified by Congress.

Upon receipt of this news, the streets of the town came alive with purposeful Indians, whose threatening mien disrupted the conference and caused the federal Commission to report to headquarters: "We have been forced to the conclusion that notwithstanding the repeated promises of the Cherokee Commission to make a treaty with us . . . conditions are such here that we have little hope of succeeding in negotiating with the Cherokees. . . . We have therefore decided to go to the Creeks."[9]

The conditions thus referred to furnished exciting copy for the newspapers. Of the many news items which appeared, that in the *Muskogee Phoenix* on June 17th is typical: "Affairs are getting in a desperate condition over in the Cherokee Nation. The full-blood element is wrought up to a high pitch over the pending negotiations with the Dawes Commission and grave trouble is apprehended should the Cherokee Commission enter into an agreement with the United States representatives.

"The full-bloods have united, burying all past differences, and have organized themselves almost as a unit in opposition to any kind of a treaty, and rumor has it that they have marked out no less than forty of the progressive citizens who are urging the treaty, and given them an intimation that their lives will pay the forfeit for disrupting tribal autonomy."

"A rumor of so serious a nature as this," it was said, "would have been given little credence had it not been for the suspicious actions and open threats made by certain of the influential full-bloods to various members of the Cherokee Commission. Those conversant with the exact condition of affairs in the Cherokee Nation at that time did not hesitate to admit that in the event of an agreement to dissolve tribal autonomy, there would in all probability have been assassinations and bloodshed and riots far-reaching and disastrous in their effects."[10]

The withdrawal of the federal commission from the Cherokee Nation left the Keetoowahs free to return home and tend their waiting crops while negotiations with the Creeks were in progress. Having failed with the Creeks, the Commission returned in August to try again to negotiate with the Cherokees.

Meanwhile, in order to forestall an agreement, the full-bloods had called a National Keetoowah Convention, which met on August 10 under the banner presented to the Keetoowah warriors by the President of the United States at the close of the Civil War.[11] Under this banner, they formulated a set of resolutions protesting against any change being made in their government and land tenure: "Be it resolved by the National Keetoowah Convention that there be a strong protest filed which is to be a protest for all time to come against making any agreement and entering into any new treaties." The resolution prayed that the United States government leave the Cherokees alone to enjoy their present form of government and to give more importance to the faithful observance of the provisions of past treaties.

"We have kept the faith with the United States and observed faithfully all the provisions of these treaties, and we desire to protest against entering into any new treaties and against any change in our present form of government."[12]

Following the Keetoowah convention, a conference called by the two commissions to meet at Tahlequah was packed with Indians, many of whom were full bloods. After listening to white men and mixed bloods express their views, the commission at last asked to hear from the full-bloods present. Three speakers were chosen and addresses made in the Cherokee language were translated into English by an interpreter. Fortunately, those addresses have been preserved in the files of the *Dallas News*, by a reporter who happened to be present and took them down in shorthand.

"It is not within the power of English translation to do full justice to these three speeches," he wrote, "yet thought after thought was regularly snatched up as it came glowing from the furnace of inimitable eloquence, and shaped somewhat to the comprehension of the commissioners by the means of skillful interpretation."

The first speaker confined his remarks to the effects of the proposed changes upon the well-being of the people. "What will become of that class of people I have the honor to represent? We know the white men. They are an overbearing race. We full bloods can never live with them; their laws are too many; they are written in big books and in a language we cannot understand. We shall never know when we are violating their laws until we are arrested and dragged away to trial. Your judges shall also be white men; they will not be able to talk to us.

"When on trial we shall be at the mercy of the white man; when convicted we shall never know the nature of the offense. If it be the intention of the great government of the United States to annul our treaties and turn the white man in upon us, it would be much the same as if the Great Father at Washington should take us up and plunge us into Hell! Death would be preferable!"

The second speaker had for his theme the sanctity of treaty obligations. In regard to a new agreement, he said he could not see the need of negotiations. "You tell us that our old treaties are not any good, but there was a time when you did not think so. When did they lose their force? What is it that has spoiled them? It is not we. We have violated no treaty, we have broken no laws. . . . Treaties never die except by the consent of both parties. The Great White Father makes treaties with people beyond the great waters and they live forever. Why should he consider treaties made with us less sacred?

". . . It is unjust to spoil our treaties. We are a small people, much smaller than we used to be. . . . The Great Father has many big guns; protection was promised us yet we know that unless we obey him they will not protect us, but will be turned upon us. Yet if resistance were practicable and it were at all availing, I should willingly pour out my blood in the defense of my people."

The third speaker was an old man. "My business has been to preach the gospel. . . . It has been my special care to look after the young men . . . and lead them to the Savior of the World . . . and in doing this I have also been in the habit of recommending to them the ways of the white man as something worthy of our imitation. But I begin to doubt whether I have been right in doing this. If . . . the commissioners . . . really mean to break faith with us . . . then their example will no more be worthy of an Indian's imitation. . . . I am not in favor of a new treaty; our old treaties are all we need. . . . All we want is peace! We only want to be let alone."

The Dawes Commission, having received at last a convincing answer to the contention that it was the full-bloods who were unalterably opposed to a change, could only reply: "What you want is beyond our power to grant. Congress has determined to make a change in the political condition of the country, and we cannot help it. We can only advise you to be wise, improve the opportunity offered you and prepare for the inevitable."[13] To the Secretary of the Interior their report stated that the full-bloods were hopelessly influenced by designing half-breeds[14] and intermarried white men and that no agreement could be reached at that time. The act of Congress extending the jurisdiction of the United States Courts over the Indian Territory after January 1, 1898, it was believed, would take care of the situation for a time.[15]

This meeting at Tahlequah proved conclusively the full bloods, crowded back into the stony wooded hills, were not being betrayed by their own tribesmen, but that the Cherokee Commission was representing the wishes of the majority of all Cherokee citizens. In justification of their failure to effect an agreement, the Cherokees addressed a memorial to the Dawes Commission on October 28 in which they reviewed the history of their case since the previous December, when they had declared their readiness to begin negotiations, and outlined the developments since that time, which had rendered impossible an agreement on terms required by the government. The absence of the Dawes Commission in Washington for four months was called to their attention. The complications arising from demands of the Delawares and the Missouri, Kansas, and Texas Railroad were reviewed, and the passage of the act by Congress extending the jurisdiction of the United States courts over the Indian Territory were referred to as an insuperable obstacle in the way of an agreement. "Scarcely anything more destructive of the completion of an agreement with your commission could have been done than the passage of this act," it declared.[16]

The warning of the Dawes Commission to the Keetoowah that their opposition to a change was futile and that they should prepare to give way to the will of a higher authority apparently went unheeded. Their sentiments remained unaltered. Only their tactics changed. The white adopted citizens, however, and some of mixed blood, realizing the utter helplessness of the situation began to readjust themselves and prepare for the inevitable.

CHAPTER 29

The Curtis Act

A year after Congress had conferred citizenship jurisdiction upon the Dawes Commission, the white population in the Indian Territory outnumbered the Indians five to one. This eager, expectant, demanding throng had interpreted the act of Congress in creating the commission and clothing it with extraordinary powers as equivalent to a pledge to reorganize the Indian country in the interest of white men. To assist the government in redeeming this pledge, the outlanders imported printing presses, set up forms, and began printing and distributing newspapers and magazines by the thousands. By 1897 there were reported to be fifty publications[1] in Indian Territory, several of which had been established for the avowed purpose of advocating allotment and a change of government.

From time to time these newspapers reported progress on the work of the ten federal surveying parties, which, under instructions from the Interior Department, the United States Geological Survey had put to work surveying Indian lands as if they belonged to the public domain before ever an agreement had been reached with any of the Five Civilized Tribes. The Dawes Commission at the same time was engrossed in compiling new citizenship rolls for the five nations in readiness for allotment.

While these preparations were going forward in the Indian Territory, Washington had not been idle. A rising young congressman from Kansas, an Indian of the Kaw tribe, had introduced in the House a bill for "the protection of the people of Indian Territory, and other things," namely: The extension of the jurisdiction of the United States Courts over Indian Territory, the laying out of townsites, and the leasing of timber, and of the farming and grazing lands of the Indians.[2] This bill was passed by the House on June 6, 1896, and sent to the Senate, where it was referred to the Committee on Judiciary to be taken up later as the basis of the Curtis Act.

These activities were all part of a concerted plan on the part of Congress to dissolve tribal governments and allot Indian lands regardless of all opposition. But the Indians had shown themselves to be less amenable than had been expected. Having surrounded themselves with a wall of opposition, they presented a stubborn resistance. Not until April 1897 did the Choctaws and Chickasaws capitulate by consenting to negotiate. A breach having been made in this wall by the Atoka agreement, the Seminole Nation surrendered and signed an agreement with the Commission.[3] The Cherokees refused to negotiate on the basis laid down by Congress.

Experience had convinced the government that the Cherokees and the Creeks, with their high percentage of full bloods, would never surrender willingly what they did not want to give up at all. For a time it was almost worth a man's life to advocate allotment in the councils of these two nations. So pronounced was the opposition and so severe the condemnation of the Dawes Commission and its methods of dealing with the Indians that Congress, in deference to public opinion, called the commissioners to Washington where they appeared before a federal investigating committee to answer charges preferred against them. As foreordained, they were exonerated, however, and sent back to Indian Territory to complete the citizenship rolls, while Congress proceeded to pass "An Act for the Protection of the People of the Indian Territory, and other Purposes," based on the Curtis bill of 1896 and the Atoka and Seminole agreements of 1897.

Briefly summarized, the Curtis Act provided for the enlargement and extension of the jurisdiction of the United States Courts for the Indian Territory so as to include all causes of action irrespective of parties; it stipulated that when the citizenship rolls of any tribe should be completed and the lands surveyed, the Dawes Commission should allot the lands, giving each citizen, as far as possible, his fair and equal share; and it gave to the Dawes Commission, and to the federal courts, jurisdiction in determining the status of a large number of claimants whose citizenship rights had been denied by tribal courts.[4]

Provision was made for the incorporation of towns and for the appointment of townsite commissions;[5] for the payment of rents and royalties due the tribes into the treasury of the United States to the credit of the tribes. It prohibited the collection of these revenues by tribal officials and the payment of any moneys on any account whatsoever to the tribal governments, such payments thereafter to be made by the Secretary of the Interior, or by his agents.

The act authorized the segregation of one hundred and fifty thousand acres of land in the Cherokee Nation, subject to the adjudication of the rights of the Delawares; made provision for the location of a United States Indian Inspector in the Indian Territory to perform any duties required by law under the direction of the Secretary of the Interior; abolished the tribal courts and prohibited all officers of such courts after July 1, 1898 from performing any act under tribal laws. Additional measures safeguarded the property rights of United States citizens, guaranteed to the Cherokee freedmen equal rights with Cherokees by blood, and provided schools for children of non-citizens.

The effect of the Curtis Act upon the Five Civilized Tribes was to paralyze their governments and to reduce them from the status of autonomous republics to that of departmental dependencies controlled by the Secretary of the Interior. The administration of their vast tribal estates, including large sums of money, was taken from the constituted authorities of the nations and assigned to federal agents, to be administered by the United States as trust funds, the largest trusts in the history of the world, in the estimation of such an eminent authority as Representative John Sherman of New York.[6]

The Curtis Act went into effect automatically. In August 1898, the Secretary of the Interior appointed J. George Wright as Indian Inspector in the Indian Territory. The inspector was to have supervisory control over the officials of the Union Agency at Muskogee,[7] including the United States Indian agent, the superintendent of schools for the Indian Territory, the revenue inspector for the Cherokee Nation, and the trustees for the Choctaw and Chickasaw

Nations. He had, also, the general oversight of the townsite commissioners and engineers, and the ten surveying parties that were engaged in surveying the lands for allotment.[8]

In addition to the supervisory control, which he exercised over federal agents, the Indian inspector was given jurisdiction over the Five Civilized tribes that was autocratic in character and vice-regal in dominion.[9]

In the reorganization of the Indian Territory under the Curtis Act, the political system which replaced the constitutional governments of the Five Tribes was a type of bureaucracy ordinarily reserved for subject nations on the point of rebellion. In it the native population had no voice. In it there was no place for Indian social or economic welfare, nor for the preservation of aboriginal languages and culture.

Federal appointments were made with no regard to the welfare of the Indian, but for personal or political reasons. Government agents, as a rule, were anti-Indian in sentiment, and inclined to deprecate whatever might serve to perpetuate native institutions and tribal patriotism on the ground of their tendency to retard progress in the work of reconstruction.

Upon his arrival the Indian Inspector, although no agreement had been reached with its people, at once assumed control of the fiscal affairs of the Cherokee Nation, affected by appointing a revenue collector to replace the native fiscal agents and relieve them of their duties and emoluments.

Under the statutes of the Cherokee Nation, taxes were levied on merchandise brought into the nation and offered for sale by non-citizen merchants; on cattle imported from the states; and on hay, gravel, timber, and coal sold to non-citizens; in addition to these were the occupation tax assessed against non-citizen agricultural and mechanical laborers, the fees for ferry charters, and the money derived from the sale of town lots.[10]

The federal revenue collector added to these taxes all moneys paid for the board of students at the male and female seminaries and the colored high school. The revenues derived from these sources minus the cost of collection, were forwarded to the

Sub-Treasury in St. Louis where they were placed to the credit of the Cherokee Nation to be disbursed by administration employees.

As decreed by the Curtis Act, the interest on the invested funds which had been paid semi-annually to the treasurer of the Nation and apportioned by him to the maintenance of government, schools, and the orphans and insane of the nation, was consigned for disbursement to the Indian inspector, who passed upon all warrants issued by the nation, honored or disallowed claims at his discretion, and made recommendations to the Secretary of Interior for curtailing the expense of maintaining the tribal governments. Whatever funds were available he applied to the payment at par of warrants outstanding against the nation, some of which had been bought by individuals in California and by financiers in Wall Street at from forty to sixty cents on the dollar.

The Inspector sent his field agents to patrol the nations of the Cherokees and Creeks in aid of the Dawes Commission, while a corps of clerks, stenographers, and attorneys stood ready to execute his orders. When Cherokee authorities notified him that, in their opinion, his jurisdiction did not extend to their nation and warned him that they would not tolerate officious intrusion on their prerogatives, he ignored them. He was under orders from above and with the impersonal precision of a robot, he addressed himself to the execution of those orders, turning a deaf ear to all arguments to the contrary.

The Cherokees did not submit supinely to what they considered a high-handed act of despotism. The authorities of the nation, holding confidently to their land patent and treaty guarantees, refused to acknowledge the right of the government to impose the Curtis Act upon them without their consent. Since they had bound themselves by no agreement to surrender their rights, the status of the Cherokee Nation had not been affected by congressional legislation.

The Secretary of the Interior, on the contrary, denied this contention and ruled that the Cherokee Nation had automatically become subject to the Curtis Act since no agreement with that nation had been ratified by Congress. The Dawes Commission, on the basis of this ruling, proceeded with the work of completing the rolls and plans for the allotment of lands.

When the Cherokees found their claim denied and practically all the functions of government usurped, Chief Samuel Houston Mayes, as a last expedient, entered suit to test the constitutionality of the Curtis Act by enjoining the Secretary of the Interior from setting aside a treaty. The Supreme Court settled the question by ruling that the Curtis Act was a legislative enactment over which the court had no jurisdiction.[11]

CHAPTER 30

The Cherokee
Allotment Agreement

The anomalous position occupied by the Cherokee Nation during the next four years was as harassing as it was ineffectual. With its claims to autonomy denied by an imperialistic government that abrogated treaty guarantees and canceled land patents at will; with its tribal courts condemned and the hands of its law shackled by federal legislative acts; with its sparsely settled areas infested with alien criminals; its legislative functions circumscribed and its executive department shorn of authority; with its cherished school system under process of reconstruction in the interests of foreigners; its revenues and invested funds consigned as a trust fund to federal fiscal agents; and the entire nation overrun by grafters, the like of which has never been seen in modern history, the Cherokees found themselves in a situation similar to that in Georgia sixty years before. Again they were surrounded by fires kindled for the purpose of "smoking them out," of compelling them to capitulate, to "give in."

Under such duress it was that the Cherokees, on January 17, 1899, consented to an agreement on the basis of the allotment of lands in severalty, share and share alike; the continuation of the executive and legislative branches of the Cherokee government until allotment had been completed; and the understanding that the Cherokee Nation should not be included in any state or territory without its consent.[1]

This agreement, when submitted to a popular vote, was approved by the people but failed of ratification in Congress, a determined protest having been filed by a group of citizens under the leadership of Reverend Walter A. Duncan.[2]

Meantime, the opposition of the Nighthawk Kee-too-wah to the agreement for allotment and the dissolution of tribal government remained unshaken. They called such an agreement a "Dawes Commission treaty" and, under the organized leadership of David Muskrat, Daniel Redbird, Wilson Cummings, and others, opposed it on the ground that it was grossly unjust for "the United States government, their trustee," to subject so large a number of people to such a revolutionary change all at once. They should be given time to prepare themselves and become reconciled to the idea of relinquishing accustomed institutions.

Thus the Kee-too-wahs reasoned, and staunch in the belief that Providence would intervene in their behalf, sought seclusion among the fastness of the hills that furnished fuel for the sacred fire they had rekindled as the signal that a national crisis again confronted them.

Here they repeatedly ignored notices to come in and enroll, so that after a time the Dawes Commission became impatient and sent out corps of workers among them to complete the census. On the approach of the enrolling crews, the Indians retreated to their cabins and closed their doors. The field workers followed them, opened doors without knocking, and crossed thresholds uninvited to demand the desired data. Such conduct tended only to aggravate race antagonism and to intensify the Indian's reluctance to surrender his tribal autonomy.

Baffled and defeated by the Sphinx-like silence they came to fear, the census enumerators retreated, claiming their lives were in jeopardy and that the Kee-too-wahs and a few mixed blood politicians were trying to defeat the will of the government. Their garbled accounts and fictitious stories, reaching Washington, tended to harden the heart of the administration against the Indians, and in order to protect and exonerate its agents, the commission invoked the aid of the courts to compel the Indians to come in and enroll. When they still remained obdurate, force was used. United States marshals went out and arrested some of the Key Men,[3] hauled them off to prison for daring to stand athwart the course of the government, "clanged the iron door upon their cell," turned the key, and left them there.[4]

This durance the prisoners chose to bear in silence, denying nothing, admitting nothing. The time for words had passed. Theirs was the attitude of a valiant people with its back to the wall standing for home and country and for the rights of free men.

When after a time, however, it had become apparent that they were following a losing cause and that their organized opposition was not only futile but destructive of the interests of the entire nation, a sufficient number to break the deadlock withdrew and joined the progressives. Thus after four years of repression under the Curtis Act, an agreement approved by Congress was ratified by the Cherokee people in an election held August 7, 1902.[5] And on August 12, Principal Chief T. M. Buffington issued a proclamation declaring its adoption.

The technical title of the agreement was, "An act for the allotment of lands of the Cherokee Nation, for the disposition of townsites therein and for other purposes,"[6] although it was commonly called the Cherokee Allotment Agreement. In general, it provided for the appraisement of lands at their true value by the Dawes Commission; for the allotment of lands and the designation of a homestead of forty acres which should be nontaxable and inalienable for twenty-one years. It ruled that white adopted citizens, married prior to December 1895, were entitled to the full rights of Cherokee citizens to participate in the allotment of lands and in the distribution of tribal funds.

A list of twenty-three items was made setting aside for a specific purpose plots of land ranging from one to one hundred twenty acres. The list included land for townsites, for town and rural cemeteries, for churches and school houses, and for mission stations. It included in addition the Council House and grounds at Tahlequah; the national jail; the *Cherokee Advocate* printing plant; the Male and Female Seminaries; the Orphan Asylum; the Colored High School; the Cherokee Insane Asylum; and the School for The Deaf, Dumb, and Blind, at Fort Gibson.

The agreement stipulated also that all funds of the tribe and all moneys accruing therefrom should be paid out under the direction of the Secretary of the Interior, and when required for per capita payments, should be made directly to each individual by an officer appointed by the United States under the direction of the Secretary of the Interior. The payment of tribal indebtedness was not overlooked. Before any pro rata distribution of the tribal funds should be made, the Secretary of the Interior was authorized to cause all just obligations of the nation to be paid. As in the Curtis Act, jurisdiction was given the Court of Claims, with right of appeal to the Supreme Court, to examine and adjudicate any claim of the Cherokees against the United States arising under treaty stipulations, upon which suit should be instituted within two years.

The railroads which had been instrumental in bringing about the change were disappointed in their expectations of securing the land grants promised them by Congress in case the Indian Territory ever became public domain. Section twenty-four provided that only lands granted by act of Congress for right of way, depots, station grounds, water stations, stock yards, or similar uses connected with the maintenance and operation of any railroad, should be reserved from allotment.

To the Principal Chief of the Cherokee Nation was assigned the duty of executing and delivering the patents to allotments made by the Dawes Commission. The signature of the principal chief and the great seal of the nation were affixed to each document which bore also the name of the Secretary of the Interior, the stamp of the United States, and the name and roll number of the allottee, together with the description of the land. More than forty thousand patents were issued to the citizens of the Cherokee Nation, although the number of Cherokees by blood was scarcely four-sevenths of that number.[7]

It will be remembered that according to the "Dark Treaty" of 1866 the Cherokee freedmen were to enjoy all the rights and privileges of the Indians and to share equally in all their land and moneys. The Dawes Commission admitted to citizenship a long list of those whose rights the Cherokees had consistently denied. More than four thousand negroes shared in the tribal lands and funds of the Cherokees.

By the time the Allotment Agreement had gone into effect, the Cherokee Nation had practically ceased to function save as a financial corporation in the hands of a receiver. The Dawes Commission was deeply engrossed in its business of completing the rolls and allotting the lands in view of winding up the landed estates of the Five Civilized Tribes; while the Indian Inspector, acting in the capacity of fiscal agent for the government and receiver for the Cherokee Nation, was liquidating its indebtedness, balancing its ledgers and auditing its accounts, as the last step toward the formal dissolution of the tribal government.

Meanwhile, Congress, by act of March 3, 1901, had conferred citizenship upon the citizens of the Five Tribes, and the country had undergone marked changes. The towns had increased in number and in population as the white population increased. In 1902 the Indian Territory had one hundred and forty-seven incorporated towns in which schools had been organized for the benefit of children whose parents were non-citizens.[8]

By that time many non-citizens had acquired title to town lots on which they had erected homes and business houses. On May 27, 1902, Congress passed an act making it unlawful to remove or deport any person from the Indian Territory who was in lawful possession of any lots or parcels of land in any town or city of the Indian Territory. On the preceding April, an act had been approved abolishing the penalty for paying the tribal taxes so much complained of, because no part of these revenues were expended for public purposes, such as roads, bridges, and schools.

The dissolution of the Dawes Commission and the withdrawal from their midst of the men who constituted its personnel elicited no expression of regret from the citizens of the Five Tribes, who had always looked upon them askance. Full blood Cherokees and Creeks especially had reason to feel relieved when they withdrew from the country.

The work of the commission had lasted over a period of twelve years and through three national administrations. When appointed by President Cleveland on November 11, 1893,[9] it was composed of three members. Later the number was increased to five, then reduced to four, and on July 1, 1905, the commission was dissolved under an act of Congress, the work having been so nearly finished as to render its services no longer indispensable. The unfinished business was taken over by a commissioner for the Five Civilized Tribes, who under the direction of the Secretary of the Interior carried it to completion.[10]

According to the Cherokee Allotment Agreement, the tribal government of the Cherokees was to have ended on March 4, 1906. As the time drew near, however, it became obvious that the work of allotment could not be completed in so short a time; consequently, a year of grace had to be allowed by a joint resolution of Congress extending the time to March 4, 1907.[11]

There was still so much unfinished miscellaneous business that Congress, on April 26, 1906, passed "An Act to provide for the final disposition of the business of the Five Civilized Tribes,"[12] which included: the completion of the rolls; the determination of the status of illegitimate children and those Cherokee freedmen whose citizenship was yet in doubt; allotment contests; the removal of a principal chief for non-performance of duties; the transference of tribal schools to the control of the Secretary of the Interior and the disposal of tribal school funds; the disposal of tribal buildings and the per capita distribution of tribal funds; also the continuance of the tribal government for all purposes authorized by law until June 30, 1914, when it was to be finally abolished.[13]

As the time drew near for the dissolution of Indian Territory, the question of statehood took on two aspects: that of separate statehood for each territory, and that of joint statehood for Indian Territory and Oklahoma Territory. Each side had its protagonists and each its opponents, the white people favoring single statehood, and the citizens of the Five Tribes, separate statehood for the Indian Territory, with a constitution and laws adapted to the needs of the Indians.

A memorial declaring for separate statehood for the Indian Territory was adopted by an intertribal council held at South McAlester as early as November 1897: "We will never consent to a union with Oklahoma. When a change of government takes place we will ask admission as a state of the Union with constitutional provisions irrepealable, protecting the property rights and political privileges of our people, the constitution to be made by our own people.

"We represent sixty-five thousand sober, industrious, and God-fearing people, owners of the entire soil of the Indian Territory by solemn treaty and patented titles, people who came into a wilderness driven by force and made it a cultivated land, people who have erected schools, churches and courts of justice and governments under which they have found safety and happiness. We appeal to the moral sentiment of a great and magnanimous nation in whose hands is our ultimate destiny and in whose national life and history we have a decent and honorable place."[14]

The opposition of the Cherokees to sharing a government under white people has been previously quoted. "We know the white men. They are a proud and overbearing race. We full-bloods can never live with them. Their laws are too many; they are written in big books and in a language which we cannot understand."[15] Death would be preferable to having "the white men turned in upon them."

True this extreme sense of apprehension on the part of the full-bloods was not felt by some of the foremost leaders of mixed descent whose broader contacts and superior education afforded them some advantage over their compatriots in dealing with aliens and alien institutions. Nevertheless, they never relaxed their vigilance and solicitude for their compatriots, who were obsessed with so great a fear for the future.

As the time for the dissolution of their nation approached, chiefs and councilors of the Five Tribes conferred often with each other on plans for organizing an Indian state strictly for Indians, of Indians, and by Indians. To this end the principal chiefs of the Five Tribes organized and entered into a compact to call a convention, formulate a constitution for the Indian Territory and, as California and others had done before them, ask for admission into the Union as a separate state.

It was left to Chief Rogers of the Cherokee Nation, and to Governor McCurtain of the Choctaw, to take the initiative. They, on July 6, issued a statement in which they urged the advisability of taking steps toward organizing the Indian Territory as a state. This policy having been endorsed by all of the Five Tribes, their officials issued a joint proclamation[16] calling for a convention to meet at Muskogee on August 21, for the purpose of drawing up a form of state government for the Indian Territory.[17] The mass meetings for the selection of delegates to the convention, which were held in each enrolling town, made no invidious distinction against non-citizens, although it was distinctly understood that the movement was initiated by the Indians for the purpose of safeguarding their own interests.

The convention was called to order by Chief Rogers, the temporary chairman, one hundred and fifty delegates presenting credentials. A permanent organization was effected with Chief Pleasant Porter of the Creek Nation as president; and Alexander Posey, the gifted Creek Poet, secretary. Robert L. Owen read a memorial from the Keetoowah Society favoring separate statehood and prohibition. The committee on constitution had as one of its members, A. Grant Evans, an English scholar and educator thoroughly in sympathy with the Indians with whom he had been associated as teacher and preacher for many years. To him was accorded the distinction of drafting a seal for the proposed state. In the main, however, the instrument formulated by the committee represented the efforts of representatives from the Five Tribes, themselves exceptionally able men, equal to the work in hand.[18]

"We the people of the State of Sequoyah, do ordain and establish this constitution:"[19] so ran the preamble. The new state, which was to be divided into forty-eight counties and twenty-one senatorial districts, was to have a legislative department of two houses styled the "General Assembly of the State of Sequoyah." Provision was made for a free public school system including higher education for boys and girls, and the right of suffrage was to be extended to women by legislative enactment. Fort Gibson was designated as the seat of government.[20] The design of the seal was a five-pointed

star, in the points of which were placed the seals of the Five Civilized Tribes. Above the star and between the two upper points
appeared the half-length figure of Sequoyah holding in his hands a
tablet on which was written in Cherokee characters the legend, "We
are Brothers." In the remaining spaces between the points were
grouped forty-five stars, emblematic of the forty-five states of the
Union at that time.

On September 8, the convention, having recessed for two
weeks, met and approved the constitution, which, in spite of a vigorous campaign of opposition conducted through the newspapers,
was adopted by a vote of seven to one when it was submitted to the
people on November 7. Thus, "without election machinery, without rival candidates to stimulate voters, and with no revenues to
defray the expenses of such an election, the total of fifty-six thousand votes cast was significant of a deep interest in the question by
the people,"[21] most vitally concerned.

In a supreme effort to secure the favorable consideration of
the government, a memorial was dispatched to Washington in
December by a committee of four, which had been appointed by
the constitutional convention to present the claims of the Sequoyah
constitution to the administration and work for its adoption.[22] The
committee had a cool reception, and the plan it sponsored was
never given a hearing. The administration did not favor separate
statehood for the Indian Territory at this time, nor at any time. President Theodore Roosevelt made his stand clear in his opening message to the fifty-ninth Congress by the following pronouncement:

> I recommend that Indian Territory and Oklahoma be ad-
> mitted as one state, and that New Mexico and Arizona be
> admitted as one state. There is no obligation upon us to
> treat territorial subdivisions, which are matters of conven-
> tion only, as binding us in the question of admission to
> statehood. Nothing has taken up more time in the Con-
> gress during the past few years than the question as to the
> statehood to be granted to the four territories above men-
> tioned, and, after careful consideration of all that has been

developed in the discussion of the question, I recommend that they be immediately admitted as two states. There is no justification for further delay, and the advisability of making four territories into two states has been clearly established.[23]

Pursuant to this policy, Congress proceeded at once to act. On December 4, a bill for the admission of Oklahoma and Indian Territory as a single state with the name of Oklahoma was introduced in the House,[24] and on January 25 in the Senate,[25] under the name of the Hamilton Statehood Bill. After much discussion in both houses it was passed as the Enabling Act. On June 16, 1906, the bill for joint statehood was approved by the President.[26]

The act provided that the people of the Indian Territory and Oklahoma Territory were to adopt a constitution and be admitted into the Union as a state under the name of Oklahoma. Delegates chosen in a general election held on November 16, 1908, met in convention at Guthrie, Oklahoma Territory, and framed a constitution, which the people of both territories ratified in an election held on September 17, 1904.[27] By presidential proclamation, Oklahoma became a state on November 16, 1907.[28]

Single statehood for the Indian Territory and Oklahoma was regarded as a great achievement by the administration, and by its protagonists in both territories, who celebrated the event with great display of musical and oratorical enthusiasm. Of all the able addresses made on that occasion, perhaps none surpass in richness of allegory the efforts of a young enthusiast inspired by high hopes of winning distinguished honors for himself in the state of his adoption.

Quoted in part, it reads:

The brightest day in all the Red Man's land has dawned. From the skies of the receding night. . . . builders of an empire have plucked the brightest star and pinned it to the azure field of Old Glory, adding new luster to the Nation's flag.

In imperishable letters a new name has been inscribed upon the banner of freedom, . . . a name now heard in the busy marts of trade, and wherever beats the Nation's throbbing heart of industry. . . . Today we stand erect, clothed with the full panoply of American citizenship. Today we have entered into our inheritance. . . . Today we begin a new era with the ideal government of the immortal Lincoln, "a government of the people, for the people and by the people." . . . And so we turn with confidence to the future, proud in the record of yesterday, secure in the belief that tomorrow will bring us . . . additional triumphs. . . . The clang of their political shackles, falling from the arms of freedmen makes wondrous music for the patriots who fought in freedom's cause. . . . It is but meet that we should pause . . . and tell them that they builded better than they knew in giving to posterity the greatest commonwealth the nation ever welcomed into the sisterhood of states, Oklahoma![29]

And . . .

The Red Man, what had he to say
To welcome in this glad new day?
Faced he the east to shout a bright sun up?
Pledged he his fealty in brimming cup?
Paeans of praise intoned his dark-eyed brood,
Their mother looking on in placid mood?
Not so. As sheep before the shearer he was dumb,
His heart bowed down, distraught, and all his senses numb.
Muted his children's voices at their play,
The while their elders went apart to pray.
The stony, wooded hills gave back no answering shout;
Idle the Council House, its ancient fires put out.
No ground remained to him in all his native land
On which to press his feet, resilient rise and stand
And, head erect, go forth once more to mend his broken
    walls,
Rebuild his schools, reconstitute his Council halls.
Athwart his path the lengthening shadows lay,
The Darkening Land, a few more moons away.

Notes

A Tribute to Rachel Caroline Eaton

1. As originally published in the *Tulsa Daily World*, August 30, 1931. In *History of Oklahoma State Federation of Women's Clubs, 1939*, and in the *Tulsa Indian Women's Club Yearbook, 1976–77*, it appeared with slightly different wording. The last line had been changed to "Renew your Council Fire."

Introduction

1. Turtle Island is the name of the continent so often referred to as North America. The name references Indigenous land and origin stories. For an example of a Cherokee version of the origin story of Turtle Island, see "A Story of Turtle Island Told by Sequoyah Guess" in Christopher B. Teuton, *Cherokee Stories of the Turtle Island Liars' Club* (Chapel Hill: University of North Carolina Press, 2012), 39–40.

2. Because the seminary burned that year, she and her fellow students' graduation ceremony was held at the Cherokee Male Seminary. Muriel H. Wright, "Rachel Caroline Eaton," *Chronicles of Oklahoma* 16, no. 4 (December 1938): 509.

3. The forced Removal of the Cherokee Nation from their homelands in the Southeast to the land commonly known today as northeastern Oklahoma. Many other Native Nations also endured forced removals.

4. Martha Berry, *Our Fires Still Burn* (2002), https://berrybeadwork.com/custom-listing/our-fires-still-burn/ (accessed July 16, 2025); Martha Berry, *Fire Carrier's Footsteps*, https://berrybeadwork.com/custom-listing/fire-carriers-footsteps/ (accessed July 16, 2025).

5. For a discussion of a Cherokee view of history and a definition of ᎣᏣᏈᏍᎩ/kanohesgi, see Heidi M. Altman and Thomas N. Belt, "Reading History: Cherokee History Through a Cherokee Lens," *Native South* 1 (2008): 90–98. I use the term (hi)stories to reflect the connection between history and story as seen in ᎣᏣᏈᏍᎩ/kanohesgi. Cherokee linguist Ben Frey notes that ᎣᏣᏈᏍᏗ/kanohesdi is another way to say (hi)story.

6. For a discussion of Nancy Ward/Nanyehi, see Michelene E. Pesantubbee, "Nancy Ward: American Patriot or Cherokee Nationalist?" *American Indian Quarterly* 28, no. 2 (Spring 2012): 177–206. See also Theda Perdue, *Cherokee Women: Gender and Culture Change, 1700–1835* (Lincoln: University of Nebraska Press, 1998).

7. All three of these were chiefs in the Cherokee Nation.

8. John Ross, Principal Chief of the Cherokee Nation, led the fight against Removal, but a smaller number of Cherokees had come to believe it was inevitable. A handful of Cherokee men signed the Treaty of New Echota in 1835, resulting in the forced relocation of the majority of Cherokees to lands in what is now known as Oklahoma. While many of Eaton's contemporaries shared her pro-John Ross viewpoints, not everyone did. Readers should view Eaton's work as one of many Cherokee voices in a diverse Nation.

9. James Mooring York Jr. and Paulyne York Vanzant, entry 170, *The History of Rogers County, Oklahoma* (Claremore, OK: Claremore College Foundation, 1979), 184–185; Ken Willhoite, "War Changed Future of G. W. Eaton," *Claremore Daily Progress*, March 22, 2008.

10. Eaton writes in this volume that the Cherokees "were familiar with the medicinal properties and food values of herbs and roots, and they knew the benefits to be derived from hot and cold water. They are said to have been among the first people known to use the vapor bath."

11. John M. Rhea, *A Field of Their Own: Women and American Indian History, 1830–1941* (University of Oklahoma Press), 158; Rachel Caroline Eaton, *John Ross and the Cherokee Indians* (Menasha, WI: George Banta Publishing Company, 1914); Rachel Caroline Eaton, *John Ross and the Cherokee Indians* (Muscogee, OK: Star Printery, 1921).

12. Eaton was hired as Dean of Women and Professor of History at Trinity University in Texas in 1916. *Trinity University Bulletin*, August 1, 1916, 5.

13. James Mooring York Jr. and Paulyne York Vanzant, entry 170, *History of Rogers County, Oklahoma*, 184–185; Wright, "Rachel Caroline Eaton," 509–510. See also Farina King, "'Loyal Countrywoman': Rachel Caroline Eaton, Alumna of the Cherokee National Female Seminary," in *This Is Herland: Gendered Activism in Oklahoma From the 1870s to the 2010s*, ed. Sarah Eppler Janda and Patricia Loughlin (Norman: University of Oklahoma Press, 2021), 99–120; Rhea, *A Field of Their Own*, 156–162; Kirby Brown, *Stoking the Fire: Nationhood in Cherokee Writing, 1907–1970* (Norman: University of Oklahoma Press, 2018), 66–116.

14. Julie L. Reed, *Serving the Nation: Cherokee Sovereignty and Social Welfare, 1800–1907* (Norman: University of Oklahoma Press, 2016), 209.

15. The Cherokee Female Seminary was modeled on Mount Holyoke Seminary, a women's college in the Northeast. For an in-depth discussion of the Cherokee Female Seminary, see Devon Mihesuah, *Cultivating the Rosebuds: The Education of Women at the Cherokee Female Seminary, 1851–1909* (Urbana and Chicago: University of Illinois Press, 1993).

16. For a further discussion of Gadugi as research practice, see Emily Legg, *Stories of Our Living Ephemera: Storytelling Methodologies in the Archives of the Cherokee National Seminaries, 1846–1907* (Logan: Utah State University Press, 2023), 223–242.

17. Rachel Caroline Eaton, "Domestic Science Among the Primitive Cherokees," *Tulsa Daily World*, September 19, 1926.

18. Wahnenauhi, *Historical Sketches of the Cherokees, Together with Some of their Customs, Traditions, and Superstitions*, ed. Jack Frederick Kilpatrick, Anthropological Papers, No. 77, Smithsonian Institution, Bureau of American Ethnology, Bulletin

196 (Washington: US Government Printing Office, 1966), 183; Narcissa Owen, *A Cherokee Woman's America: Memoirs of Narcissa Owen*, ed. Karen Kilcup (Gainesville: University of Florida Press, 2005), 46; Eaton, *John Ross and the Cherokee Indians* (1914), preface. Mabel Anderson, also a graduate of the Cherokee Female Seminary, discussed her use of oral history in her biography of Stand Watie. Anderson's political leanings differed greatly from Eaton's. Mabel W. Anderson, *The Life of General Stand Watie: The Only Indian Brigadier General of the Confederate Army and the Last General to Surrender*, rev. ed. (Pryor, OK: self-published, 1931), 8.

19. Mrs. Caroline Eaton, Oklahoma Federation of Women's Clubs Credential Card, Historic Oklahoma Collection, Oklahoma Federation of Women's Clubs, Oklahoma Historical Society, Oklahoma City; Myrtle A. McDougal to President of Sequoyah Historical Society, March 29, 1909, Historic Oklahoma Collection, Oklahoma Federation of Women's Clubs, Oklahoma Historical Society, Oklahoma City.

20. "Sequoyah Historical Society," *Claremore Progress*, April 4, 1908. In 1931, Carolyn Thomas Foreman wrote that the society had been composed of "seventy Indian citizens." It was certainly remembered as an Indigenous historical society, and it may have been the case that the advertisement in the *Claremore Progress* was written in such a way as to gain approval and recognition from Euro-American audiences. Carolyn Thomas Foreman, "Aunt Eliza of Tahlequah," *Chronicles of Oklahoma* 9, no. 1 (March 1931): 53. See also Rhea, *A Field of Their Own*, 156–157; King, "'Loyal Countrywoman,'" 99–100; Brown, *Stoking the Fire*, 72.

21. Sageeyah is located just outside Claremore.

22. Rachel Caroline Eaton, "The Legend of the Battle of Claremore Mound," *Chronicles of Oklahoma* 8, no. 4 (December 1930): 369.

23. Rachel Caroline Eaton, "Son of Daniel Boone Once Commanded Fort Wayne in Oklahoma," *Tulsa World*, December 27, 1931.

24. Ibid.

25. Rachel Caroline Eaton, "Domestic Science Among the Primitive Cherokees," *Tulsa Daily World*, September 19, 1926.

26. Eaton, "Son of Daniel Boone Once Commanded Fort Wayne in Oklahoma." See also Rachel Caroline Eaton, "Long Forgotten Oklahoma Fort Named for 'Mad Anthony' Wayne," *Tulsa World*, December 20, 1931; Rachel Caroline Eaton, "Old Fort Wayne Saw Last Military Display in Civil War Battle," *Tulsa World*, January 24, 1931. Other newspaper articles written by Eaton include Rachel Caroline Eaton, "History of Presbyterian Church," *Claremore Progress*, March 5, 1925; Rachel Caroline Eaton, "Evolution and Elevation of Oklahoma," *Tulsa Daily World*, August 1, 1926; "Fort Gibson a Shrine of Early Oklahoma," *Tulsa Daily World*, October 31, 1926; Rachel Caroline Eaton, "When the Civil War Raged Around Tulsa," *Tulsa World*, January 11, 1931; Rachel Caroline Eaton, "Civil War Left a Bloody Trail in Oklahoma," *Tulsa World*, April 5, 1931; Rachel Caroline Eaton, "Battle of Cabin Creek, Near Vinita, Was the Most Dramatic Engagement of Long and Bitter Civil War on the Border," *Tulsa World*, September 20, 1931.

27. John M. Oskison, "Author Recalls Literary Oklahoma of Yesterday as Compared to Now," *The Tulsa Tribune*, February 2, 1930.

28. Daniel Heath Justice, *Our Fire Survives the Storm: A Cherokee Literary History* (Minneapolis: University of Minnesota Press, 2006), 3–42.

29. Rachel Caroline Eaton, "Domestic Science Among the Primitive Cherokees," *Tulsa Daily World*, September 19, 1926.

30. Joseph A. Brandt to Rachel Caroline Eaton, November 18, 1935. University of Oklahoma Press Collection, Box 17, Folder 6, Western History Collections, University of Oklahoma Libraries. John Rhea also discusses some of this history in Rhea, *A Field of Their Own*, 160.

31. The Dawes Commission oversaw the registration of Indigenous people, the allotment of set amounts of land to Indigenous individuals, and the theft of supposedly surplus Indigenous land, which was then opened for white settlement.

32. Joseph A. Brandt to Grant Foreman, September 5, 1935, University of Oklahoma Press Collection, Box 17, Folder 19, Western History Collections, University of Oklahoma Libraries. During the editing process, Brandt, the editor, seemed to think Wardell's manuscript was too biased in favor of the US government, noting that the author made the United States look "benevolent" and that he failed to even acknowledge "that the Cherokees were a nation." Joseph A. Brandt to Morris L. Wardell, January 25, 1936, University of Oklahoma Press Collection, Box 52, Folder 3, Western History Collections, University of Oklahoma Libraries. After Wardell made revisions, OU Press published his book and seemingly forgot about Eaton's manuscript. Morris L. Wardell, *A Political History of the Cherokee Nation, 1838-1907* (Norman: University of Oklahoma Press, 1938).

33. Wright, "Rachel Caroline Eaton," 509. John Rhea discusses the impact of Eaton's work on subsequent scholars in *A Field of Their Own*, 161–162. Rachel Caroline Eaton also inspired my own decision to become a historian.

34. Brown, *Stoking the Fire*; Rhea, *A Field of Their Own*; King, "'Loyal Countrywoman.'"

35. John Rhea has documented the original rejection of the manuscript by the University of Oklahoma Press in *A Field of Their Own*, 158–161. Today, there is a growing network of Indigenous women scholars in academia. Farina King also encouraged the family to seek publication.

36. See, for example, William G. McLoughlin, *Cherokee Renascence in the New Republic* (Princeton, NJ: Princeton University Press, 1986); Joshua Nelson, *Progressive Traditions: Identity in Cherokee Literature and Culture* (Norman: University of Oklahoma Press, 2014); Andrew Denson, *Demanding the Cherokee Nation: Indian Autonomy and American Culture, 1830–1900* (Lincoln: University of Nebraska Press, 2004).

37. Eaton, *John Ross and the Cherokee Indians* (1914), preface; Helen Hunt Jackson, *A Century of Dishonor: A Sketch of the United States Government's Dealings with Some of the Indian Tribes* (New York: Harper & Brothers, 1881). Eaton may have also been referencing the Century of Progress International Exposition, also known as the Chicago World's Fair (1933). The family archive includes a memento from the Chicago World's Fair, and having graduated from the University of Chicago, she would likely have kept up with major events in the city. Daniel Heath Justice provides an excellent discussion of Cherokee nationalism in literature in *Our Fire Survives the Storm*.

38. Eaton, *John Ross and the Cherokee Indians* (1914), 117.

39. Elias Boudinot, "To the Public," *Cherokee Phoenix*, February 21, 1828. For further discussions of the development of the syllabary and the Cherokee Phoenix newspaper, see Ellen Cushman, *The Cherokee Syllabary: Writing the People's Perseverance* (Norman: University of Oklahoma Press, 2011); Constance Owl, "Tsalagi Tsulehisanvhi: Uncovering Cherokee Language Articles from the *Cherokee Phoenix* Newspaper, 1828–1834" (master's thesis, Western Carolina University, 2020).

40. Justice, *Our Fire Survives the Storm*, 3–42; Nelson, *Progressive Traditions*.

41. Narcissa Owen, *Memoirs*, 73–74. Cherokee activist Ruth Muskrat Bronson discussed the Trail of Tears in her own book, written for a popular audience. Ruth Muskrat Bronson, *The Indians Are People, Too* (New York: Friendship Press, 1944), 38–41.

42. Christina Berry, great-great niece of Rachel Caroline Eaton, notes, "In addition to the book's value as a history book, one chapter, Trail of Tears, was used for many years as a model of English literature at the University of Missouri."

43. The inspiration for the musical *Oklahoma!* was taken from Lynn Riggs, *Green Grow the Lilacs*, 1931. For a discussion of Riggs's play in this context, see Jace Weaver, *That the People Might Live: Native American Literatures and Native American Community* (New York: Oxford University Press, 1997): 99–101.

44. Brown, *Stoking the Fire*, 216.

45. Rachel Caroline Eaton, "Social Economy among the Indians," in The Indian Women's Club of Tulsa, Oklahoma, *Indian Women's Cookbook*, 1933, reprinted in Louis Szathmary, *Southwestern Cookery: Indian and Spanish Influences* (New York: Arno Press, 1973), 5.

46. Rachel Caroline Eaton, untitled, published as the club collect of the Tulsa Indian Women's Club, 1976–77. Courtesy of Christina Berry. See also Rachel Caroline Eaton, "Collect of Tulsa Indian Women's Club," *Tulsa World*, August 30, 1931. The version published in the *Tulsa World* reads, "Build up your Council Fire" rather than "Renew your Council Fire."

Editors' Note

1. Tiya Miles, *The House on Diamond Hill: A Cherokee Plantation Story* (Chapel Hill: University of North Carolina Press, 2010); Fay Yarbrough, *Race and the Cherokee Nation: Sovereignty in the Nineteenth Century* (Philadelphia: University of Pennsylvania Press, 2008). See also Theda Perdue, *Slavery and the Evolution of Cherokee Society, 1540–1866* (Knoxville: University of Tennessee Press, 1979). For a discussion of enslavement and Afro-Cherokee relationships from the perspective of a Cherokee enslaver, see John Ridge to Albert Gallatin, February 27, 1826, in John Howard Payne Letters Concerning Missions and the Relations of the Cherokees and the Government, 8:113, microfilm, Newberry Library, Chicago.

2. In chapter sixteen of this volume, Eaton wrote that after the Trail of Tears, the Cherokees were "converting a wilderness into homesteads and waste places into cultivated fields." This completely ignored the fact that other Nations, like the Osages, called these lands home. Eaton's article on the Cherokee-Osage battle also reveals a distinct Cherokee perspective that ignores Osage points of view,

likely due in part to her reliance on Cherokee oral (hi)stories. For an excellent discussion of Cherokee-Osage relations in this region, see Kathleen DuVal, *The Native Ground: Indians and Colonists in the Heart of the Continent* (Philadelphia: University of Pennsylvania Press, 2006), 217–226.

3. Christina Berry, "Rachel Caroline Eaton—Cherokee Woman, Historian, and Educator," All Things Cherokee, January 2, 2001, https://www.allthingscherokee.com/rachel-caroline-eaton/

Preface and Acknowledgments

1. Editor's note: William E. Dodd, "Foreword," in Rachel Caroline Eaton, *John Ross and the Cherokee Indians* (Menasha, WI: George Banta Publishing Company, 1914).

2. Editor's note: *John Ross and the Cherokee Indians* was first published in 1914 (cited in the previous note), and was later revised as Eaton's dissertation in 1919, and reprinted in 1921. Rachel Caroline Eaton, *John Ross and the Cherokee Indians* (Muscogee, OK: Star Printery, 1921).

3. Editor's note: Robert Latham Owen was elected to the United States Senate from Oklahoma in 1907 and retired from that body in 1925.

4. Editor's note: Lucy Ward Williams (born 1821 in Deep Creek, Georgia; died 1899 in Claremore, Oklahoma) was Rachel Caroline Eaton's grandmother.

Chapter 1

1. Mooney, James, *Myths of the Cherokees*, 19th Report of the Bureau of Ethnology, Vol. I, p. 15. On ceremonial occasions, they spoke of themselves as Ani´Kitu´hwagi, or people of Kitu´hwa, the ancient settlement which had been the original nucleus of the tribe. Chalaque in Portuguese, Cheraqui in French, became Cherokee in English from as early as 1708.

2. Bancroft's *History of the United States*, Vol. 2, p. 95.

3. *American State Papers*, 2, p. 651. David Brown was educated at Cornwall, Connecticut, and at Dartmouth College.

4. Editor's note: This is outdated and offensive language. Since the early nineteenth century, many Cherokees developed a diplomatic strategy of telling Euro-Americans that they used to be "primitive" or "savage" but had since become "civilized." Eaton followed that trend in order to convince Euro-American readers that Cherokees were not "savage" or "primitive."

5. Possibly owing to their free use of bear's oil.

6. Bartram, *Travels Through North and South Carolina*.

7. Ibid.

8. Editor's note: Etsauta is often spelled Echota or Chota.

9. Payne M.S., 4, 362.

10. The sacred fire was kept perpetually burning in the National Council House and in each town house, and it was regarded as an omen of calamity to have it fail for any reason. Payne M.S., 8, pp. 137–143.

11. Ibid, p. 16.

12. Editor's note: Oukah has multiple English spellings, including Uka, and more commonly, Uku. Uku is possibly a shortened form of ᎤᎦᏫᏳᎯ/ugvwiyuhi, the Cherokee word often translated as "Chief."

13. Editor's note: ᎡᎸᏗ/Elvdi or ᎡᎳᏗ/Eladi (lower) and ᎣᏓᎵ/odali (mountain) are more common spellings today.

14. Oo-too-nah Ka-nah-leh, meaning we are "big friends," connoted more than ordinary attachment between two of different clan affiliation. Editor's note: A more contemporary spelling is ᎤᏔᎾ ᏥᎾᎵ/utana ginalii. I am grateful for Ben Frey for help on this question.

15. Editor's note: John Howard Payne Papers, Edward E. Ayer Collection, Newberry Library, Chicago Illinois, vol. 4, 357–359.

16. Adair, James *A History of the American Indians*, pp. 224–26.

17. Ibid, p. 226.

18. Ibid, 227.

19. Editor's note: See note 12 above.

20. In 1785 a cession of land was made which included the town of Etsauta, or Chota. Thereafter, the capitol was moved several times. For a time the Grand Council met at Oostenauleh; in 1817 it convened at Amohe; later it was located at New Echota. Editor's note: Oostenauleh is commonly spelled Ustenali.

Chapter 2

1. *The Gentleman of Elvas*. This book was published at Evora in 1557 and was translated from the Portuguese by Richard Hakluyt of London in 1609.

2. Haywood, *Natural and Aboriginal Tennessee*, p. 227. Firearms were first introduced among them about 1700.

3. Hewatt, A. *Historical Account of the Rise and Progress of the Colonies of South Carolina and Georgia*, Vol. I, pp. 297–98.

4. Ibid, Royce, *The Cherokee Nation of Indians, 5th Annual Report of the Bureau of Ethnology*, 144.

5. Editor's note: Sir Alexander Cuming.

6. Editor's note: Cuming did not have authorization from North Carolina or from the British. See Ludovick Grant, "Historical Relation of Facts Delivered by Ludovick Grant, Indian Trader, to His Excellency the Governor of South Carolina," *South Carolina Historical and Genealogical Magazine* 10, no. 1 (January 1909): 54–68; Samuel Cole Williams, ed., *Early Travels in the Tennessee Country, 1540–1800* (Johnson City, TN: Watauga Press, 1928), 117.

7. Editor's note: Often spelled ᏂᏆᏏ/Nikwasi or Nequasee.

8. Hewatt, A., *Historical Account of the Rise and Progress of the Colonies of South Carolina and Georgia*, Vol. II, pp. 3, 9, 11.

9. Ibid.

10. Martin, *History of North Carolina*, Vol. II, p. 87.

11. *Amer. State Papers*, Indian Affairs, Vol. I, p. 431.

12. Editor's note: often spelled Chickamauga.

13. The Henderson Purchase of March 1775 was one of these: the Treaty of Sycamore Shoals it was called.

14. A large body of land was secured to the colony of Transylvania for $50.00 in merchandise. A treaty with the State of Franklin in 1784 secured from the Cherokees a large body of land under threat of forced removal or extermination by the backwoodsmen.

15. McKenney & Hall, *History of the Indian Tribes of N. America*, Vol. III, p. 343.

16. Editor's note: 1761.

17. *Amer. State Papers*, Indian Affairs, Vol. I, p. 953.

18. Ibid, p. 52.

19. 7 U.S. Statutes at Large, p. 62; Cong. Doc. 531, No. 28, p. 148.

20. Payne M. S., 8, Ridge to Gallatin, 1826; also Payne M. S., 5, Extract from Journal of the Moravians.

21. Royce, *Cherokee Nation*, p. 231.

22. Editor's note: James Adair, *The History of the American Indians*, (London: Edward and Charles Dilly, 1775), 231. Adair states, "the Cherokees had a prodigious number of excellent horses."

23. Editor's note: John Sevier, who later went on to become governor of Tennessee.

24. Mooney, *Myths of the Cherokees*, p. 82.

25. Adair, p. 230.

26. Becker, Carl, *Beginnings of the American People*, p. 23.

27. Editor's note: In her first book, Eaton cites this source as "Adair, 240–243." Eaton, *John Ross and the Cherokee Indians*, 14. Priber did not set up a monarchy, but Adair notes that Priber used the language of European monarchy to describe Cherokee leadership roles.

28. *American State Papers*, Indian Affairs, II, p. 283. Editor's note: Also spelled Ustenali. Eaton also spells it Oostenauleh in chapter one.

Chapter 3

1. Editor's note: Atta-Kulla-Kulla, or Attakullakulla.

2. Also known in English as Old Tassel.

3. Editor's note: Also spelled Scoloscuta or Uskwaliguta or Scolucutta. In English he was sometimes called Hanging Maw.

4. Editor's note: Also spelled Inoli or Inali. In English he was sometimes called Black Fox.

5. Editor's note: Alexander Cuming did not have authorization from any authority to make an alliance with the Cherokees. See Ludovick Grant, "Historical Relation of Facts Delivered by Ludovick Grant, Indian Trader, to His Excellency the Governor of South Carolina," *South Carolina Historical and Genealogical Magazine* 10, no. 1 (January 1909): 54–68.

6. Narcissa Owen, *Memoirs*, pp. 30–31.

7. Editor's note: Heavy overcoat worn by soldiers and sailors on watch.

8. Hewatt, A., *A Historical Account of the Rise and Progress of South Carolina and Georgia*, Vol. II, p. 3.

9. The land of death situated beyond the setting sun, according to Cherokee legend.

10. 7 U.S. Statutes at Large, p. 43.

11. Editor's note: While scholars still debate who Nanye'hi/Nancy Ward's father was, scholars no longer believe it was Sir Francis Ward.

12. Her first husband, a full-blood Cherokee, was killed in one of the Creek wars in which she herself participated as a warrior. Later she married Bryan Ward, the son of her father's brother. By her request they were married according to the native ceremony; afterwards, because he wished it, the Reverend Charles Cummings, Chaplain of the garrison at Fort Loudon, performed the rites prescribed by the Scotch Presbyterian church. "And here under the great oaks of the primeval forest was pronounced the first Christian marriage in the State of Tennessee." National Archives of the Daughters of the American Revolution, data compiled by Mrs. T. F. Walker, Regent of the Nancy Ward Chapter of the D.A.R. in Tennessee.

13. Editor's note: Footnote missing from the original manuscript.

14. Many stories of her life-saving prerogative have come down in the chronicles of the time. The story of how she saved the pioneer white woman Mrs. Bean is one of these.

15. Editor's note: See note 12.

16. Editor's note: There is no footnote in the original manuscript. It is also unclear whether Eaton is quoting a written or oral source.

17. Editor's note: Emmet Starr also writes that Nancy Ward was the first to practice African chattel-style slavery, though it is difficult to ascertain this with certainty. Emmet Starr, *History of the Cherokee Indians and Their Legends and Folklore* (Oklahoma City: Warden Company, 1921), 468. Most Cherokee families were involved in planting cotton and producing cloth, but most did not use enslaved labor. Patricia Dawson, "Our Hearts Are Straight: Cherokee Clothing in Early America" (PhD diss., University of North Carolina, 2023), 110–160.

18. Editor's note: Eaton notes in note 19 that scholars are unsure about Nancy Ward's date of birth and death. Ward was most likely a few decades younger than 108.

19. She was buried in the cemetery near her home, which was three miles from the modern town of Benton, Tennessee. There a stone pyramid bearing a bronze marker was erected by the Daughters of the American Revolution of the State of Tennessee on October 25, 1924. The marker bears the inscription: "In Memory of Nancy Ward, Princess and Prophetess of the Cherokee Nation. The Pocahontas of Tennessee. The Constant Friend of the American Pioneer." (Authorities do not agree on the date of her birth, nor of her death.) A company of soldiers from Benton during the World War was called the Nancy Ward Rifles. The high school at Benton is named for her. Mrs. T. F. Walker to Mrs. Witcher, Tulsa, Okla., Chattanooga, Tenn., April 18, 1926.

20. Editor's note: Black Fox, or TZℓ/Inoli.

21. McKenney and Hall, *Indian Tribes of North America*, Vol. III, p. 291.

22. Daniel Ross had married Mollie McDonald, a mixed blood Cherokee, daughter of John McDonald and his full blood Cherokee wife.

23. Mooney, *Myths of the Cherokees*, p. 38; Carroll's *Historical Collections of South Carolina*, II, pp. 97–98, 517 (1836).

24. Thompson, A. C., *Moravian Missions*, p. 341; *Amer. State Papers*, Indian Affairs, I, p. 282; Walker, *Torchlights to the Cherokees.*

25. Editor's note: Also spelled Ustenali.

26. Gude, Mary B. *Georgia and the Cherokees*, p. 24.

27. Ibid, p. 23.

28. Cong. Doc. 531, No. 28, p. 148; *Amer. State Papers*, Indian Affairs, I, p. 649; Royce, *Cherokee Nation of Indians*, p. 187; *Amer. State Papers*, I, p. 698; U.S. Statutes at Large, p. 139.

29. Morse, *Report to the Secretary of War of the United States on Indian Affairs*, Hicks to Calhoun, 1822.

30. McKenney & Hall, *Indian Tribes of North America*, Vol. III, p. 331; *Amer. State Papers*, Indian Affairs, II, p. 651. Letter of David Brown; Ibid.

Chapter 4

1. Royce, Charles C., *The Cherokee Nation of Indians, Fifth Annual Report of the Bureau of Ethnology*, pp. 214–216; Washburn, Cephas, *Reminiscences*, p. 21.

2. Roosevelt, *Winning of the West*, Vol. II, pp. 61, 67.

3. Royce, p. 20. The Louisiana Purchase was negotiated May 2, ratified by Congress October 21; the stars and stripes were raised over New Orleans December 20, 1803. Jefferson Message, Nov. 14, 1803, *Amer. St. Papers*, Mis., I, p. 350. Payne Mss., 2, p. 71.

4. *Jefferson's Writings*, Ford ed., VIII, 243, Library Edition XVI, 432–435.

5. 2 U.S. Statutes, 289.

6. Royce, pp. 202–203; Abel, Anne H. *History of Events Resulting in Indian Consolidation West of the Mississippi*, in American Historical Association, Annual Report, 1906, L. 233–438; Indian Office Manuscript Records, Secretary Dearborn to Agent Meigs, March 25, 1808.

7. Royce, p. 204; 7 U.S. Statutes, 156; *Jefferson's Writings*, Library Edition, XVI. Pp. 432–435.

8. *American State Papers*, Indian Affairs, II, p. 97–125.

9. 7 U.S. Statutes, 156.

10. 7 U.S. Statutes, p. 183.

11. *Report of the Commissioner of Indian Affairs for 1899*, pp. 77, 78.

12. Hallum's *History of Arkansas*, p. 261.

13. 7 U.S. Statutes, p. 156; reprinted in *Oklahoma Red Book*, Vol. 1, pp. 245–252.

14. 7 U.S. Statutes, 311; preamble to the treaty of 1828 gives a summary of events leading up to the treaty; Report of Jedediah Morse to the Secretary of Interior, 1822, Appendix, 365. Thomas Nuttall visited the western Cherokees in 1819 and wrote in his journal: "Both banks of the river, as we proceeded, were lined with houses and fences of the Cherokees, and although their dress was a mixture of indigenous and European taste, yet in their houses and their farms, we found a happy approach toward civilization." Nuttall's *Journal*, p. 120.

15. Pike, Zebulon. *Journal and Account of an Expedition to the Source of the Mississippi*, Appendix to Part II.

16. Nuttall, pp. 135–136; *Wilkinson Journal*, Entry of Dec. 20, 1806; Owen, Narcissa, *Memoirs*, 1831–1907, p. 40; *Traditional Background of Indian*, pp. 47–52; *Niles' Register*.

17. Editor's note: Also spelled Toan-Tuh, and often called Spring Frog in English.

18. Editor's note: Also sometimes spelled Clermont or Claremont.

19. Owen, Narcissa, *Memoirs*, p. 20. Mrs. Owen's father, Thomas Chisholm, is said to have taken part in the battle of Pasuga. He was one of the chiefs of the Western Cherokees.

20. Lieutenant James Wilkinson, who saw him in 1806 and conversed with him at the Three Forks, December 27; Zebulon Pike, *Journal, An Account of an Expedition to the Source of the Mississippi*.

21. Editor's note: Also sometimes spelled D0⸱ꝰꝑ/Anvyi. The Strawberry Moon occurs in the spring. In her article on this battle, Eaton notes that she used to gather strawberries on this site during her childhood. Rachel Caroline Eaton, "The Legend of the Battle of Claremore Mound," *Chronicles of Oklahoma* 8, no. 4 (December 1930): 369.

22. Editor's note: Also sometimes spelled Tahlonteeskee or Tolluntuskee.

23. Washburn, *Reminiscences*, pp. 23–40.

Chapter 5

1. *American State Papers*, Indian Affairs I, p. 797–804.

2. Circular Letter from Department of War to Southern Agent, June 20, 1805, Indian Office Manuscript Records.

3. McKenney and Hall, *Indian Tribes of North America*, Vol. III, p. 298 (1870).

4. Editor's note: Tecumseh.

5. Ibid. Vol. II, pp. 93–94 (1855).

6. Editor's note: Often spelled Horseshoe Bend.

7. Editor's note: Also spelled Muscogees. Muscogee is another term for Creek.

8. Drake, *American Indians*, p. 406; Pickett's *Alabama*, pp. 58–59 (Reprint of 1896); Cong. Globe, 2nd Sess., 25th Cong., p. 404; Drake, *American Indians*, p. 401; Major Ridge and Adjutant John Ross were among these Cherokee warriors. Editor's note: See also James Mooney, *Myths of the Cherokee* (Washington: Government Printing Office, 1902), 97.

9. A. H. Abel, *Indian Consolidation West of the Mississippi*, 279f.

10. March 22, 1816. 7 U.S. Statutes, p. 139; Indian Treaties (1837), pp. 185–187.

11. Parton, *Life of Andrew Jackson*, p. 356.

12. Editor's note: Also sometimes spelled Cunnessuny and Cheucunsenee.

13. *Niles' Register* 10, p. 16.

14. Abel, A. H., *Indian Consolidation*, p. 280; Indian Office Letter Books, Manuscript Records, Crawford to Meigs, May 27, 1816.

15. Editor's note: James Monroe.

16. Commission composed of General Jackson, Governor McMinn, and General Meriwether.

17. Editor's note: Also sometimes spelled Amohee.

18. McKenney and Hall, *Indian Tribes*, Vol. III, p. 299.

19. Jackson's Talk to the Cherokees, 1817, Payne Mss., 7, 31–44.

20. Payne Mss., 7, p. 45.

21. Cong. Doc. 98, no. 127, pp. 52–82 (18th Cong.).

22. *Niles' Register* 13, p. 74, Letter of Agent Meigs.

23. Cong. Doc. 98, no. 127, p. 76. Editor's note: The original quote reads, "We consider ourselves as a free and distinct nation, and that the government of the United States have no police over us, further than a friendly intercourse in trade."

24. *Niles' Register* 16:158.

25. Editor's note: John Calhoun, Secretary of War.

26. 7 U.S. Statutes, p. 195.

27. *Amer. State Papers*, Public Lands, I; Greeley, *American Conflict*, I, p. 103 (1864).

28. Later governor of Georgia.

29. *American State Papers*, Indian Affairs, II, p. 257.

30. 3 U.S. Statutes at Large, p. 688.

31. Payne Mss., 2, pp. 501–03. *American State Papers*, Indian Affairs, II, pp. 468–73.

32. Ibid, pp. 473, 494, 1834; Royce, 237.

33. Abel, *Indian Consolidation*, p. 324; Indian Office Manuscript Records, Calhoun to Campbell, March 17, 1823.

34. Both Georgia men.

35. Payne Mss., 2, p. 505. Commissioner Campbell reported to the Secretary of War that it was the desire of both parties. The Cherokees claimed it was at their request.

36. Campbell to Calhoun, *Amer. State Papers*, Indian Affairs, II, p. 464.

37. *American State Papers*, Indian Affairs, II, pp. 468–69.

38. Ibid, 475, 477.

39. *American State Papers*, Indian Affairs, II, p. 464.

40. *American State Papers*, Indian Affairs, II, p. 473; Cong. Doc. 91, No. 63.

41. Cong. Doc. 91; Sen. Doc. 63, p. 38.

42. *American State Papers*, Indian Affairs, II, p. 474.

43. *Niles' Register* 26, p. 275. Hardin's *Life of George M. Troup*, pp. 206–218.

44. Richardson's *Messages of the President*, II, pp. 234–237.

45. *Niles' Register* 26, pp. 275–276. Cong. Doc. 91, No. 63, pp. 46–48.

46. 4 United States Statutes at Large, p. 36.

47. Hardin's *Life of George M. Troup*, p. 469. Editor's note: Original quote reads, "A state of things so unnatural and so fruitful of evil, as an independent Government of a semi-barbarous people coexisting within the same limits, cannot long continue; and wise counsels must direct, that relations, which cannot be maintained in peace, should be dissolved before any occasion can occur to break that peace."

48. Ibid, pp. 411, 412.

49. Payne Mss., 7.

Chapter 6

1. *Niles' Register* 4, p. 125.

2. *Niles' Register*, 26, p. 102.

3. *Niles' Register*, 14, p. 390.

4. Payne Mss. 6 and 7; Morse Report, Hicks to Calhoun, 1822.

5. *Niles' Register* 20, p. 102

6. Editor's note: A small national police force.

7. A treasurer was first appointed in 1819 to take charge of annuities. Payne Mss. 2, p. 379.

8. Payne Mss. 2, p. 379, Letter of Ridge to Gallatin, 1826; also, Vols. 6 and 7; *American State Papers*, Indian Affairs, II, 279–83; McKenney's Letter, Ibid, p. 657; Drake, *Indians of North America*, pp. 437, 438 (1880).

9. Editor's note: This is offensive and outdated language, and Euro-Americans have a history of using this term in a racist, derogatory manner, though Cherokees, including Eaton, accepted citizens who had both Cherokee and Euro-American heritage. Cherokees traditionally belonged to their mother's clan and the Cherokee Nation regardless of their father's heritage. Euro-Americans developed a racialized notion of identity and applied it to Indigenous people, using terms such as the one Eaton uses here to refer to multiracial Cherokees. For further discussion, see Theda Perdue, "Race and Culture: Writing the Ethnohistory of the Early South," *Ethnohistory* 51, no. 4 (Fall 2004): 701–723. For a discussion on the development of southeastern Indigenous views on race, see Nancy Shoemaker, "How Indians Got to be Red," *American Historical Review* 102, no. 3 (June 1997): 625–644.

10. Also called George Gist, Sequoyah was born about 1760 at Tuskeegee town in Tennessee, near old Fort Loudoun. His mother's brother was a chief in one of the villages. McKenney and Hall, Vol. I (1858), Sequoyah.

11. For this claim to be able to make the leaf talk, Sequoyah was condemned by the medicine men of being possessed of evil spirits. He was a wizard, they said, and should be put to death. He also was lazy and shiftless, allowing his field to grow up in weeds. *Cherokee Advocate*, Vol. 5, Oct. 26, 1844.

12. McKenney and Hall, *Indian Tribes of North America*, I, p. 46 (1858).

13. Editor's note: Also sometimes spelled Ayoka.

14. *Indian Treaties*, p. 425 (1837). A very interesting account of the life of Sequoyah, written by a full-blood Cherokee, translated into English by another Cherokee, and passed upon by a Committee of the National Council, is found in Payne Mss. 2, pp. 224–249. Other accounts are found in Mooney's *Myths of the Cherokees*, 107–10; Phillip's *Sequoyah, Harper's Magazine*, September 1870, pp. 542–48; J. C. Pilling, *Bibliography of Iroquois Languages*, pp. 72–73; Foster, *Sequoyah*, 1885; *Cherokee Advocate*, reprinted in *Christian Advocate and Journal*, New York, Sept. 26, 1828.

15. *Cherokee Advocate*, Vol. 1, No. 5, Oct. 29, 1844; *Christian Observer*, May 20, 1826; Pilling's *Bibliography of the Iroquoian Language*, pp. 21–73; *American State Papers*, Indian Affairs, p. 653; Washburn's *Reminiscences*, pp. 178, 206.

16. Editor's note: This is offensive language. Many Cherokees and Euro-Americans at the time used the term "Five Civilized Tribes" to describe the Cherokee, Choctaw, Chickasaw, Seminole, and Muscogee/Creek, the large southeastern Nations removed to Indian Territory, and used offensive terms such as "wild tribes" or "savage tribes" to describe other Nations who belong to the West, including the Nations whose land the Five Tribes now sit on.

17. Honorable Champ Clark of Missouri.

18. Honorable Robert Latham Owen of Oklahoma.

19. William Potter Ross in an address to a graduating class at the Male Seminary, Ross, *Life and Times of William P. Ross*, p. 208.

Editorial Commentary for Chapters 7–15

1. Gerald Vizenor writes, "Survivance is an active sense of presence, the continuance of native stories, not a mere reaction, or a survivable name. Native survivance stories are renunciations of dominance, tragedy and victimry." See Gerald Vizenor, *Manifest Manners: Narratives on Postindian Survivance* (Lincoln: University of Nebraska Press, 1999), iv.

Chapter 7

1. Payne Mss. 2.

2. Cong. Doc. 138, No. 124; McKenney's Report of 1826, *American State Papers*, II, p. 651.

3. In 1826, there were 22,000 cattle, 7,000 horses, 46,000 swine and 25,000 sheep in the Cherokee Nation. *Niles' Register* 30, p. 145.

4. Of saw mills there were sixteen; grist mills, thirty-one; looms, seven hundred and sixty-two; cotton mills, eight; and ferries, eighteen. Ibid.

5. *American State Papers*, Indian Affairs, II, pp. 651, 652.

6. Editor's note: This is outdated and offensive language. Since the early nineteenth century, many Cherokees developed a diplomatic strategy of telling Euro-Americans that they used to be "primitive" or "savage" but had since become "civilized." Eaton followed that trend in order to convince Euro-American readers that Cherokees were not "savage."

7. *Cherokee Phoenix*, February 1828.

8. Editor's note: Orally.

9. *Niles' Register*, 32, p. 255, Meredith, *Extra Census Bulletin* 1894, pp. 113–114, 224. Editor's note: The handwriting for the footnote was somewhat unclear, but the Extra Census Bulletin for 1894 only has 70 pages.

10. Cong. Doc. 273, No. 91; Payne Mss. 2.

11. *Cherokee Phoenix*, February 28, 1828.

12. *Huntsville Democrat*, quoted in *Niles' Register* 33, p. 214.

13. *Niles' Register* 32, p. 214.

14. January 8, 1827.

15. Morse, *Indian Reports*, p. 162.

16. William Hicks was a brother of Charles Renatus Hicks, one of the earliest converts to Christianity among the Cherokees and for many years an influential tribesman, greatly beloved throughout the nation.

17. Payne Mss. 2, p. 273.

18. Editor's note: Also spelled Quatie.

19. Editor's note: Also spelled Ustenali.

20. Gude, Mary B. *Georgia and the Cherokees*, p. 33. This is known as the home of Colonel Carter's family.

21. Acts of Georgia Assembly, 1827, p. 249.

22. Editor's note: John Forsyth, governor of Georgia.

23. *Niles' Register* 33, p. 406.

24. *Gale's and Seaton's Register* Vol. IV, Part 1, p. 914.

25. Ibid, p. 925.

26. 7 U.S. Statutes at Large, p. 311 (May 6, 1828).

27. 4 U.S. Statutes at Large, p. 300 (May 9, 1828).

28. Indian Office Letter Books, Series II, No. 5, p. 33, May 27, 1828.

29. *Niles' Register* 35, p. 56.

30. Cong. Doc. 186, No. 95.

Chapter 8

1. *Cherokee Phoenix*, October 1828.

2. Dawson, *Compilation of the Laws of the State of Georgia*, 1829, pp. 29–198.

3. *Cherokee Phoenix*, October 1828.

4. Cong. Doc. 187, No. 145, p. 3; Parker, *The Cherokee Indians*.

5. Richardson's *Messages of the Presidents*, II, p. 438.

6. Editor's note: John Eaton.

7. *Natchez Statesman and Gazette*, June 29, 1829, *Niles' Register* 36, p. 258; Payne Mss. 2. "If you will go to the setting sun there you will be happy; there you can remain in peace and quietness; so long as the waters run and the oaks grow that country shall be guaranteed to you and no white man shall be permitted to settle near you." Payne Mss. 6.

8. *Cherokee Phoenix*, May 1828.

9. Eaton's Letters of Instruction to Carroll, May 30, 1829. Indian Office Manuscript Records.

10. Ibid. Carroll to Eaton.

11. Richardson's *Messages of the Presidents*, II, 456–459.

12. Editor's note: This is offensive language. Many Cherokees and Euro-Americans at the time used the term "Five Civilized Tribes" to describe the Cherokee, Choctaw, Chickasaw, Seminole, and Muscogee/Creek, the large southeastern Nations removed to Indian Territory, and used offensive terms such as "wild tribes" or "savage tribes" to describe other Nations who belong to the West, including those whose land the Five Tribes now sit on.

13. Gale's and Seaton's Register, Vol. VI, Part II, 996–1003. Index to Senate and House Journals, 21st Congress, 1st session; *National Intelligencer*, May 24, 1838.

14. Cong. Doc. 208, No. 90, pp. 1–3.

15. 4 U.S. Statutes at Large, p. 411.

16. Benton's *Thirty Years View*, 1:164. It was carried by one vote.

17. *Niles' Register*, 39, p. 106.

18. Georgia had declared her laws would go into effect there June 1, 1830.

19. *Niles' Register*, 38, p. 328.

20. Ibid, 38, pp. 404–405.

21. Ibid, 39, p. 106.

22. Ibid, 39, p. 264.

23. Prince's *Digest of the Laws of Georgia* to 1837.

24. *Niles' Register*, 40, p. 132.

25. Edward Everett, Speech in Senate, April 16, 1830. Peter Force, Printer. *Niles' Register*, 39, pp. 179–80.

26. Cong. Doc. 208, No. 102, p. 2.

27. Payne Mss. 2, p. 383; Cong. Doc. 315, No. 120, p. 543.

28. Cong. Doc. 315, No. 120, p. 529. Statement by John Ridge.

29. March 5, 1831.

30. The Cherokee Nation vs. Georgia, Peters' *Supreme Court Reports*, Vol. 5, p. 1; *Niles' Register*, 39, pp. 31, 338, 339.

31. *Niles' Register*, 40, p. 297.

32. *Missionary Herald*, March 1831, Vol. XXVII, 69–84; *Niles' Register*, 40, p. 132.

33. The Methodists and Moravians had recalled their missionaries. The American Board of Commissioners for Foreign Missions had left their missionaries to decide the question of leaving the country for themselves.

34. Payne Mss. 7, pp. 125–30.

35. *Niles' Register*, 42, pp. 40–56.

36. Letter of Elijah Hicks to a friend in Washington, March 26, 1832. *Niles' Register*, 42, p. 201.

37. Ibid.

Chapter 9

1. Payne Mss. 6; Mooney, *Myths of the Cherokees*, pp. 113–14.

2. Abel, R.H., *Indian Consolidation*, p. 402.

3. Editor's note: Often spelled Chattooga.

4. Payne Mss. 2, p. 369.

5. Cong. Doc. 315, No. 121, pp. 5–7.

6. Ibid.

7. *Niles' Register*, 47, p. 353.

8. McKenney and Hall, *Indian Tribes of North America*, Vol. III, pp. 103–106.

9. *Niles' Register*, 56, p. 342.

10. Editor's note: July 19, 1832.

11. *Niles' Register*, 42 p. 441; *Cherokee Phoenix*, July 7, 1832; Drake's *Indians*, p. 458 (1880).

12. Cong. Doc. 268, No. 71, p. 29.

13. Editor's note: Secretary of War Lewis Cass.

14. Editor's note: Lewis Cass to John Ross, R. Taylor, John F. Baldridge, and Joseph Vann, February 2, 1833, in *Memorial of John Ross and Others*, 23rd Cong., 2nd sess., 1833, H. Doc, 268, no. 71, 30.

15. Cong. Doc. 268, No. 71, p. 32–35.

16. Commissioner of Indian Affairs to Agent Montgomery, April 22, 1833. Indian Office Manuscript Records; *Cherokee Phoenix*, March 6, 1832.

17. *Niles' Register*, 44, p. 230.

18. Ibid, pp. 231, 270.

19. Cong. Doc. 292, No. 286, p. 5.

20. Editor's note: John Martin.

21. Ibid, p. 6.

22. Cong. Doc. 208, No. 57, p. 7.

23. *Cherokee Phoenix*, October 12, 1833.

24. Payne Mss. 2.

25. Editor's note: Footnote missing from the original manuscript.

26. Cong. Doc. 315, No. 120, p. 455.

27. Cong. Doc. 292, No. 286, pp. 132, 133.

28. Ibid, 141–143.

29. Ibid, 142–144.

30. Ibid, p. 40–43.

31. Governor William Carroll of Tennessee was appointed on the commission but because of illness was unable to serve.

32. Editor's note: Footnote cut off in original manuscript. In *John Ross and the Cherokee Indians*, Eaton cites "Payne Mss. 2, p. 398." See Rachel Caroline Eaton, *John Ross and the Cherokee Indians* (Menasha, WI: George Banta Publishing Company, 1914), 85n8. For modern pagination, see John Howard Payne Papers, Edward E. Ayer Collection, Newberry Library, Chicago Illinois, 2:204–205.

33. Ibid, 279–290.

34. Cong. Doc. 292, No. 286, p. 10. The Ross family sought refuge in Tennessee where they lived in an abandoned cabin for three years.

35. Payne Mss. 2 p. 381.

36. This was in range of the Georgia Guard, and the chiefs could not attend without danger of arrest. Threats had been circulated to keep them away so that the annuities when paid would fall into the hands of the opposition. Then it was expected that the majority of the people would "follow the purse."

37. Cong. Doc. 292, No. 286, p. 8.

38. Ibid, p. 6; Payne Mss. 6.

39. Payne Mss. 6; Cong. Doc. 292, No. 286, p. 10.

40. Secretary of War to Schermerhorn, Sept. 26, 1835, Indian Office Manuscript Records; *National Intelligencer*, May 24, 1838.

41. Schermerhorn to Secretary of War, Sept. 10, 1835, Indian Office Manuscript Records.

42. Cong. Doc. 315, No. 120, p. 485. Schermerhorn to Cass, Oct. 30, 1835.

43. Cong. Doc. 292, No. 286, p. 82.

44. *National Intelligencer*, May 24, 1828.

45. Cong. Doc. 315, No. 120, pp. 484 and 485.

46. Ibid, p. 485.

47. Ibid, p. 484.

48. Curry to Cass, November 3, 1835. Indian Office Letter 835, 1836.

49. Payne Mss., 2.

50. Cong. Doc. 315, No. 120, p. 513.

51. Ibid.

52. Ibid, pp. 495, 512. The Treaty of New Echota was negotiated on December 29, 1835. Everett's Speech in House of Representatives, May 31, 1838.

53. 7 U.S. Statutes at Large, p. 478 et seq.

54. Cong. Doc. 292, No. 286p. 118ff.

55. Editor's note: Cherokee Petition, February 3, 1836, in Memorial and Protest of the Cherokee Nation, 24th Cong., 1st sess., H. Doc. 286, serial 292, 114–115.

56. Editor's note: in Memorial and Protest of the Cherokee Nation, 24th Cong., 1st sess., H. Doc. 286, serial 292, 107–108.

57. 7 U.S. Statutes at Large, p. 478.

58. Cong. Doc. 315, No. 120. Numerous letters to the president and the Secretary of War. Out of a population of over 17,000, not more than five hundred men, women and children were present when this treaty was negotiated.

Chapter 10

1. Cong. Doc. 315, No. 120, p. 679.

2. Ibid, p. 599.

3. Abel, *Indian Consolidation*, p. 266.

4. *Niles' Register*, 50, p. 383.

5. Editor's note: General John E. Wool.

6. *National Intelligencer*, May 24, 1838.

7. Cong. Doc. 315, No. 120, pp. 646–48.

8. Ibid, p. 629.

9. Editor's note: Henry Clay and Theodore Frelinghuysen ran in 1844, not 1836. Ross and other Cherokees hoped that Martin Van Buren would stop Indian Removal if elected.

10. Cherokee Mss. Collection, Tahlequah, Okla.

11. Letter of John Ross in Cherokee Mss. Collection.

12. Cong. Doc. 315, No. 120, p. 807.

13. Cong. Doc. 315, No. 120, p. 807.

14. Ibid, pp. 186, 190. Report of Indian Commissioner, 1836, p. 285.

15. Cong. Doc. 315, No. 120, p. 774; also, 685.

16. *Report of the Commissioner of Indian Affairs, 1836*, p. 24.

17. This was in January 1837.

18. Cong. Doc. 315, No. 120, pp. 802–8.

19. Ibid, 24.

20. Ibid, p. 648.

21. Ibid, p. 82.

22. *National Intelligencer*, May 24, 1838.

23. Cong. Doc. 315, No. 120, p. 607.

24. Ibid, p. 68.

25. The Treaty Party had already gone west with the exception of those who remained to assist the government in carrying out the treaty. *National Intelligencer*, May 24, 1838.

26. Cong. Doc. 325, No. 82, pp. 3–5.

27. May 1837.

28. Cong. Doc. 325, No. 99, pp. 26–32.

29. *Congressional Globe*, 24th Congress, p. 477.

30. Gen. Wool to Sec. of War, June 3, 1837. Cong. Doc. 315, No. 120, p. 88.

31. Cong. Doc. 325, No. 82, p. 10.

32. Lumpkin, *Removal of the Cherokees*, pp. 229, 230. Editor's note: The original text of the quote reads, "He ought to have been put in strings and banished from the country. Although a large slave holder, Ross was well qualified to have filled a prominent place amongst the New England Abolitionists, or in the Republic of Hayti—and to one of these places I wished to see him emigrate." Lumpkin, 222.

33. Cong. Doc. 325, No. 82, p. 11.

34. Mr. Lumpkin entered the Senate in Dec. 1837, and from that vantage point wielded the fatal blows to the last lingering hopes of the Cherokees.

35. The proclamation was dated December 28, 1838.

36. May 23.

37. Cong. Doc. 329, No. 316, p. 5.

38. Ibid, pp. 1–4.

39. Cong. Doc. 315, No. 120. Letter of Henry Clay to John Gunter, Sept. 30, 1836.

40. *Cong. Globe*, 2nd Session, 25th Congress, p. 404.

41. Benton's *Thirty Years' View*, Vol. 1, p. 625.

42. *Cong. Globe*, 24th Congress, p. 477.

43. Ibid.

44. *Cong. Globe*, 25th Congress, p. 68.

45. Ibid.

Chapter 11

1. Letter of John Ross to Pennsylvania Legislature, May 1838. Cher. Mss. Records, Tahlequah, Okla.

2. Lumpkin, *Removal of the Cherokees*, p. 208.

3. May 15; *National Intelligencer*, May 24, 1835.

4. Lumpkin, *Removal of the Cherokees*, 193.

5. Cong. Doc. 330, No. 421, pp. 2, 17.

6. Ibid, p. 4.

7. There were as many soldiers as adult Indians, Payne Mss. 6, pp. 13–38.

8. Cong. Doc. 329, No. 316, p. 7.

9. Mooney, *Myths of the Cherokees*, p. 130.

10. Payne Mss. 9, pp. 23–25.

11. The same language was used in driving them as is commonly used in driving cattle and hogs.

12. Payne Mss., 9, pp. 23–25.

13. Editor's note: Also spelled Euchella.

14. Lanman, *Letters of the Allegheny Mountains*, p. 110.

15. Editor's note: The "Father of Waters" refers to the Mississippi River.

16. Ibid, 113.

17. Ibid, 114.

18. Mooney, *Myths of the Cherokees*, 131.

Chapter 12

1. Payne Mss. 9:23–25.
2. Cong. Doc. 129, No. 288, p. 36.
3. Ibid, 405; Congressional Doc. 338, 459:1.
4. John Ross to Pennsylvania Legislature. Cherokee Mss. Records.
5. The committee was composed of John Ross, Richard Taylor, Samuel Gunter, Edward Gunter, James Brown, Elijah Hicks, and Sitewakee.
6. Cong. Doc. 338, No. 459, p. 1.
7. Payne Mss. 6, p. 6.
8. Calhoun.
9. W. Shorey Coody to John Howard Payne. Payne Mss. 6.
10. Coody was one of the officers engaged in removing this detachment. The story is taken almost verbatim from his account of the incident.
11. Cong. Doc. 411, No. 1098, pp. 48–49.
12. A wagon, drawn by six horses, and five saddle horses, were provided for every twenty persons. The young people and the able bodied were expected to walk. Gen. Scott thought it would be good for their health. There were six hundred and forty-five wagons used for the transportation of the thirteen detachments.
13. At Tucker's Ferry. Mooney, *Myths of the Cherokees*, p. 132.
14. He was in charge of a detachment.
15. Wilson, Calvin Dill, "The Arrow Head," *The Memphis Commercial Appeal*, May 8, 1913. Editor's note: Eaton quotes selected lines from the poem, and this is not the complete poem. The date and name of the newspaper she referenced might be wrong. "The Arrow Head" appeared in a New York newspaper in 1912 and was also picked up by other newspapers. Calvin Dill Wilson, "The Arrow Head," *The Sun*, November 3, 1912; Calvin Dill Wilson, "The Arrow Head," *Sapulpa Evening Light*, November 22, 1912; Calvin Dill Wilson, "The Arrow Head," *The Washington Herald*, November 13, 1912; Calvin Dill Wilson, "The Arrow Head," *Kansas City Journal*, November 19, 1912; Calvin Dill Wilson, "The Arrow Head," *The Shreveport Journal*, Feb. 4, 1913; Calvin Dill Wilson, "The Arrow Head," *The Allentown Democrat*, February 11, 1913; Calvin Dill Wilson, "The Arrow Head," *The Lincoln Star*, April 12, 1913.

Chapter 13

1. Wyeth, Walter, *Poor Lo*, p. 67.
2. Narcissa Owen, *Memoirs*, pp. 39, 40.
3. He had stopped on the way to bury his wife, who had fallen a victim to disease and exposure.
4. Mooney, *Myths of the Cherokees*, p. 141.
5. Nuttall's *Journal*, p. 59.
6. Washburn's *Reminiscences* (edited by Emmett Starr), p. 40.
7. Cong. Doc. 365, No. 129, pp. 21–25.
8. Editor's note: The quotation marks on the original manuscript are unclear.
9. Editor's note: Also spelled Tollunteeskee or Tolluntuskee.

10. Cong. Doc. 365, No. 129, pp. 21–55.

11. Payne Mss. 5, p. 26.

12. Cong. Doc. 443, No. 235, p. 15.

13. Editor's note: *Memorial of the Delegation of the Cherokee Nation*, 26th Cong., 1st sess., H. Doc 129, Serial 365, 4.

14. Cong. Doc. 365, No. 129, p. 54.

15. *Niles' Register*, 56, p. 44.

16. *Report of the Commissioner of Indian Affairs, 1839*, p. 335.

17. Congressional Document 365, No. 129, p. 16; Congressional Document 368, No. 222, p. 20.

18. Cong. Doc. 365, No. 129, p. 86; Cong. Doc. 448, No. 235, p. 16.

19. Cong. Doc. 368, No. 222, p. 2.

20. Cong. Doc. 368, No. 222, p. 2.

21. Cong. Doc. 368, No. 188, p. 41; 368, No. 222, p. 2; Cong. Doc. 365, No. 129, p. 66.

22. Cong. Doc. 259, No. 34, p. 16.

23. Cong. Doc. 365, No. 129, p. 38. Gen. Arbuckle did not attend out of deference to the Treaty men who were afraid of revealing the weakness of their numbers.

24. Cong. Doc. 365, No. 129, p. 17.

25. Cong. Doc. 359, No. 347, pp. 45, 57.

26. Cong. Doc. 366, No. 188, pp. 54–56; Cong. Doc. 457, No. 140, p. 67.

Chapter 14

1. Cong. Doc. 411, No. 1098, pp. 73–81.

2. Ibid, p. 45.

3. Cong. Doc. 411, 1098, pp. 45, 73–78.

4. Cong. Doc. 411, No. 1098, pp. 71, 72; Ethan Allen Hitchcock, *A Traveler in the Indian Territory* (edited by Grant Foreman), p. 40.

5. Cong. Doc. 411, No. 1098, pp. 71, 72.

6. Cong. Doc. 476, No. 3311, p. 8; Royce, *Cherokee Nation of Indians*, pp. 300, 301.

7. Ibid, 301.

8. Cong. Doc. 476, No. 331, p. 18. The commissioners were Gen. R. Jones, Lt. Col. R. B. Mason, and Mr. P. M. Butler, agent for the Cherokees.

9. Editor's note: This is offensive and outdated language, and Euro-Americans have a history of using this term in a racist, derogatory manner, though Cherokees, including Eaton, accepted citizens who had both Cherokee and Euro-American heritage. Cherokees traditionally belonged to their mother's clan and the Cherokee Nation regardless of their father's heritage. Euro-Americans developed a racialized notion of identity and applied it to Indigenous people, using terms such as the one Eaton uses here to refer to multiracial Cherokees. For further discussion, see Theda Perdue, "Race and Culture: Writing the Ethnohistory of the Early South," *Ethnohistory* 51, no. 4 (Fall 2004): 701–723. For a discussion on the development of southeastern Indigenous views on race, see Nancy Shoemaker, "How Indians Got to be Red," *American Historical Review* 102, no. 3 (June 1997): 625–644.

10. Cong. Doc. 457, No. 140, pp. 5–14.

11. Editor's note: James K. Polk.

12. Agent McKissick to Commissioner of Indian Affairs, May 12, 1846; General Arbuckle to Secretary of War, February 26, 1846; Report of Agent McKissick, July 1846 in Report of Commissioner of Indian Affairs 1846; Cong. Doc. 470, No. 298.

13. Richardson's *Messages and Papers of the Presidents*, IV, p. 430.

14. Cong. Doc. 476, No. 331, pp. 33–39.

15. Article 5.

16. Commissioner of Indian Affairs to Major Armstrong, June 24, 1846.

17. Ratified and proclaimed by the President, August 17, 1846.

18. $5,000 going to the heirs of Major Ridge, and an equal sum to each of the families of John Ridge and Elias Boudinot.

19. 9 U.S. Statutes at Large, p. 871.

20. Ibid.

21. Cong. Doc. 521, No. 65, p. 6.

22. Cong. Doc. 511, No. 145, pp. 1–5.

23. *Cong. Globe*, 2nd Session, 31st Congress, p. 602.

24. Report of Commissioner of Indian Affairs, 1854.

Chapter 15

1. Editor's note: This is offensive language. Many Cherokees and Euro-Americans at the time used the term "Five Civilized Tribes" to describe the Cherokee, Choctaw, Chickasaw, Seminole, and Muscogee/Creek, the large southeastern Nations removed to Indian Territory, and used offensive terms such as "wild tribes" or "savage tribes" to describe other Nations who belong to the West, including the Nations whose land the Five Tribes now sit on.

2. Goode, William H., *Outposts of Zion*, pp. 67–76.

3. Laws of the Cherokee Nation, 1839–1851, pp. 87, 88.

4. Tracey, Joseph, *History of the American Board of Commissioners of Foreign Missions*, pp. 170, 171, 206.

5. MS Journal of the Union Mission in Oklahoma Historical Society.

6. Drake, *Biography and History of the Indians of North America*; Mooney, *Myths of the Cherokees*, p. 218. Pilling, *Bibliography of the Iroquois Languages*, 40–42; Report of Commissioner of Indian Affairs for 1843 (Worcester Letters).

7. Wyeth, Walter, *Poor Lo*, p. 36.

8. Editor's note: Also sometimes spelled Kaneeda.

9. Editor's note: Beattie's Prairie, or Beaty's Prairie.

10. Editor's note: James Ward was not related by blood, but was a great-grandson of Bryan Ward, Nancy Ward's second husband.

11. Editor's note: Also spelled Oochgeelogy.

12. Goode, William E., *Outposts*.

13. *Report of the Commissioner of Indian Affairs for 1859*, p. 181.

14. *Report of the Commissioner of Indian Affairs for 1852*, pp. 405–06. *Cherokee Almanac* for 1840, pp. 20–21.

15. Walker, *Torch Lights to the Cherokees*.

16. 7 U.S. Statutes, p. 195; Royce, *The Cherokee Nation of Indians*, p. 227.

17. 7 U.S. Statutes, pp. 488. Editor's note: The text of Article 10 reads, "The President of the United States shall invest in some safe and most productive public stocks of the country for the benefit of the whole Cherokee nation . . . the sum of two hundred thousand dollars in addition to the present annuities of the nation to constitute a general fund the interest of which shall be applied annually by the council of the nation to such purposes as they may deem best for the general interest of their people. The sum of fifty thousand dollars to constitute an orphans' fund. . . . The sum of one hundred and fifty thousand dollars in addition to the present school fund of the nation shall constitute a permanent school fund, the interest of which shall be applied annually by the council of the nation for the support of common schools and such a literary institution of a higher order as may be established in the Indian country. And in order to secure as far as possible the true and beneficial application of the orphans' and school fund the council of the Cherokee nation when required by the President of the United States shall make a report of the application of those funds and he shall at all times have the right if the funds have been misapplied to correct any abuses of them and direct the manner of their application for the purposes for which they were intended. . . ." US Statutes at Large, vol. 7, 482–483.

18. Laws of the Cherokee Nation, 1839–1867, September 26, 1839.

19. Ibid, November 16, 1841; Cong. Doc. 411, No. 1098.

20. Reports of the Commissioner of Indian Affairs for 1859, p. 178; for 1860, p. 183.

21. Pamphlet *Report of the Board of Education for the Cherokee Nation for 1887*, p. 1. *The Constitution and Laws of the Cherokee Nation 1839–1867*, Nov. 2.

22. Made near the site of each school by a party of Mormons on their way to Utah.

23. Which was a Methodist church, built of brick and furnished with high-backed pews.

24. $5.00 a month, payable in national warrants.

Editorial Commentary for Chapters 16–21

1. For a discussion of the centrality of the West during this time, see Heather Cox Richardson, *West from Appomattox: The Reconstruction of America after the Civil War* (New Haven: Yale University Press, 2007). Readers may be interested in Cherokee historian Mabel Anderson's account of Stand Watie. Mabel W. Anderson, *The Life of General Stand Watie: The Only Indian Brigadier General of the Confederate Army and the Last General to Surrender*, rev. ed. (Pryor, OK: self-published, 1931).

Chapter 16

1. *Report of the Commissioner of Indian Affairs for 1859*, p. 173.

2. Editor's note: This is offensive language. Many Cherokees and Euro-Americans at the time used the term "Five Civilized Tribes" to describe the Cherokee, Choctaw, Chickasaw, Seminole, and Muscogee/Creek, the large southeastern Nations removed to Indian Territory, and used offensive terms such as "wild tribes"

or "savage tribes" to describe other Nations who belong to the West, including the Nations whose land the Five Tribes now sit on.

3. *Official Records of the War of the Rebellion*, Series I, Vol. 1, p. 682; Abel, *The Indians in the Civil War, American Historical Review*, Vol. XV, p. 282.

4. Ibid. This was the very day the Southern senators in Washington adopted resolutions advising secession.

5. Abel, *The Indians in the Civil War*, p. 282.

6. *Official Records of the War of the Rebellion*, Series I, Vol. 13, pp. 490–92; and Vol. 1, p. 683; Moore's *Rebellion Records*, Vol. 2, Doc. 114.

7. *Official Rec. of the War of the Rebellion*, Series I, Vol. 1, p. 693; Moore's *Rebellion Records*, Vol. 2, p. 302.

8. Moore's *Rebellion Rec.*, Vol. 2, p. 393.

9. Ibid, pp. 393, 394.

10. *Official Records of the War of the Rebellion*, Series I, Vol. 8, p. 393.

11. *Official Records of the War of the Rebellion*, Series I, Vol. 3, p. 577.

12. Ibid, Vol. 13, p. 498–499.

13. *The Indians in the Civil War*, 284.

14. *Philadelphia North American*, Letter of S. W. Butler, January 24, 1863.

15. *The Cherokee Question*, p. 26; Royce, *Cherokee Nation of Indians*, p. 325.

16. *Official Records of the War of the Rebellion*, Series I, Vol. 13, p. 489; Sneed, *The Fight for Missouri*, p. 220.

17. Sneed, *The Fight for Missouri*, p. 230.

18. *Official Records of the War of the Rebellion*, Series I, Vol. 2, pp. 580, 581.

19. Editor's note: The Keetoowahs, who identified each other by an insignia of crossed pins on their coats, became known as "Pins" or "Pin Indians."

20. *The Cherokee Question*, p. 26.

21. Ibid.

22. *The Cherokee Question*, p. 26.

23. *Official Records of the War of the Rebellion*, Series I, Vol. 3, p. 592.

24. Ibid, pp. 596–7.

25. *Official Records of the War of the Rebellion*, Series I, Vol. 13, pp. 585–7.

26. Editor's note: Also spelled Opothleyohola.

27. *The Cherokee Question*, p. 27; Royce, *The Cherokee Nation of Indians*, p. 327.

28. *Official Records of the War of the Rebellion*, Series I, Vol. 13, p. 501.

29. *Report of the Commissioner of Indian Affairs, 1862*, 71. Editor's note: This quote appears on p. 159.

30. *Chronicles of Oklahoma*.

31. *Confederate Statutes at Large*, pp. 394–411.

Chapter 17

1. *The Cherokee Question*, 20. The correspondence between Ross and Opothleyohola, pp. 16–20.

2. Now Tulsa, Okla.

3. Editor's note: Colonel Douglas H. Cooper.

4. Editor's note: Colonel John Drew.

5. *Official Records of the War of the Rebellion*, Series I, Vol. 8, pp. 712, 715; also pp. 4–33; Britton, *Civil War on the Border*, Vol. 1, p. 65.

6. Colonel McIntosh was a Texan but not related to the distinguished Creek family of that name. He was killed at the Battle of Pea Ridge.

7. *Official Records of the War of the Rebellion*, Series I, Vol. 8, pp. 712–715; also pp. 4–33.

8. *Report of Commissioner of Indian Affairs*, 1862, 1863; Abel, *The Indians in the Civil War*, 289.

9. Ibid.

10. *Official Records of the War of the Rebellion*, Series I, 8:525.

11. Editor's note: Samuel R. Curtis.

12. Editor's note: Union General Nathaniel Lyon was killed at the Battle of Wilson's Creek in Missouri.

13. *Official Records of the War of the Rebellion*, Series I, Vol. 8, pp. 195, 482; Sneed, *The Fight for Missions*, pp. 218.

14. Near Armstrong Academy.

15. Editor's note: Union forces under Brigadier General James Henry Lane.

16. Editor's note: William Weer, also sometimes spelled Weir.

17. Moore's *Rebellion Records*, Vol. 5, pp. 549–550.

18. Editor's note: Thomas Hindman, Confederate general.

19. The supplies for his forces had been appropriated to other troops so that Pike was in great need of food, clothing, and military supplies.

20. *Official Records of the War of the Rebellion*, Vol. XII, p. 38.

21. *Official Records of the War of the Rebellion*, Vol. XIII, pp. 460–468, 489–505.

22. Editor's note: John Ross.

23. Colonel Cloud was detached with his command to conduct Chief Ross and some of the prominent men of the nation, with their families, to Cabin Creek where they joined the army which was then retreating towards Fort Scott. The national archives together with a few family treasures, chiefly portrait paintings cut from their frames, were placed onto two ox-wagons, which went under special guard. Wiley Britton, "A Day With Colonel Cloud," *Chronicles of Oklahoma*, Vol. V., No. 3, p. 311.

24. *Official Records of the War of the Rebellion*, Series I. Vol. XVI, pp. 788, 791.

25. *Constitution and Laws of the Cherokee Nation, 1839–1867*, July 14, 1865.

Chapter 18

1. Exec. Docs., 39th Sess., 11 (1246), p. IX. Editor's note: Eaton is possibly referring to *Report of the Secretary of Interior*, December 4, 1865, 39th Cong., 1st sess., H. Exec. Doc., 1, serial 1248, IX.

2. 1 & 2 Exec. Docs., 38th Cong., 2nd sess., V (1220), 177.

3. Ibid, 473. Editor's note: page numbers do not seem to match.

4. Editor's note: This is offensive language. Many Cherokees and Euro-Americans at the time used the term "Five Civilized Tribes" to describe the Cherokee, Choctaw,

Chickasaw, Seminole, and Muscogee/Creek, the large southeastern Nations removed to Indian Territory, and used offensive terms such as "wild tribes" or "savage tribes" to describe other Nations who belong to the West, including those whose land the Five Tribes now sit on.

5. *Report of Commissioner of Indian Affairs*, 1865, p. 295; *Official Records of the War of the Rebellion*, Vol. XLVI, part II, p. 1018.

6. Abbot, *History and Civics of Oklahoma*, p. 127. Editor's note: Located on the Washita River.

7. Report of Commissioner of Indian Affairs, 1865, 295.

8. Rock, Marion T., *Illustrated History of Oklahoma*, pp. 8–9.

9. Abel, *The American Indian Under Reconstruction*, pp. 65–70; *Laws of the Cherokee Nation* 1867, pp. 40–47.

10. The proceedings of the Fort Smith Council are given in full in the *Report of the Com. of Indian Affairs*, 1865, pp. 299–336; also *Annual Report of the Se. of the Interior* for 1865. H. Exec. Docs., 39th Congress, 1st Sess., II (1248); Report of D. N. Cooley as president, pp. 480–496; the Official Report, pp. 496–537, The Proceedings of Council at Fort Smith.

11. *Report of Com. of Indian Affairs for 1865*, p. 324; Abel, *The American Indian Under Reconstruction*, p. 199.

12. *Cong. Globe*, 38th Congress, 2nd Sess., 1305.

13. *The Cherokee Question*, p. 5.

14. *Report of the Secretary of the Interior for 1865*, p. 305; H. Exec. Docs., 39th Cong., 1st sess., II (1248), p. 528.

15. *Report of the Secretary of the Interior for 1865*, H. Exec. Docs., 39th Cong., 1st sess., II (1248), p. 529.

16. *The Cherokee Question*, p. 3.

Chapter 19

1. H. Exec. Docs., 39th Congress, 1st Sess., II (1248), 7. Of the 17,000 Cherokees who took part in the Civil War, 6,500 joined the Confederacy; 10,500 remained loyal to the Union and by their help saved Missouri to the Union. House Exec. Docs., 1st Sess., XII (26389), p. 1. Editor's note: Eaton redacted various phrases and sentences from the quote in the body of the text and does not use ellipses, so readers should consult the original source for more information.

2. Editor's note: Footnote missing from the original manuscript.

3. H. Exec. Docs., 38th Congress, 2nd Sess., V (1220), 174. Other reports defending the defection of the Indians: H. Exec. Docs. 39th Congress, 1st Sess., II (1248), 438, 439, in which Superintendent Sells calls attention to the fact that two-thirds of the Cherokees, one-half of the Seminoles and nearly one-half of the Creeks had been loyal to the federal government; the *Report of the Commissioner of Indian Affairs for 1864*, H. Exec. Docs., 38th Congress, 2nd sess., V (1220), 174.

4. *The Cherokee Question*, p. 10.

5. *Report of the Commissioner of Indian Affairs*, 1866, p. 67; Abel, *The American Indian Under Reconstruction*, pp. 359–370.

6. *Chronicles of Oklahoma*, Vol. 1, pp. 146, 147.

7. Abel, *The American Indian Under Reconstruction*, p. 360.

8. White Catcher, S. H. Benge, John B. Jones, James McDaniel, Thomas Pegg, Daniel H. Ross, and Chief John Ross were the delegates from the Cherokee Nation.

9. Abel, *The American Indian Under Reconstruction*, p. 361; *Chronicles of Oklahoma*, Vol. III pp. 143–146.

10. 14 U.S. Statutes, pp. 799–807; *Oklahoma Red Book*, Vol. 1, pp. 363–371.

11. 14 U.S. Statutes, p. 799.

Chapter 20

1. They "had to cultivate their own little [corn] patches with sharpened sticks and such plows and hoes as their more fortunate neighbors could loan them, and I have known a solitary horse and plow to pass from house to house over a large settlement under loan for a whole season during the first two years that succeeded the War." Address delivered at Muskogee International Fair, 1878, by W. P. Adair, *Eufaula Indian Journal*, October 9 and 16, 1878; Reprinted in *Chronicles of Okla.*, Vol. 3, pp. 254–274.

2. From a very limited variety of raw products, Indian women were capable of setting a table to tempt an epicure. The traveler, Adair, in 1776 pronounced them the best cooks in the world. For the preparation of wild meats and vegetables, they seemed to possess a special gift. Poke greens boiled with bear's bacon passed down the ages as a choice and wholesome dish for young and old in the springtime. With hog-jowl or bacon it is still served on some tables, second in choice to wild onions only.

3. *Report of the Commissioner of Indian Affairs*, 1867, p. 32.

4. Ibid, 1869, p. 397. There had been an epidemic of cholera in 1867 that proved fatal to several Cherokee citizens. Ross, *The Life and Times of Hon. William P. Ross*, p. 196.

5. Editor's note: Other Indigenous Nations arriving in Indian Territory maintained their own nationhood.

6. *Report of the Commissioner of Indian Affairs*, 1870, 284–286.

7. A double log house was made of two houses built ten feet apart, united by a single roof. The passage way between was sometimes boarded up to form a hall.

8. *Report of the Commissioner of Indian Affairs*, 1870, p. 34. Editor's note: Committee on Indian Affairs, *Investigation of Indian Frauds*, 42 Cong., 3rd sess., 1873, H. Rep. 98, 352.

9. Editor's note: Many Euro-Americans used this term to refer to Indigenous people who they believed were supposedly "uncivilized." Some Cherokees also began using this term, often disparagingly, to contrast themselves and the other southeastern nations who had been removed to Indian Territory with the original Nations belonging to the land.

10. Ross, *Life and Times of Hon. W. P. Ross*, pp. 9–10. A nursery was started to encourage the planting of fruit trees. "No finer apples are grown in the United

States than some [that come] from orchards . . . north of the Arkansas and Canadian rivers." Ross, p. 9

11. Appendix 37. *Report of Board of Indian Commissioners*. Second Annual Report, 1870, pp. 234–236.

12. *Annual Report of Com. of Indian Affairs*, 1875, p. 76.

13. Editor's note: This is offensive and outdated language, and Euro-Americans have a history of using this term in a racist, derogatory manner, though Cherokees, including Eaton, accepted citizens who had both Cherokee and Euro-American heritage. Cherokees traditionally belonged to their mother's clan and the Cherokee Nation regardless of their father's heritage. Euro-Americans developed a racialized notion of identity and applied it to Indigenous people, using terms such as the one Eaton uses here to refer to multiracial Cherokees. For further discussion, see Theda Perdue, "Race and Culture: Writing the Ethnohistory of the Early South," *Ethnohistory* 51, no. 4 (Fall 2004): 701–723. For a discussion on the development of southeastern Indigenous views on race, see Nancy Shoemaker, "How Indians Got to be Red," *American Historical Review* 102, no. 3 (June 1997): 625–644.

14. *Cherokee County Democrat-Star*, September 18, 1931.

15. *The Tulsa World*, Feb. 28, 1934; Personal information received from a number of reliable sources.

Chapter 21

1. He had some intermixture of white blood that was said to date back to the eighteenth century. He was a warm friend of Evan Jones, the abolitionist missionary, who had helped to organize the non-slaveholding Cherokees, eventually known as "Pins," into a strong society opposed to secession.

2. The law long in operation provided that improvements on land that had been abandoned for a period of two years reverted to the nation. The full text of this message is to be found in *The Life and Times of the Hon. W. P. Ross*, by Mrs. W. P. Ross, pp. 1–6.

3. *Report of Commissioner of Indian Affairs*, 1870, p. 289.

4. Ibid. There was at one time a demand for a negro state to be located in the unassigned lands of the Territory.

5. Rabs Creek, Fourteen Mile Creek, and Goose Neck Bend. At Fort Gibson there was a large group holding on to the outskirts of the town and raising cotton and corn for Cherokee citizens on the shares.

6. The Negroes located in Gooseneck Bend were politically minded to an unusual degree. Editor's note: Eaton sometimes uses paternalistic language when discussing Cherokee Freedmen, and this is offensive.

7. Articles 4, 5, and 6 of the treaty of 1866.

8. On November 26, 1866, a National Convention met at Tahlequah and adopted the amendments required by the late treaty. Additional amendments for the better functioning of the administration of the different departments of government were made at this time.

9. *Report of Commissioner of Indian Affairs*, 1867, 397.

10. Either from Kansas or Arkansas, or even Washington.

11. Sydney Clark's naive account of this movement from beginning to end was printed as it came from his own hand submitted to Luther B. Hill, in Hill's *History of Oklahoma*, Vol. 1, pp. 170–183.

12. Who were then at war in the west trying to protect their buffalo herds against wanton destruction.

13. *Report of Commissioner of Indian Affairs*, 1872, p. 237.

14. *Report of Commissioner of Indian Affairs*, 1871, pp. 236, 237.

15. Editor's note: The Delawares purchased land from the Cherokee Nation and received Cherokee citizenship but continued to maintain their own tribal sovereignty.

16. Kappler's "Laws and Treaties," Vol. II, pp. 937–42; also 618–23; 395–97; 362. The Osages were assigned a reservation between 96 degrees longitude and the Arkansas River north of the Creek Nation.

17. At the time of forcible removal of the Cherokees in 1839, some who were unalterably opposed to going west escaped to inaccessible mountains of North Carolina and Tennessee, where they remained until they changed their minds and went willingly. When individuals and groups expressed a willingness to remove, the Secretary of the Interior was authorized to defray their expenses out of a fund appropriated for that purpose. U.S. Statutes at Large, Article 15 of the Treaty of 1866.

18. The human mosquito, singing "Cousin, Cousin," they were called by the Indians.

19. Article 26 of the Treaty of 1866.

20. Benedict, John D. *History of Muskogee*, Vol. 1, pp. 220–222.

21. *Report of Com. of Indian Affairs*, 1880, p. 95.

22. In 1874 these aliens went so far as to create a disturbance in the nation when they were not allowed to participate in a per capita relief fund the Cherokee National Council was distributing to the needy members of the tribe. *Rep. of Com. of Ind. Af.*, 1875, p. 48.

23. *Report of the Commissioner of Indian Affairs*, 1876, p. 60.

24. *Report of the Commissioner of Indian Affairs*, 1880, pp. 94, 95.

Chapter 22

1. This system prior to the Civil War: It was probably owing to the influence of the missionaries that the Cherokee Nation set aside the proceeds of a tract of land in Alabama, which they sold in 1819, to be used as a school fund. The money was invested in government bonds, and the interest alone was available. In 1835 this fund was increased by the sum of $150,000 from the proceeds of another sale of land. In the Treaty of 1866 it was provided that 35% of all funds due the nation from the government or which should accrue from sale of lands in the future, should be applied to the support of common schools and for all other educational purposes to be used exclusively for the youth of the Cherokee Nation.

Not until 1839 was the first step taken to establish schools supported by the nation and supervised by native superintendents of education. In that year a committee was appointed by the Cherokee National Council to prepare a "system of general education by schools" to be reported to that body the following year. In pursuance of the recommendation of this committee, eleven primary schools were organized in 1841 with an appropriation of $5,885.00 for their maintenance. In 1843 the number was increased to 18, and three years later measures were taken for the founding of two high schools, one for girls and the other for boys. Necessarily they were boarding schools. Textbooks were furnished at the expense of the nation for the entire system. In 1861, there were 32 common schools, but the high schools had been suspended for lack of funds.

2. Ross, *Life and Times of W. P. Ross*, pp. 51, 74, 75. Chief William Potter Ross was the son of Jack Ross and nephew of Chief John Ross. He was born in 1820 at Lookout Mountain town, was reared at Mills Town, Alabama, attended Creek Path Mission School and Greenville Academy, Tennessee. At Hamil Preparatory School, he prepared to enter Princeton. In 1842, he graduated with honors at Princeton, and upon his return to the Cherokee Nation, he became clerk of the Senate in 1843 and editor of the *Cherokee Advocate* in 1844. He was a man of great talent, a scholar, orator, and educator. *Cherokee Advocate*, April 2, 1879.

3. *Constitution and Laws of the Cherokee Nation, 1839–1867*, p. 197; *Report of the Commissioner of Indian Affairs*, 1867, p. 65.

4. *Annual report of Board of Education of the Cher. Nat.*, 1886–1888, p. 30. There was no compulsory attendance law. A school was discontinued when the average daily attendance fell below thirteen. For an average above fifteen a bonus of $1.00 per month per child up to thirty-five was paid the teacher. The minimum salary was $30.00 per month; the maximum, $50.00, for primary schools.

5. Ibid, p. 11. Worcester Academy was located at Vinita; and Baptist University at Tahlequah. Later it was removed to Muskogee.

6. Later the school year was reduced to nine months, divided into terms of four and five months.

7. *Report of the Commissioner of Indian Affairs*, 1877, p. 85.

8. *Annual Report of the Board of Education for Cherokee Nation*, 1886–88, p. 31 footnote.

9. The Park Hill Seminary had been badly damaged. The weight of commissary supplies, stored in the chapel, had broken the floor through; windows were shattered and walls defaced. Schwarze, *Moravian Missions Among the Southern Indians*, p. 294.

10. *Annual Report of the Board of Education of the Cherokee Nation*, p. 29.

11. *Laws of the Cherokee Nation*, 1875 Edition; *Annual Report of the Board of Education of the Cherokee Nation*, 1887, p. 18; *Report of the Com. of Indian Affairs*, 1872, p. 35; 1880, p. 95; *Laws of the Cherokee Nation*, 1875, pp. 260, 262; Ross, *Life and Times of W. P. Ross*, pp. 79, 196.

12. As provided for by act of the National Council, Nov. 25, 1871, *Laws of the Cherokee Nation*, 1875, p. 238.

13. The Treaty of 1835 provided a fund of $50,000 for orphans, the annual income from which should be used for the education of children bereft of parents

and destitute of the means of subsistence. By the Treaty of 1886 that investment was changed so as to provide that 15% of any funds due the nation, or thereafter accrued from the sale of their lands by the United States, were to be invested and the credit applied to the orphan fund. In 1872 this fund amounted to $175,935.51. *Report of Commissioner of Indian Affairs*, 1872, p. 34.

14. *Laws of the Cherokee Nation*, 1875, pp. 263, 265.

15. The timber land furnished fuel, fencing, lumber for buildings and repairs on the farm; the grazing land supplied pasturage for the livestock with which it was equipped. There was a spring that supplied the institution with an abundance of excellent water, and a large spring house of dressed stone, so carefully prepared and adjusted as to require neither mortar nor cement. It was hexagonal in shape and was built by a native stone mason. This was the cold storage plant, in which were kept milk, butter and cheese produced on the premises; also such perishables as fruits and berries in their season. The large stone smokehouse was for curing and storing meat. The plant was largely self-sustaining. Teachers' salaries, etc. were appropriated from the annual interest on the orphans' fund.

16. Children under the age of nine years were cared for by relatives or were adopted by families. They were too young for institutional life and would have complicated the management of the school.

17. *Laws of the Cherokee Nation*, 1875, p. 258; Ross, *Life and Times of W. P. Ross*, p. 197; *Report of the Commissioner of Indian Affairs for 1878*, p. 60. The price of board was $5.00 a month, payable in advance, for which national warrants were sometimes accepted in lieu of money.

18. Preaching services were held from three to four o'clock every Sunday afternoon.

19. *Annual Report of the Board of Education of the Cherokee Nation*, 1, 1889, p. 22; Ross, *Life and Times of W. P. Ross*, p. 198.

20. *Annual Report of the Board of Education of the Cherokee Nation*, 1888–89, p. 30; Benedict, John D. *History of Muskogee*, Vol. 1, p. 271; Ross, *Life and Times of W. P. Ross*, pp. 186–201. The text of the address delivered at the dedication,—a masterpiece of Indian eloquence and optimism.

21. School opened on the last Monday in August 1889 with 200 students in attendance. The new building was entirely modern, equipped with the latest improvements in plumbing, lighting and heating.

22. *Annual Report of Board of Education of the Cherokee Nation, 1887–88*; pp. 19, 20.

23. Laws of the Cherokee Nation, 1839, 1867, 75; Reports of Commissioner of Indian Affairs for 1870, 289; for 1882, 89; and for 1887, 267.

24. Benedict, Vol. 1, p. 271; *Report of Commissioner of Indian Affairs*, 1888, pp. 104, 105; Ibid, p. 31; *Laws of the Cherokee Nation*.

25. In 1889 there were in operation in the Cherokee Nation: Worcester Academy, located at Vinita, under the auspices of the American Missionary Society; Cherokee Academy at Tahlequah, under the Baptist Missionary Society; Hogan Institute near Locust Grove, under the Cumberland Presbyterian Church; Elm

Springs, Park Hill, Spring Place, now Oaks, and Dwight under the Women's Missionary Society of the Presbyterian Church. The Cherokee Academy, removed to Muskogee in 1887, developed into Bacone University, an Indian college of a high order, possessing a clear conception of what constitutes the best type of training for the Indian in the twentieth century. Schwarze, *Moravian Missions Among the Southern Indians*, pp. 288–294; Ross, *Life and Times of W. P. Ross*, p. 199.

26. *Our Brother in Red*, October 1884; personal information received from Hon. Alice Robertson during her sojourn at Claremore in the summer of 1930. What Sibyl could have foretold that forty years from the time of this convention, the secretary of this organization would be sitting in the House of Representatives, and the treasurer in the Senate of the United States, from a state called Oklahoma.

27. 30 U.S. Statutes at Large, 495–518; also 32 Statutes, 716.

28. Editor's note: Footnote is missing from the original manuscript.

29. Editor's note: Footnote is missing from the original manuscript.

30. After the Civil War, the superintendents of education were: S. S. Stephens, O. H. Brewer, W. W. Hastings and W. H. Jackson. After the system had been changed, a board of education composed of three members took the place of the superintendents. Some of the outstanding members of this board were: Leonidas Dobson, George S. Mason, John Ross Vann, W. H. Davis, William Potter Ross, J. L. Adair, A. W. Timberlake, J. A. Spiers, G. W. Choate, R. L. Owen, W. A. Duncan, M. R. Brown, R. T. Hanks, T. B. Hitchcock, Eli Whitmire, W. V. Carey, A. E. Ivey, W. J. McKee, J. E. Butler, G. W. Mitchell, Mark Lee Paden, Connell Rogers, J. H. Thompson, J. T. Parks, J. F. McCullough, Thomas Carlile, Carlotta Archer, Theodore Perry, S. W. Woodall, D. E. Ward, O. H. P. Brewer, Albert Sydney Wyly and S. F. Parks. From the reports of the Commissioner of Indian Affairs, 1866–1902.

Chapter 23

1. Senate Journal, 39th Cong., 1st sess., 23.

2. Senate Journal, 41st Cong., 2nd sess., 382 (Parker Calendar 149)

3. See Gittinger Appendix E for list of bills and references.

4. Obviously there was a desire to get away from the name of "the Indian Territory." In 1854, Senator Johnson of Arkansas had proposed a rather complex measure for the organization of the country west of his state into three distinct territories. They were to be known as the Chelokee Territory, with the capital at Tahlequah; the Muscogee Territory, with the capital at the Creek Agency; and the Chahta Territory, with its capital at Doaksville. When these territories were ready for statehood, they were to be united and admitted under the name of Neosho. According to the report of the Committee, the object of the bill was to "persuade these tribes to become an integral part of the United States, to merge their useless nationalities in that of the America Republic, and to look forward with confidence to the time when they will constitute a portion of the Union, and add another star to its flag." *Cong. Globe*, 33rd Congress, 1st sess., 532, 956; Sen. Reports, 33rd Cong., 1st sess., II (707). The proposed Chelokee Territory was to enclose, in addition to the Cherokee Nation and the group of small tribes in its northeastern

corner, the Cherokee Neutral Lands in Kansas, the Cherokee Outlet and all that area that became known as "No Man's Land," which had been left by Texas, which upon entering the Union as a slave state she had been obligated to fix her northern boundary at 36 degrees in conformity to the Missouri Compromise. The bill got no farther than the second session of the 33rd Congress where it was lost for want of proper steering. *Cong. Globe*, 33rd Cong., 1st sess., 532, 986; 33rd Cong., 2nd sess., 53, 135.

5. 14 U.S. Statutes, 291, 294. Under the leadership of Stephen A. Douglas, in 1850 Congress adopted the policy of railroad building. In 1857 Missouri began construction of the Atlantic and Pacific. Johnson, *Stephen A. Douglas*, 169–174.

6. *A Report of the Commissioner of Indian Affairs*, 1871, p. 86; H. Exec. Doc., 42nd Cong., 2nd sess., III, 1 (1505), 982.

7. Named for Vinnie Ream, a well-known sculptress of the time who made a bust of Sequoyah which was placed in the Council House at Tahlequah. The original name of Vinita was Downingsville.

8. H. Exec. Docs., 43rd Congress, 1st sess., IV (1601), p. XXVI; Sen. Reports, 45th Congress, 3rd sess., III (1839), 3.

9. Report of the Commissioner of Indian Affairs for 1882, p. 72. "During the year the Atlantic and Pacific has been extended 60 miles west of Vinita, Cherokee Nation, and is being rapidly built toward Albuquerque, New Mexico." The corporation was later reorganized as the St. Louis and San Francisco.

10. Report of the Commissioner of Indian Affairs for 1871, p. 72; for 1872, p. 83; for 1873, p. 95.

11. Bassett, John Spencer. *History of the U.S.*, pp. 683, 686; *Report of Com. of Indian Affairs for 1868*, pp. 25, 50; for 1869, 69; for 1871, p. 40; for 1872, 128. Editor's note: "Wild Tribes" is offensive language. Many Cherokees and Euro-Americans at the time used the term "Five Civilized Tribes" to describe the Cherokee, Choctaw, Chickasaw, Seminole, and Muscogee/Creek, the large southeastern Nations removed to Indian Territory, and used offensive terms such as "wild tribes" or "savage tribes" to describe other Nations who belong to the West, including those whose land the Five Tribes now sit on.

12. Editor's note: "Treaty with the Cherokee," July 19, 1866, *Indian Affairs: Laws and Treaties*, ed. Charles Joseph Kappler (Washington: Government Printing Office, 1904), 2:945–946.

13. At this time, Okmulgee was "a town of some fifty log cabins. . . . with two or three large stores of Indian traders and a tumble-down council house in the center of a large square." The hotel was a large farm house with a hall through the center and a wide piazza on one side. *Lippincotts Magazine*, January 1870; Hill, Vol. 1, p. 129. Later the Creek Nation erected a substantial stone council house, which they surrounded by a stone wall, making a very attractive arrangement.

14. *Report of the Board of Commissioners for 1870*, Sen. Exec. Doc., 41st Cong., 3rd sess., 1 (1440) No. 26; *Report of the Commissioner of Indian Affairs for 1871*, pp. 565–572.

15. *Report of the Board of Indian Commissioners for 1870*, pp. 114–136; *Chronicles of Oklahoma*, Vol. III, No. 1.

16. Journal of the Adjourned Session of the First General Council of the Indian Territory, *Chronicles of Oklahoma*, Vol. III, No. 2, pp. 120–136; *Rep. of the Board of Indian Commissioners for 1870*, pp. 114–136; *Rep. Commissioner of Indian Affairs 1871*, p. 571; *Messages and Papers of the Presidents*, Vol. VII p. 119. President Grant objected to the Okmulgee Constitution because it did not give Congress power to pass upon legislative acts. Robert Campbell of Saint Louis, John V. Farwell of Chicago, and John D. Lang of Maine. Their report of the meeting appears later.

17. *Report of the Secretary of Interior for 1874*, H. Exec. Docs., 43 Cong., 2 sess., Vol. 1. p. 32.

18. Ross, *Life and Times of William P. Ross*, p. 162–186; *Report of Commissioner of Indian Affairs for 1875* p. 85; *Report of Commissioner of Indian Affairs for 1874*, p. 34.

19. Benedict, John D. *History of Muskogee*, Vol. 1, p. 378.

20. Editor's note: Commonly spelled Kiowas.

21. Walker, Francis A., *The Indian Question*, p. 89.

22. *Report of Commissioner of Indian Affairs, 1871*, p. 466.

23. *Report of the Commissioner of Indian Affairs, 1872*, Report of Daniel Ross, commissioner and secretary of the Indian Peace Commission, pp. 195–198.

24. The Honorable Sydney Clark was closely associated with Senator Lane of Kansas, Senator Van Horn of Missouri, and Colonel E.C. Boudinot of Arkansas in the interests of one of the railroads in Indian Territory. Hill, Luther B., *A History of Oklahoma*, Vol. 1, pp. 170–183.

25. 16 U.S. Statutes, 566.

26. *Report of the Commissioner of Indian Affairs for 1871*, p. 32.

27. There were three Oklahoma bills introduced in Congress that year; Senate Bill 27, introduced by John J. Ingalls of Kansas Dec. 2, Cong. Rec. 43rd Cong., 1st sess., 2; House Bill 151 on Dec. 4, Ibid, 66; House Bill 164, Dec. 4, Ibid, 67.

28. Pleasant Porter and D. N. McIntosh of the Creek Nation; and William P. Ross and William Penn Adair of the Cherokee.

29. They were stopped at the Missouri border after having crossed through the Indian Territory, the drovers beaten, and the herds stampeded by cattle thieves from the states.

30. House Exec. Docs., 42nd Cong., 3rd Sess., no. 110.

31. 14 U.S. Statutes, pp. 799–804.

32. 25 U.S. Statutes, pp. 783–785.

33. The Tragedy of Going Snake, which took place in 1872, is an instance of unwarranted federal interference in the Cherokee Nation. Zeke Proctor, Cherokee Indian and a veteran of the Civil War, accidentally shot and killed Mrs. Kesterson, another Cherokee citizen. Her husband, a white man, was instrumental in having a posse of United States marshals sent from Fort Smith to arrest Proctor. Proctor was under trial in the district court of the Cherokee Nation, located at the Going Snake Court House, when the federal party arrived to demand his surrender. An affray was precipitated in which eleven men were killed and twelve wounded. The United States marshal in charge of the party was among the eleven killed. *Report of the Commissioner of Indian Affairs for 1872*, p. 78; Cong. Doc. 1520, No. 287.

Chapter 24

1. From 1865 to 1879.

2. Senate Report, 45th Cong., 3rd sess., III (1839), p. 111; 20 U.S. Statutes, 313; Cong. Rec., 3rd Sess., 311–318.

3. House Report, 46th Cong., 2nd Sess., II (1936) no. 474.

4. Senate Rep., 45th Cong., 3rd Sess., III (1839) p. 3; Gittinger, *The Formation of the State of Oklahoma*, Chapter VII; In 1872, the railroad had been completed to Vinita, where construction had been stopped when it became doubtful that the Indian title to the lands would be extinguished. H. Exec. Doc., 1st Sess., IV (1601) xxvi. It will be remembered that the Missouri, Kansas and Texas, and the Atlantic and Pacific, later chartered as the St. Louis and San Francisco, had obtained from Congress promises of large land grant subsidies contingent on the extinguishment of Indian titles to these lands. 14 U.S. Statutes, 238, 239, 294.

5. Mr. Boudinot, whose spectacular conduct at the Fort Smith Peace Council can never be forgotten, and whose activities in the negotiations of the Dark Treaty of 1866 alienated even his best friends, established his residence in Arkansas, but spent much time in Washington.

6. Gittinger, 106. Payne was with Custer during the Ouachita Campaign of 1868. Colonel Boudinot was not a resident of the Cherokee Nation after the Civil War.

7. Senate Exec. Doc., 46th Cong., 1st Sess., I (1869) no. 20, p. 5; Gittinger, p. 98.

8. In addition, he averred, "Whatever may have been the desire or intention of the United States government in 1866 to locate Indians and negroes upon these lands, it is certain that no such desire or intention exists in 1879. The negro, since that date, has become a citizen of the United States, and Congress has recently enacted laws which practically forbid the removal of any more Indians into the Territory. Two years ago, Mills, of Texas, caused a provision to be inserted in the Indian Appropriation Bill [in which] . . . the removal of any Indians from Arizona or New Mexico is forbidden. These laws practically leave several million acres of the richest lands on the continent free from Indian titles or occupancy and an integral part of the public domain." Ibid, 11.

9. Senate Exec. Docs., 46th Cong., 1st Sess., I (1869) no. 20, pp. 12–20, 26.

10. Senate Exec. Docs., 46th Cong., 1st Sess., I (1869) no. 20, p. 21.

11. Senate Exec. Docs., 46th Cong., 1st Sess., I (1869) no. 20, pp. 12, 20; also 1 & 5: 24–31; *Cherokee Advocate*, April 30, 1879.

12. Ibid, pp. 24–31.

13. House Reports, 943; Cong. Record, 46th Congress, 1st sess., 634.

14. Gittinger, pp. 106–11, for Payne's activities as leader of the Boomer Movement. Also reports of the Commissioner of Indian Affairs for 1880, 1881, 1882, 1883.

15. 14 U.S. Statutes, p. 799, Articles 15, 16.

16. Editor's note: This is offensive language. Many Cherokees and Euro-Americans at the time used the term "Five Civilized Tribes" to describe the Cherokee, Choctaw, Chickasaw, Seminole, and Muscogee/Creek, the large southeastern Nations removed to Indian Territory, and used offensive terms such as "wild tribes"

or "savage tribes" to describe other Nations who belong to the West, including those whose land the Five Tribes now sit on.

17. *Laws of the Cherokee Nation 1839–1867.*

18. There were several of these cattle trails through the Indian Territory. One of them was the Baxter Springs Trail that followed the old military road from the Red River to the southwest corner of Missouri. It was said to be so infested with bandits that the drovers had to abandon it. There were the Shawnee Trails, the Eastern Trail passing through the Osage Nation to Abilene. There seem to have been several extensions of the Chisholm Trail, a fact which caused some confusion for a time in the minds of historians.

19. Much had been written on the subject of the cattle industry. In her story of Oklahoma, Muriel Wright has two very charming chapters on this subject. Buchanan and Dale, *A History of Oklahoma*, Chapter X, is equally interesting from the standpoint of the casual reader. Dale, E. E., *The Ranchmen's Last Frontier* is a more exhaustive treatment of the subject. E. E. Dale, *The Cherokee Strip Live Stock Association* is referred to frequently in this volume; Nimmo, *Range and Cattle Traffic*, p. 28.

20. *Cherokee Advocate*, March 16, 1883.

21. The graziers' license facilitated the collection of revenues for the nation and increased the amounts turned in to the treasury. In 1880, the amount was $7,200, and in 1882 it had increased to $41,000, *Cherokee Advocate*, Feb. 6, 1885; Dale, p. 64.

22. Senate Report 1278, 49th Cong., 1st sess., Vol. VIII, p. 683. On May 19, 1883, the National Council passed an act which provided that the treasurer, whenever payments were made to him by the Cherokee Live Stock Association, was to retain the money in the treasury until it amounted to $300,000, when it was to be paid out per capita under the direction of the National Council. The census was to be taken and the money paid to citizens by blood. This was called Grass Money and sometimes bread money when crops failed and there was a shortage of bread-stuff. *Cherokee Advocate*, May 7, 1886.

23. Sen. Exec. Doc. 136, 50th Cong., Vol. IV, pp. 3–4; Dale, pp. 72–73.

Chapter 25

1. Senate Misc. Docs. 80, 50th Cong., 2nd Sess., p. 20.

2. Dale, E. E., pp. 72, 73; Charles Eldred Papers, Nov. 1886 to Dec. 1888; Senate Exec. Doc. 136, 50th Cong., 2nd Sess., Vol. IV, pp. 2–4.

3. The Charles Eldred Papers. Dec. 1888.

4. 2 U.S. Statutes, 388; Cong. Record, 49th Congress, 1st Sess. 123, 1558, 1764, 2nd Sess., 286, 772, 882, 972, 1577; Gittinger, p. 140.

5. 39 *Constitution and Laws of the Cherokee Nation 1839–1867*, Art. IV, Sec. 1, 14. In this he was entirely sincere, although the Secretary of the Interior was inclined to doubt it.

6. 16 Opinion, 16, p. 407 (February 25, 1880).

7. Sen. Exec. Doc., 54th Cong., 1st Sess., Vol. IV, p. 9.

8. House Report 3768, 51st Cong., 2nd Sess., Vol. IV, p. 9; Dale, p. 73.

9. Quoted by Sec. Noble in his letter.

10. Sen. Exec. Doc., 20, 25th Cong., 2nd sess., p. 98.

11. House Exec. Doc. 51st Cong., 1st sess., XI (2724), p. XIII.

12. *Messages and Papers of the Presidents* LX, p. 69.

13. 26 U.S. Statutes, p. 1577; *Messages and Papers of the Presidents* XI, p. 97. The president had already secured from the Attorney General the opinion that the lease of the Cherokee Strip Live Stock Association was invalid. 19 Opinions, p. 499.

14. Dale, E. E. *The Cherokee Live Stock Association*, p. 71. A bill was introduced in Cong. in Jan. 1891 proposing to pay $1.25 an acre for the lands of the Outlet and if they still refused to sell, take them without further negotiations. Objections were raised to this policy on the ground that for the government to do so would violate its faith and disregard its solemn obligations. Dale, 75; Sen. Exec. Doc. 63, 51st Cong., 1st Sess., V (3200) 56. 27 U.S. Statutes, 641; Sen. Exec. Doc. 52nd Cong., 2nd Sess., Vol. LV pp. 8–9. In 1871 Cong. had ruled that there should be no more Indian treaties, and later that the U.S. had the right and authority to govern them by acts of Congress instead of controlling them by treaties. 16 U.S. Statutes, p. 566; Cong. Docs. 1520, No. 287.

15. David H. Jerome, Alfred M. Wilson, and Warren G. Sayre.

16. Elias Boudinot, Joseph A. Scales, George Downing, Roach Young, Thomas Smith, Thomas Triplet, and Joseph Smallwood, Preamble of Cherokee Agreement.

17. Article IV.

18. Arranged in chronological order the significant events of the cession of the Outlet follow:

1. Dec.14, death of Chief Joel B. Mayes, following his re-election on August 4, of that year.

2. Dec. 19, the Cherokee National Council agreed to cede the Outlet to the U.S. subject to the approval of the Cherokee people in an election to be held on Jan. 4, 1892. Sen. Exec. Doc. 56, 52nd Congress, 2nd sess., Vol. V, pp. 14, 15.

3. The people approved the cession by a small majority, Sen. Exec. Docs., 52nd Cong., 1st Sess., V (2900) no. 56.

4. 1893, March 3, terms of agreement were modified by Congress and returned to the Cherokee Nation for adoption.

5. 1893, April 3, the Cherokee people gave their assent to the modifications submitted by Congress.

6. May 17,—following, the contract was signed by the Commissioner of Indian Affairs, H. Exec. Docs., 53rd Cong., 2nd Sess., XIV (3210), 33.

7. 1893, Sept. 16,—the lands of the Outlet on report of Commissioner of Indian Affairs 1893, opened to settlement, 28 U.S. Statutes 1222; *Messages and Papers of the Presidents* XIX, p. 406.

8. The proceeds from the sale of the Outlet were released to the Cherokee Nation and disbursed per capita during the spring and summer of 1894.

19. East of the Meridian of ninety-seven and one-half degrees the lands were sold for two dollars and a half an acre; between ninety-seven and a half and ninety and a half for two dollars an acre; and those west of ninety-eight and a half for a dollar and a half an acre. Act of March 3, 1893, 27 U.S. Statutes 642, 643, 644; Gittinger, p. 167.

20. Spurious charges brought by these vociferous intruders against reputable and upright Cherokee citizens were used within the next few years to prejudice the entire country against the government and citizenship of the nation. The intruders mentioned in Article two, Sec I of the agreement were never removed. The government made no effort to comply with its contract, until the Curtis Act made it null and void.

21. A disreputable class of non-citizen lawyers who had come into the nation for purposes of graft, fattened on these contested citizenship claims.

22. Delawares and Shawnees.

23. The per capita apportionment was $265.65.

Chapter 26

1. Cong. Doc. 2915, No. 1079, p. 7.

2. Owen, Robert L. The Crisis in Indian Territory, *Muskogee Phoenix*, Dec. 17, 1896.

3. March 3, 1893. The only power given the commission at this time was to negotiate and report.

4. 27 U.S. Statutes, 645; *Okla. Red Book* I, p. 481. Each member was entitled to receive for his services a salary of $5,000. All necessary expenses were paid. A secretary, stenographer and an interpreter for each nation were provided. The total amount appropriated for the first year was $25,000.

5. He had served sixteen years in the House and eighteen in the Senate of the United States. His advocacy of allotment for the Indians had long been pronounced.

6. *The Vinita Indian Chieftain*, February 15, 1894.

7. The letter of Governor Fishback of Arkansas to the President under date of Dec. 22, 1893, complained loudly of crime in the Indian Country and its demoralizing effect upon the good people of the States. "The state of semi-chaos and the forces of governments which exist in the territory, rendering it a constant menace to the peace and order of all the States of the Mississippi Valley from the Allegheny to the Rocky Mountains suggests the very serious question whether the time has not arrived for the federal government to assert its right to eminent domain over this part of the National domain and to change its political relations with the United States." He could conceive of no valid reasons why any Indians' rights were any more sacred than those of a white man. *The Cherokee Advocate*, on January 3, 1894, analyzed the letter, giving pertinent answers to all the governor's accusations.

8. A sophism reminiscent of arguments for Indian removal.

9. Like bad children of indulgent parents, the intruders must be acceded to in their demands, else there was no telling what they might do.

10. Editor's note: This is offensive and outdated language, and Euro-Americans have a history of using this term in a racist, derogatory manner, though Cherokees, including Eaton, accepted citizens who had both Cherokee and Euro-American heritage. Cherokees traditionally belonged to their mother's clan and the Cherokee Nation regardless of their father's heritage. Euro-Americans developed a racialized notion of identity and applied it to Indigenous people, using terms such as the one Eaton uses here to refer to multiracial Cherokees. For further discussion, see Theda Perdue, "Race and Culture: Writing the Ethnohistory of the Early South," *Ethnohistory* 51, no. 4 (Fall 2004): 701–723. For a discussion on the development of southeastern Indigenous views on race, see Nancy Shoemaker, "How Indians Got to be Red," *American Historical Review* 102, no. 3 (June 1997): 625–644.

11. Rep. of the Com. to the Five Civilized Tribes for Nov. 1894. H. Exec. Docs. 53rd Congress, 3rd sess., XIV (3305), p. XLI; *Vinita Indian Chieftain*, Feb. 11, 1894.

12. *Cherokee Advocate*, Tahlequah, Cherokee Nation, March 9, 1894.

13. *The Vinita Indian Chieftain*, March 8, 1894.

14. Gittinger, Roy, *The Formation of the State of Oklahoma*, p. 189.

15. *Cherokee Advocate*, April 3, 1895; *Report of Commissioner of Indian Affairs for 1893*, p. 187.

16. Editor's note: This is reprehensible and unconscionable language. While Eaton herself uses the words "black," "negro," and "freedman," in her own writing, we acknowledge the harm that comes from printing quotations of this racial slur in its entirety. Because this is a historical document, we have chosen to keep the original language of the text.

17. *Cherokee Advocate*, April 3, 1895.

18. *Rep. of the Com, to the Five Civilized Tribes*, Nov. 20, 1894, H. Exec. Docs. 63rd Congress, XIV (3305), pp. 19–20.

19. The Seminoles sent no delegate. The Creek Nation was represented by G. W. Grayson, the Choctaw Nation by Jonas Dyer, the Chickasaw Nation by W. M. Guy, and the Cherokee Nation by C. J. Harris, W. A. Duncan, S. W. Gray, J. F. Thompson and Roach Young.

20. *The Cherokee Advocate*, Tahlequah, Cherokee Nation, Feb. 27, 1895.

21. 28 U.S. Statutes, 939. Thomas Cabiniss of Georgia and Alexander H. Montgomery of Kentucky were added to the Commission. Gen. Frank R. Armstrong replaced Commissioner Kidd.

22. *Cherokee Advocate*, Tahlequah, April 7, 1895.

23. *The Muskogee Phoenix*, May 22, 1895.

24. Sen. Doc. No. 12, 54th Congress, 1st Sess.; *Atoka Indian Citizen*, July 11; *Cherokee Advocate*, April 3, 1895.

25. House Exec. Docs., 54th Cong., 1st sess., XIV (3394).

26. House Exec. Docs., 54th Cong., 1st sess. (338) p. XCVI; Sen. Doc. 12, 54th Congress, 1st sess.

27. 27 U.S. Statutes 640; The agreement was reached in Dec.19, 1891; approved by the Cherokees Jan. 4, 1892, Sen. Exec. Docs., 52nd Cong., 1st sess., V (2900) No. 56; approved by Cong. April 3, 1893; contract signed May 17, 1893, H. Exec.

Docs., 53rd Congress, 2nd sess., XIV (3210) 33 V; *Oklahoma Red Book*, Vol. 1, pp. 469–470.

28. 29 U.S. Statutes 339, 340.

29. *Annual Rep. of the Com. to The Five Civilized Tribes for 1895*, pp. 74, 75, 76.

30. Under the Congressional Act of March 2, 1895, the survey of the lands of the Indian Territory was begun by the United States Geological Survey in April of that year.

31. Editor's note: Adapted from Henry Wadsworth Longfellow, *The Courtship of Miles Standish.*

32. *Rep. of the Com. to the Five Civilized Tribes for 1901*, p. 212. It takes an Indian to know an Indian, especially if he looks like a white man.

33. H. Report, 54th Cong., 1st Sess., 12 (3460) No. 1102.

34. 30 U.S. Statutes, p. 80.

35. *Report of the Commission to the Five Civilized Tribes for 1897.*

Chapter 27

1. Editor's note: Civil War.

2. William Penn Adair died in 1880 while with a delegation in Washington, and the National Council appointed Rabbit Bunch to complete the term. The Assistant Chiefs from 1839 to 1879 were: 1839, Joseph Vann; 1840, Anderson Vann; 1843–1851, George Lowrey; 1851, Richard Taylor; 1855, Jack Spears; 1859 Joseph Vann; 1862, Thomas Pegg; 1863 Lewis Downing; 1867, James Vann; 1871, Robert Buffington Daniels; 1875, David Rowe.

3. In 1879 the national indebtedness amounted to $187,000, and Cherokee warrants were selling at twenty-five cents on the dollar. Eight years later, the nation was out of debt and its paper was at par.

4. The highest salary that John Ross ever received was $500.00. In 1859 this was reduced to $400.00 because of a national depression. In 1866 the salary was raised to $900.00; in 1879 to $2,000.00; in 1893 it was reduced to $1,500, after which it was not changed.

5. The Constitution of 1839 provided that the principal and the assistant chiefs of the nation attend at the seat of government during the session of the National Council.

6. It was called the "Mail Hack."

7. On April 19, 1895, it was completely destroyed by fire. It was valued at $3,000 and was insured for half of its value. This fire destroyed eighteen places of business, 8 residences, 13 offices and the Presbyterian Church and the building occupied by the *Cherokee Arrow*. The fire started in Wilson's livery stable at 1 A.M. on April 19. *Cherokee Arrow* (Fire Edition), April 19, 1895.

8. In 1866 the population was estimated at fourteen thousand. *Report of Commissioner of Indian Affairs*, p. 65; for 1879, at 17,000.

9. *The Tulsa Daily World,* January 29, 1934. The original company was composed of C. W. Turner, J. B. Stapler, J. S. Stapler, John S. Scott, L. B. Bell, and E. D. Hicks.

10. *Report of the Commissioner of Indian Affairs for 1886*, p. 120.

11. *Laws of the Cherokee Nation*, 1875, p. 86.

12. Editor's note: Joel Bryant Mayes.

13. A large part of the proceedings was political dramatics, and so understood at the time by the participants.

14. Thus Coo-wee-scoo-wee District lost two good citizens, at the same time the Cherokee Nation was bereft of both Principal and Assistant Chiefs.

15. *Cherokee Advocate*, February 5, 1886.

16. *Cherokee Advocate*, July 24, 1895. Chief Harris was in Washington on July 1 in his executive capacity to remonstrate against this measure.

17. *Muskogee Phoenix*, August 26, 1897; *Report of Commissioner of Indian Affairs for 1899.*

18. His residence was at Skiatook, where he operated a general store. He also owned stores at Vera and Talala.

19. *Annual Report of U.S. Indian Inspector for the Indian Territory for 1901*, p. 122.

Chapter 28

1. This was not because their language lacked expressiveness, for when the time came for speech, there were spoken words adequate to every need. The language is rich in imagery and symbolism, but no word of profanity can be found in its vocabulary. A tribesman, if swear he must, uses English or some other foreign tongue, but, laconic by nature, he has no need of oaths, neither in politics nor religion.

2. Editor's note: The footnote is missing from the original manuscript. The original manuscript does not include an end quotation mark.

3. U.S. Statutes, 311.

4. At Eufaula, June 28, 1896, *Rep. of the Com. to the Five Civilized Tribes*, 1894, 1895, and 1896, Exhibit G.

5. In the regular session of the National Council, Nov. 8, 1896.

6. *Report of the Com. to the Five Civilized Tribes*, 1897, pp. 33, 34.

7. Editor's note: The footnote is missing in the original manuscript.

8. Editor's note: The footnote is missing in the original manuscript. Eaton refers to the Curtis Act, or "An Act for the Protection of the People of Indian Territory." This act was enacted on June 28, 1898.

9. *Rep. of the Commission to the Five Civilized Tribes for 1897*, p. 34.

10. *Muskogee Phoenix*, June 17, 1897.

11. *Report of the Commission to the Five Civilized Tribes for 1897*, pp. 34, 35.

12. *Cherokee Advocate*, August 12, 1897; Benedict, John D., *History of Muskogee and Northeastern Oklahoma*, Vol. 1, pp. 147–48. *Rep. of the Commissioner of Indian Affairs for 1897*, pp. 143, 144.

13. *Dallas News*, August 25, 1897: "The scene from a moral point of view," said the reporter, "was simply awful. It was the white man's boasted civilization brought down to lick the dust at the feet of the red man's so-called barbarism; an exhibition at which the moon might well blush and the sun hide its head forever in the Caverns of Universal night from motives of intolerable shame." Editor's note: A full report of the conference also appeared in the *Weekly Chieftain*, June 24, 1897.

14. Editor's note: This is offensive and outdated language, and Euro-Americans have a history of using this term in a racist, derogatory manner, though Cherokees,

including Eaton, accepted citizens who had both Cherokee and Euro-American heritage. Cherokees traditionally belonged to their mother's clan and the Cherokee Nation regardless of their father's heritage. Euro-Americans developed a racialized notion of identity and applied it to Indigenous people, using terms such as the one Eaton uses here to refer to multiracial Cherokees. For further discussion, see Theda Perdue, "Race and Culture: Writing the Ethnohistory of the Early South," *Ethnohistory* 51, no. 4 (Fall 2004): 701–723. For a discussion on the development of southeastern Indigenous views on race, see Nancy Shoemaker, "How Indians Got to be Red," *American Historical Review* 102, no. 3 (June 1997): 625–644.

15. *Report of the Commission to the Five Civilized Tribes for 1897*, p. 38.

16. Ibid, p. 78.

Chapter 29

1. *The Oklahoma Magazine*, May 1894; Hill, *History of the State of Oklahoma*, Vol. 1, p. 300.

2. *Tenth Annual Report of the Commission to the Five Civilized Tribes*, p. 5.

3. The Creek people did not ratify the agreement. The Atoka agreement furnished the basis for negotiations with the other tribal nations.

4. The Curtis Bill, Cong. Rec. 54th Congress, 1st sess., Vol. 3, pp. 6197, 6246; H. R. 7907; 2nd sess., Vol. XXIX, p. 873.

5. Townsite work in the Cherokee Nation was simplified by reason of the fact that the National Council had provided for the incorporation of towns and the sale of town lots. Fort Gibson was the first incorporated town in the Indian Territory.

6. *Life and Times of Tams Bixby*, p. 74.

7. The Union Agency was composed of the agencies of the Creeks, Cherokees, Choctaws, Chickasaws, and Seminoles. The consolidation was effected in July 1874. *Rep. of Com. of Indian Affairs, 1876*, p. 60. The Union Agency was then located in the vicinity of Muskogee, at that time a small railroad station.

8. *Annual Reports of the Indian Inspector for the Indian Territory, 1899–1904*.

9. For a period of ten years, J. George Wright occupied the position of a foreign governor general over seventy thousand intelligent, civilized native Americans. Among his subjects were men of education and political experience, and women distinguished for talent and intelligence, who within a century had advanced the standard of their tribe to the status of a civilized nation. From them he sought no counsel; to them he rendered no accounts. He submitted his reports and recommendations and rendered his accounts to Washington. *Annual Report of the Indian Inspector for the Indian Territory for 1899*, pp. 1–20.

10. *Annual Report of the Indian Inspector for the Indian Territory for 1899*, p. 14.

11. The Cherokee Nation vs. Ethan Allen Hitchcock, Secretary of the Interior, 1889. U.S., p. 294.

Chapter 30

1. *Report of the Commission to the Five Civilized Tribes for 1899*, p. 49.

2. Cong. Record, vol. XXXII, p. 2264.

3. Kee-too-wah is a Cherokee word meaning key, according to J. W. Duncan, once secretary of the order. Editor's note: Keetoowah, or ᏫᏍᎦ/giduwa/kituwa, refers to the Cherokee concept of the community coming together for mutual benefit. ᏫᏍᎦ/Giduwa/Kituwa was a mother town in the traditional homelands in the Cherokee Nation. The Cherokees call themselves the ᎠᏂᏫᏍᎦᏯ/anigiduwagi or theᎠᏂᏫᏍᎦ/anigiduwa, meaning, the people of Giduwa.

4. *Report of the Commissioners to the Five Civilized Tribes for 1902*, pp. 28–35. The Crazy Snake uprising in the Creek Nation was more dramatic but no more tyrannously dealt with than the Kee-too-wah rebellion.

5. *Annual Report of the Indian Inspector for the Indian Territory for 1902*, pp. 28–35.

6. 32 U.S. Statutes, pp. 716. A second agreement reached on April 9, 1900, and ratified by Congress on March 1, 1901 (31 U.S. Statutes, p. 848), was rejected by the Cherokees on April 29, 1901. The final agreement, known as the Cherokee Allotment Agreement, was ratified by Congress July 1, 1902. (32 U.S. Statutes, p. 716, et seq.)

7. The other three sevenths were white adopted citizens, Delawares and Shawnees, freedmen and spurious claimants to citizenship whose names had been placed on the rolls by the Dawes Commission arbitrarily. On the Cherokee citizenship rolls compiled by the Dawes Commission, the number of freedmen was approximately five thousand.

8. *Report of the Commission to the Five Civilized Tribes for 1902*, pp. 47–48.

9. Editor's note: Eaton originally wrote 1903, but we believe this was a typo. The correct date is 1893.

10. Tams Bixby, who had been chairman of the commission, was made Indian Commissioner and retained to complete the work of the commission.

11. Otherwise the Indian land titles would have reverted to the United States government and the lands have become public domain. In that case, the St. Louis and San Francisco and the Missouri, Kansas and Texas railroads claimed large areas of land in the Cherokee and Choctaw Nations under the provisional land grant subsidy contained in the original charter.

12. House Report 5976; Public Doc. 129; 34 U.S. Statutes, p. 137.

13. The Principal Chief William Charles Rogers, for the Cherokees, was retained in office until his death in 1917. One of his duties was that of signing allotment deeds.

14. Resolution adopted by the Five Civilized Tribes in convention at South McAlester, November 2, 1896, articles 7 and 8. *Report of the Commission to the Five Civilized Tribes for 1894, 1895, 1896*. Exhibit G.

15. Benedict, Vol. 1, p. 151.

16. *The Muskogee Phoenix*, July 6, 1905. James Norman acted as secretary.

17. Of the Cherokee, Creek, Choctaw, Chickasaw and Seminole Nations respectively. *The Muskogee Phoenix*, July 14, 1905.

18. *The Muskogee Phoenix*, August 22, 1905.

19. *Oklahoma Redbook*, pp. 623–674.

20. Ibid, p. 624.

21. *The Outlook*, March 1906; Hill, Luther B., *History of the State of Oklahoma*, Vol. I, pp. 350–353.

22. Sen. Doc., 59th Cong., 1st sess., IV (4912) No. 143, pp. 1–27; *Final Report of the Commission to the Five Civilized Tribes*, June 30, 1905; p. 79; House Doc., 59th Congress, 1st Sess., XIX (4959) p. 614.

23. *Messages and Papers of the Presidents*, Vol. XI, p. 1178.

24. H. Bill 79, Cong. Record, 59th Congress, 1st sess., p. 47.

25. S. Bill 3680, Ibid, p. 1527.

26. Sen. Doc., 59th Congress, 1st sess., VIII (4916) No. 478–482; House Report 114908, No. 4660, 4925.

27. S. Docs., 60th Congress, 1st sess., VII (5240) No. 187.

28. 34 U.S. Statutes, 267.

29. Abridged from an editorial published in the *Muskogee Phoenix*, Nov. 17, 1907.

Selected Bibliography

Editor's note: This is Rachel Caroline Eaton's original selected bibliography. While the editors made a few adjustments, it does not fulfill all the conventions of a modern standard bibliography.

I. Alphabetical List of (Primary) Sources

Abel, Annie Heloise, Editor, *The Official Correspondence of James S. Calhoun* (Washington D.C.)

Acts of the General Assembly of the State of Georgia, 1827–1837.

Adams, John Quincy *Memoirs*, Edited by Charles Frances Adams.

American State Papers, Indian Affairs, Volumes I and II.

American State Papers, Public Lands.

Annals of Congress, 1789–1824.

Annual Cyclopedia, 1861.

Annual Report of Board of Education of the Cherokee Nation for 1887.

Bartram, William, *Travels Through North and South Carolina, Georgia, East and West Florida, the Cherokee Country, the Creek Confederacy and the Land of the Choctaws, 1773–1778.*

Cherokee National Manuscript Records.

Cherokee Nation, Laws of, Adopted by the Council at Various Periods, Knoxville, 1826; 1839–1867; 1875; 1833; 1893.

Cherokee Phoenix, The, 1828–1834, Chicago Historical Society.

Cherokee Treaties, 1866.

Cherokee Question, The; Report of the Commissioner of Indian Affairs to the President on the Question of Cherokee Loyalty in the Civil War. It also contains Albert Pike's letter of February 17, 1866, and various letters and papers on the Civil War in the Cherokee Country.

Confederate Statutes at Large, The.

Confederate State Papers, The.

Confidential letter of P. M. Butler to T. Hartley Crawford, Indian Commissioner, March 4, 1842. On file in Indian Office, Washington.

Congressional Documents, Serial Numbers: 27, 64, 86, 102, 114, 115, 122, 133, 165, 171, 173, 184, 186, 187, 201, 208, 217, 268, 273, 283, 292, 311, 318, 325, 328, 329, 330, 340, 342, 348, 359, 365, 366, 368, 404, 411, 420, 425, 428, 429,

433, 434, 443, 446, 451, 457, 474, 476, 477, 488, 485, 490, 493, 495, 511, 521, 523, 526, 529, 531, 544, 547, 554, 565, 576, 618, 652, 658, 673, 690, 710, 723, 743, 751, 783, 859, 914, 965, 1070, 1232, 1337, 1339, 1360, 1399, 1408, 1409, 1433, 1437, 1464, 1515, 1520, 1608, 1630, 1645, 1648, 1655, 1790, 1822, 1823, 1833, 1861, 1898, 1991, 2006, 2028, 2031, 2068, 2070, 2073, 2076, 2087, 2108, 2110, 2162, 2167, 2171, 2174, 2255, 2259, 2261, 2274, 2303, 2329, 2339, 2360, 2436, 2437, 2443, 2456, 2517, 2519, 2559, 2600, 2612, 2613, 2674, 2688, 2752, 2807, 2887, 2888, 2900, 2901, 2951, 3046, 3048, 3064, 3142, 3346, 3470, 3559, 3858, 3867, 3868, 3915, 3916.

Congressional Globe; 23rd Congress, 1st and 2nd sessions; 24th Congress, 2nd session; 25th Congress, 2nd and 3rd sessions; 26th Congress, 1st and 2nd sessions; 27th Congress, 1st and 3rd sessions; 28th Congress, 1st session; 30th Congress, 2nd session; 31st Congress, 1st and 2nd sessions; 32nd Congress, 2nd session; 33rd Congress, 2nd session; 34th Congress, 1st and 2nd sessions; 39th Congress, 2nd session; 40th Congress, 2nd and 3rd sessions; Debates in Congress, 1829–30; 1830–31; 1831–32; Congressional records, 52nd Congress, 2nd session; 53rd Congress, 3rd session.

Dale and Raider, *Source Book of Oklahoma History*.

Evarts, Jeremiah, *Speeches on the Passage of the Bill for Removal of the Indians*, One Volume, (Boston and New York, 1830).

Gale and Seaton's Register of Debates in Congress, 13 Volumes, Washington, December 1824 to March 1837.

Gentleman of Elvas, The, Publication of the Hakluyt Society (London, 1851).

Greeley, Horace, *The American Conflict* (Hartford 1864–1867).

Indian Office Manuscript Records.

Irving, Washington, *A Tour of the Prairies*.

Irving, Pierre, *The Life and Letters of Washington Irving*.

Jefferson's Works, Library Edition.

Journal of The Union Mission (Oklahoma Historical Society, Oklahoma City).

Lanman, Charles, *Letters from the Allegheny Mountains*.

Latrobe, Charles Joseph, *The Rambler in North America (1832–1833)*.

Laws of the Cherokee Nation. Printed in English and Cherokee, 1856; 1839–1867; 1875; 1883; 1893.

Laws Relating to the Five Civilized Tribes 1890–1914. Printed by order of the committee on Indian affairs, House of Representatives, 63rd Congress, 3rd session.

Mooney, James, and Olbrechts, Frans M., *The Swimmer Manuscript: Cherokee Sacred Formulas and Medicinal Prescriptions*, Bulletin 99, Smithsonian Institute, Bureau of Ethnology, Bureau of American Ethnology.

Moore, Frank, Editor, *Rebellion Records*, Eleven Volumes.

Morse, J., *Report of the Secretary of War on Indian Affairs, 1822*.

Niles Register, Numbers 4, 6, 14, 16, 26, 36, 37, 39, 40, 41, 42.

Official Records of the War of the Rebellion, Series One, Volumes I, III, VIII and XIII.

Oklahoma Redbook, Vol. I.

Owen, Narcissa, *Memoirs*.

Payne Manuscript, 9 volumes, Containing the Cherokee Official Records before 1838, Letters of Missionaries on the condition of the Indians before 1830 and during removal; Letters of Cherokee Children in the Mission Schools to philanthropic people in the North, broadsides and publications relative to the tribe; myths and traditions of the Cherokees as related by the priesthood. (The Ayer Collection, Newberry Library, Chicago).

Report of the Commissioner of Indian Affairs, 1833–1911.

Report of the Commission to the Five Civilized Tribes, 1894–1905.

Report of the United States Indian Inspector for the Indian Territory, 1898–1907.

Report of the Trial of Stand Watie, by George W. Paschal.

Richardson's messages and papers of the Presidents, 1789–1897, 10 volumes.

Ross, Mrs. W. P., *Life and Times of the Honorable William P. Ross.*

Supreme Court Reports: Cherokee Nation vs. Georgia, 5 Peters, p. 1; Worcester vs. Georgia, 6 Peters, p.516; Cherokee Tobacco Case, 11 Wallace, p. 216; Holden vs. Joy, 17 Wallace, p. 211; United States vs. Rogers, 4 Howard, p. 567; Elks vs. Williams, 112 U.S. Reports, p. 100; 117 U.S. Reports, p. 288; U.S. vs. Kagama, 118, U.S. Reports, p. 641; 148 U.S. Reports; 20 Court of Claims, p. 449; 27 Court of Claims, p. 1.

Swain, James B., *The Life and Speeches of Henry Clay.*

Tracy, Joseph, *History of the Board of Commissioners for Foreign Missions.*

Trent, William P., and George H. Hillmon, *The Journals of Washington Irving,* The Bibliophile Society, III, p. 101.

U.S. Statutes at Large; 4, 5, 7, 9, 12, 13, 14, 15, 16, 17, 18, 19, 20, 21, 22, 23, 24, 25, 26, 27, 28, 29, 30, 31, 32, (Parts 1 and 2).

Washburn, Cephas, *Reminiscences.*

II. Alphabetical Listing of Secondary Authorities

Abel, Annie Heloise. *History of Events Resulting in Indian Consolidation West of the Mississippi.*

———. *The American Indians as Slave Holders and Secessionists.*

———. *The American Indians as Participants in the Civil War.*

———. *The American Indians Under Reconstruction.*

Adair, J., *History of the American Indians.*

Alden, George Henry, *New Governments West of the Alleghenies Before 1780.*

Bancroft, *History of the United States.* Vol. II.

Benten, Thomas H., *Thirty Years' View.*

Britton, Wiley, *Civil War on the Border.* (New York, 1899), Vol. II.

Brown, J. M., *Political Beginnings of Kentucky.*

Chronicles of Oklahoma.

Clayton, Powell, *The Aftermath of the Civil War in Arkansas.* (Vol. XIX, American Nation Series).

Dodd, William E., *Exposition and Conflict* (Vol. III Riverside History of the United States).

———. *Jefferson Davis.*

Drake, S. G., *Biography and History of the Indians in North America, 1857.*

———. *Early History of Georgia, embracing the Embassy of Sir Alexander Cummings to the Country of the Cherokees, 1872.*

Evans, General Clement A., editor, *Confederate Military History*, Vol. X.

Garrison, William Loyd, *Life of, as Told by His Children*, four volumes (New York 1885–89). Contains references to Jackson's Indian policy and to Georgia's treatment of the Cherokees.

Gilmer, George R., *The Georgians*, 1855.

Greeley, Horace, *The American Conflict.*

Gude, Mary B., *Georgia and the Cherokees.*

Hart, Albert, *The Formation of the Union.*

Haywood, J., *History of Tennessee*, two volumes, 1823.

Hewett, Alexander, *An Historical Account of the Rise and Progress of the Colonies of South Carolina and Georgia.*

Hodge, Frederick Webb, *Handbook of the American Indians*, Bulletin 30.

Hosmer, James Kendall, *Appeal to Arms* (American Nation Series).

Howard, C. E., *Preliminaries of the Revolution* (American Nation Series).

Kennedy, John Pendleton, *Memoirs and Life of William Wirt*, Two Volumes. Vol. II, Chapters XV, XVII and XIX are useful for the study of the Cherokee Case.

Lumpkin, Wilson, *Removal of the Cherokee Indians from Georgia*, two volumes, 1908.

Martin, *History of North Carolina.*

McKenney, Thomas L., and James Hall, *History of the Indian Tribes of North America*, three volumes.

McLaughlin, Andrew Cunningham, *A History of the American Nation.*

Meredith, Extra Census Bulletin, 1894.

Mooney, James, *Myths of the Cherokees*; 19th Annual Report of the Bureau of Ethnology, 1897, 1898, Part I.

Parker, T. V., *The Cherokee Indians*, 1907.

Phillips, U. B., *Georgia and States' Rights*; Annual Report of American Historical Association 1901, Volume II.

Pickett, A. J., *History of Alabama.*

Ramsey, *Annals of Tennessee.*

Royce, C. C., *The Cherokee Nation of Indians*, 5th Annual Report of Bureau of Ethnology, 1883–84.

Sargent, Epes, *Life and Public Services of Henry Clay*, New York, 1848.

Scott, Nancy M., *A Memoir of Hugh Lawson White*, 1856. Includes selections from his speeches, some of which contain criticisms of Benjamin F. Curry and Cherokee Removal.

Schwarze, Edmond, *A History of the Moravian Missions among the Cherokees.*

Thompson, Augustus Charles, *Moravian Missions.*

Walker, *Torch Lights to the Cherokees.*

White, *Historical Collections of Georgia.*

Wilson, *Division and Reunion*, 1829, 1872.

Winsor, Justin, *The Mississippi Basin.*

——. *The Westward Movement.*

III Pamphlets

Anderson, Mable Washburn, *The Life of General Stand Watie* (Pryor, Okla.).

Buttrick, Rev. Daniel Saden, *Antiquities of the Cherokees.*

Couch, Nevada, *Pages From Cherokee History.*

Cherokee National Female Seminary, Souvenir Catalog.

Murrow, Rev. J. S., *The Indian Side.*

Resolution of the Committee of One Hundred, Gov. Doc. 68th Congress, 1st session, Doc. 149.

United States Indians, Department of Interior, Bulletin 1926, No. 3.

Upham, Mrs. W. P., *Secession Among the Cherokees* (Watchman and Reflector, Boston, Mass., May 1, 1869).

IV. Newspapers

The Arkansas Gazette, Little Rock, Ark.

The Evening Post, Little Rock, Ark.

The Cherokee Advocate, Tahlequah, I.T.

The Cherokee Phoenix, New Echota, Cherokee Nation.

The Dallas News, Dallas, Texas.

The Fort Smith Elevator, Fort Smith, Ark.

The Indian Citizen, Atoka, Okla.

The Indian Journal, Eufala, Okla.

The Kansas City Times, Kansas City, Mo.

The Muskogee Phoenix, Muskogee, Okla.

Our Brother in Red, Muskogee, I.T.

The Purcell Register, Purcell, I.T.

The St. Louis Globe Democrat, St. Louis, Mo.

The Vinita Chieftain, Vinita, Okla.

The Washington Post, Washington, D.C.

Index

Note: Page numbers in *italics* refer to illustrative matter.

Corcoran Art Gallery, 188
corruption charges, 234–39
cotton, 17, 23, 26, 47, 55, 308n5
cotton mills, 294n4
Cowskin Prairie Council, 173
Cox, George, *142*
Crawford, John, 157
Crawford, William, 36
Crazy Snake uprising, 323n4
Creek Nation. *See* Muscogee Nation
Creek War, 35–36
criminal punishment, 48, 64, 113
Cuming, Alexander, 14, 20, 287nn5–6, 288n5
Cummings, Charles, 289n12
Cummings, Wilson, 271
Cunnessee (Cunnessuny or Cheucunsenee), 37, 291n12
Curry, Benjamin F., 69, 73, 76, 77, 78, 79, 80, 81, 83, 86–87, 89
Curtis, Samuel R., 305n11
Curtis Act (1896), 205, 208, 265–69, 318n20

Dameron, Henry, *142*
Dannenberg, Trixie, *143*
"Dark Treaty," as term, 181, 194
Davis, John Barber, 24
Dawes, Henry, 233–34, 318n5
Dawes Commission, 198, 233–45, 255, 258–69, 274, 284n31, 323n7
death during forced removal, 104–7, 108. *See also* disease and sickness
debt, 48, 65, 82, 83, 126–27, 153, 253, 273, 274, 320n3
Delawares, 130, 194, 231, 258, 266, 309n15
Department of Indian Affairs, 170
depression (economic), xi, xii, 320n4
depression (mental), 68, 104, 179
De Soto, Hernando, 13
Dinsmore, Silas, 17
The Discipline of the Methodist Church (Boudinot), 133

disease and sickness, 83, 104, 128, 184. *See also* death during forced removal
displacement. *See* forced removal
district organization, 20, 30, 47–48, 55–56, 110, 118–19
Dole, W. P., 168
double log house, 307n7 (ch. 20)
Dougherty, Cornelius, 13–14
Downing, Lewis, 167, 171, 190, 191, 192, 193, 194, 246, 256
Drennan, John, 126
Drew, John, 158, 305n4 (ch. 17)
drought, 101, 102, 103, 126, 149
Drury College, xviii
Duncan, Walter A., 201, 206, 257, 271, 319n19
Dwight, Timothy, 33
Dwight Mission, 33, 110, 131, 187
Dyer, Jonas, 319n19

earthquake, 28
Eastern Cherokees, 31, 34. *See also* Cherokee people
Eastern Trail, 316n18
Eaton, George Washington, xvii, *139*
Eaton, Joel Merritt, *142*
Eaton, John, 61
Eaton, Martha "Mattie" Pauline, xxiv, *143*, *144*
Eaton, Rachel Caroline "Callie," xi–xxx, *139*, 141, *144*, *145*, 146; education of, xv, xviii; *A History of the Cherokee Nation*, about, xvi, xxix–xxxvi, xxv; home of, *139*; *John Ross and the Cherokee Indians*, xvi, xviii; "The Legend of the Battle of Claremore Mound," xxii, xviii; teaching position of, xviii, *141*, 282n12
education, 46–47, 201. *See also* schools
Elvdi, 10, 287n13
emigration. *See* forced removal
Enabling Act (1906), 279–80
English language, 24, 49

Old Hop, xiii, xvii
Old Settlers, 108, 110–11, 112–14,
    116, 117, 119–20, 121, 123,
    124–25, 126, 128. *See also* Arkansas
    settlement; Western Cherokees
Oochalata (chief), 221, 246–47
Oostenauleh. *See* Ustenali
Oothcalogy (Oochgeelogy), 134,
    302n11
Oo-too-nah Ka-nah-leh (ᎣᏏᎾ
    ᏴᎬᏔ/utana ginalii), 287n14
Oowala community, *143*
Opothleyohola, 156, 159, 304n26
origin stories, xvi–xvii, 7, 281n1,
    286n1 (ch. 1)
orphans, 137, 199, 201–2. *See also*
    Cherokee Orphan Asylum
orphans' fund, 136, 181, 303n17,
    310n13, 312n15
Orr, James, 131
Osages: –Cherokee battles, xxii,
    31–33, 53, 285n2; land of, 30–31,
    53, 109, 222, 285n2, 309n16;
    reservation of, 194; schools of,
    130–31
Oskison, John, xxiv
Otarre. *See* Odali
Otoe, 222
Ouachita Campaign (1868), 315n6
the Outlet. *See* Cherokee Outlet
    Agreement and Perpetual Outlet
    West land grant
Overhill language dialect, 10
Owen, Narcissa, xxiv, xxviii, 188
Owen, Robert L., 206, 277

Pan, Robin, 257
Parker, Ely S., 170, 213
Parker, Isaac C., 236, 237
Park Hill district, 129, 155
Park Hill Mission, 118, 132–33,
    137
Parris, Richard, *142*
Pasuga (battle). *See* Battle of
    Claremore Mound

paternalism, 308n6
Pathkiller (chief), 20, 25, 57, 207
Payne, David L., 219
Payne, James Madison, 138
Payne, John Howard, 81
Peace Commission, 167–75
peaceful period, 34–35
peach trees, 23, 55
Pegg, Thomas, 163, 164, 171, 179
People's Party, 193. *See also* Downing,
    Lewis
per capita payments, 66, 78, 120, 121,
    125, 126, 231–32, 309n22, 317n22,
    319n18, 319n23
Perpetual Outlet West land grant, 31,
    218–26
Phillips, W. A., 164, 168–69
Pike, Albert, 154–55, 156, 161, 162,
    178–79
Pins, 147, 308n1. *See also* Keetowah
    Society
Pocahontas Club. *See* Indian Women's
    Pocahontas Club
political organization of Cherokees,
    47, 118–19
Polk, James, 123
Ponca, 222
poney-clubs, 65
Pope, John, 221
population statistics, 27, 149, 322n8
    (ch. 27)
Potter, William, 131
Presbyterian missionaries, 25–26, 134.
    See also missionaries
Priber, Christian, 18
primitive, as term, 5, 6, 8, 9, 53, 56,
    286n4 (ch. 1), 294n6
printing press, 50, 125, 264
Proctor, Isaac, 67
Proctor, Zeke, 314n33
profanities, 321n1
Progressive Era, xxv–xxvi
progress, idea of, xxvii–xxviii, 5–6,
    20–27
The Purcell Register (publication), 234

338

www.ingramcontent.com/pod-product-compliance
Lightning Source LLC
Chambersburg PA
CBHW020446100426
42812CB00036B/3468/J